Lina Bo Bardi

Lina Bo Bardi

Zeuler R. M. de A. Lima

Foreword by Barry Bergdoll

Yale University Press
New Haven and London

Publication of *Lina Bo Bardi* is supported by a grant from the Architectural History Foundation.

yalebooks.com/art

Designed by Luke Bulman/Thumb, New York
Set in Plantin and Univers
Printed in China through Regent Publishing Services Ltd.

Cover illustration: Teatro Gregorio de Matas, Salvador, 1986–87, interior (figure 139).
Photograph by Zeuler R. Lima.
Frontispiece: *Lina Bo Bardi*, 1991. Photograph by Juan Esteves.

The Library of Congress has catalogued the hardcover edition as follows:
Lima, Zeuler Rocha Mello de Almeida.
  Lina Bo Bardi / Zeuler R. M. de A. Lima ; foreword by Barry Bergdoll.
     pages   cm
  Includes bibliographical references and index.
  ISBN 978-0-300-15426-9 (clothbound : alk. paper)
  1. Bardi, Lina Bo, 1914–1992. 2. Architects—Brazil—Biography. 3. Women architects—Brazil—Biography. I. Bergdoll, Barry, writer of added commentary. II. Title.
  NA859.B37L55 2013
  720.92—dc23
  [B]   2013013065

ISBN 978-0-300-24422-9 (pbk.)

A catalogue record for this book is available from the British Library.

10 9 8 7 6 5 4 3 2 1

"The work is the death mask of its conception."
— Walter Benjamin, *One-Way Street*, 1928

Contents

Foreword

Lina Bo Bardi began her half-century-long architectural career not on building sites but in magazine editorial offices at the height of World War II in her native Italy. Yet she could scarcely have imagined that today, two decades after her death, her own design work would circulate as never before in lifestyle magazines, that her furniture would command high prices and even be subject to forgery, and that international artists would be invited to reflect on her work in a series of installations in the house in the Morumbi district of São Paulo where she and Pietro Maria Bardi entertained artists and intellectuals in their adopted Brazilian homeland. Lina Bo Bardi—or Lina, as she is now affectionately referred to by growing circles of admirers who never knew her—has become something of a posthumous *Starchitect*, just as the phenomena of fame and outspoken formal experimentation of the boom years of the turn of the twenty-first century are being called into question both economically and ethically.

Nothing — as Zeuler R. M. de A. Lima's insightful and sensitive account makes clear — could be more alien to the complex body of work Bo Bardi left behind. Her body of work resists any easy stylistic categorization as it moves from the most inventive embrace of new technical and material possibilities to an engagement with traditional means and images of building, not only from period to period in her life, from region to region, or even from building to building, but even within the same structure. Her own house — now referred to by most as the Glass House (Casa de vidro) — appears on arrival through the dense semitropical planting of its hillside site as a freestanding glazed pavilion raised on pilotis, partaking of the mid-twentieth-century obsession with the glazed box as observatory from Mies van der Rohe to Philip Johnson to Charles and Ray Eames to the overall dreams of transparency of the European avant-garde of the interwar period. And yet inside, this great room of floor-to-ceiling glass connects seamlessly to a grounded, grade-level neo-vernacular courtyard house of traditional construction surrounding an enclosed patio, redolent of traditional Portuguese colonial houses in Brazil and with distant echoes of the hybrid modern-vernacular work from a decade earlier of another émigré in São Paulo, Bernard Rudofsky.

No less important is an internalized dialogue and complex relationship to a site and place than the experience of MASP — Museu de Arte de São Paulo — where the heroic engineered galleries raised high above avenida Paulista created both a great urban window at street level for the view they framed of the city beyond and a plaza for impromptu events atop lower galleries of the building built into the hillside itself. Indeed, Bo Bardi's body of work — from the assertive engineering of MASP (1957–68) to the almost

Afro-Brazilian vernacular of the Casa de Benin in Salvador (1987) or the brutalist expression of the new structures of SESC Pompeia in São Paulo (1977–86) — embodies no catalogue of set solutions, no quests for universal types, no extravagant personal expressions continually reworked and honed. Here is no set of forms to form a school in the tradition of Frank Lloyd Wright, Le Corbusier, Mies van der Rohe, Louis Kahn, or Oscar Niemeyer — although devoted former associates of Bo Bardi still create fresh work in Brazil today. Rather, hers was a quest for an architecture at once of complexity and yet of humbleness, heroically unpretentious, one might almost say. Hers was not a quest for the ideal — as so often seen in the work of Mies van der Rohe, for instance — but a practice engaged with challenging situations, grappling with the realities of the present, seeking to embody rather than transcend the world as found, yet still committed to the architect as an agent of betterment.

"Architecture and architectural freedom are above all a social issue that must be seen from inside a political structure, not from outside it," she wrote in 1974, a decade after her first period of work in Salvador da Bahia, in Brazil's northeast region, ended amid the changing political scenario produced by the military coup.[1] Her life and her work became intimately aligned to one of the most complex moments in modern Brazilian history, touched deeply and directly by dictatorship and economic ebbs and flows, at once pragmatic and yet fundamentally optimistic. And while Bo Bardi did not set out to create a body of work that was autobiographical, her work was intimately tied up with her life, her passionate engagement with a set of changing circumstances and settings from postwar Milan to São Paulo in artistic ferment and to the discovery of the Afro-Brazilian culture and native expressions of the Brazilian Nordeste. Her career was a continual research for an ethics of engagement that transcended the creation of buildings to the curating of theatrical space, the staging of exhibitions, in which the very definition of the architect was at the heart of the quest.

In Zeuler R. M. de A. Lima, Lina Bo Bardi has found a thinker worthy of her own profound quest, someone able to bring her diverse corpus of works and life story into a dialogue that loses none of the profound open-ended search, unflagging commitment, and sophisticated embrace of new challenges, new awareness, new perceptions that mark Bo Bardi's oeuvre. Lima sits astride the complex relation of the past and the present just as Lina Bo Bardi herself did in her insistence that the past was always a present, that memory was always an agent, but that this presence of the past is adamantly not nostalgic. As her work came to fruition in the early 1980s with the astounding recasting of a São Paulo factory into the SESC Pompeia Leisure Center it stood at once at the forefront of adaptive reuse in Brazil and in dramatic counterpoint to the nascent postmodern notion of the "Presence of the Past" celebrated in the *Strada Novissima* of Paolo Portogeshi's influential Venice Biennale of 1980. Hers was not the creation of a stage set for the reinvention of the lost meaning of historical forms but rather the creation of the stage for the ongoing life of both the burgeoning metropolis of São Paulo and the vibrant multicultural day-to-day expressions of a country as vast as Brazil.

"If the economist and the sociologist can diagnose things with detachment, the artist must act as an element connected to active people, as well as to the intellectual," Bo Bardi explained in a key text of 1976.[2] And it is precisely this engagement with the full complexity of her work and life — from her unconventional marriage to Pietro Maria Bardi, as much a spiritual counterpart as a spouse; to her movement from designer to museum director and collector; to her joint passion for new engineering solutions and for the handicrafts of the complex ethnic and racial stratigraphy of Brazil's regions — that makes this hybrid monograph and biography the perfect narrative and analytic point of entry into a body of work that has as much to tell us about Brazil's complicated recent past as to offer suggestions for meaningful practices for today.

Lima's monograph contains no conventional biographical account, for he weaves in subtle readings of the design work into each of the vignettes that follow the continual emigrations and internal migrations of his subject both across the territory and across a voyage of discovery of different peoples and places. Shortly before her death, in one of her last interviews, Bo Bardi contrasted her engagement with Brazil with that of her husband: "Pietro's never forgotten Italy, he remembers it even today! Me no, I remember nothing; it doesn't interest me in the least. For me there's only Brazil, since it's a country I have a special affection for. A poor country, poor people, but very rich, marvelous, somewhere you could do things. Politically, Brazil's situation is very dangerous, especially right now."[3]

At first reading, that quotation would seem to ground Lina Bo Bardi's work firmly in a Brazil before the rise of the BRIC economies in the opening decade of our own century. Brazil's position in the world now commands an attention that it probably has not had — politically, economically, even architecturally — since the 1940s. That midcentury moment, when the Bardis arrived from Italy just after Brazil had entered the final stages of World War II and just before the great undertaking of Brasília, had turned all eyes on Brazilian modernism. Yet much of what Bo Bardi grappled with is as pertinent and applicable today as it was during her lifetime. Not only did she articulate and teach — during her short periods on the faculty of both the Universities of São Paulo and of Bahia, and then in her studio — a philosophy of practice that rejected "the complex of the individualistic architect," but she revealed how the architect's involvement with daily culture and with a specific environment extends beyond the design of buildings alone. It would seem that one of her greatest frustrations was the opposition she met in trying to obtain a fixed teaching post, determined in part that her larger vision of a social and political function for architecture could be achieved in teaching: "We can begin in part to create a collective consciousness of architecture in schools, the opposite of an arrogant individualism."[4] Bo Bardi spoke of a dream of creating an alternative to the reigning rationalized modernism of the Ulm School and, by extension, a popular university — a plan whose intellectual roots and allegiances are subtly researched and argued by Lima in this book of timely engagement.

Today Bo Bardi's architecture sits at a paradoxical juncture. While several of her key buildings — MASP chief among them — are in a lamentable state of delayed maintenance and insensitive alterations and suffer from aggressive misunderstanding and lack of sympathy for her forms and aims, her work continues to attract more and more attention among not only architects but a larger public. Lima reveals here the almost immediate attraction to her work, to her spirit, and to her convictions that all visitors experience in the remarkable fragment of a city that is Bo Bardi's SESC Pompeia. His analysis is itself a sign of a renewed receptivity to her thinking, and a testament to the pertinence of her work. In a period in which a fascination with the life of unplanned communities and of the favelas often courts to a naive and literal romanticism, Bo Bardi's combination of respect — "We know that favelas, slums, and shanty towns offer a sense of community and interaction superior to that of planned neighborhoods" — with a sense of engaged intervention to enhance life as found. Here is a middle ground between the modernist total plan and the dangerous and paradoxical current encounter between the romanticism of a left-leaning critique of modernism with a neoconservative laissez-faire approach to the life of the other 90 percent. When Bo Bardi speaks of a "poor architecture," she refers to an architecture of dignity made with simple forms but one still that is meant to enrich life, relations, and conditions. Lima reveals the extent to which it comes from intellectual debates Bo Bardi encountered in Bahia and to which it tends to extend the theory of the "poor theatre" and of the role of performance to new possibilities for architecture and its insertion into communities at all scales.

Bo Bardi's is neither an architecture of nostalgia for a world before modernism nor a cynical acceptance of the impossibility of change in a globalizing capitalist economy. Rather, it is a position that seeks to extend modernism and create an alliance both with everyday wisdom and with the conditions of life in an inclusive society, a legacy of a belief that work itself is an ongoing engagement in a process rather than a singular assertion of a utopian frozen moment. To unite a discussion of her life, her political convictions, and her struggles at times with authorities and the cultural establishment, with her work and its engagement with users, as Lima thoroughly demonstrates, is to enter a world in which the choice is not between formal planning and informal settlement, between design and nostalgia, but rather an architecture that is at once humble often in aspects of its expression and its acceptance and demanding in its command that the architect serve as the handmaiden to crafting the stage for the optimal social, political, and economic interactions in a world of real possibilities.

Barry Bergdoll
Chief Curator of Architecture and Design
Museum of Modern Art, New York

Preface

At the end of her life, Lina Bo Bardi used to jot down notes on small newsprint pads, leaving a trail of thoughts among many drawings and records of experiences that were meaningful to her. She yearned for an account of her development and achievements as an architect and likely expected that her remarks would yield a single narrative. She also believed that one's history is made up of the stories one tells oneself, and she sometimes took liberties to magnify their effect and drama. Among her later notes, she reported that, at age twenty-five, she had wanted to write her memoirs and that, as a young designer-to-be, she had resented not having a story to tell. This book — the first comprehensive study of her career as an architect — acknowledges Bo Bardi's unfulfilled longing and approaches her vast production from historical and critical perspectives to reveal the work of her hands and mind.

Written two decades after Bo Bardi's death in São Paulo in 1992 and nearing the centennial of her birth in Rome in 1914, this volume is published in commemoration. Above and beyond this tribute, it reminds readers of her nonconformist outlook as an insightful counterpoint to the self-indulgence of the professional "star system" and of contemporary mass culture. At the core of her legacy as an architect is not a formal vocabulary but an attitude: the search for an authenticity that could be collectively shared.

Motivated by my early curiosity as a designer and later by my inquisitiveness as a scholar, I aim in this book to provide an equitable narrative that brings Bo Bardi's work and thinking to the foreground while also unveiling her ambitions and ambiguities, as well as the changing historical and geographical contexts that framed her education and practice. This book seeks to engage professional and scholarly audiences interested in the work of key twentieth-century architects as well as readers interested in a compelling story about a woman who grew to strive for the humanization of architecture and the socialization of cultural practices. Given Bo Bardi's complex aesthetic and conceptual choices and her varied life experiences, this study does not seek to provide definitive interpretations. Instead, it offers a genealogy of her design achievements in the context of the ideological, artistic, and lived conditions she experienced (as represented by personal and political obstacles and possibilities). It carefully articulates different sources of information both critically and chronologically and invites new and future insights.

Above all, this study presents the vantage point and the probing mind of an individual, designer, and activist who approached architecture from varied and remarkable circumstances on two continents. Bo Bardi's actions offer examples of a critical framework for reassessing the uneven links modernity established with culture at large and with architecture and its recent history in particular. Her work and thought fostered the unstable negotiation between modern and nonmodern values and continuously reversed the relation between the mainstream and its margins. Her experience and accomplishments continue to offer empirical and theoretical analogies to contemporary challenges that designers face in a world undergoing global modernization — a world that struggles between the contraction of geographic dimensions and resources and the conflicting expansion of social practices and symbolic repertoires.

Bo Bardi often spent long hours reflecting, talking, and making notes before she produced colorful hand drawings, her most intimate and powerful means of expression. More than a confident modernist architect, she was a skeptical modern designer and thinker. Instead of universal values, her complex work and writing unveil the roles of plurality, otherness, and instability in the constitution of modernity. Instead of agreeable forms, she strived to embrace the contingency and spontaneity of life. She spent her own life in transit, navigating the contingencies of different locations and worldviews. Her ventures established a weaving path in and out of modern culture, materialized in the communication between innovation and tradition, abstraction and realism, rationalism and surrealism, and naturalism and history, as well as between revolutionary impulses and melancholy.

Unconcerned with contradictions, Bo Bardi merged different — and sometimes opposing — realities and values in her practice. As she did so, she also revealed aspects and conflicts that modernization tends to conceal. Instead of embracing unfettered innovation, she was sensitive to technical simplification and to national-popular values. Despite her praise of the spontaneity of nature and uneducated culture, she remained attached to Enlightenment principles such as rational logic, scientific knowledge, and free will. Aware of such ambitions and choices and also of their predicaments, she defined herself as being romantic but not sentimental.

Beyond the unusual appearance of her work there lie meaningful political and ethical concerns. Having grown up in Italy under Fascism and survived World War II, Bo Bardi followed her generation's attachment to aesthetic realism. She also set out in search of a new humanism, which she distinguished from both educated Renaissance humanism and charitable humanitarianism. Her sense of humanism was pragmatic. It acknowledged the constraints of specific situations and aspired to justice. She was especially fond of the improvisation and authenticity of simple people, whom she often saw as deprived of material means but rich in creative capacity. To her, humanity and its collective struggles were more important than individualistic aspirations, a belief she sought to foreground especially in her mature years.

Bo Bardi believed in the work of architects not only as an artistic endeavor but also as a civic duty. To her, design emerged from an understanding of the physical world and of people's living conditions, habits, and needs: architecture should ultimately be useful and meaningful to those who employ and inhabit it. In this quest, she developed extensive networks of social and professional relations with other leading architects, artists, and intellectuals both in Italy and in Brazil. She produced and kept a vast collection of sketches, notes, and manuscripts. She wrote and illustrated articles, edited magazines, created museums, and organized exhibitions, taught and lectured on architecture and design, and designed innovative furniture and buildings.

This broad spectrum in Bo Bardi's thinking and practice informs the material for this book. The text that follows is the result of a long investigative process of more than ten years collecting and analyzing extensive archival documentation, conducting fieldwork and interviews, checking information, and culling material from various sources and in different locations around the world. It employs a combined methodology, associating the analysis of Bo Bardi's design and written works with the analysis of the biographic circumstances and historic contexts in which she developed them. The chronological and cross-referential interpretation of her work gives voice to her values, principles, and choices and points to patterns and changes along her career. The field analysis unveils the situations under which her quest for humanizing architecture and her dialogue with modern design evolved, highlighting key historic and cultural developments in Italy and in Brazil along with relevant aspects of her life and of her personal, professional, and social relations.

Work on this project required many trips to places where Bo Bardi spent her life, to document her projects, all in the attempt to locate them geographically and historically, and to understand the relation between her work and her living circumstances. Although I consulted several secondary sources and bibliographic references to substantiate information, I rely on primary sources to accomplish the book's narrative goals. Many of those sources come from the vast and varied archival material in the collection of the Instituto Lina Bo e Pietro Maria Bardi, which holds most of the documents (images, drawings, manuscripts, documents, and objects) regarding the work and life of the architect. Complementary archival material about Bo Bardi and her work in Brazil came from the Museu de Arte de São Paulo, the Museu de Arte Moderna da Bahia, the Fundação Gregório de Matos in Salvador, and the library of the

Faculdade de Arquitetura e Urbanismo at the Universidade de São Paulo.

Other material comes from the Italian archives of the Fondazione Bruno Zevi and of Fabrizio Clerici, as well as the architecture library of the Università degli Studi di Firenze and the Biblioteca Nazionale di Firenze. The archives of the Rockefeller Archive Center, the New York Metropolitan Museum, and Saul Steinberg also provided much-needed resources. Most important to enriching and clarifying my understanding of Bo Bardi's life, however, were the conversations and interviews I conducted with Lina Bo and Pietro Maria Bardi's collaborators, friends, acquaintances, and family members.

This volume organizes that vast documentation into a broad and critical study of Lina Bo Bardi and aims to offer an original addition to the sparse and dispersed — and sometimes uncritical — but growing scholarship covering her work. Though a few studies have appeared in Italy and other countries, most works about her have been produced in Brazil. Since the late 1980s, near the end of her life, Brazilian newspapers, magazines, and academic journals began to publish interviews with her and short pieces by and about her. Since the early 2000s, concurrent with the research for and production of this manuscript, the international interest in Bo Bardi's work has grown and a few new publications about her have been printed. More recently, a few periodicals in Europe and the Americas have increased the international visibility of her work, as have a handful of meaningful master's theses and doctoral dissertations analyzing specific aspects of her career and design work — three of which were published in book format. But no new in-depth archival study has developed between 2006 and when this manuscript was completed in 2013, a period during which Bo Bardi's records were largely closed to consultation due to new cataloguing and facilities remodeling.

I acknowledge these studies in due references, though I do not discuss their documentation, analyses, and methods. Rather, my purpose is to critically expand their partial scope and to introduce Bo Bardi's work through the examination of original documents and a comprehensive analysis of her design work and writing, of her personal and professional experiences, and of the multiple historical and geographic contexts in which she lived. I aim to establish an inclusive, original, and enduring reference and to clarify, as much as possible, existing inaccurate (and sometimes mythical) information about her. Though the scholarship about Bo Bardi is growing, it sometimes presents — given the reproduction of unverified data and insufficient analysis of primary sources and oral documentation — persisting misinterpretations. Such problems have contributed to naturalize her discourse and to create and to perpetuate an imprecise understanding of her work and personality, which the meticulous research for this study intended to elucidate. Despite such ambition, I acknowledge the occasional lack of evidence for conclusive interpretations and limited space for longer analyses, and consequently invite other scholars to open new investigations.

Though this book offers clear descriptions to provoke imagination and curiosity about the places, thoughts, events, and realizations that constituted Bo Bardi's experiences, it also relies on graphic images to show her accomplishments. The accompanying illustrations consist of three complementary categories: archival documents selected from reproducible sources;[1] photographs of her works; and exclusive digital analytical models, which I have produced as a parallel research project to this manuscript intended to represent and to map her architectural work built in Brazil between the early 1950s and the early 1990s. Together, this graphic material illustrates the works of her hands and mind as well as makes possible the analysis and understanding of complex spatial, formal, and structural logics.

This book is likely not the history Bo Bardi would have told of herself out of many stories, but it acknowledges her rich imagination and adventurous actions: the account of a designer dedicated to collective life and a woman who was at the same time insightful and impudent, gloomy and restless. This study does not look for a single overarching insight about her work and life. Rather, it keeps alive the ambiguities she brought into her practice. To some who knew her, Bo Bardi struggled for her beliefs. To others, she was a troublemaker. As such she was both part of the establishment and an outsider: an insurgent in noble garb.

Acknowledgments

This book is the result of countless hours of reclusive research, thought, and writing, but it also rests on the support of many individuals and organizations. So many people generously gave of their time, their knowledge, their reminiscences, their resources, their solidarity, and their friendship to make this project possible. I feel deeply grateful to them.

At the Instituto Lina Bo e Pietro Maria Bardi, I found a great historical treasure. I began conducting my systematic archival research in 2002 and continued it through the conclusion of the manuscript. In this treasure — comprising thousands of fascinating papers, drawings, and photographs — I found an inconspicuous but unforgettable note Bo Bardi wrote. In it, she contradicted the philosopher Michel Foucault by saying that history should not transform documents into monuments. I tried to keep this note in mind as I assessed her professional and personal records.

Three generations of board members and a helpful staff at the Instituto have worked against many odds to preserve and to disseminate the legacy of the exceptional Bardi couple in their promotion of Brazilian art and culture. They have granted me invaluable access to extensive documentation and information about Lina Bo Bardi, as well as permission to publish illustrations. I particularly appreciate the support of those who assisted me more closely with the research over the years, including Yannick Bourguignon Carvalho, Graziella Bo Valentinetti, Daniela Rodrigues de Araújo, Liana Perez de Oliveira, Anna Carboncini, and Malu Villas-Bôas.

Many knowledgeable archivists and librarians in Italy, Brazil, and the United States provided generous access to original information. Among them are Emanuela Termine at the Fondazione Bruno Zevi, Eros Renzetti at the Fabrizio Clerici archives, Maíra Moraes and Ivani di Grazia Costa at the Museu de Arte de São Paulo, and Amy Fitch at the Rockefeller Archive Center. They and many others who worked anonymously but no less willingly and resourcefully helped me identify essential primary evidence during many of my detective-like adventures.

This volume was also made possible by the prompt and enthusiastic embrace of my book proposal by Michelle Komie, my editor at Yale University Press. She patiently followed me in the long process to the book's completion, encouraging me and thoughtfully guiding the evaluation and production procedures, including blind peer reviews, which offered validation and meaningful insights into the project. I am also grateful to Laura Jones Dooley, my manuscript editor, who helped me polish the text with great sensitivity, to Sarah Henry, who carefully supervised the book production, and to Luke Bulman for his insightful graphic design.

I conceived this comprehensive study in concert with my academic activities, and I am thankful to Bruce Lindsey and Carmon Colangelo, deans of the School of Design and Visual Arts at Washington University in Saint Louis, who supported my pedagogical and research endeavors and granted me a leave of absence to work on the project in a more concentrated manner.

I am grateful to the Graham Foundation for financial support regarding the production of this book and the Rockefeller Archive Center for a research grant.

Though this book presents an original narrative, its content stems from shorter essays I wrote and lectures I gave about Lina Bo Bardi with the support of several journal and magazine editors and event and conference organizers around the world, each of whom offered me opportunities to experiment with different theoretical and methodological frameworks.

In addition to those dialogues, in the more than ten years that I have worked to make this book a reality, I have developed friendships and engaged in inspiring intellectual exchanges with scholars and designers of varied interests in architecture, culture, Lina Bo Bardi, and the events surrounding her. Without their stimulating conversations, this book would have been deprived of the full and rich life I hope I have given it.

I am grateful to Andreas Huyssen, who generously welcomed me into the world of comparative literature and who encouraged me to pursue the extensive research for this book; to Marcelo Carvalho Ferraz and Isa Grinspum Ferraz, who opened their minds and hearts as continuous sources of information and confident support; to Vera Pallamin for her friendship and indispensable guidance in the study of architecture, culture, and philosophy; to Maristella Casciato, who showed me the initial road to Rome and followed up with valued suggestions during the preparation of the manuscript; to Adachiara Zevi, for her generosity in supporting my research, for housing me in her father's towerlike *pensatoio* (Bruno Zevi's thinking quarters), and for introducing me to rich aspects of the artistic and intellectual life of Rome; to Britt-Marie Schiller, Lourdes Henares, and members of the Saint Louis Psychoanalytic Institute, who helped me explore the labyrinth of Bo Bardi's inner world; to Jussilene Santana, who engaged in a prolific dialogue about the cultural and political life of Salvador in the 1950s and 1960s; to Barry Bergdoll, whose enthusiastic interest in the study of architecture and cities in Brazil and elsewhere in Latin America has offered me invaluable opportunities for discussing and disseminating Bo Bardi's work; and to my friends in Florence, Rome, and Milan, who have captivated me with their warmth and knowledge and have helped make their country feel like home.

Aside from the archival documentation, I found enlightening pieces of the mosaic that composed Lina Bo Bardi's world in thorough and priceless interviews with Edmar de Almeida, Graziella Bo Valentinetti, Claudio Valentinetti, Marcelo Suzuki, Francesco Tentori, and Riccardo Mariani. Along the way, colorful details were added in conversations with several people who shared meaningful professional or personal experiences with Bo Bardi, including André Vainer, Giancarlo Latorraca, Hélio Eichbauer, Caetano Veloso, and Carlos Nelson Coutinho. I also had welcome opportunities to share helpful information, material, and ideas for this book with well-informed and passionate scholars, writers, and designers such as Anat Falbel, Hugo Segawa, Sandra Vivanco, Cathrine Veikos, Michelangelo Sabatino, Max Risselada, Mary McLeod, Silvana Rubino, Franco Montanari, Alessandra Criconia, Elisabetta Andreoli, Carlos Eduardo Comas, Paula Lupkin, Edward Dimendberg, Robert Duffy, Ana Beatriz Galvão, Maria Cristina Cabral, Márcio Correia Campos, Renato Anelli, and Cassiano Elek Machado. I am also grateful to Maria Luíza L. Soares for having kindly opened her house (originally designed for the Cirell-Czerna couple) for documentation and notes.

The research and production of this book counted on the resourceful assistance of Deborah Costa during the initial phase of archival research in São Paulo and on Nelson Kon's generosity in making his photographic work available for consultation and reproduction. Photographer Juan Esteves kindly offered his arresting photograph of Lina Bo Bardi to be used as the frontispiece. Likewise, the archives of the Instituto Bardi, the Fondazione Bruno Zevi, the MASP library, and Instituto Moreira Salles granted permission to reproduce images from their collections. My research assistants Maria Eva Contesti, Roberto Deseda, Brian Michener, Justin Beadle, Michael Heller, Emily Oster, David Orndorff, and Joshua Canez brought their outstanding design skills into the project I carried out to translate Bo Bardi's buildings into digital images. In due course, the fresh view of many enthusiastic graduate students in my architecture history seminar dedicated to Lina Bo Bardi helped me fine-tune the reception and narrative of this book.

On a more personal note, the preparation for this book and my writing routine counted on constant presences in my daily life. I found needed relief and critical insight in my peripatetic strolls with our walker hound, cheekily and warmly named Lina Bobarky: a constant reminder of how to live in the present. I am greatly thankful to my friends, in whom I find, even from far away, indispensable safe harbors and sources of joy; to Deanna Benjamin for her invaluable teaching about creative writing as she deeply and insight-fully dove into my manuscript throughout the writing and editing processes and for accompanying me into the fas-cinating woods of beauties and dangers that comprise the English language; to Gary Hirshberg for being a loyal and caring ally in exploring the challenges and the delight that lie much beneath the surface of my mind. And to my par-ents, Urgel and Elza, for giving me unconditional logistical support and encouragement. Most important, I thank both of them for providing me with unique lifelong and wide-ranging educational opportunities — all of which directly and indirectly led into this project. I am especially grate-ful to Edmund Sprunger — for instilling in me the belief that the exercise of writing should aspire to offer the reader both clarity and truth (always with a good deal of drafting, editing, and revising); for his constant belief that this long project was worth pursuing, in particular during its most difficult moments; and, above all, for his loving support and companionship.

Prologue

In April 1989, architect Lina Bo Bardi was honored with the first exhibition of her work. She was seventy-four. The Universidade de São Paulo — the same school that, three decades earlier, had denied her a permanent teaching position — hosted the show. Students and architects viewed photographs of her latest projects alongside several of her chairs and colorful sketches. Highlighted was her ongoing proposal for the urban revitalization of the historical center of Salvador, the first colonial capital of Brazil. Only recently had Bo Bardi begun to receive recognition for her long and prolific career as a designer — a career that began with her education in Rome, where she was born in 1914. After her professional experiences in Milan during World War II, she moved, in 1946, to Brazil, the country of her adopted citizenship. She would die there in 1992. Crowning the São Paulo exhibition, which closed less than a week later, was her final lecture, which was also the first time that the mostly young audience had seen her in person. It was a rare public appearance.

Bo Bardi arrived late for the event. A large crowd chatted impatiently in the brightly lit auditorium. Constrained by arthritis, she walked slowly down the school's ramps and entered the lecture hall through the right door. She climbed the side steps leading onto the bare stage with some difficulty. There, a few guests welcomed her at the table. She accommodated herself, and as she spoke into the microphone with her husky, Italian-accented Portuguese, the audience hushed. Though fragmented and without a climatic denouement, her presentation was well paced, frank, touched with European erudition, and packed with statements of her beliefs. Her opening remarks showed her concern about architectural criticism. Perhaps rebutting the narrow formalism that had kept her unusual work from being fully accepted by modern Brazilian architects, she spoke against a tradition that she traced back to the Enlightenment as a "set of classical rules that were codified in books and erudite treatises."[1] She was also concerned about contemporary architectural education.

As she had strived to reconcile different impulses in her work and thinking, Bo Bardi warned: "I would not say that those rules are as dangerous as Gropius thought, but they may disturb the creative education of architects when they are not well understood historically." Instead, she suggested, "it is necessary to consider the past as a historical present, still alive, a present that helps us avoid traps," and to "forge another 'true' present," reminding students that "this ability is not only taught in books." At the end of her lecture, she recommended, "When we design, even as a student, it is important that a building serves a purpose and that it has the connotation of use. It is necessary that the work does not fall from the sky over its inhabitants, but rather expresses a need." Before accepting questions from the audience, she concluded: "You should always look for the ideal, decent object, which could also be defined by the old term 'beauty.'"[2]

Bo Bardi welcomed the audience's remarks. She enjoyed conversation. When asked how she worked, she responded somewhat romantically that she did not have an office, worked in the silence of the night, and spent her days on the construction site, "where the collaboration among all professionals is total." When asked how a professional pedagogy could be created in which architects would serve all people, not merely the affluent classes, her answer was brisk: "The question is beautiful, but it is also a little naïve. Architects, like other professionals, . . . depend on the country's socioeconomic structure. In order to change, one needs to make a revolution." Still, she acknowledged, idealism "is very beautiful, worthy of a man, of a real person." Then she reported on her personal experience: "I never worked for the affluent classes."[3]

As the dialogue continued, Bo Bardi offered a synthesis of her personal and professional path since leaving Europe and brought up her controversial political views. In response to a question about the dilemmas between democracy and authoritarianism, socialism and capitalism, and private and public initiatives, she said: "In Brazil, I have always done everything I wanted." She stressed her point by adding, "I never faced any obstacles, not even as a woman. That's why I say I am Stalinist and anti-feminist."[4] She did not explain what she meant by such provocative assertions, which journalists published in newspapers, contributing to her personal mythology. The audience did not know that Bo Bardi saw Stalin, not as a political leader, but as a hero in the liberation of Italy from Nazi-fascism. They also did not understand that what she had opposed about feminism was the women's liberation movement, which, for all its legal struggles, she considered a bourgeois dispute. In fact, she admired an earlier generation who fought for equality, adding that, among the poorer classes, women always strove side by side with men.

When the conversation ended, the guests surrounding Bo Bardi on the stage stood up and applauded, as did the audience. She remained seated. The clapping filled the space and echoed within the concrete walls of the auditorium. She crossed her arms and pressed them down against her chest, resting her elbows over the sheets of paper piled on the table. This was the same stance she had taken when she had presented her proposals for Salvador's historic Pelourinho District to city administrators a few years earlier. Then she had sat, arms crossed and covering the drawings she had

prepared, and listened in silence to their political speeches. When they had finished, Bo Bardi had risen up, told them they were mistaken about their architectural approach, and pushed her colorful sketches to the center of the table, asserting that this was how it should be done.[5] This time — at her final lecture — she remained quiet.

The audience finally left the auditorium to visit the exhibition in the hall above, where they glimpsed the most recent examples of the working process of a designer who had an inclusive view of architecture and practiced it accordingly. The simple displays, set up on a wooden frame that reminded many observers of her previous curatorial projects, traced different aspects of Bo Bardi's work. They suggested how she developed an ample view of architecture with incursions into varying fields, associating its practice with everyday culture and its experience with the theater of life. As she said in the lecture and often throughout her career, she was against the idea that architecture and design education were problem-solving endeavors. Architects, she believed, do not need to know how to solve everything. They need to know how to think innovatively about where to look for solutions. Above all, she believed that architects should embed their choices in the search of collective freedom and solidarity instead of competition.

The exhibition at the Universidade de São Paulo focused on a small selection of Bo Bardi's drawings and objects, so visitors could not see the broad and original intellectual and artistic body of work that had emerged from her prolific but discontinuous and circuitous trajectory. Nor could they see that the work she had developed as an architect, designer, illustrator, writer, editor, and curator had emerged from her transit between two countries and, especially, among different cities: Rome and Milan, in Italy, and São Paulo, Salvador, and, to a lesser extent, Rio de Janeiro, in Brazil. In both countries, she had witnessed significant moments of cultural and economic modernization marked by strong political tensions and unequal social realities. In those different and unique cities, she gathered the varied and rich resources that drove her thoughts and actions.

Bo Bardi had been exposed to multiple, contentious definitions of design and architecture since her early education. In the mid-1930s, when she began her professional education in Rome, the architectural culture of Italy was thriving, but with little consensus. By the time she graduated in 1939, however, Italian modern architecture was in crisis and the nation was about to enter World War II. She decided to leave Rome, following her Milanese classmate and boyfriend Carlo Pagani to the more progressive north, expanding the varied artistic and intellectual threads she would weave continuously throughout her career. Away from what she described as the stale environment of the capital, she received her second education in Milan, where she developed an editorial career and some design experience as a freelancer struggling to create constructive alternatives and to humanize design amid massive physical, social, and moral devastation.

Leaving Italy permanently was not in Bo Bardi's mind when she decided, rather impulsively, to marry the influential Italian art dealer and journalist Pietro Maria Bardi in 1946 and join him in a commercial venture to sell his art collection in South America. But in the new land across the Atlantic Ocean, she found a novel environment and unmatched opportunities, collaborating with her husband in the creation of a museum that would become a powerhouse for the renovation and diffusion of modern culture in Brazil. Bo Bardi's first decade in São Paulo was also the springboard for her independent career in her mature years, especially after she emerged from her husband's shadow to become a museum director in Salvador. With innovative ideas about culture, design, and education, she entered an almost mythical region of the country, the Nordeste, for which she developed a great cultural and intellectual affinity.

The opportunities for cultural renewal that Bo Bardi encountered in this remote and archaic region offered her a stimulating context and new partnerships for materializing her longtime quest for an authentic expression of design and architecture. Personal and political conflicts, however, kept her from working in Salvador after the 1964 coup d'état, which installed a two-decade-long military regime in Brazil. Back in São Paulo, both disappointed and angry, Bo Bardi sought out alternative work. The new facilities for the museum directed by her husband kept her busy until it was completed in 1968. In the following years, the harshest period of Brazil's recent history, Bo Bardi's political and aesthetic positions became more radical, placing her irrevocably at a crossroads that yielded changes with long-lasting consequences to her work and to her relationship to Brazilian architecture.

Bo Bardi's involvement with radical theater productions and socially experimental projects led her to develop distinctive contributions to design. This interest surfaced in the mid-1970s, when she was already in her early sixties, and lasted until the end of her life, when Brazilian and international architecture struggled with profound conceptual crises that had been unresolved since the end of World War II. "Despite the great years being over," she declared at the time of her São Paulo exhibition, "I continue working."[6] And by continuing to work, she enlarged her personal experience and knowledge and amplified the cultural geography of the places in which she developed her ideas and projects.

Her writings and wide-ranging designs are insightful and engaging yet also ambivalent and idiosyncratic, and they cannot be easily classified into a single framework. Bo Bardi searched for strong design concepts and relied on a simple formal vocabulary. Still, her output was not systematic. Though fewer than twenty of her architectural projects were built, their social and conceptual meaning is deep, broad, and in direct communication with the many other types of design she developed. Her work was based more often on experimentation and on the laborious process of developing and materializing programs that nurtured collective life than on the desire to produce a coherent professional portfolio. She invited those who read her articles, attended her lectures, or experienced the spaces she designed to consider, as she did in several talks in the 1950s, "architecture not as built work, but as possible means to be and to face [different] situations."[7] She strove to produce work that embraced how people live.

Bo Bardi was more loyal to an emancipating concept of modernity than to the abstract, formal language of modern architecture. Her thinking and practice were situated at the intersection of different worldviews: north and south, city and hinterland, privilege and deprivation. She balanced that thinking and practice between modern and traditional values, the past and present, abstraction and social realism. She moved from the hesitant but ambitious outset of her career in Italy into professional and intellectual maturity in Brazil, especially in the Nordeste, where she "learned that beauty, proportions, all these things are not important."[8]

Her life's trajectory does not explain her work but made it possible. And it would be misleading to assume that Bo Bardi's personal history single-handedly provides explanations of her efforts. Still, her work and life deeply informed each other in many varied contexts. She remained faithful throughout her distinctive career to a process of self-renewal despite (or perhaps because of) the discontinuous means she employed, the unusual paths she pursued, and the wide-ranging collaborations she embraced. As Bo Bardi declared to a journalist who interviewed her about the exhibition honoring her work in 1989, "I didn't make myself alone. I am curious and this quality broadens my horizons." Without hesitation, she added: "I am somehow special."[9]

A Girl in Pants

Lina Bo Bardi could not have foretold in her youth that she would become an influential architect, let alone one who achieved recognition outside her native country and in a field controlled by men. Born in Rome into a family of limited financial resources shortly before Italy joined World War I, she grew up during the ascendance of Fascism and came of age during World War II. Yet despite the social and emotional turmoil of these years, she had the imagination and resolve to challenge conventions, adjust herself to changing situations, and accomplish her ambitions.

A good example of her fluctuations and adaptability is suggested by her name. Her original birth certificate, dated December 5, 1914, reads Achillina di Enrico Bo, carrying her father's name, following the tradition of the time. Transcripts reissued after World War II read Achillina Giuseppina Bo and Achillina Bo.[1] Her childhood nicknames were Lina and, at home, Linuccia. She called herself Lina Bo especially during college and before she wed Pietro Maria Bardi, and even after her marriage, she used that name when she wished to affirm her individuality. In her adopted country, Brazil, she is known as Lina Bo Bardi, sometimes as Dona Lina (Ms. Lina) or just Lina. For all of its fleeting qualities, she favored this short and unassuming childhood name in the same way that she prized simplicity in the works she developed throughout her life.

Reliable records about her childhood and adolescence are scarce. Still, there is evidence in documents and accounts by those who were close to her that her family environment, the transformations of Rome, and the political and cultural life of Italy all offered a stimulating and challenging context for her early years. The young Lina had good reasons to feel socially alienated as a girl and particularly as a teenager with a budding desire for independence. She grew up surrounded by serious economic and political problems and was raised in a culture in which most women, especially among lower-income families, were limited to submissive social roles. Fascism reinforced those stereotypes by placing its dominant and ambiguously modern model of the mother-woman (domestic, strong, and productive) against the crisis-woman (urbane, decadent, and barren).[2] On the professional front, including in the burgeoning field of architecture, the division of labor was no different and presented great disadvantages to women, but they did not intimidate her.

At home, Lina had two contrasting models: a conventional mother and a lenient father. When she and her younger sister, Graziella, were born, their parents lived modestly in an apartment building on the unsophisticated and inconspicuous via Otranto, located near the stark Vatican walls. The district of Prati di Castello, as many called the new urban development along the lowlands west of Castel Sant'Angelo and across the Tiber River from the old historic center of Rome, was the setting of her early life. Whereas public employees moved into the more prosperous area along the nearby via Cola de Rienzo, her family lived off the less predictable income of her father's occupation as a small contractor.

For all the efforts to either normalize or dismiss her early years, Lina seems to have been a melancholy and anxious child. In an interview at the end of her life, she stated, "I was so frightened for being born, I decided never to have children."[3] She also wrote to an old friend that she didn't like to go back to Rome "because it br[ought] back the terrible frustrations of my childhood."[4] "Damn old Rome," she exclaimed in protest, describing her hometown as an old, stagnant place, "one of the moldiest cities in the world; full of ruins."[5] She also recalled in her biographical notes, written late in life, how, "fifteen days before my birth, I experienced the earthquake of Avezzano in my mother's womb," claiming that her gestation and the earthquake were no coincidence.[6] In reality, though an earthquake did violently strike the area a few miles from her mother's family's village in the Abruzzo hills, it took place a few weeks after her birth. The inflated association she made between the events suggests a powerful allegory to her own imaginative, detached, and attention-seeking temperament. Like the earthquake, Bo Bardi's existence and perhaps her presence in the architectural community were not to be ignored.

Although young Lina showed signs of nonconformity, her mother, Giovanna Adriana Grazia, tried to enforce conventional gender habits. She sent Lina to the after-school Fascist youth groups Piccole italiane and Opera nazionale Balilla, though they were incompatible with her character and ambitions. Lina strongly resented women's conventional social passivity, yet her mother had internalized traumatic memories regarding transgression. As a toddler, Giovanna had been the victim of an impulsive mother, Elisa Gasparetti, who had plotted to kill her husband, Lina's maternal grandfather, Giuseppe Grazia, after she fell in love with another man. Unsuccessful, Elisa went to jail, and according to the laws of the time, Giovanna and her sister Velia were sent there with her. A few years later, the girls were taken into a Catholic school and eventually settled with their father in the Abruzzo region. They never saw their mother again.

In spite of Giovanna's painful childhood memories, young Lina grew up fascinated by the audacity she heard in the stories about the grandmother she never met.[7] She seems to have developed, early on, her proclivity as an adult to be independent and ingenious but also volatile and defiant.[8] She constantly upset her watchful mother with her capricious insubordination to conventional rules. Giovanna used to say, "Lina always goes in the opposite direction," with a frown and a hand raised and rotating in the air to suggest that there was something unusual with her daughter.[9] As Lina grew up mistrustful of conventional female social roles, she leaned away from her mother's strict and conventional figure and toward the warmer and more exciting and tolerant male figures in her family, especially her maternal grandfather, her uncle, and her father.

Her grandfather, Giuseppe Grazia, lived in the Abruzzo countryside. Though Lina's family did not travel much, she enjoyed a few summer trips to the Ligurian, French, and Adriatic coasts and to the central hills to visit Giuseppe, who was a *medico condotto* and provided health services to peasants and their livestock.[10] As he had missed the opportunity to care for his daughters, he took young Lina along on his short trips around small farms. Late in life, she talked fondly about how he and his clients, who were simple people, welcomed her with special attention and treats, associating them with a romantic experience of rural life that persisted throughout her adult years in Brazil.[11]

Another significant figure in Lina's early life was her uncle Natale Alberto Simeoni, whom she called Uncle Natalino.[12] He was likely her first active connection with the world she later came to occupy. Simeoni was a journalist, songwriter, and playwright with Fascist convictions and close acquaintances with futurist artists and authors. He lived a bohemian existence and, after his wife died, left his daughter, Mariella, to be brought up by Lina's parents. For many years, Simeoni frequented the Bo household, and when the girls were old enough he took them to see French, German, and American movies and to experience the cultural attractions of Rome. Against Giovanna's approval, he introduced Lina to popular theater and variety shows, the unpretentious settings of which enticed her curiosity and shaped her youthful aesthetic repertoire.[13]

Her father, Enrico Bo, tempered their household with a certain anarchistic free will. An extroverted and passionate man, as well as a fantasist and skirt chaser, he likely offered young Lina a model for being inventive and for warding off difficult emotions.[14] He was also likely her model of a contrarian, a *bastian contrario*, as her family members referred to him, deliberately and facetiously questioning what other people said or did.[15] Enrico also had an artistic knack, and Lina described him as having good technical, manual, and visual skills.[16] In his youth, he held several menial jobs and moved around central Italy, working with typography and home utensils and even making toys for a time. Once married, he settled in Rome, building and renovating simple houses in growing working-class districts like Testaccio. When World War I began, he was not conscripted because he had legs of unequal length. His military release kept him close to home and allowed him to develop his entrepreneurial verve and to bring his technical knowledge and visual sensitivity to his construction work, as he tried to add a bit of comfort and a piece of backyard to each small building. Unlike many Italian men who went to the front, he was present in the life of his toddler daughter.

Lina idealized her father as a man of "good humor, predilection, and love."[17] As an adult, she never hid her preference for his imaginative personality and attention and seldom talked of her mother. It seems that Enrico was mostly dismissive of his wife's strictness and disappointment in their older daughter's nonconformity. As a result, he had a more assenting influence in young Lina's life and was particularly supportive of her budding artistic interests. Besides running a small business that eventually improved his family's living standards, Enrico dedicated his free time to painting — his favorite occupation. He produced compositions that emulated futuristic, metaphysical, and folksy themes in a dreamlike atmosphere with elaborate images filled with everyday characters. Later in life, he befriended Giorgio de Chirico, who even painted a quick portrait of Lina as a young adult.

Enrico's experience with mechanical inventions and technical drawings and his interest in painting were important points of connection with his daughter, as he helped Lina develop basic artistic skills such as principles of perspective, copy and observation drawing, and the use of color, which in turn seem to have helped her withdraw into a world of images whose secret passages only she knew.

Her earliest recorded watercolors date to 1924, when she was nine. Lina quickly learned to draw steady lines in pencil and to combine layers of bright colors, just as she would do later in life. Until 1926, while she lived in the congested Prati neighborhood, picturesque themes pervaded her drawings. More than artistic quality or creativity, they show a growing awareness of perspective, layered color planes in different hue saturations, and variations of light and shadow. Almost invariably, they depict idyllic landscapes with small buildings and lush vegetation, a few urban scenes and, sometimes, human figures. Whether these are copies of book or magazine illustrations, outlines done by her father, or images of her own invention is difficult to determine. Still, they offer a hint of the colorful palette and liveliness she would later bring into the design and representation of buildings covered with plants and naturalistic materials.

In the late 1920s, her early picturesque drawings yielded to representations of human figures, almost all feminine, in light-hearted themes, such as a few with the German title *Moderne Tanz* (modern dance), as well as more dramatic and melancholic studies, including a large series of solitary females. These compositions are charged with high contrast — extremes of light and color, darkness and brightness, movement and serenity, evoking containment and longing, self-assurance and abandonment. Like many of the illustrations she would produce in her early professional life, these drawings seem to have derived from other sources, likely developed from fable books or fashion magazines. In one composition, a woman wearing a colorful dress emerges dramatically from wavy waters and climbs onto a rock atop which a flower shines like a full moon at night. In another, an elegant woman wearing a white fur coat and carrying a small dog shines in the dark against a house with a lit window. The protagonists in her watercolors — whether copies or her own creations — appear in carefully studied poses, resembling the affected and self-conscious attitudes in which Lina let herself be photographed both as a child and as an adult and even produced in a self-portrait as a young teenager (figure 1).

If her early drawings suggest an aloof attitude at home, her school life was probably not very different. She attended grade school at Liceo Pianciari on via Stefano Porcari and middle school at Regio Liceo Ginasio Terenzio Mamiani on viale delle Milizie, both in Prati di Castello. According to her sister, Lina saw traditional education as having limited horizons and felt personally and socially uneasy in it.[18] Lina seems to have experienced difficulty with emotional attachment in her childhood. Though as an adult she praised Voltaire's idea of virtuous friendship, close friendships did not come easily to her. They had to be somehow unique in order to justify the effort. The only early acquaintance she seems to have kept into adulthood was her extravagant friend Fabrizio Clerici, who also studied architecture but became a surrealist painter. As a schoolgirl, according to her sister, Lina expected constant compliance with her ideas, and past her first impressions or after signs of disagreement or disappointment, her unconditional enthusiasm for a person could easily turn into cruelty and deception.[19]

Lina did not stand out as a student, but her imagination worked intensely. She worked hard on her drawings during her free time. The old monuments and neighborhoods around her were another interest. "As a kid I was afraid of all the beauty in Rome," she reflected later in life, "and I asked myself, 'Why is everything in ruins? There must be an explanation.'"[20] She was aware of the city's intense physical transformation into a vital political and cultural center of the Fascist administration, though she was less aware of their significance. She noticed the rapid transformation

1. Lina Bo Bardi, untitled, 1933. Watercolor and pencil on cardstock,
28 × 22 cm. ILBPMB Collection.

of squalid historic quarters that today are sanitized tourist destinations with the same awe that she viewed the city's old structures. As a conscientious adult, she would not spare her disapproval of the destruction of the blocks occupied by low-income residents between Piazza San Pietro and Castel Sant'Angelo, near where she grew up.

By the late 1920s, the marks of Fascism were pervasive throughout Rome. Though Lina was too young to have any opinion about the regime, she would be reminded of it constantly in the years after leaving Prati di Castello. As her father's income as a contractor improved, he moved his family to via delle Alpi and soon thereafter to viale di Villa Massimo, both in the more affluent and relatively new northeastern district of Nomentano.[21] It was in this new area that Lina spent the years of her secondary school and professional education. Coincidentally, their building lot shared a wall with the backside of Villa Torlonia, the neoclassical estate that was Benito Mussolini's residence for almost two decades after his ascendance to power in the early 1920s. From there, he not only controlled his political operations but also changed Italian society and the capital's urban and architectural landscape.

It was in the shadow of her neighbor's Fascist state that Lina came of age as a young woman and a designer. The end of World War I brought meaningful fashion changes to middle-class and affluent women. Younger women experimented with shorter skirts and sleeves, transparent stockings, and soft fabrics. Seaside vacations became more common, as did simpler and briefer swimming suits and suggestive poses, which Lina, as seen in the summer vacation photographs she kept of her youth, liked to imitate.[22] With the ascendance of Fascism after 1925, however, state policy dictated the condition of women in Italian society. Aside from her mother's conventional outlook, Lina grew up exposed to a regime that demoted women, through the provision of mass social and health services and pervasive propaganda, to the roles of mother and housewife. Such roles did not favor the young woman who aspired to lead an independent professional and personal life.

In 1929, during Lina's final year of middle school, the Italian Ministry of Education issued a new dress code for female students and teachers: a dark-colored dress with a hem below the knee, a high neck, and long sleeves. The rule of moral austerity was mandatory and enforced by school principals and parents.[23] "I used to wear white stockings all the way up under my navy-style dress, because my mother said girls under seventeen looked vulgar wearing pants."[24] But Lina also experimented with a progressive image. She saw no reason to follow the conformist roles imposed by the regime and perpetuated at home. "I secretly bought a pair of slacks and, just after leaving the house, I put them on to go to Liceo Mamiani," she reported late in life. In spite of her initial enthusiasm for the new trousers, she added: "I tripped over and fell onto the ground. It rained and I ended up full of mud. At home, they interpreted it as divine punishment for my rebellion."[25]

Whether her social disobedience had to do with her upbringing or with the pervasive Fascist ideology is unclear. Still, Lina was clear that no household chores or mothering were in her future plans. She wanted a professional education, but as Fascism redefined the boundaries between private and public life, even educated women found few alternatives for autonomous expression. Outside conventional domestic roles, artistic activities available to women were limited to writing stories or romance novels, producing illustrations, or practicing interior design, which is in fact how Lina would start her career a few years later.

Since just breaking rules would not suffice, she needed education to advance her goals. Because of her middling grades, Lina was not admitted to the *liceo classico*, or classical lyceum, which offered access to universities and prestigious careers in law and philosophy to the Italian elites.[26] Her best option for a secondary diploma was the *liceo artistico*, or art lyceum, a school aimed at forming teachers with theoretical and practical education in the visual fields, including a basis in art and architecture history, theory, and drawing. In 1930, she enrolled in the Liceo Artistico di Roma and attended it until 1934. The school, which still exists, was located in a neoclassical complex around an intimate horseshoe-shaped plaza on via di Ripetta. The building also contained the Accademia di Belle Arti (Fine arts academy) and, during Lina's first years there, provisionally housed the school of architecture and its traditional curriculum until 1932.[27]

Lina's lyceum education "included studying architectural canons from Vitruvius to Vignola, shadow theory and geometric drawing," and she substantially improved her drawing technique and learned academic artistic conventions.[28] She gained confidence and skill, producing good observation drawings of objects and human figures, though her work was not especially outstanding in the context of what was expected from students. During this period, she also produced watercolors in vibrant hues depicting several characters in action, using slightly stylized forms that recall cartoons or modernist book illustrations more than academic subjects. These drawings depict popular scenes in collective urban spaces, ranging from a man writing a letter for an illiterate woman in a plaza to crowds participating in colorful festivities (figure 2). Lina's motivation for choosing such theatrical narratives is unclear. Some of them suggest a visual dialogue with her father's works, while others strongly suggest her imitation of printed illustrations. Whatever the source, these urban drawings reveal Lina's enthusiasm for inhabited spaces and show her exploring complex three-dimensional compositions with visual accuracy. As she would later insist, architecture and cities do not exist without life, and as a teenager, she looked not for the shape of isolated objects and buildings but for the atmosphere and life that their presence made possible.

Lina's daily references changed with her new school and neighborhood. Studying at the lyceum in the historic city center offered her more than an opportunity to hone her artistic skills. It gave her increased mobility and exposure to ongoing urban, architectural, and political transformations in the capital. Diagonally across the street from her school stood one of Mussolini's most significant urban renovation projects: the recovery of the imposing Mausoleum of Augustus and the reconstruction of the demolished areas around it. Half buried for centuries with weeds growing in its cracks and buttressed by tenements, the monument was an example of the refined classical composition and construction techniques of Vitruvius, whose work Lina studied in the lyceum. It was also one of the sites where leading Roman urbanists and architects such as Gustavo Giovannoni and Marcello Piacentini exercised the theories that supported the city's new master plan to sanitize and reclaim poor and dilapidated urban areas and to restore the capital's monumental splendor.[29]

Lina would soon meet Giovannoni and Piacentini as senior professors at the Scuola di Architettura (School of architecture) in Rome, which she entered in the fall of 1934. Giovannoni was a prominent architectural historian and town planner, as well as dean of the school. He was well known for his theories about *ambientismo* (contextualism), which proposed to ground visual and experiential qualities of urban space into contextual situations, and for his method of scientific restoration, which promoted the preservation of ancient monuments based on rigorous documentation and their integration into the urban fabric.[30] Aside from teaching, Piacentini was an active architect and the president of the powerful Sindacato nazionale fascista architetti (National fascist union of architects). Focused on a modernizing agenda for the regime, he was less concerned than Giovannoni with historic preservation but wary of the rationalist and functionalist architectural trends coming from the north of Italy and elsewhere in Europe. Together Giovannoni and Piacentini were involved with the renovation of professional practice and education in Italy, but they resisted the direct influence of international artistic avant-gardes, proposing instead to incorporate Italian traditions into contemporary practice. They initially embraced

picturesque and spontaneous ethnographic references. As the Fascist regime became more authoritarian, Giovannoni advocated the monumentalization of Rome and Piacentini pursued, in collaboration, a simplified version of classicism. Together, they planned to change the face of the capital.

While in artistic lyceum, Lina observed the transformations taking place in the city brought about by those designers' ideas and by Mussolini's pickax. She also heard exciting news about another assertive personality and an architectural diatribe he helped galvanize and that would eventually transform her professional education and personal life. Among the frequent stories her uncle Natalino told her parents about Rome's public life, those about a controversial critic and journalist especially drew her attention.

"Bardi is crazy!" She overheard her uncle talking about Pietro Maria Bardi, the controversial critic who had created havoc in the Roman architectural milieu with an exhibition about modern architecture in the spring of 1931. Bardi had rapidly built a prolific career as a journalist and art dealer in Milan, and in 1930, he strategically moved his art gallery to the capital and maneuvered himself into Mussolini's circle of influence. Soon after, he became the director of the state-run Galleria di Arte di Roma (Rome art gallery) on via Vittorio Veneto under the auspices of the Sindacato nazionale fascista belli arti (National fascist union of fine arts).[31] Bardi's move to Rome quickly turned him from a press and trade expert into a key cultural player in the unfolding of modern Italian art and architecture.

During the decade preceding Lina's arrival at the school of architecture, Italian architects and critics operating under the ascending Fascist regime had engaged in a heated debate about functionalist ideas, industrial production, and popular and classical traditions. Though their dispute was tainted by complex political colors and interrupted by the crises that led to World War II, it held long-lasting influence on the modernization of Italian architecture. By the time Lina began her professional studies, three main threads patterned the irregular and rich fabric of modern Italian architecture, as well as of the sensibilities shared by her generation. Among the principles at stake were the reference to rural and vernacular traditions, the increasing association between nationalism and classical order, and the cosmopolitan references to abstract rationalism and industrial logic. To varying degrees and with different consequences, Lina was exposed to all of those strands.

The event described by her uncle Natalino referred to a bold gesture prepared by Bardi. The shrewd young gallery owner capitalized the energies of the young and vibrant MIAR group (Movimento italiano architettura nazionale, the Italian movement for rationalist architecture informed

2. Lina Bo Bardi, *Summer Watermelon*, c. 1929. Watercolor, gouache, and pencil on cardstock, 31.1 × 24.9 cm. ILBPMB Collection.

by the work of architects such as Le Corbusier and Mies van der Rohe) to stage the *II Mostra di architettura razionale* (Second exhibition of rationalist architecture). In his polemical *Rapporto sull'architettura (per Mussolini)* (Report on architecture [for Mussolini]) Bardi claimed that modern architecture should ascend to the official stature of architecture of the state and opened fire on academic architects and critics. He illustrated his manifesto with a juried selection of projects by young rationalist architects, especially those who had recently graduated from the Istituto Politecnico (Polytechnic institute), the engineering school in Milan. Right at the center of the exhibition, he displayed his infamous *Tavolo degli orrori* (Table of horrors), a Dadaist photomontage, with pictures of historicist and eclectic works designed by traditionalist Roman designers including Piacentini and Giovannoni.[32]

Though Bardi's plans eventually backfired, the controversy temporarily garnered Mussolini's sympathy. Bardi's actions as a curator and a journalist joined the rationalist movement in an attack against the older generation, enhancing the disputes among different groups striving for the modernization of Italian architecture. Above all, Bardi

helped put rationalist architecture in daily headlines. Lina was just seventeen at the time and did not see the exhibition, but at the end of her life she said she secretly promised herself not to lose track of the provocative man her uncle talked about with such enthusiasm.[33]

It is unlikely that Lina followed Bardi's steps closely, but her interest in architecture was certainly growing during her years in the lyceum. Her works became more elaborate, and her artistic technique improved. She continued to sketch picturesque urban scenes not very different from those the regime was destroying. For all the technical development of her work, she had little interest in academic and decorative arts. She didn't see herself becoming "a flower painter," as she used to say, or an art teacher like other women of her generation. After graduating, many of her colleagues from the Liceo Artistico moved to the Accademia di Belle Arti. Unlike them, Lina wanted, against her family's will, to attend the new Facoltà di Architettura (previously named Scuola), which had just moved out of the neoclassical estate on via di Ripetta to a new integralist building at Valle Giulia, north of the historic Villa Borghese.[34] Even her father, who wanted her to attend the Accademia, discouraged her plans. Yet she was adamant.

In 1934, at nineteen, the girl Lina started to become Lina Bo, the young woman occupying a new vantage point, penetrating the almost exclusively masculine world of architecture. She was confident about her possibilities, and even though there were only a handful of female students — and no female professors — in the building, she felt at ease among her male colleagues and instructors. She had struggled to step off a conventional path and was excited to step into a new and challenging career. Though she sensed the cultural controversies beyond her academic education, she was not fully aware of the complex, pluralistic, and heated dispute regarding the development of Italian architecture that had occupied most professionals and critics during the previous decade. But as she moved from the lyceum to her professional education, Lina moved from the margins toward the center of the architectural and cultural discourse, eventually finding herself in the midst of the debate. Like Achilles, the deity whose name she bore on her birth certificate and who cross-dressed to achieve his goals, Lina Bo would eventually find herself — this time against her will — wearing trousers in order to obtain her diploma.

On Becoming an Architect

Just before she turned twenty, in the fall of 1934, Lina Bo crossed the park of Villa Borghese toward the steep and curved sidewalks of via Antonio Gramsci to a set of steps. She climbed them eagerly to a small yard preceding the front door. This passage would lead her out of a life of domestic conformity and into the architecture school's new building, which was painted terra-cotta to emulate ancient Roman buildings. Despite her family's resistance, she was finally getting closer to defining an independent professional career.

In the fifteen years since its opening in 1920, the Roman architecture school had stayed connected to the academic, fine arts tradition and away from the ideas proposed by the European avant-gardes. It had enforced a pedagogical framework that coincided with the urban and infrastructural modernization largely sponsored by the Fascist regime and by the school's founders and leaders, Gustavo Giovannoni and Marcello Piacentini. Still, the institution had not completely objected to modern scientific knowledge, given its deeper roots in a long-standing debate to overcome the separation between creative and technical training in both architecture and preservation.[1] While Lina Bo was studying at the art lyceum, modern Italian architecture was experiencing an intellectually vibrant, aesthetically pluralistic, and politically convoluted period, with Roman architects standing mostly on the conservative side of it. However, by the time she entered the school and especially on her graduation in 1939, architecture, like the rest of the country, was in crisis.

For all the futurists' fascination with the industrial world, Italy remained largely isolated, poor, and agrarian in the early twentieth century, and its modern architecture emerged comparatively late to its industrialized neighbors. The call for a return to order among Italian architects after World War I had led to several experiments ranging from an interest in rural buildings and classical traditions to abstract forms and new technologies.[2] Despite the country's seclusion, however, several architects — particularly those of a younger generation living in growing manufacturing centers such as Turin and Milan — absorbed the varied aesthetic innovations taking place in areas north of the Alps.

The Fascist bureaucracy embraced these innovations in the early 1930s, gathering the most active creative and intellectual figures and keeping them close to Mussolini's regime.[3] By the time Lina Bo began architecture school, Mussolini had constructed a large network of public buildings and even created entire towns. However, instead of achieving a common language, Italian architects established themselves in different camps.

Among the groups leading the renovation in Italian architecture was an older generation that embraced traditional values, closer to academic principles and including Giovannoni, the prolific historian, preservationist, urban planner, and proponent of ambientismo. He trained architecture students in his philological method of historic preservation, bridging historical narrative and scientific rigor. His organic ideas were largely informed by the Viennese urbanist Camillo Sitte, and he did not believe that functionalism suited the Italian reality.[4] According to Lina Bo's college transcripts, she did well in his courses, and though she did not subscribe to his traditionalist mindset, his method became an important gauge in the adaptive reuse projects she would develop later in Brazil. She would also remember his warning against reconstructing ruins to their original state and the need to interpret the contemporary state of different historic works with the support of archival documents and architectural fragments.[5] Rather than a preservation or a strict modernism, she would become interested in an invigorating dialogue with history.

Another group of influential architects took a mediating position between tradition and modernization. A little younger than Giovannoni, they included the new dean of the architecture school in Rome, Marcello Piacentini, and his followers.[6] Industrial innovation, scientific logic, and even historic rigor was of less interest to Piacentini than the spectacular potential of ancient Roman architecture. Standing midway between the neoclassical Novecento group and modern rationalism, he devised the simplification of classical principles and forms to represent the monumentality of new public buildings. His geometric, simplified classicism promoted simultaneously the values of nationalist *italianità* (Italianness) and traditionalist and imperialist *romanità* (Romanness) enforced by the Fascist bureaucracy at the time. Though aware of the ideas proposed by prominent European modernists like Walter Gropius, Le Corbusier, and Mies van der Rohe, Piacentini did not fully embrace their principles. And although he flirted politically with functionalism, he had no tolerance for rationalist Italian architects and critics, considering them excessively radical and arrogant.[7]

Still, Piacentini's efforts to prevent the dissemination of avant-garde ideas coming from the north did not keep young Roman students from being exposed to them, even if from a distance. While architecture students seldom traveled, they were aware that Milan and Turin played host to younger professionals and critics who turned to international references.[8] The economic and industrial advantages of those cities as well as their distance from the capital allowed for increased private investments and closer contact with a more cosmopolitan culture, opening young architects to rationalist principles and abstract forms that had been circulating in European professional periodicals since the late 1920s.

By the time Lina Bo began studying architecture, the small but prolific MIAR — with architects organized in regional groups — had made a name throughout the peninsula. Their activities were based on the successful experiences of newly graduated architects from Milan's Istituto Politecnico. They were interested in the experiences of the Bauhaus and Russian constructivism, and above all, they embraced Le Corbusier's writings. Still, MIAR members promoted new technologies and logical clarity without underestimating the past. They believed that Italian architects should approach modernism with the classical substrate of their culture.[9]

In negotiating for Mussolini's recognition and favor, young rationalist architects received resounding support from three of the most active critics in Italy: Giuseppe Pagano, Edoardo Persico, and Pietro Maria Bardi. These critics collaborated in finding patrons to sponsor the work of MIAR members and in creating magazines and exhibitions promoting rationalism, such as Bardi's show containing the *Tavolo degli orrori* in 1931, and rebuffing traditional ideas.

Bardi was a young, wily, prolific, and self-taught journalist. He had lived in Turin and Milan in the late 1920s and played an important role as a proponent of modern art and architecture. Passionate and clever, he befriended shrewd politicians such as Mussolini and preeminent architects such as Le Corbusier and became an important mediator between Italian rationalists and the CIAM (International congresses of modern architecture).[10] He published virulent, enigmatic articles, some of them anonymously, and although he became a member of the Fascist Party in 1926, he would soon start a rivalry with its culturally conservative wing, after which he became an independent journalist and gallery owner, propelling his lifelong career as an adventurous art dealer, critic, and editor.[11]

Between 1933 and 1936, while Lina Bo moved from the art lyceum to the architecture school, Bardi and Massimo Bontempelli published *Quadrante*, a magazine that ran thought-provoking articles about architecture, town planning, cinema, arts, and industry. It made history for its innovative graphic design and openness to European avant-gardes. Above all, it played a central role, along with its more erudite competitor *Casabella*, in the dissemination of modern Italian architecture. Though he had now moved to Rome, Bardi continued to strongly support architects in and around Milan, where the rationalist movement eventually retreated.[12]

His efforts ranged as far as Argentina, where in 1934 he set up an exhibition of modern Italian architecture just before leaving his position as director and curator of the state-run Galleria di Arte di Roma on via Vittorio Veneto. At the time, he was falling out of favor with Mussolini, and so he was starting to look discreetly for new markets for the works in his private art gallery among the South American influx of wealthy Italian immigrants. During his ship's layover at the Brazilian port of Santos, he hired a driver to take him to São Paulo, which would become his home thirteen years later. After returning to Rome, he moved with his wife and two young daughters to a new apartment on via Bartolomeo Piazza 8, fewer than five blocks from Lina Bo's residence.[13] Even had she known Bardi, Lina Bo could not have imagined she would eventually marry him and move to Brazil. Her thoughts were elsewhere as she prepared for her first semester as an architecture student.

Lina Bo's personal accounts about her professional education are sparse, and she kept hardly any documental and visual records of it. The intellectual, artistic, and political mosaic in which she was trained as an architect before and after graduation is complex and cannot be reduced to a single insight. Still, before being introduced to rationalist logic and developing her sensibility to everyday and popular repertoires at the end of World War II, she was immersed in a classicizing value system during these formative years. Her education at the liceo artistico and, more important, the Roman Facoltà di Architettura exposed her to an academic and historicist framework she downplayed rhetorically but did not refute aesthetically, then or throughout her life. Despite her emotional reservations about her hometown, she did not hesitate to say, when she was older, that "Rome was a great school of architecture."[14]

For all her defense, during her mature years, of the social and political tenets brought forward by the European artistic avant-gardes, there is not enough evidence to confirm her adherence to them as a student. Still, she internalized the varying sensibilities of modern Italian architects who did not resist tradition as much as they rejected aesthetic conservatism and its affiliation to decorative arts.[15] Unlike young architects coming out of the Istituto Politecnico in Milan, Lina Bo was immersed in a historicist pedagogical setting and a less industrialized but also highly symbolic city. In a letter remembering that he had met her shortly after transferring to her school from Milan in 1938, her boyfriend and classmate Carlo Pagani described seeing her project with a "double bed displayed diagonally" in a room, a fact he considered to be "an error from the functionalist point of view."[16] Though she did not subscribe to the architecture most commonly associated with the Fascist regime, either, Lina Bo never neglected the understanding that architecture and design both exist within a historical context.

She would have to wait until after graduation to leave Rome and to find full exposure to rationalist and progressive ideas, which she informally called her Milanese education. Still, her Roman education was an integral part of the design sensibility she would develop over time. It offered her a distinctive awareness of traditions that became useful in her first professional experiences during World War II and particularly in the critical work she developed in the final decades of her life in Brazil. Classical themes such as formal symmetry, hierarchy, axial compositions, platonic geometries, and simple solid volumes with little continuity between interior and exterior spaces were part of an architectural vocabulary to which she was extensively exposed and which she never fully abandoned.

According to her biographical notes, most of Lina Bo's five-year formal professional education in Rome followed the orientation given by Giovannoni and Piacentini. She referred to the first two years under their leadership as a pedagogical challenge that combined technical training and courses about the capital's historical architecture.[17] She noted, "Many students ran out of steam after the first year because [of the] *biennio delle matematiche* [two-year core program in sciences]" taught by professors from the engineering school.[18] The following years of her *triennio d'applicazione* (three-year practical program) were dedicated to building systems and design, which continued to emphasize Giovannoni's scientific restoration method.[19]

Lina Bo took courses in art history, history of styles, and history of criticism, in which she studied classical, Renaissance, and mannerist writings and treatises by Vitruvius, Vico, and Vignola.[20] She also studied elements of composition and design, freehand observation drawing and documentation, and perspective and descriptive geometry, all of which focused on the relation between history and design. Another class was theory of architecture with Enrico Calantra, who, she remembered, taught her that conceptual ideas are historic constructs. She talked about him as having an "essential and anti-rhetorical intuition, and a method devoid of false enthusiasm but rich in a profound sense of human inquiry, which accompanied me for my whole life."[21]

Her professional education focused on historic investigation as a base for new buildings and provided little exposure to innovative projects.[22] Her transcripts indicate that she excelled in drawing, monument documentation, restoration, set design, and art and architecture history but not particularly in composition, which was how architectural design was defined in academic terms. The only two remaining design works kept in the archives from her youth, besides her graduation project, are a remodeling plan for piazza Navona based on art deco geometries (and perhaps designed during her lyceum years) and the preliminary study for a two-story rectangular house design created at the architectural school (figure 3). Without notes or precise dates and contexts, the competency of the works remains unclear. In the house design, however, the simple geometry and the way she organized the bedrooms on the second floor in a row with a single loaded corridor leading to stairs suggest a basic awareness of simple geometries and logical layout. Still, her lower floor and site plan in black ink with bright orange poché along the walls show the building as a solid and isolated object, a traditional practice that would recur in her later work.

More than revealing the extent to which she focused on the architectural debate about modern architecture, the limited information about her college works and transcripts suggests that she was not single-mindedly interested in building design. She seemed instead to embrace the model

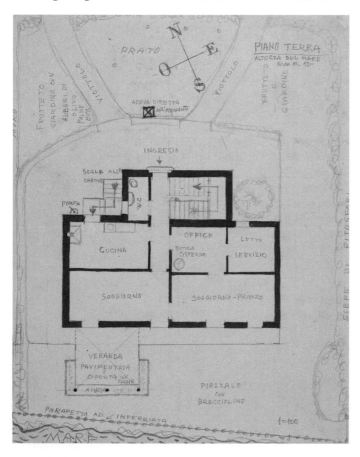

3. Lina Bo Bardi, *House Project (Ground Floor)*, no date. Pencil and gouache on paper, 28 × 22 cm. ILBPMB Collection.

of a generalist designer — an *architetto totale* — as promoted by Giovannoni. Her training in artistic, technical, and architectural principles — with courses in restoration, building design, and urban planning, which had been dominant since the school's creation — marked her mindset and career as a polymath.[23] Italian architects in general and in her school in particular did not follow Walter Gropius's recommendation to Bauhaus students to forget the history books.

Despite having sometimes downplayed her Roman experience, she recognized, late in life, the influence her education at the school of architecture had on her. "Bravi," she said, not only of Piacentini and Giovannoni but also of her other professors, and added: "Many of them were very intelligent."[24] She remembered Vincenzo Fasolo's classes on Greek, Roman, and Renaissance architecture. He was an academic designer and historian who believed that modern architecture should stem from classical canons and was also known for his warm personality. Students in his classes were asked to create freehand drawings on site and complex analytical axonometric and exploded-section drawings in the studio.[25]

Lina Bo fondly remembered Arnaldo Foschini's design classes, which covered the elements of composition.[26] The other professor she recalled was Enrico Del Debbio, who taught observation drawing and the study of Roman monuments.[27] Both were well-known practicing architects and fully aligned with Piacentini's simplified classicism and Giovannoni's urban renovation ideas. Still, she emphasized that engineers such as Professor Lucio Silla, who taught introductory technical courses, were stylistically more tolerant than Piacentini.[28]

Though she enjoyed Silla's classes and received a high grade in her final exam, he made an enduring impression on her as a female student. He was known for making obscene comments in class. According to Lina Bo, he liked to compare a dynamometer to frescoes at Pompeii, presumably the ones regarding Priapus, the Greek-Roman deity of fertility, easily recognizable for his permanently erect phallus. Her male classmates suggested that she should skip Silla's first lesson because of this. She recalled that she not only attended but "listened to Professor Silla's risqué comments without batting an eye."[29]

The fact that there were only a handful of women among the 120 students at the school did not seem to bother Lina Bo. She could be aloof sometimes but was not timid. She did not talk about her romantic life but mentioned enjoying the fact that some of her male classmates liked to flirt with her.[30]

Among them was her boyfriend, Carlo Pagani. Just over a year older than Lina Bo, he was a well-heeled, enthusiastic

Milanese student who transferred to the Roman school in the beginning of 1938 after completing his fourth year at the Istituto Politecnico. Pagani had been invited to complete his studies in Rome by an influential relative, Monsignore Chiappetta, the Vatican's chief architect-engineer, who promised him a professional position on graduation.[31] In Milan, Pagani had studied under architect and designer Gio Ponti, who was not as strongly against rationalism as Piacentini and who advocated a middle path between modernization and tradition, especially in the relation between industrial production and handicraft. After graduating, Pagani would change his plans and return to Milan to work for Ponti and invite Lina Bo to join him, where she would be introduced to a broader view of both architecture and politics.

Lina Bo and Pagani studied architecture during a period when many Italians were realizing the false promises of Fascism. The political scene worsened as Mussolini nurtured imperialistic ambitions, and an ideological crisis at the core of modern architecture in Italy soon followed.[32] The changing situation propelled some of the most self-conscious designers and critics to reconsider their ethical and aesthetic compromises with the Fascist regime and to assert another way of establishing continuity among modernity, national identity, and traditions that would be deeply influential after Lina Bo's graduation.

Before then, her worldview seems to have been more limited. While she struggled with her introductory science courses and daily walked past Villa Torlonia, her neighbor Mussolini invaded Ethiopia, and as the nation prepared for war and absolute rule, so did the culture it supported. Mussolini occupied Addis Ababa in May 1936, announcing the foundation of the Fascist Italian empire. His appetite for monumentality and nationalism increased, with Rome as the full embodiment of the imagery of Italy's majestic past.[33] Rationalist architecture had little place in this new script, especially after radio and cinema emerged as more efficient vehicles for propaganda.

But the predicament of modern architecture in Italy had been visible even before the Fascist hierarchy abandoned rationalism in favor of classical monumentality. In the early 1930s, critic Edoardo Persico began drawing attention to the illusion of Fascism's promises.[34] Persico was among the few who had resisted the ideology from the outset as well as one of the few to anticipate the crisis of Italian rationalism and, by extension, of the modernist movement. He tied this crisis to architects' inability to establish a clear framework to deal with the social dimension of architecture and to propel deeper cultural and political transformations.[35]

Just before his premature death in 1936, Persico made an important advancement.[36] He asserted that the purpose of abstract aesthetics, technical simplification, and sanitation, though essential in addressing the realities of mass society, was not to serve efficiency but to welcome human life and to help society define and share collective values.[37] Persico planted the seeds of a self-critical realism that would bud a decade later among Lina Bo's generation during the efforts of postwar reconstruction. She never mentioned his name, but his views had a delayed and indirect, though meaningful, effect on her way of thinking and later work.

Persico's critique coincided with the creation of new Fascist towns and a growing focus on the value of rural communities. At the time of his death and while Lina Bo studied Renaissance and baroque architecture, a few Tuscan architects began focusing on Italy's rural heritage, comparing the economy and straightforwardness of the peasant house to the tectonic functionality of modern architecture.[38] Their work gained prominence when Giuseppe Pagano, Persico's collaborator, placed rural architecture at the center of the 1936 Milan Triennale, the testing ground for modern architecture. In association with Guarniero Daniel, Pagano reintroduced the theme of vernacular architecture with an evocative exhibition titled *Continuità e modernità* (Continuity and modernity) and a photographic essay titled "Architettura rurale" (Rural architecture).[39] At the time, Italy was experiencing a slight though elusive economic revival, which coincided with the highpoint of rationalist architecture production in the country.

The 1936 exhibition rejected the early 1920s culturalist views of ambientismo and *architettura minore* (vernacular architecture) by presenting rural building techniques as the authentic tradition for rethinking modernization. It also differed from Gio Ponti's previous Triennale of 1933, *Stile e civiltà* (Style and civilization), which associated rationalism with a simplified classicism. Pagano published his new ideas widely in *Casabella*, and even Bardi, who had differences with both Pagano and Persico, planned to dedicate an issue of *Quadrante* to the rural house before the magazine folded in 1936. Pagano's and Daniel's work on rural architecture stressed objectivity, economy, and the technical simplicity of rural buildings in a way that Lina Bo would later evoke in the editorial work she would organize with Bardi in Brazil.

For all their critical advancements in combining rational logic and rural architecture, rationalist designers' desire for revision soon met official resistance. After the end of the 1936 show, members of the Sindacato nazionale fascista architteti transferred control of the Triennale to the state bureaucracy, and new exhibitions focusing on nationalist propaganda and expansionist diplomacy left little leeway for revisionary views. The debate proposed by Persico would be delayed until after the end of World War II, when it found new energies and, coincidently, when Lina Bo would become committed to it through her editorial work in Milan.[40]

The political and cultural obstacles surrounding Lina Bo as she attended architecture school seemed just as discouraging as the hardships on the familial and emotional front. "My mother kept saying I was not going to graduate," she complained, after she had missed final exams because of helping Pagani with his graduation work.[41] In addition, the imminent threat of World War II and corresponding bombardments prompted her family to move temporarily from Rome to the safer Abruzzo, where her maternal grandfather had lived. Lina Bo planned to leave Rome and follow Pagani to Milan, but she needed to present her thesis project in order to receive her diploma and get a job.[42] Under pressure, she organized herself and "worked like crazy, day and night" to conclude her work.[43]

On December 1, 1939, four days before her twenty-fifth birthday, Lina Bo presented her work to a jury of professors. Following the school's protocol, she had to wear a Fascist uniform, including dark wool pants, which she borrowed from a male colleague. Cross-dressing in gender and politics, she showed up at school carrying her drawings and model. Her project had the official title *Nucleo assistenziale*

di maternità e infanzia (Maternity and childcare welfare unit), which later in life she fancifully called "a hospital for single mothers."[44] The only available visual documentation recording it are three photographs of the architectural model showing three long buildings lined up with one another on a flat lot (figure 4). They are complemented by a few smaller, one-story buildings in an orderly layout with bordering walls, trees, and a few streets and driveways. At first glance, her hospital project might be seen as an unequivocally rationalist idea, but on a closer look more ambiguous references are revealed. Lacking drawings, the model looks more like a sample platter of formal experiments than a single statement about architecture.

According to the pictures, the central asymmetrical building is the only one that fully breaks from classical principles. Like the most accomplished rationalist projects, it explicitly incorporates pilotis to raise part of the building off the ground. It also has separate and contrasting solid and hollow volumes with different shapes and connected by walls and canopies. Given the general layout of volumes, walls, and courtyard, one can imagine that Lina Bo intended this central building to be the day care center, offering the indoor and outdoor spaces common to state-sponsored facilities at the time.

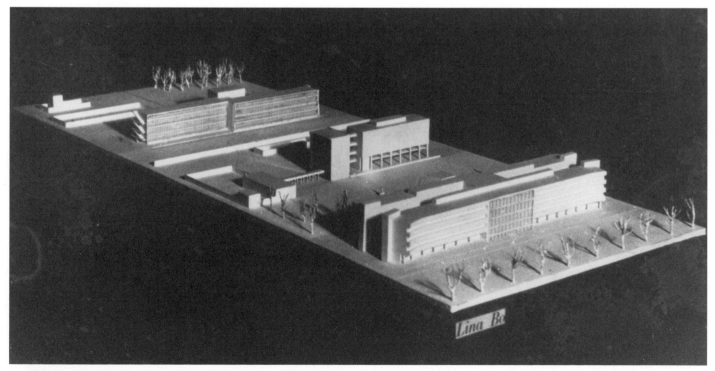

4. Lina Bo Bardi, *Graduation Project Model*, 1939. Photographic reproduction. ILBPMB Collection.

In contrast, the larger building, facing what seems to be a main thoroughfare, is organized in two pairs of parallel and symmetrical wings marked by extended balconies with slightly curved ends. The wings are connected through a vertical gridded volume that adds monumentality to the building. Its footprint suggests single-loaded corridors giving access to modular rooms, likely indicating the maternity hospital. The third, shorter building at the other end of the ensemble is the least elaborate one. Its symmetrical and glazed elevation is interrupted only by a volume with a horizontal marquee reserved for the entrance. The simplicity and repetitiveness of the composition suggest that she may have intended it to serve either administrative or medical purposes.

Later in life, Lina Bo mentioned having two references in mind when designing those structures. She compared her orthogonal project to Alvar Aalto's tuberculosis sanatorium outside Paimio, Finland.[45] However, this analogy — like many of her inflated reminiscences — seems to be only generic if not remote. In spite of the language of white plastered volumes that was pervasive among rationalist projects, her plan does not present the complex asymmetrical layout and forms seen in the Finnish hospital. She also declared that she had followed, with great interest, the construction of a project by architect Luigi Piccinato for a special maternity hospital in the countryside near Rome. According to her, his project housed Italian single mothers whose babies had been born abroad.[46] Although Piccinato designed a little-known *Casa della madre e del fanciullo* (Maternity and day care center) in 1937, it was in Treviso, outside Venice, not around Rome.[47] It is probable that she retrospectively confused it with one of his highly advertised projects during those years: the new town of Sabaudia. It did have a hospital and a maternity hospital with a day care center, representing the usual Fascist Opera nazionale maternità e infanzia (Maternity and child care welfare units). However, both buildings were designed by architect Angelo Vicario, not Piccinato.[48] Though Lina Bo's project bears no resemblance to Vicario's small units, his large, nearby hospital was organized in a tripartite scheme of long buildings, which her plan does recall.

Bo Bardi's later description of her composition as a hospital for single mothers might suggest some provocative insight, but in fact this was a pervasive Fascist institution that reinforced women's child-bearing identity. Moreover, she was not the only or even the first student in the school to develop such a proposal. Several plans presented in the late 1930s illustrate the Fascist stamp on the school's curriculum. Nonetheless, at the time she was one of only ten female graduates, some of whom had been interested in similar themes, such as Maria Ferrero, who presented a Children's Sanatorium at the Sea in 1931, and Maria Calandra, who designed a School Center in 1934. Her only female classmate among forty graduates in 1939, Giuliana Fagiolo, went for a more conventional theme: a Beaux-Arts Academy. Child and health care programs were also chosen by several male students in the years before Lina Bo graduated, from a Children's Orthopedic Institute by Mario Tecchio in 1935 to an Elementary School and a Tuberculosis Sanatorium by Lillo Barbera in 1938.[49] Her graduation project may have been less irreverent than she later made it appear.

Though she had, according to her sparse biographical notes, "a beautiful project," the jury, which included her professors Piacentini, Foschini, and Fasolo, was not impressed.[50] Her grade, 106 out of 110 points, according to her school transcripts (108 out of 110, according to her), was an average grade and less than the exceptional result she probably expected.[51] She later said that the jury resented that her project "did not respond to the strict guidelines established by the [Fascist] regime, which required that any architecture be designed with bricks established by the autarchic system."[52]

Four days after her evaluation, she complained in a letter to Pagani that "Foschini removed the 110 that Piacentini would have given me," adding that "Fasolo [was] the most enthusiastic one" about the project.[53] However, Piacentini, as the school's dean, was known for systematically giving students lower grades if they did not subscribe to the school's aesthetic orientation.[54] In her later years, she suggested that he told her sternly, "I grant you the diploma, wondering if it will ever be useful to you."[55] That comment most likely had less to do with her project than with the fact that she indeed chose to make it useful and did not abandon her professional ambitions for a traditional family, even though her prospects were uncertain.

Soon after making her presentation, Lina Bo left Rome. Her mother feared the impending war, but her father offered to send money for a year so that she could pursue her goals. With her family's financial support and her artistic skills in hand, she set herself up for a professional and personal adventure that would be far from ordinary. In her observations about that period made at the end of life, she noted, "I never wanted to be young. What I really wanted was to have a history. At the age of twenty-five, I wanted to write my memoirs, but I didn't have the material."[56] Upon her graduation, she began collecting them.

One month after presenting her graduation project, Lina Bo made a short trip to Milan to verify her potential professional prospects. On the way, she stopped in Venice to take the *esame di stato*, the test that granted her professional certification, and was approved.[1] She finally moved to Milan on April 23, 1940, and, perhaps as an auspicious sign of change, temporarily dyed her raven black hair red.[2] She took a room at the Pensione Corecco, a simple boardinghouse not far from its contrasting neighbor, the ornate train station. It did not take her long to walk from there to the small office space Carlo Pagani had rented in a building on the then-unfashionable but central via Gesù. According to his recollection, they exchanged their first kiss in the front yard of that building. Her romantic life and independence most likely justified her personal notes about Milan suggesting that she was not bothered by the escalating tensions leading to World War II. Instead she seemed excited about the city where she would get her second, cosmopolitan education. "All of Italy was boring," she wrote, "except for Milan."[3] She was serious about being recognized as an Italian architect, and soon after her arrival, she designed her professional stationery. It was simple but proud, two juxtaposed rectangles with Italy's national colors. The red rectangle to the left held her name, "lina bo," and the green rectangle to the right, her title, "architetto." Underneath them lay a single line with her address and telephone number, all in the contrasting strokes of lowercase Bodoni.

Though her reminiscences maintain that she had unsuccessfully tried to work as a draftsperson for Giuseppe Pagano, it was Pagani, who was teaching at the Istituto Politecnico and collaborating with his mentor, Gio Ponti, who offered her most of the professional opportunities she would have during her six-year sojourn in Lombardy.[4] And though she did not work in Ponti's office, as she suggested in her biographical notes, she initially worked as a freelancer on commissions and graphic assignments that the prominent designer handed over to Pagani.[5] With an influential grip on the Milanese publishing circles, Ponti's efforts to survey Italian handicraft, to associate it to industrial production, and to promote the continuity between tradition and modernity in the Italian house became significant conceptual references for Lina Bo.

In their practice, Pagani had the professional contacts and often controlled tasks, reinforcing traditional gender divisions of labor. He enjoyed public exposure while Lina Bo worked in the private sphere of the office. Such constraints, however, did not limit her ambitions. In fact, she used the opportunity to refine her visual and writing skills, but she struggled to keep a leadership position in their partnership after he was sent to fight the war in Corsica in 1943. During that period, their professional collaboration became strained and their romantic relationship evolved into a convoluted friendship. As a woman and an outsider in a new city, Lina Bo initially found it hard to assert herself as an independent professional, but it would not take her long to make herself known.

Within two months of Lina Bo's arrival in Milan, Mussolini entered the war. It was June 10, 1940, and the British would bomb the city eight times between then and Christmas. Lina Bo continued with her daily chores, but the war deeply marked her personal life and first professional experiences. She faced the adversity of becoming an architect, as she remembered, "when nothing was built, only destroyed."[6] The alternative was to work as an illustrator and graphic designer. Instead of developers, large publishing houses were often architects' best clients during the war. Many Italian publishers expanded their editorial lines toward interior decoration and women's magazines, taking advantage of the new reproduction technique of rotogravure, which allowed for extensive color printing. The demand for graphic designers increased correspondingly, with Gio Ponti controlling a substantial part of that professional market, especially through his office and his position as director of *Domus* (the magazine he created in 1928 to promote Italian architecture and industrial and interior design).[7] In the fall of 1940, Pagani introduced Lina Bo to Ponti, and in January 1941, Ponti launched a new magazine, *Lo Stile*, which would come to benefit these two young architects.

But before he brought them onto *Lo Stile*, Ponti published two short, illustrated articles by Lina Bo and Pagani in the November and December issues of *Domus* in 1940. The first text, "Stanza per due ragazzi" (A bedroom for two boys), suggested ways for improving domestic space and furniture layouts.[8] The second, "Un giardino disegnato da Bo e Pagani" (A garden design by Bo and Pagani), featured one of her India ink drawings illustrating an imaginary park with naturalistic, classical, and modernist elements.[9] In it, she showed her early interest in plants and her preference for working with small-scale elements and for organizing images in typological groups, a method that would materialize in her later projects as a curator. Soon after these first *Domus* articles, Lina Bo and Pagani joined in Ponti's launching of *Lo Stile*. Another frequent contributor was Pietro Maria Bardi, who was struggling to find writing commissions in Rome and flattered Ponti by calling his new magazine "rich, new, and original," and saying, "Nobody would have guessed to get so much for only ten liras."[10]

Lo Stile emulated *Domus* but had a more popular appeal and a less professional and educated flair. Despite the increasing hardships imposed by the war, the magazine

5. Magazine cover, *Lo Stile* 11 (November 1941). Zeuler R. Lima Collection.

aimed to educate the new urban middle classes to avoid gaudiness and focus on simple means and forms without losing the sense of taste and liveliness that were signs of civility.[11] Reading its lighthearted articles, one would hardly assume they were produced under the pressure of German advances or at a time when Italians were living under dire material deprivation. The new magazine was politically conservative but visually progressive. This was a medium for graphic experimentation, and it offered great opportunities for Lina Bo to explore different design formats in the many pieces she produced between January 1941 and July 1943. She freely combined and transformed visual elements from varied sources. During this period, architects traveled little and copyrights were largely disregarded as magazines had entered the era of rapid reproducibility. While many young Italian professionals struggled to find work during those difficult years, Lina Bo leaned against her desk and carefully touched up pictures collected from international magazines that came from Ponti's office.[12] Among the countless

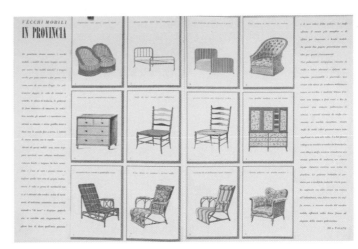

7. Article about the recovery of old furniture written and illustrated by Lina Bo and Carlo Pagani. *Lo Stile* 11 (November 1941), 20, 21, with folded flaps. Zeuler R. Lima Collection.

6. Article about the use of fabric designed and illustrated by Lina Bo in *Lo Stile* 11 (November 1941), 40. Zeuler R. Lima Collection.

documents she collected in her life are several works that show how she systematically cut photographs from those publications and glued them onto separate pieces of paper. Once dry, she would use gouache to paint over them, adjusting and tranforming them into new illustrations.

Her collaboration with Pagani intensified after Ponti appointed him editor-in-chief of *Lo Stile* in May 1941. By then, Pagani had moved the magazine's editorial office to the space he shared with Lina Bo on via Gesù 12. Her chief responsibility was to prepare printing layouts and illustrations, but she also wrote a few articles. In addition, she helped Ponti illustrate magazine covers (figure 5). Between October 1941 and December 1942, she also contributed to a few collective covers under the acronym "Gienlica," which combined the initial two letters of each author's first name — Gio Ponti, Enrico Bo, Lina Bo, and Carlo Pagani.

Lina Bo and Pagani cosigned several small, illustrated articles in *Lo Stile* with suggestions for interior design (figures 6, 7). Their first piece, titled "Arredamenti"

(Furniture), had a brief introduction followed by several pages of sketches.[13] Other articles ranged from "L'acquario in casa" (A fish tank at home), published in October 1941, to "Mobili di Bo e Pagani: Armadio semplice" (Furniture by Bo and Pagani: simple closet), issued in February 1943. Another article, "Un arredamento a Milano" (Decoration in Milan), in the September 1942 issue, was her first publication featuring a finished interior design project, one they created for Pagani's brother's apartment.[14]

Lina Bo received her first solo byline in *Lo Stile* in October 1941. In a single-page book review, she praised the German functionalist architect Otto Völckers's book *Das Grundrisswerk* (Foundation work) for its prolific documentation of a large collection of building layouts. She wrote, Völckers's "ordering of plans regard less the modernity of isolated buildings than the degree to which they positively address required needs." Notably, she announced in this first article that "architecture is . . . the expression of human life, and it has a profound moral content," a key point she would reiterate many times in her long career.[15]

Along with *Lo Stile*, Ponti created two other magazines that involved Lina Bo and Carlo Pagani: *Linea*, a fashion magazine later renamed *Bellezza*, and *Vetrina e Negozio*, dedicated to retail projects. Again Pagani coordinated editorial and graphic design tasks, and Lina Bo was in charge of page layout and illustrations. Pagani's connections to publishers from the Mondadori family also opened up new possibilities and personal contacts for them. The two contributed to *Tempo* (also known as *Il Tempo Illustrato*), which followed the model of *Life* magazine, and *Grazia*, a popular Italian women's publication.[16] They also made a small contribution (an article titled "Ambienti per bambini," Children's rooms, and inventively illustrated by her father, Enrico Bo) to *Cordelia*, another magazine catering to a female audience.[17] Lina Bo seems to have included her father, now retired, pursuing his interest in painting and living with her family in Milan, as often as possible in her editorial endeavors.

For *Grazia*, Lina Bo and Pagani cosigned a weekly one-page column titled "La casa" (The house) with interior design suggestions illustrated by lively watercolors. Starting in August 1941, their articles ranged from "In campagna" (In the countryside), where, they wrote, "you can allow some craziness . . . such as matching yellow and purple," to "L'antico nella casa d'oggi" (Old objects in today's house), which provided detailed instructions on refurbishing existing pieces.[18] The frivolous character of some of their articles occasionally made Lina Bo feel awkward, but they gave her the financial independence she desired and the professional experience she needed. They also foregrounded some of the aesthetic principles that would pervade the work she developed later as an architect, including her interests in interior and furniture design, in formal and technical simplification, and in the continuity between figurative and abstract motifs.

Besides working with Pagani, Lina Bo developed independent illustrations and sketches, many of which have survived without notes. For example, she illustrated a novel by Tuscan writer Enrico Pea, *Magoometto*, published serially in the weekly *L'Illustrazione Italiana* in 1943.[19] She also made several caricatures of her family and created an allegorical image, the 1943 India ink drawing titled *Camera dell'architetto* (The architect's room), suggesting the artistic value system of her formative years (figure 8). The drawing shows a desk, a chair, and an armoire filled with models of buildings and monuments both historical and modern. Their juxtaposition recalls the eclectic sensitivity and dilemmas Italian architects faced in bridging traditions with new aesthetics. With no hierarchy, a functionalist house was given no more evidence than a classical monument or an obelisk in the composition.

Between the spring and summer of 1943, when Pagani was drafted into the army, Lina Bo had to run their business by herself. She was now twenty-eight, with new responsibilities that gave her more autonomy and greater exposure in editorial circles. But more responsibility also brought distress. She kept several notes that show how she struggled to manage her schedule and that she faced an emotional breakdown as the war advanced. In the letters Pagani sent to her while he recovered from an injury in a military hospital, he talked about ending their collaboration with Ponti and starting their own magazine. He told her to proceed in his absence and whom to contact for assistance. While his professional tone was positive, his personal comments showed nostalgia for a romantic relationship that had turned sour in the months before his departure.

In December 1942, in a fractious letter over money, Lina Bo wrote to Pagani that she considered "any link and future between us dissolved," and she proposed to "calmly give closure to our common work and reassess our relationship."[20] According to Pagani's immediate response, their quarrel involved more than financial disagreements. Their problems had started a year earlier as the result of his jealousy and were compounded by interference from her family.[21] Though Pagani continued to work with her and, until 1946, to send her letters — sometimes in a rather inconsolable tone — she no longer had a romantic attachment to him. Her personal records point to relationships with a few other mature and powerful men. Above all, they show evidence of a fact reported by those who knew her well throughout her life: that she took pleasure in seducing but not in being seduced.

As Lina Bo collaborated with Gio Ponti as a freelancer, she seems to have attracted more than his professional interest. Though he maintained sporadic but formal correspondence with her until his death, during the difficult war period he wrote her at least one evocative and nostalgic letter describing moments of "our life full of nuances, delicacy, and tenderness," missing her presence, and lamenting her silence. Even more meaningful was a series of telegrams and letters she exchanged with her former professor Marcello Piacentini, thirty-four years her senior, which indicate that they became close between the spring of 1942 and the spring of 1943, while he still enjoyed great prestige in Italian professional circles. She traveled a few times to Rome, where she met with him, and though their communication was initially professional, the tone soon changed. Piacentini anticipated they would "do great things together" and talked about a deep and physically intimate friendship and about leaving

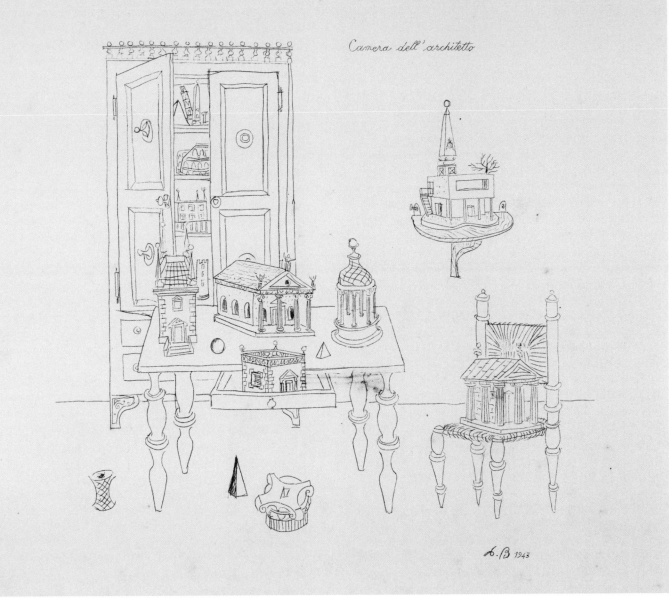

Camera dell'architetto

8. Lina Bo Bardi, *The Architect's Room*, 1943. Lithograph on cardstock, 25.3 × 35.2 cm. ILBPMB Collection.

their feelings "behind veils."[22] In March 1943, according to Piacentini, she wrote him a "sweet and melancholic eight-page letter," which he saw as a "prodigy of sincerity [and] abandonment." He wondered, "You, like no other woman," before signing the letter with a kiss and writing, "My whole life has been completely transformed like in a dream."[23]

Their liaison, however, would not last much longer as Piacentini's increasingly heartbroken letters offering to console her sadness and dismay also describe her as being distant. According to her biographical notes, on a trip to Rome in May 1943, Lina Bo met Piacentini's younger rival, Pietro Maria Bardi. She had been sent by Ponti to interview Bardi about an apartment building designed by Luigi Piccinato where he kept a studio office. In her notes, she described Bardi as "young [forty-two years old and fourteen years her senior], elegant; he had an oriental flare," and added: "I did the interview, we walked kilometers to artists' houses, to see paintings and works of art." Despite these notes, the beginnings and development of the relationship that would lead to their marriage remain unclear. Their accounts about that period are both diverse and evasive. The circumstances were complex, given that he was married.[24] According to Pagani's records and Lina Bo's sister, the relationship started with a fight over a drawing he had lent her for the publication of an article, perhaps the one that took her to Rome in May 1943.[25] One thing is certain: Lina Bo was attracted to Bardi's striking public figure and found in his articulate and shrewd personality a unique and intellectually exciting ally for her ambitions.

No matter the circumstances of their first encounter, Lina Bo produced the article about Piccinato's building. Published as "Casa e nuclei abitativi a Roma" (House and housing units in Rome) in July 1943, it inaugurated her writing in architectural criticism and simultaneously concluded her contribution to *Lo Stile*. The article also showed her embrace of the critical discourse about rationalism that had been reemerging since Edoardo Persico's death almost a decade earlier. She stressed how living needs were more important than stylistic choices and how Piccinato keenly responded to the site constraints and vegetation, carefully selected materials, and responded to natural light and ventilation. She praised his ability to make the most of the material and technical limitations imposed by the war, emphasizing how "necessity defined the plan layout." She also subscribed to Ponti's editorial line regarding good taste, remarking on something that would continue to upset her for many years. She valued the way the residents had been "attracted by pure beauty, by the architecture's clear simplicity," but criticized them for "not having been inspired by it in their choice of furniture and decoration," pointing disdainfully to the "Louis XVI imitations . . . or, even worse, nineteenth-century velvet armchairs, . . . silver trinkets, and little ceramic pieces" she saw in the units she visited.[26]

After these complaints, Lina Bo highlighted aspects of Piccinato's building that announced the basis of a value system she would develop as an architect in Brazil. These elements were at the core of her future quest for an architecture that could be simultaneously modern, simply built, and responsive to local realities and daily life. She wrote that "architecture did not emerge from the modern or intrinsic character of materials but, in reality, from the indisputable practical and aesthetic needs that render it natural, spontaneous, useful, and also beautiful."[27] She started to question her editorial jobs for *Lo Stile* and began to assert her values more clearly.

In the meantime, as Mussolini began to lose his grip on Italy in 1943, Milan once again became the target of air raids. Constant escapes to bomb shelters and the dramatic sight of parts of the city in flames and of crumbled buildings weighed on Lina Bo, magnifying her distress. She complained in a letter to Pagani, "My work with Ponti is morally almost unbearable . . . , and his superficiality makes me sick."[28] Soon after that, Pagani was released from the military hospital in Livorno, returned to Milan, and resigned from his position as *Lo Stile*'s editor-in-chief. Despite their worn-out romantic relationship, she followed him professionally, resigning from the magazine and, consequently, losing her main source of income.

Summer arrived, but it did little to ease everyday life. The defeat of Fascism on July 25, 1943, turned Italy into a puppet state under Nazi military forces. British attacks intensified as Milan became a stage for massive German occupation and underground resistance. On the morning of August 13, Lina Bo and Pagani discovered that the building in which their office was located on via Gesù had been severely damaged.[29] Under the rubble lay most of their work.[30] Amid such hardships, leaving *Lo Stile* was risky, but it was also auspicious. Within three months, publisher Gianni Mazzocchi invited Pagani to be in charge of *Domus*. Pagani had the right credentials, but he was still in military service and thus exposed to constant combing operations by Nazi troops. The solution was to have Lina Bo join him as coeditor and to have her travel to the town of Bergamo, an hour east of Milan by train, where Mazzocchi had relocated his editorial and printing offices after the *Domus* headquarters were destroyed in Milan. As a woman, moreover, she was better suited to move back and forth between the two cities without raising suspicion about the kind of information she would be transporting. Under these new circumstances, she appeared for the first time in print and at age twenty-nine as coeditor with Pagani of the January 1944 issue of *Domus*. But before then, between November and December 1943, Mazzocchi had introduced them to their new audience through two articles in the magazine. Those assignments finally allowed Lina Bo to veer toward a discourse that better expressed her values and aspirations.

The first article, "Architettura e natura: La casa nel paesaggio" (Architecture and nature: The house in the landscape), was published in November 1943. A one-page introduction, signed "L.B.," announced the reemergence of critical rationalism left open by Persico and Pagano and was followed by several illustrated pages. Lina Bo asserted that "the realistic investigation of the modern world . . . has taken architecture to the relationships among ground, climate, environment, and life" and grounded that investigation in "the most spontaneous forms of architecture: rural architecture." Like many architects of her generation, she imbued traditional buildings with modern attributes. She continued, "The primordial instinct of the shelter that inspired the hut made out of straw and branches, the conic and cubic refuges in stone blocks can be found today in the profound evolution of houses," preserving "the 'purity' of spontaneous and primordial forms from which they derive."[31] Disregarding authorship, copyright, and geographic accuracy, the illustrations were not Italian. They were not even European. Instead they represented houses in the United States, probably extracted from the magazine *California Arts and Architecture*, which sponsored new ideas in residential design and had held an exhibition on that vernacular topic the year before.[32]

Through her introduction, Lina Bo was announcing themes that would guide her residential projects more than a decade later. In the following issue of *Domus*, she published "Alla ricerca di una architettura vivente" (In search of a living architecture). Signed with just four small initials — L.B.C.P., this article was actually a complete (and perhaps unauthorized), verbatim Italian translation of Albert Frey's 1939 book *In Search of a Living Architecture*, which included several photographs and drawings, some of them re-created by Lina Bo.[33] Though little in their two first articles came from original research, Lina Bo and Carlo Pagani revealed their interest in anonymous and vernacular architecture (*architettura minore*) as well as in the continuity between tradition and modernity and between architecture and landscape.

Together, they coedited more than a dozen issues of *Domus* during the final, difficult years of World War II. Articles by various authors covered such subjects as house design, decorative arts, and art in general. Among them is the short essay by the young editors titled "Case sui trampoli" (Houses on stilts), which is a collage of images and citations, including a side-by-side typological comparison between functionalist light-frame houses on pilotis, designed by Le Corbusier and Frey, and a small wooden house built on stilts by a fisherman at the shore of Lake Maggiore, which unmistakably displayed "the traits and proportions of the most expressive modern architecture."[34] In it, one can find much of the desire to reconcile rationalism, naturalism, and simplification found in the work Lina Bo would later develop in Brazil.

She wrote only a few pieces as coeditor of *Domus*, but made many graphic contributions, touching up pictures and laying out pages that featured innovative design elements such as cutout holes and a drawing of a hand with a pointing finger to emphasize specific parts of the page, icons that recurred throughout her career. Among her limited solo contributions, she produced a ten-page article titled "Sistemazione degli interni" (Interior layout). In an almost pedagogical tone, the piece advocated for new furniture forms for a new house and a new life. The article also confirmed her embrace of the anti-academic position she would maintain throughout her career. She attacked the traditional approach of her formal education as being devoid of social purpose. To her, the art academy had "created a fictitious life (art for art's sake) [leading] to sterile aesthetic speculation." Simplicity, clarity, and efficiency were attributes she used to describe the modern house, whose main purpose was to "provide for a convenient and comfortable life," against formalist and decorative impulses.[35]

Domus increasingly embraced rationalism, but it was less progressive in its observations than its more politically engaged peer *Casabella*, to which Pietro Maria Bardi had started to contribute. The young editors failed to recognize fully that the new house and new interiors they described, prescribed, and illustrated in their pages were radically different from the immediate human needs around them. Moreover, the references they collected — although carrying a more modern and cosmopolitan veneer — still served the same social groups Lina Bo so often criticized for having obsolete values and frivolous tastes.

An exception to this editorial line was the independent series *Quaderni di Domus*, organized by Lina Bo and Pagani and published in brochures that accompanied selected issues. Instead of focusing on house projects, *Quaderni* presented special features, sometimes emblematically printed in light brown newsprint, on such timely topics as housing, human needs, and everyday culture ranging from François de Pierrefeu's and Le Corbusier's 1942 book *La maison de l'homme* (The house of mankind) to a war report titled "Centri di attesa per 'senza tetto'" (Homeless shelters).[36]

As the devastation of war came to a close, Lina Bo caught up with the harsh realities around her and the country. Besides acquiring more professional experience with *Domus*, she gained exposure to the revisionary debate that postwar reconstruction would spark. However, because of spiking production costs and the difficulties imposed by Nazi occupation, Pagani suggested in December 1944 that Mazzocchi suspend the magazine. *Domus* was not published in 1945 and returned only in January 1946, after the war had ended, with a new editorial line coordinated by architect Ernesto Nathan Rogers.

Meanwhile, Lina Bo, idle as she witnessed the changes in her country, felt compelled to revise her beliefs and her professional discourse, although it would take her at least another two decades to completely turn her value system inside out and to materialize it as innovative design and architecture.

Basta!

By early 1945, the heart of Milan had been heavily damaged by air raids and the outskirts remained under attack. "The years that should have been of sunshine, blue skies and happiness, I spent underground, running, and taking shelter from bombs and machine guns," Lina Bo would later write.[1]

Everything from paper to food was rationed. Thousands were homeless, including some of her friends. Her parents and sister had temporarily left their large apartment on the upper floor of the eclectic Palazzo Bolchini located at piazza Francesco Crispi 3 (now named piazza Filippo Meda), not far from the cathedral.[2] Lina Bo lived with the Mondadori family, and Enrico Bo let some of her young friends live in his home.[3] In the meantime, Nazi forces had established a communications office on the ground floor of the building where her family lived.

The empty apartment soon became an abode for young artists seeking shelter and amusement, including painters Fabrizio Clerici and Felicità Frai and writer Raffaele Carriere. Lina Bo called them "sfolatti" (the evacuees) and also, jokingly, "the most incredible bums."[4] She and Pagani also developed some projects there after leaving *Domus* magazine, but despite their stern downstairs neighbors, the general climate was more one of carousing and drinking than of work. Carriere liked to call it "Pensione Eldorado."[5] When Pagani was away either on the front lines or involved with the liberation movement, Lina Bo struggled to complete her work, receiving letters from editors complaining about delays.[6] She was also emotionally vulnerable and, according to Pagani, capricious.[7] Among those who attested to her complex disposition was Valentino Bompiani, an influential Milanese publisher, who called her "la dea stanca" (the tired goddess).[8]

Though late in life Lina Bo sometimes claimed to have participated in the resistance like Carlo Pagani or the leading Milanese architect Giuseppe Pagano, who died in a concentration camp, there is no concrete evidence that she took part in the underground movement.[9] She brushed shoulders and sympathized with active members of the resistance. She even told a story about having used her family's car to take a few partisans across the French border, but neither Pagani nor the records of the well-organized Comitato di liberazione nazionale (National liberation committee) confirmed her participation.[10] According to Pagani, her general political views "evolved over time, leaning toward the profound self-critical revision" that Italian architects embraced at the end of World War II, "with strong emphasis on social criticism" but no direct collaboration with the armed struggle.[11]

For all her overstatement about the resistance, she did actively engage in the reemerging cultural debate in Italy as the remains of the Fascist regime crumbled and the German occupation ended. Aside from championing political causes, architects developed a parallel cultural struggle to the country's liberation. Anger and hope leveraged their efforts to address the revision of rationalism tied to urgent housing and urban problems. As the mass of evacuees built more and more squalid temporary shelters on the peripheries of cities like Milan and Rome, architectural periodicals began to propose emergency solutions.

Lina Bo, Pagani, and Carriere began to think about a low-cost magazine covering contemporary Italian issues after *Domus* was suspended in December 1944, but their plans were postponed by the war. Still, they gathered a small number of young Milanese architects to discuss the future.[12] They named their group Organizzazione architetti associati (Associated organization of architects) and met in Pagani's makeshift office on via Borgonuovo 9.[13] A few months later, just before Italy surrendered to the Allied forces on May 1, 1945, their informal assembly expanded to fifteen architects, and they founded the MSA, Movimento studi architettura (Architectural study movement).[14] World War II was over, but the social situation in Italy was catastrophic, and the young architects anticipated a collective, daunting task of reconstruction.

One week after the end of the conflict, Pagani and Lina Bo received a commission from the newspaper *Milano Sera* to document living conditions along the Italian peninsula. In the company of photographer Federico Patellani, they traveled south on a road survey that was interrupted halfway because of logistical difficulties. She remembered being afraid as they navigated around blocked roads amid large contingents of withdrawing occupying forces.[15] Instead of finding concrete sources expected by MSA members to propel the revision of modern architecture and infuse it with fresh, local, and authentic meaning, Lina Bo found only devastation. She returned to Milan disappointed in the situation and in the prospects for the future. They never published the intended newspaper article but kept several pictures of their disheartening journey.

Still, not everyone had lost hope. Rather, postwar Italian culture gained new energy from a sensibility driven by the rediscovery of local, arcane values and practices of the country's different regions.[16] Though these new architectural and urban ideas would not fully materialize in Lina Bo's work until several years later, the investment in humanitarian action, the romantic belief in the good-heartedness of the common folk, and the immersion in frugal aspects of daily life presented an antidote to two decades of Fascist rule. The ideas about rooting design in everyday life and anonymous architecture pioneered in the mid-1930s by Enrico Persico and Giuseppe Pagano reemerged along with increased attention to the needs of the disenfranchised Italian population.

While, in Milan, physical devastation and repressed cultural energies encouraged a reemergence of critical rationalism within the growing MSA group, in Rome, political challenges about democracy and social programs nurtured a cultural movement founded on empirical realism.[17] Among the pioneers in the capital was the young and charismatic Bruno Zevi, returning from his education and exile in the United States with a new geopolitical agenda and an enthusiasm for the ideas of Frank Lloyd Wright. Zevi, with whom Lina Bo and Carlo Pagani would eventually associate, helped to fill the intellectual and political void left by Persico and followed his uncompromising steps, becoming a member of the antifascist Partito d'azione (Action party) and founding and leading APAO, Associazione per l'architettura organica (Association for organic architecture).[18]

Though Lina Bo gradually distanced herself from Milan and the emerging architectural debate led by the MSA, she helped Pagani organize a large, multidisciplinary, and collaborative professional meeting in the final months of 1945. Their immediate goal was to bring together architects, engineers, economists, and sociologists to discuss strategies for Italy's reconstruction. They also hoped to engage popular support for their movement by prompting other meetings around the country. Preparatory discussions included Ignazio Gardella, Ernesto Nathan Rogers, and other professionals who would become influential in the postwar architectural debate in Italy and in Europe. Finally, about eight hundred people convened in Milan for the Primo convegno nazionale per la ricostruzione edilizia (First national congress for building reconstruction) between December 14 and 16, 1945.[19] Nathan Rogers's dramatic and urgent opening lecture led a long list of presentations on topics ranging from traditional and new building technologies to urban planning models. Among the presenters was Lina Bo, recently turned thirty-one and the only woman to make an official public address, titled "La propaganda per la ricostruzione" (Publicity for reconstruction).

Lina Bo spoke briefly but incisively about how the press could be employed in the service of public causes. While her participation in the resistance was questionable and the full authorship of her presentation is unclear, the political view she represented was precise. Following Nathan Rogers's appeal for collective effort, she emphasized the ineffectiveness of newspapers, radio, and monthly magazines in the rebuilding debate and insisted, "It is necessary to fire up [public opinion], creating interest for whatever Italy needs to do." It would be "useless to create plans . . . without moral participation," she said. She suggested that the movement start "by making peasants who sit in the sun outside their miserable houses understand there are cleaner and better-lit houses where work and life are more serene." In line with Nathan Rogers, the newly appointed editor of *Domus* magazine, she declared, "We need to create consciousness about the house of mankind, which is the base of any civilization."

Her ten-minute presentation embraced the postwar debate about providing good-quality housing and embracing social causes that resurfaced among architects of her generation.[20] Their focus on housing, which Lina Bo tangentially pursued but did not fully realize throughout her career, revived the search for an aesthetic synthesis between modern, urbane architecture and anonymous, rural buildings. More than developing a rigorous anthropological understanding of specific conditions, designers like Lina Bo and many of her contemporaries aimed at infusing rationalism with historical, national, and everyday values. The result was a pluralistic discussion and a hybrid vocabulary that filled the pages of major publications, ranging from Nathan Rogers's revival of *Domus*, temporarily renamed *Domus: La casa dell'uomo* (Domus: The house of mankind), to the pragmatic guidelines of the *Manuale dell'architetto* (Architect's manual) organized by Mario Ridolfi, member of APAO.

One of these publications was a new, low-cost magazine that Lina Bo and Carlo Pagani had conceived during the war and had organized in the preceding months with Bruno Zevi. It was slated to launch a few weeks after the convention. The defiant intellectual tone of her presentation, which resonated with the focus of this publication, suggests that her address may have been a collective effort. Even so, her confrontational disposition and her collaborative style were noticeably similar to how she would approach her writing and, later, her design work in Brazil. For all her initial enthusiasm, Lina Bo's involvement with MSA dwindled after the reconstruction convention in December 1945. She began to work collaboratively with Zevi and Pagani and to spend more time in Rome, where Pietro Maria Bardi, with whom she had become involved, had opened a new private art gallery.

From the fall of 1945 to the summer of 1946, the focus of her time in Milan and Rome was to prepare the publication of the new magazine with the support of Editoriale Domus. Before Nathan Rogers took over the relaunch of *Domus* magazine, publisher Gianni Mazzocchi had offered Pagani his old job back, but Pagani declined, suggesting the alternative project that he, Lina Bo, and Pietro Maria Bardi had been discussing informally with Raffaele Carriere, Elio Vittorini, and Irenio Diotallevi since 1944.[21] After the war, only Pagani and Bo — and initially Bardi — remained

interested in the project and invited Zevi, likely with Bardi's recommendation, to sit on the editorial board.

On the group's behalf, Lina Bo wrote their first letter to Zevi from Milan on July 6, 1945, two weeks before a planned trip to Rome to meet him. She complimented him on his recent book, *Verso un'architettura organica* (Toward an organic architecture), as essential "for taking architecture out of the swamp." In this regard, she noted, they wanted to closely connect the two cities if they were to do anything about it. She highlighted their goal, which resembled her convention address: "To make architecture accessible to everybody so they can realize the kind of house where they want to live, . . . [and] to have critical judgment. This is what we plan to do through our magazine and through fair publicity." They envisioned a forum for debate among architects, journalists, writers, and artists to "address all the issues regarding architecture," announcing a viewpoint that she would maintain until the end of her life: "architecture as 'life.'" In the same letter, she suggested that the biweekly magazine would be simply named *A*.[22]

Zevi, the youngest of them, plunged headlong into the project, seeing the magazine as an instrument for his own political and professional ambitions. Though he could not take an official position in the publication until he left his job at the US Information Service (USIS) in Rome, he would soon take command of the initiative. Mazzocchi cautiously signed a publishing agreement on October 15, 1945, establishing Pagani as editor-in-chief in Milan and placing Lina Bo and Zevi on the editorial board. According to the contract, the journal would be a biweekly, two-color publication in large format (27 × 36 cm, 10½ × 14 in.), printed on sixteen pages of matte paper.

A couple of weeks later, Zevi wrote a commanding letter to Bo, Pagani, Bardi, and Ortensio Gatti insisting that they should abandon their previous projects and worldviews and occupy the political vacuum left after the war.[23] He contested architectural functionalism and accused Italian architects of inflating their praise of technology in reconstruction. Instead, he proposed "an organic social renaissance."[24] He was motivated by Persico's antifascism and his notion that architecture offered a litmus test for the degree of a country's civility, as well as by Walter Gropius's idea that architects should have an ample vision of collective values.[25] He saw the magazine as an "adventure into reality," one more political than intellectual, a call to "rail against the crowd." "Accusation must be our major motivation," Zevi wrote, "and the word accusation starts with A."[26]

The production and editorial offices, headed by Pagani in Milan, moved to Editoriale Domus on via Monte di Pietà 15. Zevi remained in Rome overseeing the small staff at

9. Magazine cover, *A* 2 (March 1, 1946). Fondazione Bruno Zevi Collection.

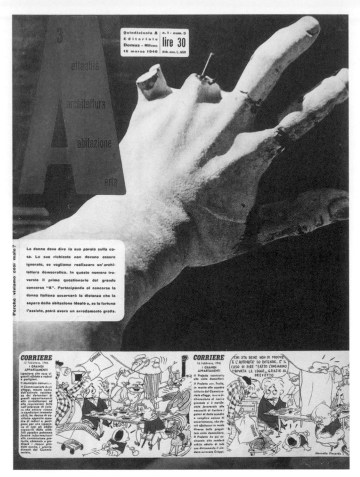

10. Magazine cover, *A* 3 (March 15, 1946). Fondazione Bruno Zevi Collection.

the local *Domus* office on via Veneto. Lina Bo was based in Milan until the summer of 1946, living with her parents, who had moved back into Palazzo Bolchini after the end of the war, but according to Pagani, her participation in the production of *A* was limited. There is little record of her actual work for the magazine other than a few illustrations and the initial correspondence. The editorial and graphic work were officially in the hands of architects Luciano Canella, Aldo Buzzi, and Egidio Bonfante. Still, her name appeared in the credits on the opening page, and according to Zevi, Lina Bo produced unsigned cover vignettes in collaboration with her father.[27] She never signed any articles for the magazine, but according to the correspondence between Zevi and Pagani, she participated in editorial discussions with her customarily barbed remarks.

The first issue of *A* was released on February 15, 1946. A large black-and-white picture offered a backdrop to the cover and announced the main topic, which appeared in the centerfold. The single-lettered title, a large, solid capital

"A," stood out at top left containing the words "attualità / architettura / abitazione / arte" (news / architecture / housing / art).[28] At the bottom of the cover page, a vignette added humor and sharp social commentary on the disparities in Italians' economic and living conditions. This general framework provided the graphic standards and the varying content that shaped the magazine's identity (figure 9).

The first issue opened with a short article by Irenio Diotallevi on the recent convention for reconstruction, highlighting several presentations but not Lina Bo's address about the role of the press. Pagani wrote a piece titled "Valmontone è un paese distrutto" (Valmontone is a destroyed village), reporting on the tragic conditions of homelessness, material deprivation, and squalid, cramped housing on the outskirts of Rome, accompanied by compelling pictures by Federico Patellani, who had joined him and Lina Bo on their earlier excursion to devastated areas of the country. The second issue featured Zevi's recent experience at Harvard University, transcribing his lunch interview

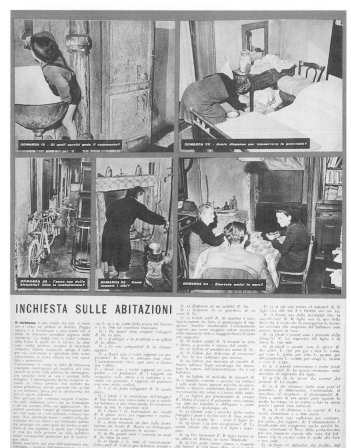

11. Article about reconstruction and democracy in *A* 3 (March 15, 1946), 3. Fondazione Bruno Zevi Collection.

12. Article about housing inquiry in *A* 3 (March 15, 1946), 4. Fondazione Bruno Zevi Collection.

with Siegfried Giedion alongside examples of prefabricated houses from the United States and followed by excerpts about urbanism by architect Josep Lluis Sert. The furniture and interiors column was written by Augusto Magnani and Arrigo Benedetti, and again Lina Bo's name did not appear in any of the articles. The following issue, illustrating the signs of war devastation on its cover, focused on debates about reconstruction and democracy and about the need to address Italy's staggering housing problems (figures 10–12).

The magazine came out every two weeks between February 1 and May 1, 1946, despite problems of limited resources, distribution, and sales. After the initial six issues, Zevi left his appointment at USIS and officially took the editorial position, keeping most records in his personal archives. He agreed with Lina Bo and Pagani that the magazine needed to change to become more accessible to a larger audience. They invested in a more colorful publication and removed the words "attualità, architettura, abitazione, arte" from the cover, replacing them with the

more popular subtitle *Cultura della vita* (The culture of living), which coincided with Lina Bo's interest in approaching architecture broadly as lived experience. The seventh issue, published on May 25, 1946, carried not only the new title but also a new anonymous column planned by Zevi titled "Attacco" (Attack). Given the delicate and polarized Italian economic and political situation, Mazzocchi was concerned about the magazine's limited sales and, especially, its progressive leaning. Zevi was instead convinced that *A: Cultura della vita* would make a name for itself. However, only two more issues came out, on June 1 and 8, 1946 (figure 13).

Just before the magazine folded, Lina Bo finally appeared as a protagonist, posing in a feature as a fictitious interior designer advising a client. The pictures (with her trademark eye and pointing finger) illustrated an unsigned centerfold article, which she most likely wrote (figure 14). The tone of "In cerca di mobili" (Looking for furniture) resonated with previous articles she had published with Pagani for *Lo Stile* and *Grazia* and had a humorous twist.

13. Magazine cover, *A* 9 (June 8, 1946). Fondazione Bruno Zevi Collection.

14. Article about furniture selection featuring Lina Bo Bardi in *A* 8 (May 24, 1946), 8. Fondazione Bruno Zevi Collection.

The images illustrated the story of a young woman seeking advice from her "friend Giorgina, who [was] an architect and kn[ew] about house and furniture." Giorgina, played by Lina Bo, appeared showing examples of modular furniture produced in series. "Their main purpose is to be useful," her character says.[29]

Introducing a belief that would accompany Lina Bo for another two decades, the fictitious but no less professional Giorgina adds that "in Italy, there is no industrial production of furniture; it is in the hands of craftsmen who are not able to design them." She continues, "We should place Italian craftsmen in small industries and have furniture designed by technical experts, but this is a long story and if you are interested we can talk about it another time."[30] Giorgina convinces her friend. Over and over, Lina Bo would insist on a similar lesson, and she would later even try to create an experimental school of design in Brazil that subscribed to that idea.

In the ninth and last issue of *A* magazine, Lina Bo's name is no longer present, but Pagani and Zevi published a provocative article about birth control, family planning, and sexual ethics, which generated some polemics. Their pragmatic view displeased Lombard churchgoers, and although the editorial team had prepared five more issues, Mazzocchi, a devout Catholic, canceled the experimental periodical.[31] He offered them *Casabella-Costruzioni*, but neither Zevi nor Pagani accepted his terms, and that well-established magazine ended up in the hands of architects Franco Albini and Giancarlo Palanti (a few years later Palanti would move to Brazil and share a short design partnership with Lina Bo).

While working for *A: Cultura della vita*, Pagani organized a large fair of low-cost furniture for Riunione italiana per le mostre di arredamento (RIMA, Italian Group for Furnishing Exhibitions). It was the summer of 1946, and he invited Lina Bo to design a stall for new materials. The exhibition took place at Palazzo dell'Arte, the traditional

15. Lina Bo Bardi, *Rhodia Stall at RIMA Exposition*, Milan, 1946.
Photographic reproduction. ILBPMB Collection.

venue housing the Milan Triennale. It displayed prototypes intended for industrial production and mass consumption, focusing on flexibility and space-saving concepts, under the slogan "Una casa migliore vuol dire vita migliore" (A better house means a better life). This show preceded the first postwar Triennale organized by Piero Bottoni on the theme "Una casa per tutti" (A house for everybody).[32] Both shows aimed to educate a large audience about the virtues of merging conventional knowledge with industrial production for domestic use, a concept well accepted among Lina Bo's generation.

Lina Bo's design for the furnishing exhibition was the last independent work she produced in Italy before leaving for Brazil. It was a showcase for Rhodoïd, or celluloid acetate, a cutting-edge material created by Rhône-Poulenc laboratories a decade earlier. "Ah, Rhodia!" she later remembered. "They paid me well and gave me a piece of fabric for a red dress."[33] Rhodoïd, an inflammable

transparent fabric, is made from purified cellulose, a petroleum-free alternative to plastic. The stall was sponsored by *Domus*, then under Nathan Rogers's editorial control, and showed the work of three female designers: architect Lina Bo and textile artists Gegia Bronzini and Fede Cheti, who researched and produced modern fabric designs based on rural weaving traditions.[34]

According to a watercolor study and the remaining black-and-white pictures, Lina Bo's stall was likely as multicolored as her drawings. It brought together craft, art, and industrial design in a simple installation with light glass cases and shelves that gave industrial products the status of objects in a modern art gallery. Around them, she created the ambience of a factory, a rural location, and a school all at the same time, anticipating the elements and approach to many other exhibitions she would later design: distance from the walls; simple hangers, display cases, and pedestals;

typological association of different materials; and juxtaposition between handwork and industrialized goods.

The stall was also theatrical (figure 15). A detached panel covered the back wall with a rolled-out bolt of fabric in a busy floral pattern, evoking a summer pasture. On opposite sides, she placed a tree and a series of striped masts, bringing to mind rural festivities with maypoles, a theme that would be recurrent in her curatorial design in Brazil. Perpendicularly to the long floral panel, she displayed a blackboard with drawings and handwritten notes in chalk explaining the need to choose appropriate fabrics for the house as she had done for articles in *Lo Stile* and *Grazia*. Her words were unequivocal: "Vi ricordate?" (Do you all remember?) and, in large capital letters, "Basta!" (Enough!), likely a reference to the garish taste of conservative and uninformed people but perhaps also the expression of deeper and more complex emotions.

After this project, the professional collaboration between Lina Bo and Pagani ended in the summer of 1946, as did their collaboration with Zevi for *A: Cultura della vita*. She maintained a friendship with Zevi for several decades, but she and Pagani drifted apart as he continued his own design and editorial practice in Milan. In spite of what seems to have been an awkward separation, she never forgot the design and political lessons she learned from her work with Pagani and from coming of age professionally during those short, intense, and stressful six years in a daunting but exciting wartime environment.

As she left the professional circles of Zevi and Pagani, she moved toward the promise of a more exciting life in Pietro Maria Bardi's company in Rome. She had started to collaborate with him in his private art gallery, Studio d'Arte Palma, opened in the spring of 1945, shortly before the war's end.[35] As the devastated Roman landscape loomed through the windows of his upper-floor gallery at piazza Augusto Imperatore — the same one Lina Bo daily saw being transformed during her years at the art lyceum, Bardi considered the possibility of expanding his commercial reach abroad.[36] He wondered if a South American country, where emerging capitalist elites would be willing to invest in artistic commodities and a cosmopolitan cultural enterprise, might provide a profitable and safe temporary alternative to his predicaments. Perhaps Lina Bo could join him on a long trip, he suggested.

While Bardi was in search of commercial alternatives for his art gallery and connoisseurship, he also found himself in political purgatory. A wave of postwar suspicions and accusations from both sides of the spectrum arose against his early alliances with the Fascist regime. He was welcome neither among bureaucrats with Fascist inclinations who

had not forgotten his disagreements with Fascist leaders nor among left-leaning intellectuals and architects who had not forgiven him for failing to redeem himself — as many others had — from his alliances during the 1930s.[37] Bardi would not engage in the collective mea culpa or submit to personal scrutiny, and he feared a witch-hunt and the revocation of his professional license to act as an art dealer, critic, and journalist. He hoped some time abroad would do away with his problems. Lina Bo hoped for respite from the harsh war years.

Since his visit to Brazil in 1934, Bardi had become acquainted with intellectuals connected to the Brazilian embassy in Rome, including Ambassador Pedro de Moraes Barros and literary critic Mário da Silva Brito, whose work Bardi had published in *Quadrante*. Silva Brito was also interested in modernism and shared other personality traits with Bardi, such as his impudence and penchant for womanizing. Once Brazilian diplomatic representation was reestablished in Rome after the end of the war, Bardi reconnected with his Brazilian acquaintances. At this time he learned of an eccentric and shrewd Brazilian journalist and entrepreneur, the press baron Francisco de Assis Chateaubriand Bandeira de Mello, who aspired to create an art museum not only to improve general education in Brazil but above all to give him national and international reputation as a philanthropist.[38] It was hard to imagine finding a more convenient prospective deal for Bardi's business. Chateaubriand directed the leading press syndicate of Brazil, Diários Associados (Associated dailies), and during the 1930s and early 1940s had wielded enormous political power and control of public opinion, with the illicit financial help of President Getúlio Vargas's authoritarian regime.

With those possible connections in mind, Silva Brito arranged for Bardi to have three commercial shows, starting in late 1946, to present artworks from Bardi's gallery in prominent venues in Rio de Janeiro, Brazil's political and cultural capital at the time. One venue was the new, glazed lobby of the emblematic Ministério de Educação e Saúde (MES, Ministry of education and health), which had become a modernist icon of great international visibility, especially after the Museum of Modern Art (MoMA) of New York had organized a comprehensive exhibition portraying the building as a special feature in the genealogy of modern Brazilian architecture three years earlier.

In light of such exciting prospects, Lina Bo found a trip to Brazil, and perhaps other South American locales, very attractive and potentially invigorating. The future of her relationship with Bardi was uncertain, as were her professional prospects in Italy. She was a talented young illustrator and designer but had worked mostly in the shadows for

Pagani and Zevi. She had no architectural design experience, and the possibilities of developing an independent career as a woman architect were limited in Italy. Traveling to South America for a time seemed like an ideal option for both her and Bardi.

More than just a romantic partner, Bardi, who was fourteen years her senior, represented the association with a fascinating, well-established man and the promise of a stimulating future. Lina Bo admired Bardi's intelligence and daring demeanor and took pleasure in seducing an important public figure. He was flattered by her youthful physical vigor and stimulated by her capricious boldness and ambition. Still, her parents would not approve her travel out of the country alone with a man, let alone a married one. The solution, Bardi and Lina Bo decided in the summer of 1946, was to get married. Divorce was not an option, so Bardi had his marriage annulled and permanently left his wife and two grown daughters.[39] On August 24, 1946, in a short ceremony at the registry office of the city hall located on the lower backside of piazza del Campidoglio in her hometown, Rome, the thirty-one-year-old Achillina di Enrico Bo became Signora Lina Bo Bardi.

Exactly one month later, they boarded *Almirante Jaceguay*, a small but luxurious Brazilian passenger ship, and headed to Recife and Rio de Janeiro.[40] As the ship sailed from the Bay of Naples, Lina moved to the portside. She found a spot with a good view from which she began to document her journey with sketches. Among them she drew sunken ships still untouched since the war's end and the potent and unpredictable Vesuvius, which had erupted violently in March 1944 and now quiescently watched her as she sailed away.

The *Almirante Jaceguay* sailed across the Atlantic Ocean for about two weeks carrying the Bardis to the tropics. More than a honeymoon, their trip was a commercial venture. Their initial plan was to stop in Brazil for exhibitions of works from Bardi's Roman art gallery and perhaps continue to other cities in South America.[1] However, they would soon find additional travel unnecessary. After a brief stop in the northeastern city of Recife, their ship sailed south and, on October 17, 1946, entered the monumental Guanabara Bay surrounded by granite rocks descending into the water. The natural landscape gradually gave way to the city until the center of Rio de Janeiro, marked by the brand-new modernist highrise of the Ministério de Educação e Saúde came into focus. Pietro Maria Bardi was scheduled to open his first exhibition in its glazed foyer within a month. He and Lina Bo Bardi, now carrying her husband's name, disembarked with their voluminous and precious luggage: two large containers holding fifty-three paintings along with pieces of furniture, books, and art objects.[2]

Three days after their arrival, Bo Bardi produced an elaborate watercolor of the historical park Passeio Público from the view of her corner window in the legendary Hotel Serrador at the heart of the vibrant Cinelândia theater district (figure 16).[3] This was her first record of the city. Framed like the glass cover of a curio cabinet, her drawing registered the coexistence of different but recognizable worlds — formal and spontaneous, affluent and poor — that would nurture her identification with Brazil and populate her cultural repertoire and imagination. In the background of the picture, lush trees, cinema marquees, and billboards surround the crowds as they move through traffic in the rain. At the center, two men sit atop wooden boxes on a colorful truck carrying groceries as if on a carnival float. Bo Bardi unexpectedly found herself in a large, cosmopolitan city, one that was exuberant, self-indulgent, and full of contrasts. She soon realized that the country had no middle class. As she said late in life, "There [were] only two aristocracies in Brazil: that of the land[owners] and that of the people."[4]

While Bo Bardi took her time to observe the new city, her husband was busy. He had only a few weeks to organize his two initial exhibitions. The first, aimed at establishing his reputation among potential Brazilian art collectors, exhibited early Italian paintings and was housed in the lobby of the ministerial building in November 1946. The second, set up in the fashionable Copacabana Palace Hotel in December, offered European furnishings to a commercial clientele.[5] A few months later, the Bardis would prepare a third exhibition, again held in the MES lobby.

16. Lina Bo Bardi, *Passeio Público Park, Rio de Janeiro*, October 20, 1946.
Watercolor and India ink on paper, 24.2 × 22.3 cm. ILBPMB Collection.

The time and place for Bardi's enterprise could not have been more opportune nor the cultural environment more familiar. In the late 1930s, Rio de Janeiro, then the capital, had become the epicenter of the Brazilian modernist movement (started a decade earlier in São Paulo) with the MES building as its flagship. In her biographical notes, Bo Bardi referred to her first vision of it as a "large white and blue ship against the sky."[6] Designed and built between 1936 and 1945, the highrise epitomized architects' efforts to consolidate modern architecture in Brazil and to associate that architecture with a modern nation-building project.[7] She retrospectively compared it to "the first message of peace to our generation after the World War II deluge."[8] On another occasion, she said, "I felt I was in an unimaginable country, where everything was possible. I felt happy, and Rio had no ruins."[9]

Unlike Rome and Milan, Rio de Janeiro had not experienced war atrocities. Still, Brazil, as Bo Bardi would eventually realize, did share some of Italy's social, cultural, and political features. Like Italy, Brazil was a young nation formed in the nineteenth century and peripheral to the capitalist system; its economy was largely based on agricultural production; and the country was politically and culturally polarized. Brazil was also emerging from an authoritarian and populist regime — the Estado Novo (New state), which established Getúlio Vargas as an absolute ruler until October 1945 — and struggling to make its new democratic constitution become a concrete reality. Since the early 1930s, President Vargas had been a charismatic and centralizing figure in Brazilian politics. Like Mussolini, he had galvanized the population with promises of modernization, legitimizing architecture's symbolic role in the affirmation of a restructuring and growing nation. However, unlike in Italy, functionalism prevailed among Brazilian architects during this dictatorial period.

When the Bardis disembarked in this new country of familiar appearances, the Estado Novo was over, but Vargas's symbolic legacy was everywhere, particularly in the way mainstream cultural discourse was used to promote brasilidade (Brazilianness), a by-product of his populist personality cult. Like Mussolini, Vargas had played ambiguous cultural roles.[10] He treated cultural production as an official, state-building affair, capitalizing on the existing pluralistic ideological climate of renovation that emerged in the 1920s and 1930s along with anti-academic impulses and the influx of European avant-garde ideas among Brazilian artists and intellectuals. By the mid-1940s, owing to its promotion by the regime, the remarkable work of Carioca (Rio native or resident) designers like Lucio Costa, Affonso Reidy, Roberto Burle Marx, and Oscar Niemeyer had become hegemonic.[11]

The introduction of modern architecture in Brazil in 1925 is credited to architects Gregori Warchavchik and Rino Levi, both of whom studied with Marcello Piacentini in Rome and began work in São Paulo following the celebrated 1922 Semana de Arte Moderna (Modern art week). In 1930 in Rio de Janeiro, Lucio Costa was appointed dean of the Escola Nacional de Belas Artes (National school of fine arts) and, with Warchavchik's initial help, carried out a short-lived curricular reform there.[12] Having first rejected the Beaux-Arts style for neocolonial architecture, Costa began to promote functionalist ideas, especially those broadcast by Le Corbusier. He was pressured by older academics to resign, however, and retreated to professional practice. Costa would later return to officially advocate his modernist ideas within Vargas's state apparatus, not as an educator, but as director of the research office of Serviço do Patrimônio Histórico e Artístico Nacional (National historic and artistic heritage department). His unusual position was possible because of the state's interest in the cultural management of modernization associated with conservation practices. This political framework allowed Vargas's bureaucracy to control the preservation of historic symbols and simultaneously to use them to ground a national project of modernity that took place at the expense of history. Vargas managed this symbolic capital through the creation of an interconnected network of institutions that gave his centralized state a leading role.

After 1934, the Ministry of Education and Health and its longtime minister Gustavo Capanema played a central role in sponsoring reforms and absorbing modernist ideas into federal administration. Able to stay above the ideological fray, Capanema had promoted the modernization of public health care and educational and cultural institutions, yielding a building boom that offered new jobs and public employment to architects. Though he did not agree with totalitarian European models, his influence over Vargas on architectural patronage was analogous to that enjoyed by Piacentini over Mussolini. Capanema's able negotiations paradoxically allowed progressive and moderate artists and intellectuals like Costa to benefit from the increasingly authoritarian nationalist and populist agenda sponsored by the Estado Novo.[13]

Though not without his critics, Costa enjoyed Capanema's full support, and he galvanized a group of young architects who would consolidate and disseminate modern architecture across Brazil.[14] He placed functionalist architecture at the vortex of a stylistic genealogy that shared unique demands of geography and climate with works from the past, framing the contemporary production as a historical event of aesthetic continuities. There was less need to forsake the past than the pluralism of modern movements in Brazil. The contribution of regional architects would be subsumed under a hegemonic definition of Brazilian modern architecture legitimized by ministerial leaders in Rio de Janeiro.[15] Together, modernist architects, artists, and intellectuals who worked under Capanema's patronage presented themselves as self-elected representatives of Brazilian society, taking responsibility for the management of the nation's cultural heritage, its modernization, and its dissemination.[16]

It was no coincidence that the new MES highrise — which critically translated Le Corbusier's ideas into the tropics — had ascended to monumental status. It institutionalized rationalist principles in the Brazilian professional milieu, legitimizing the official version of the country's cultural roots and national identity. Neither was it a coincidence that the small group of architects who designed the building, including Costa, his colleague Affonso Eduardo Reidy, and his former students Jorge Machado Moreira and Oscar Niemeyer, enjoyed great renown when Bo Bardi arrived in Brazil.[17] The *Brazil Builds* exhibition, which Nelson A. Rockefeller had helped organize at MoMA in 1943 for cultural and geopolitical reasons, gave Brazilian architecture both international visibility and a seal of approval.[18]

The country's political culture and cultural policies continued to be intimately connected. After Vargas resigned in 1945, the state apparatus, the cultural management agencies, and many bureaucrats he had set in place survived practically unscathed.[19] Modern architects and planners continued to benefit from state-sponsored projects and from the national boom in urbanization and real estate speculation, giving Brazilian modern architecture a sense of pervasive normalcy. With Costa's strategic support, Niemeyer's acclaim as a demiurgic designer turned his lyrical abstractionism into the highest artistic aspiration for the new monuments and the everyday urban fabric of a hesitant democracy in Brazil. Meanwhile, a small group of Brazilian architects continued to embrace more anonymously the notion of a historically and geographically grounded architecture, an idea initially promoted by Costa but soon demoted to a less relevant position. The aspiration to modesty could not keep up with the self-confident, although solipsistic, formal expression celebrated in the many public buildings designed by Niemeyer and his colleagues.[20] Still, simpler, contextualized works helped keep a particular sensibility for aesthetic reconciliation and continuity alive by infusing modern buildings and standardized elements with traditional meanings and shape, which opened the way for the hybrid work Bo Bardi realized after the 1950s.

Given widespread enthusiasm for rationalist projects but also the favoritism played out in their interdependent professional network, few Brazilian designers dared to question the country's selective and self-acclaimed representation of modern architecture. After World War II, however, a more critical reception of modern Brazilian architecture was shaping up internationally, especially as a result of Europe's struggle with its world-shattering cultural and political past. Even as, in the 1950s, Brazil's booming economic development and the presidency of Juscelino Kubitschek would lead to the construction of the new capital, Brasília, international critics would raise concerns not just about formal expression of Brazilian modern architecture but also about its purpose.

This was the climate when Lina Bo Bardi arrived in Brazil, but it would take time before she grasped its implications. In her first few months in Rio de Janeiro, she met a few of the official Brazilian protagonists of modern architecture. Like other young foreigners with no building design experience, however, she did not draw their particular attention. Bo Bardi's neorealist sensibility, with its roots in local, everyday life-ways, did not align with leading Brazilian architects' interest in cosmopolitan nation-building. Through their plan, they hoped to transform the country's long-standing underdevelopment and marginal condition in the capitalist world even while keeping its cultural idiosyncrasies. Later in life, Bo Bardi recalled hearing Costa say to her, "You're so dull, so many drawings," while explaining that sometimes Brazilian architects just sketched with a stick on the dirt to explain a construction detail to the foreman.[21] Her first encounter with Oscar Niemeyer was no warmer. "Europeans make things seem too complicated," he told her.[22] Bo Bardi claimed to have been impressed more by the surprising lilac suit Niemeyer was wearing than by his opinions about architecture, unburdened as he was by the experiences of the war and the dilemmas of functionalism.

More than showing a special interest in or understanding of Brazilian architecture, Bo Bardi described her encounter with the unfamiliar daily life of Rio de Janeiro with great enthusiasm: "I felt I was in an unthinkable country, living in a humane and cordial atmosphere."[23] She was impressed by people's brusqueness on the city's streets and took their lack of polish as refreshing evidence of their genuine distance from both the idea and values of European civilization.[24] Her fascination with this cultural contrast and her idealization of a simple people untouched by hubris and greed were probably more revealing and enduring about Brazil's effect on her than her memories of the modern MES highrise.

The Bardis' first contact with the ministry building was their approach to it from the corner square a few blocks from their hotel. Like everyone, they had to walk diagonally toward the slender, double-height pillars elevating the office tower and casting long shadows on the plaza. They reached the building's transparent public lobby, walked up the intimate, helicoidal enclosure of the ceremonial stairwell, and emerged into the brightly lit, glazed space of the large auditorium foyer, where they set up their exhibition. The foyer offered ideal conditions for Bardi's curatorial ideas. There were no opaque walls to hang pictures, only a neutral, open space where the paintings were displayed on stylized, orthogonal wooden easels.

Through his first show of early Italian paintings, Bardi introduced himself into the incipient Brazilian art market as a connoisseur. His familiarity with the naturalism and humanism of the Renaissance introduced a definition of modernity to the Brazilian public beyond the one claimed by the international avant-gardes and a few Brazilian literary critics.[25] With this exhibition, he and Bo Bardi unknowingly established an architectural precedent to the permanent building for the Museu de Arte de São Paulo (MASP) — a project that would materialize two decades later as a free-plan glass volume without partitions, lifted from the ground by several glass easels, and visually open to the surrounding landscape.

Among the visitors to the early Italian painting exhibition, Bardi expected to meet the eccentric Brazilian press magnate Assis Chateaubriand.[26] A self-made man from the northeastern region of Brazil, Chateaubriand lived in Rio de Janeiro and knew of Bardi's activities through the Brazilian ambassador to Rome.[27] Imaginative, contentious, unscrupulous, and eight years Bardi's senior, Chateaubriand had an almost unmatched presence on the Brazilian scene. He wielded great influence — and interference — in politics, electoral campaigns, and art patronage. He was the undeniable leader of the Brazilian press, and his controversial role is often compared to that of US media magnate William Randolph Hearst, an enthusiast of fascism whose corporation had a branch office in the same Hasenclever building in which Chateaubriand housed Diários Associados in downtown Rio de Janeiro.

Chateaubriand had been responsible, beginning in the 1920s, for many modernizing projects in Brazil. Still, he had an unprofessional and unpredictable managerial style. He also used his press network to manipulate government officials and economic elites via insults, blackmail, and even violence. His public and personal attacks ranged from obtaining political favors to extorting money to support his pet projects, such as his plan to create an art gallery or museum to disseminate art appreciation and education.[28] Inspired by international philanthropists, he had a small private collection of works by modern Brazilian painters and, without a clear artistic vision of his own, was searching for collaborators to realize his dream.[29] Before the Bardis' arrival in Rio de Janeiro, he had begun discussing the foundation of an art museum with Brazilian industrialists, hoping that such a museum would foster the development of modern art in the country.[30]

In fact, just before the Italian painting exhibition, Chateaubriand had asked Nelson A. Rockefeller to train a young Brazilian painter at MoMA to be a museum director. After meeting Bardi at the exhibition opening, however, Chateaubriand changed his mind. Bardi's connoisseurship, experience, and shrewdness captivated Chateaubriand and prompted him to buy a painting on December 13, 1946, turning *Madonna Worshipping the Child and an Angel*, by Biagio d'Antonio, into the first international blockbuster acquisition for his planned museum.[31] Without delay, Chateaubriand sought to buy more artworks and invited the Bardis to an elegant dinner, where he asked Bardi whether he was interested in participating in his enterprise. Through their conversation, Bardi confirmed that Chateaubriand was as eager and determined a man as he had imagined. At the same time, Chateaubriand realized that he might have found a man with artistic knowledge, entrepreneurial verve, and astute personality willing to become his ally. Bardi accepted the proposal, and with that gesture, his and Lina Bo Bardi's professional adventures in Brazil began.

The prospect of spending more time in Brazil to help set up a new museum greatly appealed to her. "I was so excited with Rio de Janeiro, with Brazil," she said retrospectively. "And I told Pietro: 'let's stay here. Let's never go back.'"[32] She imagined Brazil as a land "where everything was possible," a "privileged space for artistic creation," and a "new place for utopias."[33] In the meantime, Bardi was more practical. Enlisting Chateaubriand's powerful influence, he achieved in the early months of 1947 what he had done so well in the previous two decades. He met with local artists, purchased and sold artworks, and promoted himself professionally as a way of verifying the possibility of gradually transferring his art business from Italy to Brazil.[34]

Alongside the development of Bardi's plans, the commercial and cultural partnership between the two men started to take shape. Chateaubriand abandoned his previous plans to create an art museum with philanthropists in São Paulo, including the industrialist Francisco Matarazzo Sobrinho and his wife, Yolanda Penteado, and intellectuals who represented the local elites. He also abandoned the idea of having a strictly modern collection — like the one by his mentor Rockefeller — after purchasing additional Renaissance paintings from Bardi, who saw no conceptual need to divide artistic production into strict chronological and geographic categories.[35] This division made even less scnse, considering that they did not yet have a significant collection and, according to Bardi, that the museum should be a pedagogical venue rather than a specialized depository of artworks.[36]

Thinking about a potential future in Brazil, Bo Bardi also tried to make herself known as an architect and editor. In February 1947, she signed her first article in a Brazilian publication. The piece, titled "Na Europa, a casa do homem ruiu" (The house of mankind collapsed in Europe) came out in *Rio*, a monthly magazine owned by press tycoon Roberto Marinho, Chateaubriand's chief business competitor.[37] This publication offered regular short contributions by well-known Brazilian literati and artists, but on the whole it provided lighthearted entertainment to an affluent audience. The occasion of Bo Bardi's article could not have been more peculiarly timed. Her critical and somehow gloomy piece was printed during the celebration of Carnival and in sharp contrast to cheerful articles about gala dinners, parties, elegant travel destinations, high fashion, and the kind of superficial values she criticized in her text.

Unlike anything Brazilian architects would find in a local magazine, her article's opening page showed a large picture of an Italian bourgeois interior with gaudily ornamented furniture that had been destroyed during an air raid. "Things from the past were buried under the debris," announced Bo Bardi's caption. "It is necessary to compensate the future of bad taste with [the modern things] it feared and avoided." The article title appeared at the center with her typographic twist: the word *ruiu* (collapsed) visually translated her idea into shattered letters. She signed the piece with her maiden name; in a small side box, a picture showed her confidently posing on the deck of *Almirante Jaceguay*. Beneath her picture was a caption describing her as "architect Lina Bo, from the board of *Domus* magazine, from Milan and presently in Brazil," and announcing that she "wrote this magnificent article especially for *Rio* magazine." In fact, she no longer represented *Domus*, but with no one to check her references, this less-than-accurate description established her as a respectable and independent expert, especially in a new country where professional machismo was as widespread as in her native Italy.

Despite the apparent coincidence between the title of her article and the new editorial line of *Domus: La Casa del Uomo*, under Ernesto Nathan Rogers, the house she described as having collapsed was different. Bo Bardi likely meant to address the house as a social representation, a container of commodities, or a stuffy display of ornamented and contrived furnishings and interiors, all of which she had critiqued in her last article for *Lo Stile* three years earlier. This was a topic she persistently addressed as she tried to spread the belief she had assimilated from her rationalist Italian colleagues that modern design should be followed by the plainness, efficiency, and flexibility of modern furniture and, above all, by a change in values and attitudes. It may not be a coincidence that half of her short article ironically presented meticulous descriptions and a few caricatures of the excess of Italian middle-class houses and apartments. Her position (and her hope) was that the traditional house, a stage for social travesty and academic ostentation, had collapsed with the war.

With great idealism, she stressed in her article, "While bombs mercilessly demolished human works, we understood a house must exist for human 'life'; it must serve and comfort instead of theatrically displaying useless vanities of the human spirit." She reminded Brazilians that, in postwar Europe, "for the first time, people must rebuild houses, in city centers, along rural roads, in villages; and, for the first time, 'people think about human beings,' rebuild for human beings." In her opinion, not only had the war destroyed the myth of urban monuments stressed in her early education, but it had also destroyed monumental interiors. In one of the alternative illustrations she offered, two operable multi-use closets, like those portrayed in articles she had written with Carlo Pagani, supported the idea that new furniture should serve human activities because the modern house should be an ally to human life. "In Europe, reconstruction is on the way," she said, "and houses are simple, clear, and modest," suggesting that Europeans "were embarrassed by their old houses, as if they had publicly exposed their own weaknesses and vices."

This early article announced Bo Bardi's perspective as different from the prominent Brazilian architects and set up the tone of her lifelong quest in the work she would gradually develop as a designer, architect, and curator. Still, her somber claims may have been lost in the vivid pages and cover of the magazine and muted by the ongoing festivities of Carnival. It would take her a few years to publish another piece and several more to materialize her independent experiments in what she considered to be purposeful architecture. In the meantime, and for at least a decade, she closely followed the steps taken by her husband, beginning with his involvement with Chateaubriand's plan to create an art museum.

She followed Bardi as he plunged ahead into a completely new world opened up by his adventurous boss.[38] They discussed creating the art museum in Rio de Janeiro with Chateaubriand, and Bo Bardi started a preliminary design for a small venue for it in the capital's historic downtown — her first project in Brazil — but the study was left unfinished. In early 1947, the couple found a potential setting for the enterprise: a small, Beaux-Arts, four-story commercial building on the narrow and then-fashionable rua do Ouvidor. According to her drawings, the new museum had to stand out in the small canyon of shop windows, and the old facade of the building that she had meticulously drawn and all of its eclectic ornaments — those "publicly exposed weaknesses and vices," as she had put it in her recently published article — had to be veiled. Similarly, the old interior should be erased and rebuilt with "simple, clear, and modest" elements.[39]

Her project, titled "Museu de arte e balcão dos Diários Associados" (Art museum and Diários Associados showroom), proposed to hollow out the narrow and deep site, which measured about eight meters (26 ft.) in width by forty meters (131 ft.) in depth, and to replace it with an airy structure absent of internal partitions. The facade wall would remain, though it would be covered with a tall, shallow glass case projecting out to the sidewalk. Inside this glass case, Bo Bardi suggested floor-to-ceiling panels with horizontal wooden slats placed against the facade to cover columns, balconies, and a balustrade and to provide a neutral background for the display of paintings and sculptures on the upper floors, not unlike a monumental shop window set against the stage of the traditional commercial strip. She also suggested removing the three doors at street level in order to establish visual and spatial continuity between the gallery and rua do Ouvidor, like a modernist arcade attracting people to its interior filled with artistic events. At the boundary between the gallery and the sidewalk, she proposed a small planter with vegetation, reinforcing the spatial continuity between interior and exterior spaces and creating an enclosed semipublic space at street level. A long ramp flanked by two panels simultaneously created a linear exhibition display and led visitors from the ground floor onto a small mezzanine above (figure 17). From there, they would have ascended a double-flight staircase to the main exhibition hall and, on the top floor above it, a restaurant and a bar.

The Bardis envisioned an innovative gallery, but Chateaubriand was not convinced that his museum should be located in Rio de Janeiro. During their discussions, Bardi opened a third art exhibition in May 1947. This time, having the art museum in his sights, he exhibited modern Italian paintings, a favorite subject. Again, he obtained permission to use the gleaming transparent public hall of the MES highrise in the historic center of the city. This occasion most likely took both him and Bo Bardi back to Italy to select and ship the material since his Roman art gallery was still in operation and their prospects of staying in Brazil, though promising, remained uncertain.

As the Bardis organized this third exhibition, one morning Chateaubriand made his final decision. He walked up to their hotel room and announced, without ceremony, that they were going to São Paulo because that was where the money was.[40] He made it clear that, though he currently lived in Rio de Janeiro, he intended to house the new museum in the building he was constructing for his press corporation Diários Associados in São Paulo.[41]

Lina Bo Bardi argued fruitlessly with her husband to stay in Rio de Janeiro. He accepted Chateaubriand's proposal to create and direct the museum, and they gathered up their belongings and moved to São Paulo.[42] To leave the vibrant cultural life of the capital for what amounted only to the promises of an emerging but still provincial industrial center was a great disappointment to Bo Bardi. From the outset, she made clear her displeasure with the move.[43] With its cultural conservatism and social provincialism at the time, the city reminded her of the Rome of her youth. "Here [São Paulo]," she said in one of her last interviews, "I found all the musty smell that there was in Rome," which was "one of the stalest cities in the world."[44] Yet despite her initial resistance in moving, São Paulo would soon become their permanent residence, offering them both unmatched professional and personal opportunities.

During her first ten years in Brazil, Bo Bardi's life and, above all, her professional and intellectual development would be intertwined with Bardi's endeavors. From the privileged vantage point they would soon occupy and with the freshness of ambitious newcomers, they fortuitously entered Brazil's changing cultural panorama to become two of its main protagonists. Still, Bo Bardi would remain connected to the Italian and European architectural debates, staying particularly attuned with their quest to give modern architecture a humanizing face, a desire that informed her thinking and work throughout her life in Brazil. Instead of shifting her affiliations, she was about to expand her cultural geography.

17. Lina Bo Bardi, *Study for Art Museum on Rua do Ouvidor, Rio de Janeiro, Entrance Perspective*, 1947. Watercolor and India ink on paper, 49.9 × 52.2 cm. ILBPMB Collection.

On their arrival in São Paulo in the Brazilian fall of 1947, the Bardis discovered that they had overestimated Chateaubriand's readiness to begin work. They would also soon learn that his private collection was not enough even to start a small gallery. Moreover, the new highrise designed to house Diários Associados on the central rua Sete de Abril was under construction.[1] São Paulo was not as impressive as Rio de Janeiro, but since Bardi's first visit in 1934, the city had become a booming commercial and industrial metropolis. Though its social life was provincial and its cultural options were limited, there was a small group of active modernist artists and intellectuals in the city surrounding industrialist Francisco Matarazzo Sobrinho, and a few of them had participated in Capanema's group during Vargas's regime. Still, Bardi was surprised to find only one commercial art gallery in the city, let alone a cosmopolitan art museum.[2]

The opportunity to create a center for renovating the city's cultural life and connecting it to the international art world was exceptionally auspicious. It was also becoming competitive. Matarazzo, who until recently had collaborated with Chateaubriand, was trying to create a museum of modern art — which would eventually unfold into the International São Paulo Art Biennial in 1951 — with the help of their common, influential friend, Nelson Rockefeller. Chateaubriand took an independent direction after following Bardi's recommendation to create a museum-cum-school grounded in art historical knowledge instead of exclusively promoting modern abstractionism. The growing differences between the two patrons and their supporting groups would become more and more evident in the cultural establishment of São Paulo in the following years.[3]

Acting as an art dealer and promoter rather than as a conservator, Bardi benefited from the postwar revision proposed by UNESCO's International Council of Museums (ICOM), determining that new museums should have a dynamic pedagogical and cultural purpose rather than act simply as specialized depositories of artistic production for contemplation.[4] He imagined a place for lectures, art appreciation courses, temporary exhibitions, and a juxtaposition of art works and objects of diverse origins and times. Bardi suggested calling it simply Museu de Arte de São Paulo (MASP, Museum of art of São Paulo), and Chateaubriand accepted it, giving him carte blanche to establish a multifaceted collection along with educational and editorial programs.[5]

With few resources and no previous experience with museums, Bardi set out to create a new institution from scratch and in less than four months. He claimed to be building a museum on virgin soil. Chateaubriand's right-hand man, journalist Edmundo Monteiro, was enlisted to manage the museum administration and fundraising campaign, while the press magnate himself pressured the local elites to donate money by threatening to publish embarrassing personal stories about them.[6] Meanwhile, Bardi put his expertise into practice, acquiring outstanding works from struggling European collectors and New York art galleries and soon forming the largest collection of Western artworks in South America. These were the circumstances under which, at the age of thirty-two, Lina Bo Bardi became responsible for translating Bardi's conception into the museum's layout and, later, his ideas to create an art institute and a magazine.

With no designated workspace, the Bardis initially spent their time in the makeshift museum headquarters across the street from the construction site, in an old house where Chateaubriand kept his editorial office.[7] The elevators did not yet work when MASP received its first visitors on October 2, 1947.[8] Guests had to pass through a temporary entrance on the ground floor, whose facade Bo Bardi skillfully covered with a large white wooden panel with a sliding door and two glass cases displaying the museum's activities to passersby. In record time, she adapted the whole floor above the lobby into four sectors. A large hall for temporary exhibitions faced the street. The center of the floor was initially used for exhibitions. When the museum later expanded to a second floor, the exhibition hall was replaced with a multiuse auditorium, whose detached vaulted ceiling resembled an interior design project Bo Bardi had done with Carlo Pagani a few years before. The teaching facilities were placed on the backside and included a small lecture hall between the museum administrative offices and a small gallery that held temporary exhibitions.[9] Everything in the museum conveyed a fresh approach. For example, Bo Bardi used an Italian prefabricated system of pipes and simple clamps to display artworks. According to Bardi, paintings should leave the walls, where they functioned as ornaments, for easels, which suggested where they were produced.[10] Art was to be displayed as human work, not as props in a bourgeois interior. After unsuccessfully searching the city for modern furniture, Bo Bardi designed folding chairs of jacaranda with stretched canvas seats that could be stacked to provide more flexible use to the lecture hall (figure 18).[11]

Bardi's curatorial and pedagogical framework was a novelty in Brazil and strongly influenced the work his wife would develop later and independently. Interested in creating a pedagogical museum, Bardi first exhibited a panorama of art history from its origins to the mid-twentieth century brought from his Roman gallery. The material, containing reproductions of iconic art and architecture works, was used for courses in art history and exhibition design, targeting a young audience and forming docents and assistants for the museum.[12] Bo Bardi's first independent project for MASP was an exhibition about the history of chair design with several pieces ranging from pre-Renaissance Tuscany to Le Corbusier and Alvar Aalto.[13] She advertised the exhibition in a newspaper article titled "Uma cadeira de grumixaba e tábua é mais normal do que um divã de babados" (A chair of Brazilian cherry and simple boards is more acceptable than a couch with trimmings), which unmistakably introduced the simplification she would pursue in her later design work.[14] Even more clearly, the exhibition contrasted the picture of a man sitting on a rock next to the picture of a woman in a gaudy armchair, which, according to her, "was more suitable to an elephant than to a human being."[15]

As the museum expanded in the late 1940s and early 1950s, it became a new cultural center in São Paulo, with great visibility in the city and through its magazine (figures 19, 20). Aside from organizing educational and art and design shows ranging from Roberto Burle Marx to Le Corbusier, Bardi created a children's art club and small cinema school. He made many plans with Bo Bardi's help,

18. Lina Bo Bardi, foldable chair in wood and leather, 1948. Photograph by Nelson Kon.

such as outfitting a traveling semitrailer gallery to circulate temporary art exhibitions throughout small towns or creating an art institute in Florence that never saw fruition.[16] Still, he successfully organized other activities ranging from a lecture series with international critics — for example, Siegfried Giedion and Germain Bazin — to the publication of art books.

The immediate success of MASP's programs did not go unnoticed by Matarazzo and his supporters, who decided to move quickly with their plans to create their own art center in São Paulo. With donations and help from Rockefeller and MoMA, in March 1949 Matarazzo's group opened the Museu de Arte Moderna (MAM, Museum of modern art), located a few floors above MASP in space rented from Chateaubriand.[17] Following his landlord's example, Matarazzo hired a European connoisseur — the Belgian art critic Léon Degand, a major promoter of abstract art — to direct the new museum.[18] While MAM focused on abstract art and supported the emergence of concretist Brazilian artists, MASP continued to favor naturalism and realism along with pluralistic historical approaches to art and culture.[19] Their differences nourished the city's cultural renovation, but personal and ideological disputes increasingly turned industrious competition into injurious rivalry, affecting the Bardis' museum activities.

As the cultural debate stabilized in Rio de Janeiro and heated up in São Paulo in the late 1940s, Chateaubriand continued his questionable fundraising tactics to finance the acquisition of works by such artists as Édouard Manet, Paul Cézanne, and Vincent van Gogh. Bardi recognized the signs of international economic recovery and realized that he had little time left to acquire affordable masterpieces, so he frequently traveled to Europe and the United States looking for good deals.[20] With a growing permanent collection and new educational programs, MASP needed more space.

19. Article about MASP on rua 7 de Abril, featuring Burle Marx's exhibition, in *Habitat* 8 (July–September 1952), 76. Zeuler R. Lima Collection.

20. Article about MASP on rua 7 de Abril, featuring Burle Marx's exhibition, in *Habitat* 8 (July–September 1952), 77. Zeuler R. Lima Collection.

With the help of local young designers, Lina Bo Bardi took charge of designing MASP's expansion on rua Sete de Abril, which ended up occupying four floors of Diários Associados headquarters building. A new gallery hall above the existing museum stressed the free plan of the building. Light plywood panels supported by steel cables and thin metal legs appeared to hover inside the museum space, as they had done in several of Bardi's earlier exhibitions. She aimed at "an atmosphere . . . allowing the visitor to create a mental framework adequate to the understanding of artworks, with no distinction between an early piece and a modern one." [21] As in her preliminary study for Chateaubriand's museum in Rio de Janeiro, wooden slatted panels alongside the large windows facing the street controlled ventilation and lighting, which even included colorful fluorescent lights to accentuate the effect of the art history panels. She also created a *vitrina das formas* (form display case), which would become a constant reference in her independent curatorial work. A long glass case glowing with interior diffused lighting and supported by a slender metal frame spanned the hall, welcoming visitors to the permanent collection and separating the exhibition areas without breaking the floor's spatial continuity.

On July 5, 1950, MASP had a second official opening to celebrate its expansion with Chateaubriand's guest of honor and role model, Nelson A. Rockefeller. In his keynote address, Rockefeller referred to the museum as a "citadel of civilization," a term Bo Bardi would later paraphrase to define her largest project, SESC Pompeia cultural and leisure center, a "citadel of freedom." [22] MASP's renovated facilities suggested the dynamism of a museum that was intended to be comprehensive and to exist in continuity with the city's cultural and everyday life. Early paintings, modern pieces, decorative arts, architecture design, utilitarian objects, and natural and manmade forms were carefully juxtaposed, "deliberately presented to cause shock as a way of awakening reactions of curiosity and investigation." [23]

The Bardis knew, however, that exhibitions would not suffice to educate the taste of São Paulo's growing middle class. In conjunction with the newly expanded MASP, they launched the Instituto de Arte Contemporânea (IAC, Contemporary art institute) and a new cultural publication, *Habitat* (figure 21). The magazine, first issued at the end of 1950, would give Bo Bardi many opportunities to voice her criticism and hope as a survivor of cultural and physical war ruins. The IAC, modeled after the Chicago Institute of Design and the Bauhaus, began operations in March 1951 and occupied two of the four museum floors in the Diários Associados building. Students were exposed to a wide-ranging curriculum, including workshops in printmaking, drawing, painting, sculpture, industrial design, and advertising along with seminars in art history, cinema, and literature. There was even a dance group and a youth orchestra. [24]

MASP's art institute was officially dedicated to training "young students for a career in the industrial arts, enabling them to design objects whose taste and rationality for forms could match progress and modernity." [25] Bo Bardi was among the international faculty, teaching in the industrial design program after trying to create a small commercial furniture workshop with Bardi and another émigré, Carlo Palanti, whom they knew from Milan. In spite of its collective efforts, the art institute discontinued activities in late 1953 because of funding problems and the failure to create productive links with local businesses and industries to invest in product design. [26] Still, IAC pioneered a pedagogical model that promoted courses about industrial design in Brazil, including at the Universidade de São Paulo, where Bo Bardi would teach between 1955 and 1956.

Unlike the art institute, the magazine had a longer life, filling in an editorial gap in Brazil. The first issue of *Habitat: Revista das Artes no Brasil* (Habitat: Brazilian arts magazine) appeared in October 1950, when Bo Bardi was thirty-five. Chateaubriand supported the magazine, but it was the commercial venture of publicist Rodolfo Klein. The Bardis had formulated the idea of the magazine at MASP's inception and originally planned it as a joint venture between São Paulo and Rio de Janeiro led by themselves and other artists and architects including Oscar Niemeyer. [27] That partnership, however, never took place, since, according to Bo Bardi, Niemeyer believed that the "alliance between Rio and São Paulo made no sense and each group [should] stay on its own place." [28]

Aside from disseminating the work at MASP, *Habitat* aimed to stir the cultural debate by covering contemporary Brazilian architecture, art, and culture. The Bardis' title choice was "close to architecture, which [they] interpreted as having not only artistic value but also an artistically social purpose." It also shed light on "the work produced by those who express themselves with integrity through the popular arts," a perspective that would increasingly influence the way Bo Bardi defined her personal approach to architecture and design. They reported on subjects ranging from "a wattle-and-daub hut [and] native pottery" to "a baroque church, and the Ministry of Education and Health in Rio de Janeiro," and they did not forget "anonymous and renowned artists and artisans of native, African, European origin — in short, all who contributed and continue to contribute to art in Brazil." [29]

8 **HABITAT**

revista das artes no Brasil

21. Magazine cover, *Habitat* 8 (July–September 1952), issue featuring Lina
Bo Bardi's study for a museum at the seashore. Zeuler R. Lima Collection.

The magazine lasted until 1965, but the Bardis edited only the first ten numbers between 1950 and 1952 before they supervised it from a distance until, after five subsequent issues, they yielded the editorial work to critic Geraldo Ferraz in 1954.[30] During the Bardis' tenure, *Habitat* was subdivided into sections starting with an editorial topic about art, architecture, and significant events followed by short essays from guest contributors. The end pages of each issue were reserved for a collective column called "Crônicas do Alencastro" (Alencastro chronicles), which offered anonymous vignettes and criticism about São Paulo's cultural and social life. There was much improvisation during that period. Texts were often written by more than one person, including their young assistants, Flávio Motta and Luís Hossaka. Language and style were often disregarded, and mistranslations gave the collective project an Italianate accent. Many articles were left unsigned, though Motta attributed a series of them to Bo Bardi.[31] She also coordinated design and production while Bardi handled editorial matters, and her team touched up images from other national and international publications for internal and cover illustrations. Her Italian publishing experience was put to good use.

The magazine gave Bo Bardi the opportunity to begin expressing herself independently. Attuned with Italian neorealist sensibilities of her generation, she saw in *Habitat* a vehicle to explore, in constant dialogue with Bardi, the ideas of autochthonous Brazilian design and architecture associated with simplicity and purposefulness. In addition to producing short pieces about modern art and architecture, she documented rural architecture, popular culture, and everyday artifacts in Brazil, all of which eventually became part of her design vocabulary.

She opened the first issue of *Habitat* with an article about houses designed by João Vilanova Artigas, a growing leader in São Paulo architecture. She presented his work as being both human and homely, revealing "the first glaring of a new era: the era of human solidarity."[32] Another essay, illustrated with a house in the jungle — likely a collage of undisclosed sources — and unsigned but attributed to Bo Bardi, announced: "Amazonas: O povo arquiteto" (Amazon: the people as architect) and foreshadowed similar articles. "The true sense of work in Brazil," it read, "should start with the people in the hinterlands." She specifically noted the "extremely functional, pleasant, and aesthetic architecture surrounded by everyday life scenes manifesting the contentment of simple people."[33] A few years later, Chateaubriand would hyperbolically comment that "an artist with such lucidity as Lina Bo immediately saw in the aboriginal the raw material for new artistic inspiration."[34]

Still in the first issue, an essay signed "P. M. Bardi" talked about the pre-Enlightenment Italian theorist Carlo Lodoli, whose work anticipated the notions of functionalism and truth of materials embraced by modern architects in general and by Bo Bardi in particular.[35] Bardi evoked Lodoli's idea of a rational chair to combat the indiscriminate use of ornamental forms in design and architecture, in a way that resonated with the virtues pointed out in the Amazon house, in popular Brazilian artifacts in other articles for the magazine, and in his wife's writing.[36]

The second issue of *Habitat*, published in January 1951, extended the humanistic leaning of the inaugural number. Bardi's editorial, "Para uma nova cultura do homem" (Toward a new culture of mankind), referred to a report released by the International Council of Museums suggesting international cooperation between art museums and their experts for humanitarian aims.[37] In line with the report, Bo Bardi's poignant essay "Bela criança" (Beautiful child), one of the most significant of her career, established important premises that would guide her intellectual and professional viewpoints for the next four decades.[38] Her piece, illustrated with a large photograph of the iconic MES building, prefaced a series of works by up-and-coming Brazilian architects. It appeared in tandem with an article by architect Abelardo de Souza, who differed from the dominant Carioca discourse and critically suggested that Brazilian architects should abandon European models for a humanized approach based on local climate, materials, lifestyle, and the legacy of inventive historic building solutions.[39]

In Bo Bardi's assessment, the "new Brazilian architecture has many defects: it is young; it didn't have much time to stop and think." She suggested a personal way for developing contemporary Brazilian architecture, a way that sat between the blind embrace of formalism and modernization and the growing intolerance of international critics toward Brazilian architecture. She wrote: "The battle must be targeted against this dangerous generalization — against this defamation of the spirit of modern architecture, which is a spirit of intransigence and love for mankind and which has nothing to do with exterior shape and formalistic acrobatics." She agreed with Bruno Zevi's position against "formal complacencies" but disagreed with his opinion that "Brazilian architecture already present[ed] the road to a new academy."[40]

Lina Bo Bardi idealistically proposed that modern Brazilian architecture should derive "from the wattle-and-daub of solitary men who carefully cut the branches from the jungle, and from the rubber tapper's house made out of wooden floors and thatched roofs." To her, anonymous vernacular architecture "contain[ed], in its furious resolu-tion of making, a sense of pride and a poetry that belong to the man . . . who does not know the great cities of civiliza-tion and of museums, and who does not have a millenary cultural heritage." She believed that the meaning of Brazilian architecture could not be achieved until "its spirit [became] the spirit of mankind; until its quest [became] the quest for the values of life in evolution," inspired by "the intimate poetry of the Brazilian land."[41] Her search for a new humanism and the hybrid architecture and design she would gradually develop did not rule out either her adher-ence to the rationalist principles and the heroic hope of the modern movement or her sensitivity to local and popular repertoires.

A few Brazilian architects, such as Lucio Costa, had experimented previously with simple materials and local techniques in the 1930s and 1940s. Later, Rino Levi and Vilanova Artigas flirted with organic architecture in the 1950s. However, those incursions into traditional archi-tecture in Brazil were overshadowed by the prevailing Corbusian influences that Bo Bardi questioned in her article "Bela criança."

After a short writing hiatus, she returned to the third issue of *Habitat* with two collaborative, unsigned short pieces.[42] The first, "Por que o povo é arquiteto?" (Why are common people architects?), suggested, "Poor people are architects because they do not share the extravagant ideas of rich people about the house."[43] The second, longer article, titled "Casa de sete mil cruzeiros" (The seven-thousand cruzeiro house), was presented as empirical evidence of her previous claim. The illustrated essay reported on a week-end visit to a family living in the semirural outskirts of São Paulo. The story's protagonist was a woman who worked for a brick factory, where she produced the material for what Bo Bardi saw as a mythical rural house. "Everything was orderly, precise, well measured, correct, in the right place," she wrote, associating it with "the natural taste of people from the countryside, a fact that strongly contributed to add beauty, rationality, and intelligence" to the construction.[44]

Bo Bardi was strongly influenced by literature and exhi-bitions relating modern architecture with rural traditions that marked the renovation of Italian architecture during and after World War II. That experience informed the initial editorial line of *Habitat* and, a few years later, her work as a designer. She had left Italy, but the architectural debate in her native country remained her main reference during this period in São Paulo. Her articles were closely attuned with ideas from the 1930s and early 1940s as well as with newer ones, such as those presented in the *Mostra sull'architettura spontanea* (Spontaneous architecture exhibition) presented

by Italian architects including Giancarlo de Carlo and Giuseppe Samonà at the 1951 Milan Triennale. Like Bo Bardi in Brazil, they emulated Edoardo Persico's pioneering idea that architecture was part of a movement to welcome human life and to help society define and share collective values.[45] They sought to revise the recent legacy of modern architecture within the framework of a new humanism — the same argument Bo Bardi asserted in her early articles and throughout her career — calling into question the diver-gence between abstract and naturalist art — just as Bardi often did — and promoting the study of vernacular build-ings and the notion that a house was essentially a building to be lived in.[46]

She discontinued writing articles for *Habitat* when she began developing projects for Bardi and Chateaubriand, and, after completing the ninth issue of *Habitat*, she and Bardi took a year's leave from the magazine in 1953 in order to take care of a series of exhibitions of MASP's collection abroad. Motta took over as editor-in-chief and published the last of the series of Bo Bardi's unsigned essays, "O povo é arquiteto" (The people as architect), about the virtues of anonymous architecture. "Common people are born with architecture in their blood," she wrote, "because they are born with the innate spirit of searching, of needs, opportunities, and functions of life." She praised popular practical solutions and architectural sensitivity as some-times "seem[ing] more logical than the way architects invent deformed structures in their search for hermetic subtleties or extravagant forms." "Thatched roofs," she pronounced, alle-gorically foreshadowing several house studies she would later produce, "have nothing to be jealous of the most beautiful roofs."[47]

Bo Bardi returned temporarily to *Habitat* as editor-in-chief for the January–February 1954 issue, which included her and Bardi's final contributions to the magazine. Besides publishing a project for Chateaubriand's new press head-quarters in which she had collaborated with Pier Luigi Nervi, she joined in the criticism against the second edition of the São Paulo Biennial.[48] While architect Abelardo de Souza, who often contributed to the magazine, criticized Gropius's and Aalto's recent lectures during the event, she reiterated Bardi's disapproval of the Biennial's lack of public commitment to mass education.[49] She also registered her political thoughts concerning the social role of architects.

Her short piece titled "Casas, eles também precisam" (They also need houses), which resembled articles she had edited in support of the efforts of Italian reconstruction, was in tune with Brazilian architects' growing research about housing. In it, Bo Bardi questioned reactionary laws, economic inequities, and the lack of organization between architects and the building industry. Above all, she paid tribute to Giuseppe Pagano, whom she presented as a heroic figure while paraphrasing his declaration that "a curbstone in an anonymous neighborhood is worth much more than a monument."[50]

Bo Bardi's last contribution to the magazine appeared in the column "Polêmica" (Controversy), in which she criticized the opening of the new neogothic Cathedral of São Paulo. "Another lost cause," she declared, describing the church as "an inflated skin with a ridiculous cupola on top." More than a farewell article, this piece expressed her yearning to be the kind of architect she was still struggling to materialize in practice. As she observed and criticized, with guilt, the church's elaborate European appearance, she wondered about missed opportunities to ground its design in Brazilian traditions and practices. She proposed the examples of the "cathedrals of fishing or rural villages next to a cemetery full of wild plants" and of the "works of naïf painters, still able to communicate with the people, instead of imported works swollen with aesthetic rhetoric." She wondered about "other cathedrals, with white-washed walls or unfinished brick; poor, miserable churches," such as those she would design two decades later.[51]

This fifteenth issue of *Habitat* marked the end of the Bardis' editorial work but not their engagement in the cultural battles emerging in São Paulo. They co-signed an editorial letter with their publisher, a declaration printed on the first page, registering that they had presented a critical panorama of Brazilian art and design without denying their irreverent and unforgiving approach. They also justified their decision to leave the magazine by saying that their work had a contingent, short-lived, though intense controversial character, but they feared they had become repetitive and lost the readers' interest. They candidly announced being aware that their "attitude certainly surprised those people who tirelessly tapped each other's shoulders" and refused to participate "in the excessive optimism regarding the grandiosity of certain architects elevated to national monuments."[52]

Their resignation letter also mentioned several trips they were scheduled to make to Europe and the United States to organize exhibitions with masterpieces of MASP's collection. At the time, Bardi and Chateaubriand were concerned with accusations by detractors that some works in the museum collection were counterfeit. To dispel the rumors, they needed internationally recognized experts to certify the artworks' authenticity. With the end of the Bardis' tenure, the publisher, Rodolfo Klein, turned *Habitat* into a magazine that focused on architecture even though it continued to cover general cultural and artistic subjects.

Still, they left the magazine with pride and hope, asking at the end of their letter: "How many true artists, from the native Brazilian artisan to the primitive painter, from simple foremen to young architects, benefited from our revisionary proposal?"[53]

Leaving *Habitat* did not interrupt Bo Bardi's quest to develop a Brazilian architecture. During her time at the magazine, she produced several design and architecture projects in tandem with her curatorial assignments for the museum. For all the qualities of that initial work, it would be several more years before she could translate the aspirations she expressed in the pages of *Habitat* and transition from the direct influence of Italian rationalism into an architectural language of her own that was as much reverential of the political approach of the early modern movement as it was of hybrid vocabularies and humane goals.

Ventures and Adventures in Design

The late 1940s and early 1950s were a phase of inaugural realizations in Lina Bo Bardi's development as a designer and an architect, though it would take her time to materialize the independent viewpoint she conceptually elaborated in *Habitat*. Her initial compliance with Pietro Maria Bardi's cultural interests and business relations in São Paulo and her lingering connection to the Italian architectural debate kept her interested in a critical rationalism, while the lack of reliable commissions during this period limited her output. Still, she rehearsed her dissonant voice, expressing her desire to humanize architecture and to keep culture, life, and nature close together as she attempted to make herself heard by Brazilian architects.

Though Bardi claimed to have planted MASP on virgin soil, the cultural life of São Paulo was quickly changing.[1] The same was true concerning architecture and design, with the emergence of a younger generation who sought alternatives to the hegemonic Carioca group, as well as the influx of other immigrant architects and a booming construction market. While foreign architects contributed to change the city's image, preeminent native Paulistano architects became resolutely involved in the renovation of their practices and of the cultural life of São Paulo in the mid-1940s. However, instead of orbiting around MASP, they contributed to the creation of MAM and Matarazzo's cultural initiatives. The two institutions, along with the Bienal Internacional de São Paulo (International São Paulo art biennial), helped to project São Paulo both locally and abroad, stirring up the ongoing symbolic and political disputes over postwar national modernization.

Although the MES building built in Rio de Janeiro became a national modernist architectural icon, São Paulo also had its own feature building. Edifício Esther (Esther building) — opened in 1938 and located on praça da República, a block from the two new museums — was the only remarkable rationalist mixed-use building when the Bardis arrived in the city. Above all, it also served as an informal and vibrant business and cultural center that included, beyond commercial offices, Rino Levi's architecture studio and the apartments of modernist architect Vital Brasil (one of the building's designers) and modernist painters Emiliano Di Cavalcanti and Noemia Mourão. Below the street level, but not less relevantly, the lower floor housed the nascent local chapter of the Instituto de Arquitetos do Brasil (IAB, Brazilian institute of architects) along with the Clube dos Artistas Contemporâneos (Contemporary Artists' Club).

Architects in São Paulo were slower than their Carioca counterparts to accept rationalism. Not only had they not shared in the support of the Vargas regime for almost fifteen years, but design education was limited to engineering programs until the Universidade de São Paulo created an independent architecture school in 1948.[2] Beyond the early experiments of Gregori Warchavchik beginning in the late 1920s, the most active designers in building and engineering catered to an expanding but conformist real estate market, often downplaying technological innovation with academic reminiscences.[3] Only by the mid-1940s, before and during the time the Bardis arrived in the city, did Paulistano architects begin to establish an autonomous and pluralistic professional culture around the IAB.

Rino Levi, Eduardo Kneese de Mello, Osvaldo Bratke, and João Vilanova Artigas were among the most prominent of them, and Lina Bo Bardi and her husband attempted to establish professional relations with them, but their connection with Chateaubriand tended to keep them in a different camp. Levi, like Warchavchik, had studied in Rome several years before Bo Bardi and had become familiar with European rationalism, incorporating it in his residential and commercial buildings. The other designers studied architecture as part of their engineering degrees in São Paulo. Kneese de Mello created *Acrópole* magazine in 1938, publishing primarily residential projects. Bratke was involved in urban development and upscale residential projects informed by both Brazilian popular architecture and rationalism. Artigas, who became deeply involved in the Brazilian Communist Party, designed residences and public buildings and, after flirting with Frank Lloyd Wright's organicism and the Carioca school until the mid-1950s, would lead the embrace of raw concrete structures in the renovation of mainstream Brazilian architectural discourse, a technique Bo Bardi would later apply to her most preeminent designs.

While Brazilian architects tended to control the cultural scene, the influx of foreign designers in São Paulo during and after World War II contributed to the modernization of the city's architectural landscape, though in a largely pragmatic and anonymous way. Immigration brought eastern European architects such as Adolf Franz Heep, Lucjan Korngold, and, briefly, Bernard Rudofsky to Brazil, as well as several Italians like Bo Bardi, though slightly older than she was.[4] Among them were Daniele Calabi, whose house the Bardis temporarily rented in the leafy neighborhood of Pacaembu, and especially Giancarlo Palanti, whom they knew from Milan. These immigrant designers developed significant projects and careers that related their previous experiences to the reality of Brazil. Though they long remained marginal to the cultural establishment, they created a small but important tributary in the renovation of the architectural mainstream in Brazil.[5]

Bo Bardi and architects like her would eventually help revive the intellectual impulse of early Paulistano modernists to converge local, national, and international references, assimilating and transforming different cultural values and practices. However, her concrete application of those impulses would have to wait until the late 1950s, when she received her first independent commissions. In the meantime, her design work would be contained within Bardi's circle of influence. She was in her mid-thirties and professionally unexperienced as a building designer. Her husband was in his early fifties and had a commanding voice; after just a short time in Brazil, he realized that his cultural and commercial prospects in this new land were better than in Italy.

By 1948, the Bardis had decided to remain in Brazil, and they soon transferred Bardi's Roman art gallery to São Paulo, renaming it Estúdio Palma.[6] They rented a glazed office in a modernist building on rua Dr. Bráulio Gomes facing the new central library plaza and conveniently located two blocks from MASP.[7] They also invited Valéria Piacentini Cirell, an interior designer who was married to Renato Cirell Czerna, the Brazilian half-brother of Bo Bardi's Italian friend Fabrizio Clerici, to collaborate with them.[8] The Bardis saw Cirell as a liaison between them and their potential Paulistano clientele.

In addition to selling paintings and art objects to the elites, the Bardis created a small firm in partnership with architect Giancarlo Palanti to design home and commercial interiors and to manufacture modern furniture. They called it Oficina Paubrá (Paubrá workshop, shortening the Portuguese word for Brazilwood). Palanti was almost ten years older and more experienced than Bo Bardi, having collaborated with Giuseppe Pagano in exhibitions, edited *Domus* and *Casabella* magazines, and otherwise immersed himself in the Milanese design milieu since the early 1930s. With Palanti in charge of most projects, their design partnership and their participation in MASP's art institute helped to renovate the image of interior and furniture design and education in São Paulo and to merge rationalist and local Brazilian vocabularies and materials.

Though their collaboration started in early 1949 and lasted less than two years, Bo Bardi considered it "the first attempt to manufacture modern furniture (not at an industrial scale) out of cut plywood sheets (instead of Alvar Aalto's folded pieces) and other local materials" in Brazil.[9] While Palanti followed an industrial aesthetic, Bo Bardi chose simplicity and economy of means, following Bardi's references to Carlo Lodoli's pre-Enlightenment theories about functionalism. A chair designed as a "simulated 'mechanical' object," she wrote in *Habitat* at the time, was as misguided as the "contemporary reproduction of a Louis XV chair."[10] Her wooden and steel-frame chairs, which evoke the hammocks used in Brazilian riverboats, are a good example of her integration of an innovative production process with local and traditional materials (figures 22, 23).[11]

Among the interior design projects in which Bo Bardi and Palanti collaborated were retail stores that grew with the industrialization and upscale consumer market in São Paulo, several of which were a short distance from MASP and Estúdio Palma. Their portfolio included one of the Olivetti Technostores Palanti had designed for his Italian client in Brazil. It also included the interior layout of Galeria Ambiente, a modern design dealer that carried some of Bo Bardi's and Palanti's armchairs. In addition, they designed an auto show display for Studebaker, a couple of imported fabric and plastic stores on rua Sete de Abril — great novelties in the city — and the restaurant Prato de Ouro (Golden plate) on rua Conselheiro Crispiniano.[12]

While Palanti's exacting hand and rigorously plain geometries dominated the composition of their collaborative work, the effect of Bo Bardi's spontaneous freehand and undiscriminating imagination could be seen in the irregular but vibrant details in such designs as in her less finished chair prototypes and the unstructured inflatable mannequins in the Plavinil plastic store. In addition, colorful striped poles such as those she used in her 1946 project for the Rhodia stall reemerged in the auto show, becoming a recurrent theme in her design. They also appeared in a couple of house studies and in the two murals adorning the otherwise plain restaurant with their abstract figures, emulating one of the paintings her father produced during his war refuge in Parma.[13] Bo Bardi and Palanti also developed a few studies for single-family houses. Though they were never executed, they announced some of the hybrid features that would become concrete for the first time in Bo Bardi's own house and, especially, in the independent work she would develop after the late 1950s.

As the Bardis became committed to living in São Paulo, having a permanent house seemed the next logical step. Moreover, Bardi was now implementing the IAC and wanted to create work-live studios like those forming in US art schools in the style of the Bauhaus Meisterhäuser (Master houses) in Dessau, Germany. His idea was to host resident artists and their teaching workshops in the outskirts

22. Lina Bo Bardi, *Studies for a Three-Legged Chair, Palma Studio*, 1948. Ballpoint pen and color pencil on paper, 27.7 × 21.3 cm. ILBPMB Collection.

23. Lina Bo Bardi, three-legged chair in wood and leather, Palma Studio, c. 1948. Photograph by Nelson Kon.

of São Paulo. In 1949, as he and Chateaubriand looked for land to build the workshops, Warchavchik suggested a visit to Morumbi, a new subdivision he and Bratke had helped to design and develop in the picturesque hills of a former tea plantation south of the Pinheiros river valley. Using state-of-the-art infrastructure, streets were created to preserve the old farmhouse and chapel, the natural topography, and a patch of woods, which Bo Bardi remembered as being inhabited by small animals, birds, orchids, and araucaria pine trees.[14]

Morumbi seemed the perfect place for the museum's residential workshops. Its urbanistic plan combined the organic layout of Garden City planning common to São Paulo at the time with the model of Case Study Houses to produce affordable and efficient homes, which Bratke had recently seen in the United States. After a few visits, the Bardis decided it could also be a good place to live.[15] Though Chateaubriand had reserved several lots for the live-in studios, his plan fell through, likely due to financial constraints and uncertainty about the art institute's future.[16] The couple ended up purchasing only two lots on the north side of the subdivision on rua Trinta (Thirtieth Street,

renamed General Almério de Moura) in Bo Bardi's name on December 19, 1949.[17] She later reminisced that they had expected their house to become a large studio for the museum and though that never happened, their home did become a meeting place for many artists.[18]

Bo Bardi worked on the house project for more than a year, even though she would not be registered as a professional architect in Brazil until 1955. Construction began after Warchavchik filed drawings for a city permit, approved on July 5, 1951.[19] Contrary to the general belief that construction ended in 1951, archival records suggest that it was not completed until at least April 1952.[20] Nevertheless, it was the first house in the neighborhood. It was also Bo Bardi's first built project. At the border of a modern booming metropolis and the remains of an archaic agricultural society, she would finally have concrete opportunities to combine rationalist architectural references with her reverence for nature and simple things.

She designed the house, still in existence today, with the surrounding landscape and many plants in mind (figure 24). Approachable from below like an ancient acropolis but looking like a mid-twentieth-century California house, a glazed

24. Lina Bo Bardi, *Study for House in Morumbi*, c. 1951. India ink and color pencil on paper, 10.9 × 11.8 cm. ILBPMB Collection.

25. Lina Bo and P. M. Bardi house in Morumbi, São Paulo, 1949–52,
view from the northeastern side showing main glazed volume. Photo by
Nelson Kon.

26. Lina Bo and P. M. Bardi house in Morumbi, São Paulo, 1949–52,
interior view with dining room and internal patio in the foreground.
Photograph by Nelson Kon.

volume atop ten long, thin posts protrudes out of a promontory (figure 25). At the time, this position led to its popular name, the "Glass House," and allowed for an ample view of the river valley, but over the years, the vista was obscured by tall trees. Past the steep driveway that ends underneath the house as a carport, the main entrance follows a light steel staircase with marble steps. The first short flight accentuates the view, while the landing reverses it toward a small, dark vestibule that leads into the house.

Inside, the house reveals its openness and transparency through the wide, floor-to-ceiling glass windows that enclose the main volume and five of the ten steel posts that traverse the floor slab (figure 26). Soon after the house was completed, the Bardis furnished the large living room with artworks, objects, books, and a few chairs Bo Bardi designed (she refused to have sofas), including her celebrated bowl chair with its simple four-legged steel support and an upholstered and stackable concave seat containing two circular cushions (figure 27).

Similar windows line an interior light well created around orthogonal openings on both floor and ceiling slabs. This well brings daylight into the center of the building and lets a tree grow through it from the garden below. It also subdivides the large glazed hall into four contiguous areas: a

large living room spanning twenty meters (66 ft.) along the southeastern side, an entry hall in the center, a library on the northeastern side, and a dining room on the southwestern corner. This pavilionlike structure, which is usually the only part of the house visible from the outside, accounts for just half of the building. The other part, enclosed by masonry walls into two long and compartmented volumes with shutter windows and mediated by a patio, sits on the same floor behind the wall that backs the interior of the glazed block (figures 28, 29).

The frontal image of the house soon became a model for the advertising campaign promoted by Companhia Imobiliária Jardim Morumbi (Jardim Morumbi real estate company) to sell the remaining almost two hundred lots.[21] Their slogan was "Architecture and Nature," a theme that was dear to Bo Bardi, and announced: "A new factor starts to rule in contemporary architecture and aims to study nature and every moment of man's everyday life."[22] Simultaneously, Bo Bardi published articles in *Habitat* about Morumbi and, later, about her finished house, advocating that the neighborhood should follow strict architectural norms so that history would not remember its future residents as "people with a lot of money and also bad taste," which could "hardly be covered by such lush nature."[23]

27. Lina Bo Bardi, Bardi Bowl chair in steel and leather, c. 1951. Photograph by Nelson Kon.

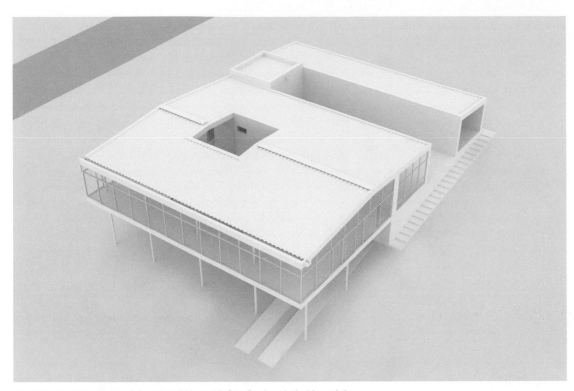

28. Lina Bo and P. M. Bardi house in Morumbi, São Paulo, 1949–52, aerial
view. Computer rendering. Zeuler R. Lima Collection.

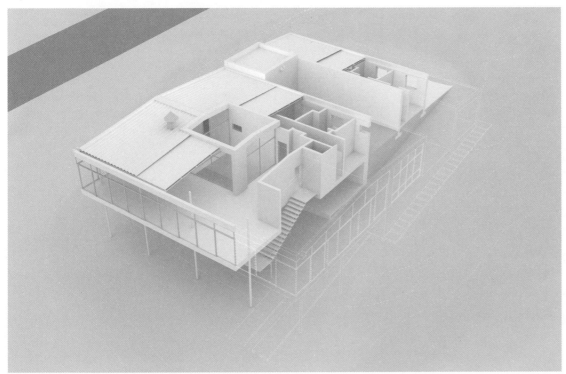

29. Lina Bo and P. M. Bardi house in Morumbi, São Paulo, 1949–52,
sectioned aerial view. Computer rendering. Zeuler R. Lima Collection.

In addition to having an open and sharp appearance, the house was equipped with novel domestic appliances that were very uncommon in Brazil at the time, suggesting an idealized housewife that was far from the reality of wealthy Brazilian housewives and their maids as well as from Bo Bardi's unconventional lifestyle.

The advertising campaign and publications about the subdivision set up the reception of a rationalist and crystalline house that effaced the visibility of both its complex design process and its hybrid features. In reality, the building reveals rear service quarters with white masonry walls and trellised shutter windows resting on the ground and rooted in the simple, popular rural traditions that Bo Bardi prized (figure 30). To complement those rural references, of which it is practically impossible to have a full view, Bo Bardi added to the small backyard "two brick and adobe ovens built by *Caboclos* [mestizo peasants]" (figure 31).

As she explained to *Habitat* readers in 1953, it was "a moment in which popular architecture establishe[d] an agreement with contemporary architecture."[24]

A more careful look at the drawings Bo Bardi produced during the design process makes her desire for reconciling different repertoires even clearer, though they shed little light on how much her husband's and even the developers' opinions may have interfered in the process. Her first study board, with its drawings and simple notes made on tracing paper, sets up a synthesis of the rationalist layout, including an elevated volume at the edge of the slanted lot, a panoramic living room, light wells with trees, and services at the rear. The same drawing also provides information about her initial intention to work with natural materials, a practice that was suppressed over the months it took to conclude the design but one that would persistently reemerge in projects she developed independently after the late 1950s.

30. Lina Bo and P. M. Bardi house in Morumbi, São Paulo, 1949–52, view from the southeastern side showing rear service volume. Photograph by Zeuler R. Lima.

She initially wrote notes for an unusual structural frame: "wood sitting on conglomerate or stone."[25] The image recalled articles she had published for *Domus* in 1944 about subjects such as her own comparison of modern and traditional houses on stilts and Max Bill's 1942 house in Bremgarten, Switzerland, with wooden posts sitting on rounded stones, a solution to the scarcity of industrial materials during the war.[26] Just as Bo Bardi did not lose contact with her native country, she seems also to have continued to follow the Italian architectural debate. The ideas for her house also parallel those represented in the 1948 Triennale, which was titled *La casa* and confronted rationalism with simple materials and construction techniques and traditional typologies, infusing modern ideas with local and everyday meanings.[27]

Though Bo Bardi initially addressed nature and climate concerns, such as protecting the house from sunlight and storm water by using different roofs and verandas, those ideas were soon abandoned for the glass-box scheme. She left no written evidence of the reasons for such changes, but she seems to have ended up endorsing the subdivision's stylistic model rather than the physical and spatial specificities of the landscape that would sustain the building and life in it. According to her drawings, she increasingly privileged the panoramic view and the idea of building the house around a tree over and above the accommodation of the building to the irregular topography and challenging orientations, which exposed the transparent volume containing the living room and library to direct sunlight for several years until large trees grew around it on the west and north sides.

After experimenting with several square and rectangular layout variations around the theme of a glazed horizontal volume and free plan around a tree, Bo Bardi arrived at a basic scheme for her house, with two major changes to the

31. Lina Bo and P. M. Bardi house in Morumbi, São Paulo, view from the southeastern side showing rear service volume and brick ovens. Photograph by Zeuler R. Lima.

Ventures and Adventures in Design

original rustic, single volume. One variation was structural and done with the help of engineer Tullio Stucchi. Given that the house was too big to be supported by thin tree trunks, it was built with hollow concrete slabs and steel posts measuring only seventeen centimeters (6½ in.) in diameter, advanced technical solutions for the time.[28] The other substantial change regarded her initial program distribution as she broke away from a single volume crowned by a pitched roof. Instead, the final house layout was organized in three parallel bays that were separated into two complementary volumes.

The larger, mostly transparent volume that exists on the east side contains the open floor with living areas embracing a light well and a tree and a long, narrow, compartmented bay that includes the bedroom area and part of the kitchen. The smaller, mostly opaque service volume contains a large pantry, a semiopen laundry room, three small bedrooms, and a bathroom. These two areas are connected by an extension to the kitchen that, under closer scrutiny, contradicts the house's simple formal logic with a slightly jagged volume that separates the otherwise rectangular plan into two areas. Together the two main volumes of the house configure a scheme that overlaps a doughnutlike diagram with a U-shaped plan containing light wells with vegetation and folded roofs, features common to other modern houses in São Paulo at the time — such as the sketches for a house with butterfly roof done on Vilanova Artigas's stationery that she kept in her records. The open spaces in Bo Bardi's project provide cross-ventilation and natural light but are short of serving as patios or terraces as proposed by other architects in São Paulo, given that they are not directly accessible from either the house or the service block on the same level.

In spite of her many publications about her project, Bo Bardi left no written records regarding the contrasting relation between the service volume and the main body of her impressive and intriguing house. It is certain, however, that she and Bardi expected to use it to host receptions for artistic and intellectual groups in the city and that they needed live-in servants.[29] Though the Bardis treated their servants generously and though their house challenged the architectural taste of affluent São Paulo neighborhoods, the design preserved the traditional gender and class divisions of wealthy Brazilian homes. It would take Bo Bardi at least another decade to begin fine-tuning the connection between her aesthetic quest and the ethical discourse she professed in her articles for Italian magazines and *Habitat*.

With no need to impress visitors, design magazine readers, or potential subdivision buyers, the service quarters soon gained new company. The additions Bo Bardi designed around the main house — a small, detached housekeeper's house resembling the rear part of the house, a new garage covered with mosaic replacing a metal car porch, and, much later, her cabinlike office — were her refuge for experimenting with traditional and organic materials and forms. In a way similar to how her own achievements had circled the men in her professional life, the servants' quarters and the additions continue to orbit, almost invisibly, in the shadow of the main house, reducing the complexity of the whole estate to simply the image of a glass house.

Though the house in Morumbi marked her first steps as a building designer, during its construction in 1951, Bo Bardi was involved in a few preliminary projects serving Bardi's and Chateaubriand's interests, including a fair pavilion, a multiuse highrise, and a seashore museum. MASP was growing, and so were the business and political contacts of Diários Associados. Early that year, Bo Bardi helped the museum set up the *Exposição da Agricultura Paulista* (São Paulo state agriculture exposition) at Parque da Água Branca, advertising agricultural modernization.[30] Her work consisted of designing a gateway to the park in latticework, a machinery display surrounded by striped maypoles, a tensile pavilion for movie projections, and the poster for the event. Of these, only the pavilion was not built. The other pieces attested to the coexistence of natural, traditional, and modern elements, especially in her colorful poster, which summarized the tone of the show: it depicted the outline of passive bovines facing a helicopter resolutely advancing toward them as it sprayed insecticide against the boundless landscape of the page.

As agriculture was modernized so, too, were communication media, getting Bo Bardi involved in Chateaubriand's plans to open the first television station in Brazil and to create new headquarters for his Diários Associados in São Paulo. He imagined a smaller version of Rockefeller Center and Radio City Music Hall on a downtown lot next to Major Quedinho overpass.[31] Bo Bardi had already produced similar studies for Chateaubriand in 1947, but his plans were halted during the creation of MASP. Her first project was attuned to recent works such as those Rino Levi and Giancarlo Palanti were developing in São Paulo with glazed volumes adjusted to sloped topography, setback restrictions, and generous pilotis and gardens.

The second version of the project, likely motivated by the launching of Chateaubriand's television station in September 1950, was more elaborate and named Taba Guaianazes. This time, however, Chateaubriand assigned the project to the supervision of Pier Luigi Nervi, whom Bardi had invited to lecture on reinforced concrete at MASP.[32] His son, Antonio Nervi, and Bo Bardi collaborated

Vista da sala de exposições, no fundo a área aberta para exposição de esculturas

Vista do lado da praia

32. Lina Bo Bardi, article about museum at seashore in *Habitat* 8
(July–September 1952), 8. Zeuler R. Lima Collection.

vinte metros. A lage inferior e a superior serão formadas por elementos pré-fabricados. No corpo do edifício são estudadas uma área aberta para exposições de peças ao ar livre e uma área interna, sôbre a qual olham as salas das aulas; o auditório, delimitado por paredes móveis, é independente da estrutura. O acesso ao edifício é feito através de uma rampa.

Os materiais para o acabamento serão o cimento natural alisado e envernizado para os pórticos, enquanto o corpo fechado será revestido de Neve Brasil; as aberturas serão de alumínio

Arquiteto Lina Bo Bardi, Museu em São Vicente. Vista da área aberta das exposições e de uma das paredes externas, móvel, do auditório

33. Lina Bo Bardi, article about museum at seashore in *Habitat* 8 (July–September 1952), 11. Zeuler R. Lima Collection.

with studies and project development for two auditoriums, apartments, offices, and a hotel on the site.[33]

In addition to her preliminary 1947 ideas, Bo Bardi produced at least two design schemes that appear to be independent of the final project that she developed with Nervi. Her new studies emphasized monumentality by seating the building on a plinth. One study consisted of circular theaters inside a cylindrical base and a matching glazed tower above. In another colorful sketch Bo Bardi took advantage of the topography with a large base for the auditoriums topped by two glazed midrise buildings with roof gardens and long flower beds, inaugurating the intense use of vegetation that she would explore in future projects. The planting idea reappeared in the final version coordinated by Nervi with an elaborate concrete frame supporting two tall towers around the theaters. Seeking to maximize natural light and ventilation in contrast to the dark internal streets of Le Corbusier's Radiant City, they designed flexible apartments with abundant hanging gardens.[34]

In the sketch's margins Bo Bardi commented on Nervi's theater roof: "A clear span of seventy meters [230 ft.], [and] calculated in pre-stressed lamellate concrete, resembling corrugated cardboard."[35] This was a technical solution she would use in many subsequent projects, ranging from her concurrent study for a low-cost movie theater pavilion to the prefabricated elements for adaptive reuse projects in the late 1980s. Though Taba Guaianazes was never built, likely because of the lack of funding, her collaboration with Nervi was a remarkable learning experience about the use of reinforced concrete and about construction drawings.

Bo Bardi's proximity to Nervi also enhanced her appreciation of the structural features of architecture. About this same time, in 1951, Charles Dantas Forbes, the mayor of the coastal city of São Vicente, approached her husband to create an art museum, likely as part of his election campaign.[36] Both Bardis jumped at the opportunity. She saw it as the expansion of her recent design experiences, and he considered it an opportunity to give his innovative museological project an architectural face. According to their description, "The City of São Vicente decided to build a museum at the sea shore, at the beach, a place where cities that want to attract tourists generally build an elegant casino," praising the mayor for his recognition that "a museum is as important as a school."[37]

Illustrated with sketches, a model, and photomontages, Bo Bardi's project combined elements from both the glazed part of the Glass House and the layout of MASP on rua Sete de Abril. Above all, the project's structural logic and simplicity evoked one of Mies van der Rohe's masterpieces, the then-recently designed (and still unfinished) Crown Hall in Chicago. Her interior drawings and collages recalled metaphysical paintings by her father's friend Giorgio de Chirico, prefiguring the simple, open spaces of many of the exhibitions she would later organize. The result was a horizontal, semiglazed volume lifted from the beach with access from underneath. She described it as an enclosed block with "the facade opened over the ocean, a side with no sun exposure."[38] The program was nonetheless simple: an exhibition hall sided by a terrace, a large auditorium enclosed by moveable walls, and services and classrooms organized around an opening in the floor through which a tree would grow (figures 32, 33).

Though it would have been practically unfeasible on sandy ground, Bo Bardi raised the building on stilts because of "the proximity to the sea and humidity, which are harmful to paintings," and because the structure "did not completely occupy the lot, allowing for views of the sea from the road." In order to lift the building from the ground, she proposed "a bearing structure formed by five sets of reinforced concrete beams measuring twenty-five meters [82 ft.] between columns and placed twenty meters [66 ft.] from each other, equivalent to the Crown Hall. Both upper and lower slabs [would be] built with prefabricated components." In addition, she selected four basic materials for the external finishes: "polished and varnished concrete for the beams and the columns, the enclosed body covered in white marble, window casement in aluminum," and glass.[39]

Not only did Bo Bardi's design for the seashore museum combine elements from other projects she developed during this period, but it prefigured the work she would start to develop a few years later, when Bardi and Chateaubriand began to look for a site to raise MASP's permanent facilities. The São Vicente museum incorporated timely international references and foreshadowed an important transformation in Brazilian architecture. Soon after her unrealized museum study, architects such as Vilanova Artigas and Affonso Reidy abandoned polished materials and started to design large spanning structures in raw concrete and rough finishes.

It would not take long for Bo Bardi to catch up with their aesthetic renovation and to appropriate it into her own rules and terms.

Between Crisis and Opportunity

Although Bo Bardi's first five years in São Paulo expanded her experience and allowed her to see her first building project materialized, her promising design practice temporarily halted. In the interim, she observed her new country undergo significant cultural, social, and political transformations ranging from new national economic development policies to the crisis of early modern Brazilian architecture with the emergence of new critical voices. Above all, she remained involved with her husband's activities and growing controversies, which led to the beginning of the long and fragmented design process for one of her career's milestones: MASP's permanent facilities on avenida Paulista.

With no other design work in sight and after moving into her house in Morumbi in 1952, Bo Bardi wrote a few articles trying to engage the debate about Brazilian architecture, though her theoretical formulations were not yet evident in the designs she produced in dialogue with Bardi and Palanti. She organized several art exhibitions at MASP, but the museum was starting to face setbacks. Meanwhile, Bardi turned *Habitat* into a vehicle for his own diatribes, with inflamed editorials written with Bo Bardi's help that defended the museum's mission while attacking whoever disagreed with his approach. The group surrounding Matarazzo and MAM was the couple's main target.

MASP's initial advantage over MAM began to suffer with Matarazzo's creation of the International São Paulo Art Biennial. Ideological disagreements aside, Bardi could hardly compete with funding by the Federação das Indústrias do Estado de São Paulo (FIESP, São Paulo state industry coalition) and strong logistical support from Rockefeller through MoMA in New York City and the International Basic Economy Corporation (IBEC) offices in São Paulo.[1] Still, the Biennial plan faced a concrete problem: MAM's facilities a few floors above MASP were inadequate to host such a large event. The solution was to build a temporary pavilion. In agreement with the city of São Paulo, the Biennial committee occupied the historic site of Belvedere do Trianon (Trianon terrace), a small park located south of downtown on avenida Paulista, then the most affluent boulevard in São Paulo.

The park overlooking the city on the north side consisted of a large, eclectic structure housing a civic hall with a ballroom and restaurant built halfway into the slanted lot and covered with a terrace surrounded by ornate pergolas and a balustrade. Until popular cultural events began to be held there in the 1940s, Trianon Terrace hosted the most elegant social and cultural meetings in São Paulo, including the gestation of the 1922 Semana de Arte Moderna (Modern art week) movement and many political campaigns. It was time for the local elites to try to regain control over the use of a symbolically and visually charged plot of land. Nothing was more useful to their purpose than the new Biennial. Architect Eduardo Kneese de Mello from MAM's executive board led the construction of the temporary exhibition pavilion with wood and brick over the existing terrace.[2] Whereas the plain white facade on avenida Paulista aligned with the sidewalk, the side facing the valley contained several slender posts suspending the second floor above the original terrace and keeping its vista open to the city.

Concerned by the competition, the Bardis published an editorial in *Habitat* criticizing the choice to follow the Venice Biennial's autocratic model instead of creating a "forum of active and intelligent people."[3] Moreover, they suggested through a scathing anonymous letter, "Had we imagined the kind of architecture they would build, we would have proposed to transform those follies on the old terrace into an architectural monument."[4]

Despite the Bardis' resistance, the show was a great success both locally and internationally. After the pavilion was dismantled, the whole terrace was demolished. The place that had been, for forty years, the center of affluent social life in São Paulo suddenly became a razed urban block, creating a dispute over the use of the site that would end up yielding MASP's transfer to its current permanent location a few years later with a bold project designed by Bo Bardi herself. Before that, Matarazzo's group jumped ahead and proposed to build a Palácio das Artes (Arts palace) on the vacant lot, in order to move the Biennial Foundation and MAM from Chateaubriand's building in the congested downtown to the bourgeoning district along avenida Paulista.

In April 1952 Matarazzo and his architect friends from the IAB convinced the city's department of public works to organize a closed competition between only two architects: Affonso Reidy, the celebrated author of the Museu de Arte Moderna (Museum of modern art) of Rio de Janeiro (completed in 1954), and José Augusto Bellucci, a competent architect with only modest exposure. The competition highlighted the need to create "a viewpoint that allows the appreciation of the gigantic urban panorama . . . toward the city center."[5] According to official competition records, Bellucci submitted only a preliminary study. In contrast, Reidy's work was more detailed and was seen as a "fortunate solution to a complex problem," which included keeping the open vista.[6]

The proposed Palácio das Artes was part of Matarazzo's larger plan to build several cultural facilities in strategic development areas in São Paulo to celebrate the four hundredth anniversary of the city's foundation, planned for January 25, 1954. He hoped to finance these projects with gifts from foreign business groups, but despite negotiations

with the local branch of the US Chamber of Commerce to support the arts palace, he was unsuccessful.[7] Reidy's project for Trianon Terrace therefore was never built.

The site on avenida Paulista remained vacant for several years as the Matarazzo group focused attention on the construction of a much larger cultural and leisure project concerning the Fourth Centennial celebration: the Parque do Ibirapuera. Among the buildings planned by Oscar Niemeyer and his team was a new version of the Palácio das Artes, which would house the Biennial Foundation facilities, enlarging the scope of Reidy's abandoned project.

Bardi did not waste the opportunity to use *Habitat* to ignite the fire of the emerging cultural wars in the city, attacking both the Biennial and the anniversary celebration.[8] More than once, he engaged Bo Bardi's graphic and architectural skills to illustrate his points, including a proposal described as an "ideal project, free of charge, for the building of the '*Exposição do Quarto Centenário*' (Fourth São Paulo centennial exposition) at Parque do Ibirapuera," published in April 1953.[9] She illustrated a short, unsigned article with a collage showing the interior of a vast, glazed pavilion composed of white slabs held by regularly but sparsely distributed thin columns and objects and machines, resembling both the couple's house in Morumbi and the design for the seashore museum. The article disparaged the quadricentennial celebration committee and described Niemeyer's building complex under construction at Ibirapuera as "an embarrassment, a provincial, ignorant, and reactionary humiliation."[10]

Responses to the Bardis' overconfident polemics and Chateaubriand's supportive manipulation came in the form of a counteroffensive to discredit their work. Journalists and respected Brazilian critics continued to write articles questioning the legitimacy of the masterpieces purchased by Bardi and generated offensive rumors about his political past as a prominent adviser to Mussolini in the early 1930s.[11] Bo Bardi found herself caught in the cultural crossfire and accused of being a foreign troublemaker.[12]

The Bardis tried to reverse such accusations by showing their commitment to their adopted country. In April 1953, they became Brazilian citizens and renounced, by law, their Italian nationality.[13] She was now thirty-eight, he fifty-three. In addition, they spent the next four years organizing a tour of MASP's collection in renowned European and American art museums to authenticate the artworks. With the help of Louvre director Germain Bazin, the Bardis set up the first show at the Musée de l'Orangerie in Paris on October 10, 1953, that included several panels with photographs documenting MASP's facilities and exhibition displays.[14] The exhibition continued to other European cities, including

Brussels, Utrecht, and Bern, receiving unanimous acclaim from European connoisseurs, before moving to the United States in 1957. Brazilian critics remained silent: no compliments but also no more deception about the collection.

During this period, the Bardis left *Habitat* to dedicate themselves to promoting the museum and, by extension, their future in Brazil. They continued to stir up controversies not only about art but also about architecture. Among them was Bo Bardi's decision to publish a notorious lecture presented by their friend Max Bill (the Bauhaus-trained designer and artist whom they had befriended since brushing shoulders with him at the 1945 reconstruction congress in Milan) at the school of architecture of the Universidade de São Paulo on June 9, 1953. In it, Bill announced that Brazil "risk[ed] falling into the most horrible antisocial academicism in regard to modern architecture," holding that "architecture should be understood as a social art." He was particularly unforgiving to Niemeyer and his followers, whom he saw as "following a doctrine that is not applicable [to the country] unless there are significant corrections." Coinciding with Bo Bardi's articles in *Habitat*, Bill believed that, more than the creation of forms, "the role of architects in modern society was to make the environment that surrounds human beings harmonious and inhabitable." [15]

Max Bill's lecture caused discomfort in academic and professional circles around the country, but with little direct reaction, and in January 1954 architects Ernesto Nathan Rogers, Walter Gropius, and Alvar Aalto raised similar concerns in their keynote presentations at the Fourth Conference of Brazilian Architects during the second Biennial.[16] They, too, found little resonance among Brazilian designers, with the exception of conference members representing the Architecture and Tradition Committee. Rogers, Gropius, and Aalto asserted the need to "develop a national architectural expression [based] on the satisfaction of the material and spiritual needs of the Brazilian people." Moreover, they proposed, "This process should start through a self-critical revision of current architectural principles, avoiding preconceived models and stylistic exaggeration." [17]

A few months after his trip to São Paulo, Nathan Rogers collected testimonies from four international designers — Walter Gropius, Oe Hiroshi, Max Bill, and himself, each having visited the architecture conference and the art exhibition — and published them in the *Architectural Review* as a collective essay titled "Report on Brazil." [18] The article brought about a more nuanced and critical coverage of Brazilian architecture than the elated international articles published in the early 1940s. Comments ranged from favorable to hostile, but all agreed on criticizing the formal excess of Brazilian architecture (especially by Niemeyer) at the cost of technical and social issues.[19] Altogether, however, Bill's controversy and the international report on Brazilian architecture had a beneficial side. They prompted Brazilian architects and critics, albeit gradually, to take stock of their situation in the transition between Getúlio Vargas's authoritarian and populist legacy and President Juscelino Kubitschek's development policies in the late 1950s, and especially to become more politically engaged in the following decade.

The focus of the growing debate among Brazilian designers was how — during a period of intense modernization and urbanization, coupled with the increasing evidence of social, economic, and environmental problems — to advance architecture at the service of collective welfare.[20] From that moment on, issues concerning formal excess, technical simplicity, national identity, urbanization, social housing, and public space started to gain prominence. New voices emerged, bringing an undue and difficult revision of Brazilian architecture to the fore. Bo Bardi finally began to find an environment in Brazil that seemed familiar to her early professional experience and aspirations and to the predicaments faced by Italian architects after the end of World War II.

The hegemonic architectural discourse from the Vargas era was in crisis, allowing the pluralistic character of modern Brazilian architecture to become temporarily more visible. As Brazilian cities grew, new architecture schools in different areas of the country disseminated modern values and diversified professional principles and practices. Among them, two prominent groups representing the cultural sectors of the Brazilian Communist Party disputed the ideological revision of modern Brazilian architecture. The group around architect Demétrio Ribeiro, who lived in Porto Alegre and advocated social agendas for housing and city planning, argued that the revision should incorporate national, popular, and traditional themes. The group around João Vilanova Artigas, who lived in São Paulo and considered Ribeiro's ideas nostalgic and paradoxical, advocated a cosmopolitan approach. The constellation of factors that increasingly gave São Paulo national prominence along with Artigas's skills and charisma benefited the latter discourse, giving him and his followers control over a nascent hegemonic language of Brazilian brutalism.

Conceptually, Bo Bardi stood somewhere between the positions advocated by those revisionist groups. She admired Artigas but subscribed to the national-popular principles pursued by Ribeiro's group, though there is no evidence that she knew of their work. In a 1955 letter to Bruno Zevi, which he published in his magazine *L'Architettura: Cronache e storia* (Architecture: Chronicles and history), Bo Bardi wrote: "The Brazilian architect [was] a young man called to arms with no plan; he put himself to work with courage and generosity," but with little knowledge about the complexity of the problems he faced. She made exceptions for those, including herself, who were sensitive to the "extremely simple and fresh constructive solutions, modesty allied to a festive sense of life." She concluded hopefully, saying, "Today, young people are leaving the university aware of this change," and adding, "A new Brazilian architecture could begin now." [21]

Bo Bardi's hope for the new generation of students was not abstract. In February 1955, she was hired for a year to teach at the Faculdade de Arquitetura e Urbanismo at the Universidade de São Paulo (FAUUSP, School of Architecture and Urbanism, University of São Paulo), where Rino Levi and João Vilanova Artigas were active and influential professors. [22] Her approach and experience at the time may have been more in tune with Levi than with Artigas. Levi, who was also a graduate of the architecture school in Rome years before her, thought buildings should be designed from the inside out and considered it to be a place of everyday life. Vilanova Artigas, however, was more interested in a Communist discourse and saw Bo Bardi's ideas about simple objects and popular culture as folkloristic and nationalistic. [23]

Though Bo Bardi's interior design course was titled "Decorative Composition," she questioned its traditional meaning and focused on furniture design based on the activities she had pursued in the previous fifteen years. In line with Levi and MASP's art institute, she believed that education should start from the practical side of life and within a historical perspective. [24] In early 1956 her contract was renewed for another year, but in August she requested a semester's leave of absence to "travel abroad in order to complete research in higher education institutions in Italy and in France." [25] This justification was likely related to her application to a chaired professor position in architecture theory announced for the second semester of 1957. [26] The application required a thesis and a new course program, which she prepared during her semester-long leave, though mostly this time allowed her to help Bardi with the exhibition tour.

On August 28, 1956, she traveled to Italy to set up the final exhibition of MASP's collection in Europe. [27] After prior stops at the Tate Gallery in London and the Düsseldorf Kunstmuseum, with additional acquisitions along the way, the paintings were displayed in the Palazzo Reale in central Milan. [28] Bo Bardi returned to Italy later that year, when she and Bardi left Milan on a road trip to the Iberian Peninsula. [29] Along their journey through Spain and Portugal, she photographed old rural constructions, small villages, and sculptural vegetation rising amid dry, rocky landscapes. Their stop in Barcelona was memorable. There, Bo Bardi saw and documented, for the first time in person, the works of architect Antoni Gaudí and his collaborators, who used the technique of *trencadis*, the brightly colored mosaic made of tile shards. In both anonymous and designed works, she found material evidence for her desire to integrate nature and architecture, building and image, and modernity and tradition. She returned to Brazil after Christmas with renewed enthusiasm and a thesis draft in progress.

Meanwhile, MASP's collection was shipped to the United States for an exhibition at the Metropolitan Museum of Art in New York. However, as the Bardis later learned, this decision proved to be a miscalculation. [30] They arrived in Manhattan on March 19, 1957, for the exhibition opening, which received much public acclaim. [31] Bo Bardi stayed until April 13 and during her trip had the opportunity to visit the Guggenheim Museum, experiencing Frank Lloyd Wright's architecture for the first time. [32] She also toured different areas of the city, carrying a camera and taking many pictures of old and new buildings, including several of the Lever House on Park Avenue, many of which she used as illustrations in the thesis she was preparing for the application for the chaired professor position.

The exhibition closed on June 2, 1957, but the collection could not leave the United States. Chateaubriand had received a subpoena charging him for a large debt he had contracted from the Guaranty Trust Company of New York to pay for artworks purchased from Georges Wildenstein's galleries in New York City and Paris. Chateaubriand's gambling managerial style had backfired this time: he had offered MASP's collection as collateral for his loan, and the art dealer now expected to regain possession of artworks whose value had multiplied several times. [33] After a few months spent scrambling to find a solution, Chateaubriand worked out a deal with President Kubitschek, who used public funds to pay off the debt he had contracted in the name of MASP. [34] The collection was returned to São Paulo in November, but Kubitschek made Chateaubriand sign an agreement, to Bardi's dismay, that separated MASP from the fiscal and administrative tutelage of Diários Associados Press Corporation. After ten years dedicated to the creation of the museum, the Bardis saw new challenges emerging on the horizon.

Following her return from New York, Bo Bardi had no regular occupation. Her university contract had not been renewed for the 1957 term. She continued to work on her application for the chaired position, which was due in September, while also producing four projects and studies that marked the transition of her affiliation to a predominantly rationalist vocabulary — which she called her "Swiss-Milanese education" — into experiments with naturalistic and humanistic approaches.[35] These projects coincided with the waning of her partnership with Bardi and yielded new collaborations and autonomous work.

Among those transitional projects was an unidentified study for a beach house, which advanced ideas from Bo Bardi's own house and previous low-cost house studies, including a single volume lifted from the ground with a rationalist layout separating social and private areas and enclosed with different materials, recalling ongoing projects by São Paulo architects such as Oswaldo Bratke. Another project was her entry for a furniture competition promoted by the town of Cantù, one of the main centers of furniture production in Italy.[36] She proposed a simple construction system with plywood pieces that resembled her experiments with Palanti. Also in line with that previous collaboration, she designed a medical office for Dr. Felloni de Mattos in São Paulo. This small, executed project revealed her attention to detail and to simple forms with industrial materials. Her signature centerpiece was a dried tree branch on a conic cement base covered with stones, announcing her yen for the integration of natural and manmade forms.

Most important, this transitional period, more precisely July 1957, saw Bo Bardi's completion of a preliminary study for MASP's new facilities on avenida Paulista. Though this proposal was put on hold until 1960 because of the museum's administrative and fiscal crises, her initial ideas explicitly suggested hybrid directions in her design work, combining a bold, raw concrete structure with hanging gardens. Still, in the long and interrupted process of the design and construction of MASP's new facilities (the museum did not open until 1968), she gradually altered the project to accommodate technical obstacles, erasing the naturalistic and spontaneous elements that significantly differentiated her original ideas from other emerging brutalist buildings that changed the course of Brazilian architecture in the second part of the twentieth century.

At different times Bo Bardi, Bardi, and Chateaubriand each claimed to have made the decision to transfer MASP to its permanent location. In 1989, for example, Bo Bardi suggested in her lecture at the Universidade de São Paulo that, after she learned of the city's plan to build public bathrooms on the lot formerly occupied by the Belvedere do Trianon, she proposed relocating the museum. She mentioned having asked Edmundo Monteiro, director of both the museum and Chateaubriand's media conglomerate, to work out a deal with the mayor, exchanging the use of the lot for providing media support for his upcoming presidential campaign. She even mentioned having prepared a colorful (supposedly lost) drawing of her idea overnight.[37]

The facts point to a more complex set of conditions, agents, and actions that converged to enable MASP's transfer from rua Sete de Abril to avenida Paulista, with neither a single leader nor a clear, preconceived plan. Even Bo Bardi's own archival records demonstrate that her preliminary study included several drawings, photocopies, photographs, a physical model, photomontages, and watercolors that would have required several weeks of work before July 1957. Moreover, the mayor's campaign for president did not happen until 1960, when Bo Bardi was often away from São Paulo for long periods.

The initial phase of studies for MASP in 1957 was short but apparently intense. Bo Bardi's first sketches show a tall, glazed pyramidal structure with four large columns meeting at the vortex of the building, a scheme that suggests either that she was unaware of the site restrictions to keep the vista unobstructed at that point or that she did not have a specific lot in mind. In two of these sketches, she showed a solid helicoidal structure — comparable to Wright's Guggenheim Museum, which she had recently visited — inside the pyramidal structure and covered with plants. She noted that it should "not give the impression of a church but that of a greenhouse," or, even more imaginatively, a "mountain under the tropical sun."[38] However, she soon abandoned those ideas and turned to her 1951 studies for the São Vicente museum for alternatives.

Bo Bardi left almost no records about her design decisions during this phase, but her drawings and model photomontages provide enough evidence to suggest that the formal and structural schemes were determined from the outset: a solid, rectangular prism elevated by piers above a semiburied platform. She experimented with red transversal beams on lateral piers, as in the seashore museum, before rotating and reducing them to two sets of beams connected to two large columns straddled between each end of the slanted lot.[39] This scheme gave the impression that the exhibition hall was hanging from the upper beams eight meters (26 ft.) above the terrace, allowing for the unobstructed vista toward the city. In reality, she added two beams between the two internal floors, which were invisible from the outside and supported most of the load of the elevated building.

After her initial studies, the open plaza separated the museum into two communicating parts: a semiburied plinth for public facilities, emulating the old civic hall, and the elevated volume containing the museum galleries and offices (figure 34). Bo Bardi offered the wide space produced

34. Museum of Art of São Paulo, study model, c. 1960. Photographic reproduction. MASP Collection.

between the two parts as a new stage for cultural life in the city, a gesture meant to meet an urban ordinance. Most of the walls of the elevated block were originally opaque. The plinth accommodated a semicircular auditorium into the site's topography, creating the terrace covered with vegetation and, according to one of her studies, even a fan-shaped pavilion following Nervi's use of pleated reinforced concrete. The elevated exhibition hall looked solid and had only ribbon windows for the offices on the lower floor and sheds in the pleated concrete roof for the upper gallery. She would insistently pursue this scheme with several variations and different kinds of epiphytes and other plants until 1965, when technical obstacles led her to accept the glass enclosure that would be built.

According to Bo Bardi, her husband was not enthusiastic about her preliminary ideas. "It's the beautiful dream of a woman," she declared him as saying, "but the museum will keep its agreement with Fundação Armando Álvares Penteado [FAAP] and transfer the collection to the building on rua Alagoas" in the leafy neighborhood of Pacaembu.[40] Bardi's decision had to do with the profound institutional crisis MASP faced in the struggle to retrieve its artworks from New York. The financial rescue deal Chateaubriand

worked out with President Kubitschek separating the museum from Diários Associados meant that MASP needed, almost literally, to reinvent itself if it was to survive. Bardi looked for a new location, initially believing that the solution would be to connect the museum with an educational institution, and signed an agreement with FAAP, a fine arts school and cultural center that was under development with a large endowment left by Armando Álvares Penteado, a prominent São Paulo coffee baron, entrepreneur, and art patron.

Soon after the collection returned to Brazil, the Bardis installed it on panels similar to those used at MASP in the foundation's building, but the new partnership did not last long. Questioning FAAP's curatorial style, Bardi broke the deal and returned MASP's artworks to rua Sete de Abril.[41] Under the terms of their agreement, however, he now ceded the educational programs to the foundation.[42] With little space and no programs, Bardi organized a few itinerant exhibitions of the collection around Brazil until he could find a solution to the crisis. It is likely that during this waiting period he intensified negotiations with the mayor about the site on avenida Paulista.

Between Crisis and Opportunity

71

The Bardis and Chateaubriand had won the battle against the defamation against MASP but not the cultural war with local groups, especially MAM and the Biennial Foundation. Bardi recognized that the impact these groups had on the city's life could not be ignored, especially after the creation of Parque do Ibirapuera in 1954.[43] Not only had the park become a new cultural venue, it had helped to reorganize the distribution of symbolic capital around the city. Gradually, the congested historic center where both MAM, MASP, and other cultural institutions originally started lost its prominence to new urban developments, and avenida Paulista (located halfway between downtown and the park) consolidated its prominence as the city's new commercial and cultural center, making the former Belvedere do Trianon lot even more attractive since Matarazzo's group had built their Palácio das Artes at Ibirapuera.

According to Bo Bardi's personal notes, in "1960, Pietro establishe[d] agreement for Museum construction on Paulista," adding: "Breaking ground."[44] However, she would have to wait at least three years to revisit her preliminary design. With no other commissions on the horizon, she worked on her application to the chaired professorship open at the Universidade de São Paulo, a challenging and frustrating experience that would unexpectedly allow her to start exploring a new trajectory hundreds of kilometers away.

With the MASP project on hold, Lina Bo Bardi, now forty-two years old, completed the long essay about architectural theory that was due in September 1957 with her application for the position at the Universidade de São Paulo. In it, she asserted beliefs regarding architecture that would inform a few lectures and two house projects that she produced in 1958 as well as later work, maintaining a dialogue with her contemporaries both in Italy and in Brazil but also setting herself apart from them.

More than an academic piece, her ninety-page thesis aspired to being a treatise or a manifesto, starting with its title: "Contribuição propedêutica ao ensino da teoria da arquitetura" (Introductory contribution to the teaching of architectural theory).[1] She published it as a small book, illustrating it with several black-and-white images taken from various sources and touched up, as she had done in her previous editorial work. Although the essay served her application well, she would dismiss it after the 1960s when she radicalized her political position.

Though not a particularly rigorous scholarly piece, "Contribuição propedêutica" remains her largest body of theoretical work. It sheds light on themes in her previous writing and in her developing design practice, focusing on "architectural theory . . . at the service of everyday life." She gave special attention to the relations among architecture, nature, and society, defining architecture as both "an art that must seriously take into account the land in which it takes place" and as "the projection of civilized man in the world."[2]

Her approach was based on the 1914 book *The Architecture of Humanism* by British scholar Geoffrey Scott, who claimed that the conceptualization of architecture was not separated from lived experience.[3] Like Scott, she refused to teach a theory of styles as she had received in her education. Instead she aspired to embed architecture theory in a "humanistic sense . . . above formalist idealism, outdated positivism, and scientific-materialist interpretations . . . but aware of its responsibilities."[4] Hers was a theory with action in mind.

"Contribuição propedêutica" is organized in two equally long sections: "Problemas da teoria da arquitetura" (Issues of architectural theory), which sorts historical and contemporary citations organized under nine topics, and "Problemas de método" (Issues of method), which outlines her pedagogical program. More than educating critics, she expected to educate architects to develop critical conscience. So she wrote her essay with more personal opinion and imagination than analytical detachment.

She dedicated the first section to the importance of theoretical knowledge as a way for students to understand how the creative process is rooted in history and place and imbued with collective responsibility. In her reference to Lodoli's moral functionalism, Bo Bardi said architecture should be concerned with "the rigorous consideration of a structure suitable to life without renouncing formal external harmony," an idea she inherited from Bardi. Nature was, to her, a source of fundamental design principles. "Architecture," she wrote, "takes inspiration from the nature that governs it and that gives it the materials and the necessary instruments to shape it harmoniously." She illustrated her embrace of nature with examples such as Gaudí's organic structures and Wright's hemicycle houses and condemned a mimetic artistic approach though, in her practice, this relationship would have ambivalent results. She cautioned professors "not to abandon the boundaries of nature and of natural laws" and quoted Nervi's reference to philosopher Francis Bacon that "nature, to be commanded, must be obeyed."[5]

Bo Bardi did not abandon modern reason, though she questioned the distance architectural rationalism had traveled from its social purpose. The solution, to her, was to promote architecture's reconciliation with science, though architects should "become, above all, the designer[s] of the house of man." She concluded her introductory theoretical approach with a discussion about the social role of designers. She suggested that architecture schools in democratic societies should be the main centers for innovative and "free research, intellectual discussion, and exchange." Recognizing the instabilities in the ongoing revision of modern architecture in the 1950s, she cautioned against sentimentality. She claimed — as she would do until the end of her life — that architecture was not the self-centered expression of an individual's desire but part of a collective effort that extends toward the city and the geography beyond it.[6]

The second section of "Contribuição propedêutica" is more programmatic in regard to her pedagogical approach. It is separated into one short introductory passage and three longer ones focusing on specific topics and potential teaching methods and assignments. In her view, professors should allow students to be propelled by uncertainty, helping them develop a sense of "moral responsibility and avoid exhibitionism." The role of such an instructor would be to "gradually offer critical conscience and historic and technical maturity to an architect," she noted.[7]

She openly questioned her friend Bruno Zevi's notion of interior space, as she had done in personal letters to him. To her, the definition of architecture should not be limited to space. Instead, it should "equally consider the circumstance of 'inhabiting,' [with] man [as architecture's] constant 'physical' protagonist." "Man's fate is to dwell," she wrote, further

hinting at changes in her design practice as were visible in the preliminary study for MASP and in two almost simultaneous residential projects she would soon design. Architects and their education, she professed, "must remain in contact with life in its most ordinary sense."[8]

To Bo Bardi, drawing — like human beings, history, and nature — had a prominent place in architectural education. "Architecture, as an art of design, lives off drawing," she stated. "However, not in the sense of an artwork [but] in the [mathematical] sense it had in the Renaissance." She insisted on avoiding pictorial representation, criticizing students who "draw in 'threaded lines' when not in impressionistic chiaroscuro" and architects who use "spectacular presentation." Instead, she called for simplicity, citing Giuseppe Pagano's instruction "to draw with one's left hand." To her, drawing had a moral purpose: "Professional ethics start with artistic modesty."[9]

Bo Bardi also addressed teaching methods in architecture theory. She wanted to free architectural education from dichotomies between theory and practice, past and present, architecture and building. Theoretical knowledge was more than a tool for design; it was the basis for making informed, ethical, and historically coherent decisions "connected to life" and for "prioritizing man as the protagonist" of architecture. She argued for a new humanism in architecture in which the designer is a "mediator of man's way of living," imbued with scientific knowledge and, above all, "moral responsibility."[10]

In her opinion, like many European critics of the time, modern architecture had dangerously arrived at a "comfortable formalism." She urged education to promote a rigorous method linked to concrete realities. The role of theory in this process, then, should be to understand the "environmental, moral, and social conditions of specific spaces." Brazil, in her view, offered matchless opportunities for architects as mediators of everyday culture, as she had already suggested in *Habitat*. With great optimism, she concluded her essay by recommending that students be introduced to a "vast horizon instead of partially looking into a single direction" and that they create works instilled with the sense of an authentic national character instead of a "vague and abstract cosmopolitanism."[11]

With these ideas in mind and the new book in hand, Bo Bardi applied for the chaired position at the Universidade de São Paulo.[12] She turned in her submission on September 21, 1957.[13] She knew, however, that her application would not be well received by some faculty members, who saw her as difficult.[14] She also faced a technical obstacle. Lacking a copy of her diploma from the Facoltà di Architettura in Rome (supposedly lost in the 1943 bombardment of the office she kept with Carlo Pagani in Milan) and having just three days to complete the documentation, she hired an attorney to sue for a writ of security.[15] A long judicial and bureaucratic battle arose, suspending her public examination until early 1959.[16] Meanwhile, she tried to gain more teaching experience to prove her qualifications for the position. She also developed new design projects and traveled to the north of Brazil for the first time.

In the months between her job application and during the development of her legal appeal, Bo Bardi visited Salvador, the capital of the northeastern state of Bahia, three times. On her first trip, February 1, 1958, she unofficially represented MASP. With Chateaubriand's help, she was hosted by Odorico Tavares, head of Diários Associados's local office and an enthusiastic and astute art collector who planned to create an art museum in the city.[17] On this short trip, she met local artists under Tavares's tutelage, including architect and professor Diógenes Rebouças, the leading local modern architect, and sculptor Mário Cravo Júnior, who introduced her to other artists and intellectuals and to the city's Afro-Brazilian culture and traditions.

The trip was also promising in architectural terms. Cravo asked her to design a simple house and studio for him. However, because he had no money for the construction, her colorful sketches for a simple house covered with rough finishes and roof gardens around a large patio were never realized. With more luck, she met Gilka Felloni de Mattos Nogueira, sister of the physician whose office Bo Bardi had recently designed in São Paulo and wife of Rubem Rodrigues Nogueira, a conservative politician.[18] Turning a blind eye to her client's political life, Bo Bardi agreed to design the couple's private house on a small lot in the area

south of Salvador known as Chame-Chame (figure 35). This commission came while she was developing another residential project in São Paulo, initiated six months before, for Valéria Cirell, once Bardi's collaborator in his short-lived Estúdio Palma (figure 36). After purchasing a small lot on rua Brigadeiro Armando Trompowsky (originally rua Cinco) just about three hundred meters (984 ft.) from the Glass House, Cirell and her husband would soon become the Bardis' neighbors in Morumbi.

Both clients gave Bo Bardi freedom to experiment with the architectural ideas about which she had been writing. She began the two projects with a related combination of orthogonal geometries and naturalistic elements and completed preliminary studies for them simultaneously in the second half of 1958, as her drawings suggest. However, their final versions, though based on similar principles, were completed in different periods and looked substantially different from each other. These two residential projects — both customized and bearing naturalistic references — have often been overlooked in relation to the industrialized features of the Glass House. While her own house was attuned — at least in its frontal volume — with the mainstream architectural discourse in Brazil, the other two houses were not. In addition, the Cirell and the Chame-Chame Houses remained mostly unknown, especially the Cirell House in Salvador, which was completed around 1964 but did not survive the boom of residential highrises that burgeoned in the area along avenida Centenário and, in 1986, was torn down and replaced by a taller building. Still, both houses genuinely represent the aesthetic searches that Bo Bardi pursued at the time, as expressed in her desire to distance herself from strict rationalism and to pursue references to

35. Chame-Chame House, Salvador, 1958–64, view from the eastern side. Photograph by Hugo Segawa.

36. Valéria P. Cirell House, São Paulo, 1957–58, view from the southern side. Photograph by Zeuler R. Lima.

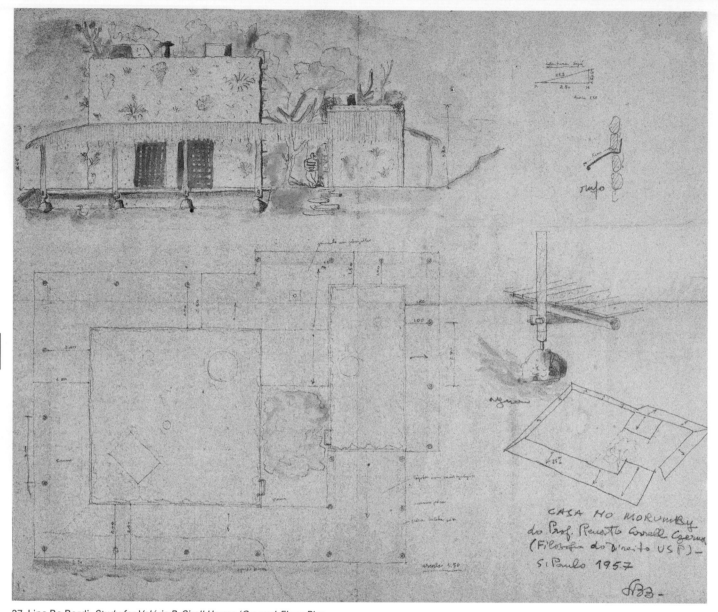

37. Lina Bo Bardi, *Study for Valéria P. Cirell House (Ground-Floor Plan, Frontal Elevation, and Details)*, 1957. Watercolor and color pencil on blueprint, 54.6 × 63.8 cm. ILBPMB Collection.

38. Valéria P. Cirell House in Morumbi, São Paulo, 1957–58, aerial view from the southern side. Computer rendering. Zeuler R. Lima Collection.

39. Valéria P. Cirell House in Morumbi, São Paulo, 1957–58, view from the southern side. Photograph by Nelson Kon.

anonymous buildings and the relation between architecture and nature.

There could not have been a more convenient place to start experimenting with her innovative concepts than near her home. However, despite such closeness and the fact that the Cirell House hints at Bo Bardi's first sketch for her own house, her two projects in Morumbi could hardly be more different. Instead of the transparent enclosure framing the surrounding vegetation in the Glass House, Bo Bardi designed solid, textured masonry walls with vertical gardens enveloping a surprisingly bright interior. Nestled in a bowl-shaped site at the edge of araucaria forest, the Cirell House also differs from the ornate mansions that mushroomed in Morumbi over time. Completed around 1959, the original house was smaller than the one Bo Bardi initially designed. It still resembles a simple cabin despite 1970s renovations conducted by a local interior designer after Valéria Cirell's death.[19]

The design process for the Cirell House likely started in late 1957, but its first approved version dates back to June 1958, after Bo Bardi had begun to travel to Salvador.[20] She produced many meticulously documented drawings and sketches, ranging from cupboard layouts to the house's concrete framework. Her initial scheme consisted of two levels with side verandas and partially elevated from the ground. However, she substantially changed it to accommodate a smaller layout and a different footprint, incorporating the adjacent lot where her design for a cylindrical guesthouse nicknamed "La Torraccia" (The little tower) would be built in 1964. Though Bo Bardi left no written records about the reasons leading to the house's built scheme, several undated sketches indicate that she experimented with solid volumes covered with plants and organized around a fireplace, as suggested by Wright — whose works and theories interested her at the time — and related to site strategies deployed by organic architects (figure 37).

The exterior of the Cirell House built in the late 1950s consisted of two separate midsized blocks with walls covered in small stones, glazed tile shards, and sculptural tropical plants. Resembling rocky formations erupting from the ground, such as the ones Bo Bardi had recently seen in the south of Brazil on a field trip to Vila Velha park with the MASP staff, the stark volumes were originally surrounded by a wooden deck and porch structure with treelike columns and thatched roofs — quickly replaced with regular ceramic tiles — that sat on concrete foundations covered with stones. The house layout was rationalist, but its bulkiness and coarse finish aspired to the scarce means of rural architecture and to the naturalistic appearance of works by Gaudí, which Bo Bardi had recently visited (figure 38).

She used the surrounding verandas to partially shade the building and to expand the interior space (figure 39). They originally created an external, covered circulation connecting the house with a small service block in the back, which was enlarged and incorporated into a single volume during its later renovation. Unlike in her own house, Bo Bardi avoided openings subject to strong sun exposure, and she added a shedlike skylight over the double-height living room. She resourcefully used inexpensive market-brand hung-sash windows — replaced with temperate glass during the renovation — and rotated them horizontally to fit into the low walls. To further protect the openings, she had sliding trellised shutters placed on tracks against the gravel-covered walls, similar to those she proposed decades later at SESC Pompeia leisure and cultural center.

Once inside, the Cirell House reveals a surprisingly light and open space, with the spatial plainness and solid enclosure of Italy's old buildings around which Bo Bardi had grown up. She magnified the experience of the small interior by inserting a wooden mezzanine spanning diagonally across the masonry volume (figure 40). With this gesture, the house simultaneously gained the scale of a larger building and the ambience of a cottage with a subtle hierarchy among living, work, and sleeping areas. She organized the open interior space both spatially and structurally around the fireplace, which supported the long tree trunk holding the mezzanine (figure 41). She made the upper level accessible through a lateral helicoidal staircase — always a spatial and sculptural event in Bo Bardi's works — placed around another polished tree trunk and protected by a tubular metal railing.

The originally built version of the Cirell House perceptibly heightened some of the values Bo Bardi had articulated in her articles for *Habitat*, in her recent thesis, and in lectures she gave in Salvador. Like some of her Italian contemporaries, she expected to revise and humanize rationalism by deriving naturalistic and handmade elements from her personal observation of popular, local practices. It is not a coincidence that the Cirell House had little recognition at the time, especially considering the enthusiasm for the industrial modernization of São Paulo and the construction of the new capital, Brasília. Nonetheless, this project, though simple and often disregarded, materialized her desire that a Brazilian house, even a middle-class one, should resemble simple, anonymous buildings. Its formal vocabulary recalled her analogies with "the rubber tapper's house made out of wooden floors and thatched roofs," as well as the simplicity of the inexpensive house built by the woman brick worker Bo Bardi wrote about in *Habitat* in 1951.[21]

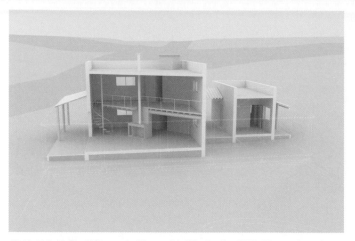

40. Valéria P. Cirell House in Morumbi, São Paulo, 1957–58, sectioned view from the southern side showing interior. Computer rendering. Zeuler R. Lima Collection.

41. Valéria P. Cirell House in Morumbi, São Paulo, 1957–58, view from the southern side. Photograph by Nelson Kon.

Unlike the cubic Cirell House, the house she designed more or less simultaneously for the Nogueiras in Salvador was intended to be camouflaged into the site. Organized, in the built version, as a series of almost concentric walls and terraces emerging from the ground, the general volume of the Chame-Chame House was laid out like the body whorl of a shell covered with pebbles, ceramic shards, and ivy. Being primarily accessible by car, like the Glass House, the most prominent view of the house was from the corner with rua Ary Barroso emerging from the lower part of the neighborhood where rua Plínio Moscoso made a full turn. Before it was demolished, the house had leaned out over the wide curve, giving it full visual exposure to the north and causing it to appear much larger than it was.

Bo Bardi's initial ideas for the house in Salvador were more similar to her previous residential projects than its final curved shapes revealed. After returning to São Paulo from her first trip to Salvador in February 1958, she started the project with an entirely orthogonal geometry. The Chame-Chame subdivision was just as hilly as Morumbi in São Paulo, and the corner lot was small but slanted like a promontory. To meet such conditions, the first drawings she presented to her new clients a few weeks later contained elements of both the Cirell and the Glass Houses. She initially consolidated the whole program for Salvador into a cubic layout with different levels and verandas at the center of the steep site and split the house into a grounded volume on the back with cantilevered terraces toward the front that made the volume appear horizontally as if to hover above a car porch.

The first perspective she sketched with pencil on tracing paper for the Chame-Chame House precisely matches a photograph, taken by Peter Scheier, of the Glass House

standing as the Acropolis on the hill soon after it was built (figure 42). A careful comparison between the two images shows how the large balconies surrounding her first study for Salvador coincided with the slabs of her own house. As she traced that framework, she added naturalistic elements, such as small stones on the walls and plants on and around the building, in the same way she had covered the exterior of the Cirell House. She even replaced the steel pilotis in the photograph with a sculptural column shaped like a tree trunk to support the main cantilever, though she seems not to have been informed about the existence of a large jackfruit tree on the site, as it appears to have been quickly marked in with ballpoint pen on a later occasion.

After receiving her first drawings at the end of March 1958, the clients wrote to Bo Bardi approving of her study with great enthusiasm, but she did not go back to the drawing board immediately. Instead she prepared herself for a second trip to Salvador to present lectures in the middle of April. On that trip, she likely had the opportunity to revisit the site and rethink some of her decisions, especially after seeing the large tree, which she considered priceless.[22] Between April and July 1958, after returning to São Paulo, she abandoned her preliminary Chame-Chame design for a new scheme that evolved out of several attempts to have the building organically match the lot's natural conditions.

In a letter to her clients, Bo Bardi talked about her successful experiment with roof gardens in the Cirell House and her intention to have the external walls covered with mortar and shards of traditional blue-and-white tiles evoking maritime themes.[23] Above all, she proposed an irregular shell-shaped scheme bent around a small, semienclosed entry patio (figure 43). These radical changes in the Chame-Chame House project seem to have been motivated

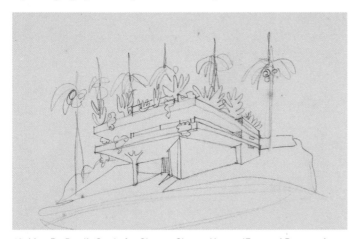

42. Lina Bo Bardi, *Study for Chame-Chame House (External Perspective, First Version)*, c. 1958. Pencil on tracing paper, 27.4 × 50.2 cm. ILBPMB Collection.

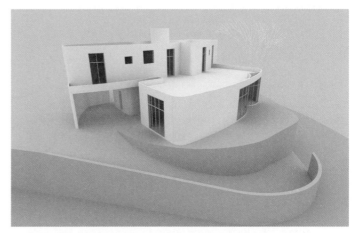

43. Chame-Chame House, Salvador, 1958–64, aerial view from the western side. Computer rendering. Zeuler R. Lima Collection.

by the acknowledgment of the jackfruit tree as well as by her evolving formal vocabulary as she traveled back and forth between São Paulo and Salvador, and between theory and practice. For example, after having seen Gaudí's and Wright's work, she revised the opinion she had expressed in *Habitat* years earlier about another house in Salvador that "the obsession with twisted shapes is . . . , by nature, a mistake," believing that "one can experiment, satisfy a temptation, but . . . the most rational way is the straight line."[24]

The few available photographs and drawings of the Chame-Chame House show a two-story building sitting on a plinth covered with climbing fig vines and topped by a cylindrical water tower (figures 44, 45). Like the Cirell House and a new garage built at the entrance of the steep driveway at the Glass House, the whole building was covered with gravel and a regular, small-clustered pattern of tile shards resembling flowers and Gaudí's works. The curved geometry of the house most likely came from her free interpretation of Wright's hemicycle house type, which she discussed in her thesis and lectures in Salvador. More than addressing Wright's climatic concerns, however, the typology allowed Bo Bardi to create small interstitial spaces and to embrace the jackfruit tree, which seems to have died after construction — perhaps because the foundations damaged the root system — leaving its dried trunk behind. The flat concrete roof and the terrace accessible from all bedrooms over the front volume were originally meant to be covered with dirt and plants, but neither idea was ever executed, likely leaving much to be desired concerning the thermal insulation necessary under the tropical sun of Salvador.

Once past the threshold of the entry door, the visual references to Gaudí and Wright yielded a cozy and softly lit hall (figure 46). As in the Glass House, the hall was a key distribution point, offering four options: to move forward toward the small but ample living room with its wide, horizontal window; to open the door to the right and enter the library; to turn left and arrive at the large service areas in the back and the independent street access; or to move upward to the bedrooms. The ascent was possible through a half-swirled staircase with long, slanted steps that negotiated the crammed space as she would soon devise for the criss-crossing ramps she designed for MASP's Civic Hall. In the floor above, three small bedrooms and the couple's suite had enough space for sleeping but not much more, resonating with the functionalist principle of minimum existence.

As Bo Bardi designed the final version of the Chame-Chame project, she also prepared one of her lectures in Salvador in which she asked, "What does organic, natural architecture mean?" In response, she said that it was not an architecture "determined a priori, [but] an 'open' architecture that accepts nature, that makes itself comfortable, and that seeks to camouflage itself into it, like a lizard lying on

44. Chame-Chame House, Salvador, 1958–64, view from the western side. Photograph by Hugo Segawa.

45. Chame-Chame House, Salvador, 1958–64, view from the upper terrace. Photograph by Hugo Segawa.

rocks in the sun." In the margins of her notes, she sketched a small reptile, invoking the languid walls she drew for the Chame-Chame site.[25]

Although the Cirell and Chame-Chame Houses looked different, they were both pioneering attempts to materialize significant independent premises Bo Bardi articulated in her articles, thesis, and lectures. She was loyal to the idea that, in order to overcome the crisis of modern architecture, designers should embrace an economy of means, modesty, and responsibility toward people and place, which was not very common among most Brazilian architects at the time. Like the work of designers such as Fransciso Bolonha, whose vacation houses resembled Lucio Costa's early attempt to associate modern vocabularies with traditional techniques and natural materials, Bo Bardi's efforts remained isolated from the cosmopolitanism pursued by most of her colleagues. She would later describe her work as *arquitetura pobre*, simple architecture.

More like her European and especially Italian contemporaries, Bo Bardi saw rustic appearance and modesty as the representation of dignifying forms of inhabitation. And yet, she, like them, could not escape an ethical and aesthetic challenge: as architects infused geometric modernism with a naturalistic and rustic architectural language, they struggled to keep the impulse for conceptual renovation from being reduced to merely visual, pictorial appearance.[26]

The same is true regarding her departure from Gaudí's and Wright's references to nature. Whereas those celebrated architects focused on the relation between natural shapes and the physical and structural properties of different materials, she conceived the Cirell and Chame-Chame Houses more as placeholders for images of simplicity than as concrete means for developing the technical clarity she stressed in her lectures.

For all the ambiguity driving those two houses, Bo Bardi's critical quest would fully blossom in her discovery of Salvador, to which she returned in April and in August 1958 and where she would take longer sojourns in the following years. Her second trip to Salvador was short but significant. It brought the promise of renegotiating her values, her personal autonomy, and her professional practice. Architect Diógenes Rebouças, Odorico Tavares's protégé who taught architecture theory in the Escola de Belas Artes (Fine arts school) at the Universidade da Bahia (University of Bahia), invited her to return to Salvador and present three lectures on "Space and Architecture" between April 17 and 21.[27]

Although she was unknown in the city, her thought-provoking presentations, covered in the press by Tavares, attracted the curiosity of architecture students and faculty.[28] She proposed a critical dialogue with Zevi's theories of space and the relation between nature and architecture,

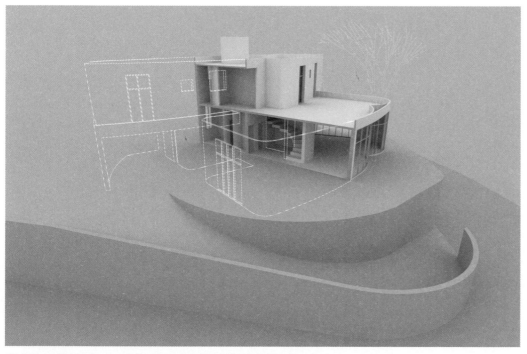

46. Chame-Chame House, Salvador, 1958–64, sectioned view from the western side. Computer rendering. Zeuler R. Lima Collection.

Theory and Action

contrasting them with works by Gaudí and Wright, whose projects left enduring memories among viewers.[29] She especially praised Gaudí's "extreme constructive rigor and his love for the most humble detail, which make the ensemble of his work transcend formal and spatial issues in the history of modern architecture and achieve high human values."[30]

Thorough handwritten lecture notes suggest that Bo Bardi's basic premises derived from the extensive material she had collected for her thesis, *Contribuição propedêutica*. Among them was a hand-drawn diagram representing two parallel evolutionary lines in Western architecture. On the one hand, her proposed lineage went from the Renaissance to rationalism (highlighting Le Corbusier) and its critical revision after World War II. On the other hand, it went from Baroque architecture to Frank Lloyd Wright.

In her first talk, she defined architecture as "an 'adventure' in which people are called to intimately participate as actors," defining the design process as "firmly connected to man, both alive and true." Following the same line, she insisted that "the architect is, above all, a human being linked to true lived experience," and she presented Gaudí's approach as an antidote to traditional architectural theories.[31] Though no notes about her third lecture have been found, her second presentation came entirely from her thesis. On April 19, she presented Geoffrey Scott's *Architecture of Humanism* to describe the dilemmas of rhetorical criticism and then showed pictures of Gaudí's work she had taken in Spain, calling him "one of the best representatives of the spatial issue." Moreover, she presented her criticism of Zevi's book *Saper vedere l'architettura* (Architecture as space: How to look at architecture) and his notion of interior space. "Man is always the protagonist, and interior space is secondary," she insisted to the audience, praising instead Gaudí and Wright as examples of humanized architecture.[32]

Bo Bardi refused self-referential and rhetorical models of criticism, and she aspired, as she announced in her lectures, to become an "intellectual and an architect who triumphs over the mathematical, abstract spirit — which belongs to the simple expert — and is prepared to start a new humanism."[33] In those words, as well as in her writing and projects in the late 1950s, lay the kernel of a crisis, of a change of heart, and of a shift in her belief system. Her travels between São Paulo and Salvador increasingly sharpened the dialogue she maintained between thinking and practice and among her lectures, writing, projects, and exhibitions. Her irreverent questions had not yet taken on political overtones, but she was gravitating toward emerging movements for the socialization of culture led by left-leaning groups in Brazil.[34]

After Bo Bardi's successful lectures, Rebouças invited her to teach his architectural theory course in the architecture program in Salvador. Her prospects as a chaired professor at the Universidade de São Paulo remained uncertain, her work with her husband at MASP had become peripheral, and their marriage was in crisis. The invitation would benefit both Bo Bardi and Rebouças: he could take a leave of absence and she could substantiate her teaching experience.[35] So she decided to accept his offer and spent a few months in Salvador. Meanwhile, her job application was halted and her postponed examination never happened. Perhaps she was discreetly let go from the Universidade of São Paulo, or she may have decided not to pursue the chaired position further.[36] What is certain is that her sojourns in Salvador proved very productive. There she would find a different country with new partnerships and cultural situations for negotiating her aspirations and identity as both a Brazilian designer and a public intellectual.

Eyes Wide Open

Lina Bo Bardi had been in Brazil more than a decade when she arrived in Salvador in early August 1958 to substitute teach for Rebouças. It was her third time there. At forty-three and with her work at MASP and the Universidade de São Paulo on hold, she faced an uncertain future. Yet Salvador, the former colonial capital in the state of Bahia, was emerging as a new, albeit unlikely, center of avant-garde movements, and the opportunity to spend more time there was appealing. So, unlike her previous short visits, she stayed in the city until November 1958.

The historic buildings, ruins, demolitions, new construction, and areas of great popular and ethnic vitality of Salvador reminded Bo Bardi more of the Rome she grew up in than of São Paulo. Politically isolated during Vargas's regime, the city remained provincial in spite of its impressive past as the first capital of the Portuguese empire. Now, however, triggered by the exploration of oil wells in the area around the bay and prompted by President Kubitschek's efforts to industrialize the Nordeste, the once-sleepy town was attempting a late entry into the national process of industrialization. Bo Bardi was arriving at a city of over half a million people situated between the sea and the arid *Sertão* (the legendary northeastern hinterland) and between the desire for modernization and deep-seated, archaic traditions.

While the oil industry propelled economic development in the bay area, unemployment and eviction forced a migration of unskilled farmworkers from their rural homes into urban areas such as Salvador.[1] Many also fled for Brazil's southern region. In the Nordeste, authoritarian landowners maintained — as they still do — tight control of an oligarchic and patrimonial political system in both the cities and the countryside, while thousands of impoverished people struggle to escape chronic drought. Those regional realities imprinted the Brazilian social imagination of the time with both ideological and idealistic representations. No other place in Brazil raised more conflicted sentiments and revolutionary hopes than the Nordeste, and Salvador was one of its symbolic centers.

President Kubitschek's economic master plan in the late 1950s was especially concerned with the region's stagnation. While the construction of the new capital, Brasília, was his chief symbolic achievement, the Nordeste was his main challenge. In 1959, he created SUDENE, Superintendência do Desenvolvimento do Nordeste (Northeast development authority), to promote industrial and infrastructural development, to minimize social conflicts, and to contain political dissidents.[2]

As federal officials and scholars attempted to implement a regional development plan, artists and intellectuals invested in a debate ranging from the validation of popular, everyday culture and the critique of folklore to the promotion of land reform and the eradication of illiteracy. Together, the political, scientific, and artistic narratives that framed the Nordeste as a unique region fueled a singular historic moment in Brazil in the mid-1950s and legitimized new modernization impulses.[3] The region's barren landscape offered a stage on which the common people would come forth as the ideal protagonist for artistic creativity and political protest.

The romantic association between everyday hardship and the cultural authenticity of inhabitants of the northeastern backlands soon gained revolutionary overtones among left-leaning Brazilian intellectuals. Such images were ubiquitous in social-realist Brazilian art, literature, and cinema and in the cultural wars of an increasingly convoluted era that ended in a coup d'état in 1964.[4] Bo Bardi's exposure to those progressive narratives in Salvador would gradually give her aesthetic quest a political dimension. There, she would step out from the shadow of her husband's direct influence and gain intellectual and artistic autonomy.

Although her sojourn in late 1958 was short, it would open up a longer and more meaningful experience than she first expected. She taught architectural theory classes and gave several lectures at other university and cultural venues while studying the project for the Chame-Chame House. She also edited a weekly cultural page in *Diários de Notícias*, part of owner Chateaubriand's and director Odorico Tavares's long-standing campaign to create new audiences and a modern art museum in the city. Her editorial work allowed her to establish collaborations outside the city's architectural milieu, notably with artist Mário Cravo Júnior and the director of the Escola de Teatro (Drama school), Eros Martim Gonçalves.

These experiences prompted her return in 1959 to help Gonçalves organize an exhibition about Bahia during the São Paulo Art Biennial. This work became a stepping-stone to her being hired in 1960 to direct the museum of which Tavares and Chateaubriand had been dreaming for several years. Simultaneously, her husband, Bardi, arrived at an agreement with the mayor of São Paulo to build the new venue for MASP on avenida Paulista. Since her first visit to Bahia in 1957, Bo Bardi traveled frequently, for almost six and a half years, between São Paulo and Salvador, maintaining contact between the two museums while also making trips to other states and the backlands of the Nordeste. She never forgot the patriarchal, chauvinistic, and politically provincial environment of Salvador and would retrospectively define the final and longest, though increasingly convoluted, sojourn there as her "five years among white men."[5]

First, though, she plunged headlong into her teaching activities on August 11, 1958. She wrote long notes for her first four lessons and met students twice a week for two hours, dividing lessons into two sections: a fifty-minute lecture with drawings on the blackboard and slide projections followed by time for practical exercises, which included documenting objects and buildings in the historic center of Salvador with simple line sketches.[6] Using her thesis *Contribuição propedêutica*, Bo Bardi talked about the character of buildings, industrial design, and the relation between space and architecture. She also cited Gaudí, Wright, and Zevi, as she had done in her three lectures in Salvador four months before, and reiterated her desire for the humanization of architecture based on "everyday life space and not metaphysical abstractions."[7]

Along with her architectural theory course, she was invited to give lectures in the dance and the engineering programs. She invoked previous presentations, saying that, just as in dance or theater, "man is the protagonist of space," insisting this time, "Until a person enters the building, climbs its steps, and seizes the space in a 'human adventure' that develops in time, architecture does not exist."[8] She also summarized many of the aspects she developed in depth in her three-month course and stressed the close and fruitful relation between architecture and engineering, as well as between art and everyday life.

The view of modernity she presented was informed not by a functionalist machine aesthetics but by a longing for a re-enchanted rationality. She suggested going beyond spatial and formalist interpretations of architecture and, again, remembered Nervi's quotation of Francis Bacon: "Nature, to be commanded, must be obeyed."[9] Above all, and showing the influence of her initial readings of Antonio Gramsci, she called for the emergence of "new intellectuals" able to respond to "true culture, to life itself."[10] Once again, Bo Bardi advocated for a new humanism, believing that "a new master will be free to enter the true life of technique and art."[11]

On September 27, 1958, a few weeks after she spoke to engineering students, she gave a lecture at Casa de França (French cultural center) in Salvador titled "Arquitetura e natureza ou natureza e arquitetura" (Architecture and nature or nature and architecture), a theme to which she would return in a similar talk a year later at the São Paulo Art Biennial. She reiterated points from her thesis and even from her introduction to the article "Architettura e natura" edited for *Domus* in 1943.[12] Her notes, written in a flavorful mixture of Portuguese and Italian, focused on the evolutionary diagram she laid out about modern Western architecture, establishing two parallel lineages comparing rationalist and non-rationalist developments. She again discussed Zevi's recent book about organic architecture and his theories of space and, in contrast to her previous criticism, presented them as useful for establishing a critical debate about architecture in Brazil.

She turned to the idea of "perfect correspondence between architecture and the environment" while also questioning her formal vocabulary, evidenced not only by her lecture notes but also by the ongoing changes to her studies for the Chame-Chame House. "Organic architecture," she wrote, "tries to mimic nearby nature, surrendering to it without offering resistance or wishing to dominate it. It accepts nature and loves it. It derives its taste from primary and rustic materials."[13] As she prepared her talk, she made a small sketch of the back access of Wright's Jacob Second House, showing not its concave transparent side but the horizontal convex volume, recalling the shapes of her revised project. "Organic architecture fascinates me," she acknowledged in her lecture notes, echoing Enrico Persico's old claim for the revision of rationalism, "but non-organic architecture is the prophecy of a future in which people will passionately love nature, trees, beautiful rocks, hills, and great green planes that will enter their houses with no opposition."[14]

While her presentations expressed previous theoretical and professional concerns about architecture and design, her everyday life in Salvador offered exciting prospects. Just as Bo Bardi was renegotiating her identities, so too was Salvador re-creating its self-image. To her, the city was the "synthesis of Portuguese Baroque, African erotic mysticism, and the bare tragedy of the backlands," and the process of cultural modernization that started in the late 1940s made it a promising place for her aspirations.[15]

When she arrived in Salvador, programs ranging from experimental park schools to a cinema club created by pedagogue Anísio Teixeira, then state secretary of education and health, were already in development.[16] Aside from substantially controlling the local press through his partnership with Chateaubriand and deep connections with local and regional politics, Odorico Tavares ran the only modern art gallery in the city and galvanized a small group of artists, including Mário Cravo Júnior, whom Bo Bardi quickly befriended. The few local modern artists strived to incorporate abstract and social-realist themes and to organize the city's first regular modern art exhibitions.[17] Active student and semiprofessional groups from literature to fine arts and from drama to cinema also offered decisive contributions to the modernization of the city's cultural life.

Salvador was becoming a center of great artistic vitality and aesthetic innovation and began reaching out to southern Brazil.[18] While amateur groups promoted experimental activities and informally started to occupy the space of artistic and intellectual expression, the Universidade da Bahia established guidelines for cultural renewal associated with economic modernization and local political interests. University president Edgard Rêgo dos Santos sponsored significant artistic and scientific renovation, astutely nurturing creative audacity, until he resigned in 1961 during a period of increasing political polarization.[19] The programs he supported would broadly influence Brazilian culture in the following decade.

Bo Bardi was not the only outsider to land in this unique place. Santos handpicked artists, professionals, and scholars from around the country — many of them modernist European émigrés — to accept jobs at the university and to participate in his new programs. In 1954, German conductor Hans-Joachim Koellreutter became the first director of the music school, leading a small orchestra of fourteen musicians. He was followed two years later by another wartime émigré, Polish choreographer Yanka Rudzka, who directed the dance school, and Italian set designer and director Gianni Ratto, who taught at the drama school.[20] In 1956, Santos appointed Eros Martim Gonçalves dean of the drama school. Santos wanted to create a collaborative performing arts program to be housed in the state's Tetro Castro Alves, then under construction near the university, but his plan was never fully implemented.

In this ebullient cultural environment, Bo Bardi would meet Gonçalves shortly after returning to Salvador in August 1958, and he would become her closest ally in the city until he left in 1961. Gonçalves was a cultured and traveled man with wide-ranging interests and a demanding temperament. Like her, he had acute visual sensibility and an interest in integrating formal productions with community life. Lacking a stage for his productions, he appropriated alternative spaces, including the drama school patio and other venues in the city.[21] He was an insightful designer of sets and costumes as well as an avid collector of everyday artifacts, which he hoped to organize into a museum.

Unlike Gonçalves's appointment, however, Bo Bardi's three-month university contract was linked not to Santos's academic reform but to Chateaubriand's and Tavares's interest in creating a museum that could promote Salvador as a center of modern culture to the rest of the country. Still, she would enthusiastically embrace the innovative impulses in the city as she tried to affirm her identity as a Brazilian designer and intellectual. For that purpose, she devoted a great amount of time to a new editorial project — the Sunday newspaper section *Crônicas* (Chronicles) in

Chateaubriand's *Diário de Notícias*, which started less than a month after her arrival in Salvador and continued while she taught at the university. The weekly page was commissioned by Tavares and Juracy Magalhães, an army general, career politician, and first president of the national oil company, who was also preparing his gubernatorial campaign in Bahia with an eye on the region's modernization.[22]

Relying on her previous experience, Bo Bardi rolled up her sleeves and began work. Without the help of typographers, she produced some of the most innovative graphic design pages in the Nordeste at the time.[23] Emulating *A* magazine, she gave it the long title *Crônicas de Arte, de História, de Costume, de Cultura da Vida* (Chronicles of art, history, mores, and life culture), and, in case the content was not clear enough to her readers, she subtitled it *Arquitetura, Pintura, Escultura, Música, Artes Visuais* (Architecture, painting, sculpture, music, and visual arts) (figure 47). Like many of her other editorial projects, *Crônicas* was shortlived — she edited only eight issues. It was confined to her first long sojourn in Salvador, but it set up the tone and alliances for her return.

Aside from its pompous headings, the page was simple, modern, and dynamic and covered local, national, and international issues. It included a short opinion piece on the top left-hand side of the page, which Bo Bardi wrote but did not sign, with a photographic op-ed alongside it provocatively titled "Olho sobre a Bahia" (An eye on Bahia), which was also unsigned and likely cowritten with anonymous contributors, just as she had done for *Habitat*.

Weekly themes focused on social and urban problems ensuing from the rapid modernization of Salvador and the region. *Crônicas* also carried contributions by Koellreutter, Ratto, and Gonçalves, along with translations of texts by Italian art critics, photographs, artworks, vignettes, collages, and caricatures drawn by Bo Bardi. Her editorials were concise, critical, and expressive and, being published hastily, exuded spontaneity and included several typos. Her style was not always refined, but the free and ambiguous associations between texts and images suggested her surrealistic aspirations and her irreverence at their best.

With eyes wide open on Bahia, the first issue, published September 7, 1958, was a critique of the urban and cultural modernization of Salvador. Bo Bardi's first op-ed, "Cultura e não-cultura" (Culture and nonculture), praised everyday practice over the isolated activity of educated individuals. Making unquoted references to Gramsci's notion of national-popular culture and to the role of public intellectuals, she asked: "Why doesn't the new humanist, who is able to understand and solve human problems, replace the *literati* with his technical basis?" She commended the common

people's ability to solve existential and material problems with limited resources, proposing to safeguard this respectable, "most genuine force in the country." "It would be useful to remember the words of a philosopher of praxis," she continued, suggesting (but not citing) Gramsci: "Don't bend as you talk to the masses, 'Mr. Intellectual,' straighten up your back."[24]

In the second issue of *Crônicas*, published a week later, Bo Bardi's unsigned opinion piece, "arquitetura ou Arquitetura" ("architecture or Architecture"), played with small and capital initials, audaciously challenging a self-critical testimony that Niemeyer had written in the ninth edition of his new magazine *Módulo* about the country's new capital (figure 48). "Where is that which is human in Niemeyer's statement?" she asked. The picture of his model for the new National Congress she used to illustrate the page offered an unmistakable answer, defining Brasília as "suffocated by forms, by compositions, by the aura of monumental European squares." Instead of his architecture for the new capital, she praised the "simplicity, human proportion, and the modest and poetic sentiment of life" in Niemeyer's earlier work. In contrast and with her eyes on Bahia, she presented a picture of the historic town of Cachoeira taken by young architect Ennes Silveira Mello, one of her editorial collaborators, in the hinterland of the state (figure 49). She insisted that "designers who look at architectural magazines sitting at their desks and don't have eyes for reality will be the creators of abstract buildings and cities." Architects, in her view, "must prioritize not their formal individualism but their awareness of being useful to people through their art and experience." "This," she concluded, "is the true meaning of today's architecture."[25]

The next edition presented Bo Bardi's refusal to separate culture into educated and popular categories in her short essay, "Inatualidade da cultura" (Outdated culture).[26] Though she did not talk about popular art at the time, she tentatively defined what culture meant to her.[27] She was against a "crystallized meaning and favored the intensification and expansion of the notion of culture," which would increasingly be expressed in her work, particularly after her final and longer five-year sojourn in Salvador.[28] She also wrote — as a result of her initial contacts with Gonçalves — a short article titled "Exposição pedagógica na Escola de Teatro" (Pedagogical exhibition at the drama school). Attuned with the school's line of work, Bo Bardi announced the strong aspiration she came later to develop on her own. In her essay, she suggested that the exhibition was "a first step in the creation of a museum of cultural customs, a drama museum, the point of departure for a school of any

Cronicas

de arte, de história, de costume, de cultura da vida

Arquitetura
Pintura
Escultura
Musica
Artes Visuais

2

Diário de Notícias — Cidade do
Salvador, 14 de setembro de 1958

arquitetura ou Arquitetura

O depoimento auto-critico do arquiteto Oscar Niemeyer, publicado no número 9 (volume segundo), da revista "Modulo", deu lugar a várias controvérsias, mas, pelo público interessado, quer dizer pelos arquitetos, tem sido interpretado como uma "confissão", uma espécie de "mea culpa" arquitetônica.

Mas o que diz em seu depoimento o arquiteto Oscar Niemeyer? O que ele diz é o seguinte, praticamente: — "Depois que se voltei da Europa muito mudou minha atitude profissional. Até àquela época estava desanimado, pela convicção de que o arquiteto exercia num meio em que imperava a injustiça social fosse uma atividade transitória, impossibilitada de resolver os problemas do povo. Assim, combatido, ancorava a profissão com espírito esportivo, com negligência, aceitando trabalho em demasia, confiando na minha capacidade de improvisação, satisfazendo caprichos da classe mais favorecida, que aceitava em mim o "realize". — E o depoimento continua, anunciando a superação dessa crise moral arquitetônica e o propósito de recusar qualquer trabalho em mental, de se dedicar, exclusivamente, a obras importantes, como, por exemplo, os edifícios governamentais de Brasília, projetados por encargo do Presidente da República.

Por essas obras, o arquiteto Niemeyer está procurando soluções compactas e geométricas, simples e elementares, à realização das quais se dedica com extremo cuidado. O depoimento acaba, citando como "a própria essência da arquitetura, a antiga definição de Le Corbusier: "l'architecture est le jeu, savant, correct e magnifique des volumes, assemblés sous la lumière", confirmando que o fim de sua obra será de comunicar "um pouco de beleza e emoção".

Mas o que é a arquitetura, senão o meio mais eficaz para combater com o exemplo a mesma injustiça social que obrigava o arquiteto Niemeyer a contribuir a aumentar (dada a sua popularidade e ascendência sobre a juventude), no campo da arquitetura, aquela mesma injustiça que tanto o feria! Não é o arquiteto moderno construtor de cidades, bairros e casas populares, um combatente ativo, no campo da justiça social? O que cria no espírito firme e convencido a dúvida moral, a consolidação da injustiça humana, pela impossibilidade de resposta, em consequência uma posição de luta para a contenção de um fim positivo, moralmente positivo?

A posição de revolta do arquiteto Niemeyer, ao fazer a contrária daquilo que ele teria podido fazer, enfrentar a especulação imobiliária para servir-se dela como uma arma, contra a própria especulação (a sua celebridade e fama permitindo), a uma posição de artista destligado de problemas sociais, uma possível de "l'art pour l'art", este possível é reafirmada hoje pelo seu depoimento que cita como base da arquitetura moderna a já citada definição de Le Corbusier! Faltando pela mesmo Corbusier, aliás, hoje superada. Onde está o humano no documento de Oscar Niemeyer? Bufotando pelas formas puras compostas, pela evocação de praças monumentais europeias, obras de gênio ao serviço dos Papas e dos Grandes da humanidade, testemunhas dum tempo desaparecido para sempre.

A injustiça social existe, mas os problemas não se resolvem, passando a sôbre êle a responsabilidade. Ao Museu de Caracas, nos edifícios de Brasília, definições de uma mesma Niemeyer, como de uma concepção, de uma pureza irrevasível, não preferimos à Igreja da Pampulha, a casinha de Vassouras que se impuseram à atenção internacional, pela simplicidade, a proposição humana, o sentimento modesto e poético da vida, que denunciava aquela mesma condição de desânimo, o combate entre o homem social e a arquitetura, que Oscar Niemeyer, no seu depoimento afirma ter superado, indicando como fim arquitetônico uma possível formal que nega todos os valores humanos e todas os quintos da arquitetura nacional. — ARQ.

Arquiteto OSCAR NIEMEYER: maquete do Palácio do Congresso Nacional em Brasília

Foto ENNES S. MELLO e SILVIO ROBATTO

 ## Ôlho sôbre a Bahia

É uma rua de Cachoeira, mas igual a tantas outras ruas desta Cidade do Salvador e Cachoeira é ainda Salvador e uma cidade não é nenhum compartimento estanque, ramifica-se, cresce... cria galhos, folhas e raizes e devagar sai dos confins e torna-se adulta como qualquer organismo vivente. O arquiteto planificador tem que basear o seu projeto sobre este desenvolvimento natural das formas arquitetônicas, urbanísticas, criadas pela necessidade da vida cotidiana. O projetista que olha as revistas de arquitetura, sentado na prancheta e não tem olhos para a realidade, será um criador de edifícios e cidades abstratas, projetadas para uma humanidade que existe somente na sua fantasia e os homens reais obrigados a habitar casas e cidades nas quais serão estrangeiros, se abandonarão ou serão transformados numa humanidade amorfa. O arquiteto de hoje mesmo se for um bom arquiteto obterá os mesmos resultados dos obtidas para especulação imobiliária: a ausência de características ou nada. A significação íntima da vida de uma cidade é sempre moderna enquanto atual. Ao arquiteto compete estudá-la e compreendê-la e traduzi-la em formas modernas e eficientes. O homem, a mulher que passam nesta rua, têm os seus determinados problemas materiais e espirituais. A abertura que é o próprio casa e os homens reais nada. A abstração não nasce social e a arquitetura, que olha os seus determinados problemas materiais e espirituais. A abstração casa e os próprio teto moderno expressão máxima de responsabilidade social, enquanto conjunto de obras públicas, terrenos e capitais públicos, quer dizer de obras expostas ao julgamento e à vida de todos, tem que pôr na base de sua própria projeção são o individualismo formalístico, mas a consciência de ser útil aos homens, por meio de sua arte e de sua experiência. Esta é a verdadeira significação da arquitetura de hoje.

Problematica da Arte Moderna

Texto e desenho de Mario Cravo Jr.

A atmosfera saturada e hermática dos nossos dias beneficia tão somente uma dicta de indivíduos saturados de literatura que passam a existir através dos auto-elogios. Os tremendos problemas do nosso século e os mais elementares, palpitantes, enquanto a vez, o impacto da problemática de todas as culturas dá estágio em nossos dias no escópio espaço de tempo de duas ou três gerações tão devido aos meios de contato fácil assim como a divulgação imediata proporcionada pelo rádio, livros, jornais e revistas...

Turris Eburnea!

O sr. Dufy não recebe ninguém. É uma defesa contra as senhoras gráfinas, diletantes de arte ou um ato de sabedoria? Talvez os dois. O pintor Dufy, pintor da Côte D'Azur e do Sweepstake talvez não gostasse de sociedade. "Vives não gostasse de pseudo-artistas intelectuais...

Mᵉ DUFY
ne reçoit pas

Carta a Claudio Santoro

H. J. Koellreutter

CLAUDIO foi reunido com enorme prazer a tua verdadeira alegria que recebi teu telegrama aceitando o nosso convite para reger a Orquestra Sinfônica da Universidade da Bahia. Considero esta e os Semi-nários Livres de Música der-se na mesma Universidade que tive a censura de construir e realização de um ideal pelo qual venho pugnando desde quanto tempo dos meus aprendizo na minha classe de composição...

CLAUDIO SANTORO regendo a Orquestra Sinfônica de Bratislava

Conclui na 2a. pág.

DOMINGO   Desenho de B.B.

ANTOLOGIA

Carta do Rio

A publicação, domingo passado, de uma carta vinda das mais puras camadas populares, nos contendo saborosa de humanidade e de poesia, agradou a muitos e a outros desagradou. Não entendem alguns porque publicar estas tão erradas? Falam certamente da ortografia, mas bem contraria não perceberam a chama que encontramos nela...

DOCUMENTOS: *Escola de Belas Artes, 1900*

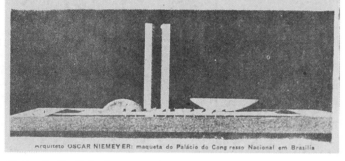

48. Lina Bo Bardi, "architetura ou Arquitetura," *Crônicas, Diário de Notícias*, Salvador, September 14, 1958, 1. ILBPMB Collection.

49. Lina Bo Bardi, "Olho sobre a Bahia," *Crônicas, Diário de Notícias*, Salvador, September 14, 1958, 1. ILBPMB Collection.

kind of human research."[29] A small and fruitful seed was planted that day.

As Bo Bardi multitasked teaching and revising the Chame-Chame House project, she continued to prepare weekly materials for *Crônicas* until it was discontinued at the end of October. Between the fourth and seventh issues, she focused on the activities promoted by the university's performing arts programs and on a critical assessment of the urban renewal of Salvador with one eye on the debate about functionalism and the other on the threat to architectural heritage. "This is not Salvador," she wrote in the fourth issue, calling it a "city built by speculation, with no love and no hope, where people get used to solitude and indifference, where they forget to see other people."[30]

In the following week, she wondered whether conservation would be enough to deal with those fast changes, recalling how Fascist architects replaced popular Roman neighborhoods with "squalid rhetorical and imperial architecture."[31] In the sixth edition, she sharpened her political tone and suggested the creation of a federal program for low-cost housing.[32] Though she left only notes about her initial theory lessons, one has to wonder to what extent she may have brought up those issues during the remainder of her course. Meanwhile, in *Crônicas*, she talked about the relation between school and life as a means for achieving a new humanism with no sentimentality and for "preserving Bahia's [Salvador's] human scale, its human proportions, the antirhetorical aspect of its buildings, its squares, and its streets." Ultimately, she insisted on "not replacing man with an idea."[33]

In addition to considering urban issues, the fourth issue of *Crônicas* marked Bo Bardi's first recorded collaboration with Gonçalves, still dean of the drama school. She published an essay in which he proposed to invert the understanding of the cultural relations between Europe and the former American colonies by valuing genuine popular manifestations. In the two following numbers, she published more contributions by Koellreutter, Gonçalves, and Ratto about music and theater. She even embraced a heated controversy with young filmmaker Glauber Rocha, who criticized the promotion of avant-garde culture within a provincial and institutional setting but who would eventually become like a disciple to Bo Bardi.[34]

In Gonçalves's interest in popular cultural performances and artifacts, Bo Bardi found a match for her interest in design and handicraft. It was also a match for her initial readings of Gramsci's critique of folklore, which were the focus of the last issue of *Crônicas* on October 27, 1958, a few weeks before she returned to São Paulo. Under the title "Arte industrial" (Industrial art), she published an op-ed showing ceramic figurines produced by Severino of Tracunhaém, an artisan from a small town in the backlands of the Nordeste. Opposing the idea of folklore as a depository of nostalgia, her text was as much a public provocation as it was the sign of the changing values she began to develop in Salvador and would later apply to her curatorial and architectural projects.

Through Gramsci's writings, Bo Bardi saw great liberating potential in everyday life and popular culture. She stressed that neither artists nor intellectuals have superior power or knowledge, nor was culture something handed down by them. Rather, impatient with sentimentality, she reiterated their responsibility toward the common people and her belief in social emancipation through everyday life practices. She declared herself modern and intended to amplify the scope of modernity in search of a new humanism, in agreement with Gramsci and in opposition to the elitist humanism of the Renaissance.

"Handicraft," she suggested following Gramsci, "is the expression of a time and a society." She saw the end of an artisanal era as producing a split between technicians and makers, which directly related to the separation of modern designers and builders. "Each one is on his own," she lamented, concluding, "Workers are debased by the lack of ethical satisfaction in the face of their own work." Criticizing sentimentality but not romantic idealism, Bo Bardi wrote that popular art "when truly popular is art with a capital A."[35]

Her short essay established the foundation of many of her future projects and collaborations in Salvador, from small exhibitions to the proposal for a center for design documentation and education, aiming at the transition from handicraft into manufacturing with an inherently Brazilian identity. It also reflected her dialogue with Gonçalves and with Cravo Júnior about their interest in everyday culture and their collections of popular artifacts and documents. To her, the main issue regarding handicraft production in Brazil should consider "the immediate collection of every old and modern artisanal material that exists in each country for the creation of a living museum, a museum that could be dedicated to 'Handicraft and Industrial Art' and that would constitute the source of historical-popular culture of a country."[36]

Bo Bardi believed that industrialization should aim not at individual work and profit but at the creation of a common good based on a collaborative and collective workforce. From Gramsci's theory of praxis and his notion that culture emerged from everyday struggles, she started to hone her ideas about industrial design and collective everyday culture that would mature in the last decades of her life. Though she was not related to socialist and communist groups in Brazil at this time, her thoughts would eventually meet their efforts to promote what Gramsci defined as a national-popular collective will. This overlap would be particularly strong during and after her last sojourn in Salvador and through her contact with leaders from the groundbreaking Movimento de Cultura Popular (Movement for popular culture) in Recife in the early 1960s.

While Gramsci saw no opposition between modernity and tradition but instead between different power groups, Bo Bardi gradually and intuitively strived to expose those oppositions in increasingly hybrid works. It is no coincidence that she illustrated the pages of *Crônicas* with strongly contrasting images. At the center of the eighth issue, for example, she placed a large picture of a hand pierced by an arrow with an idealistic caption claiming, "The hand, while it worked, created mankind," paired with, "The millenary experience of hand work will lead the machine."[37]

With no other records or explanation than a small note after the eighth edition stating, "The editor who created [*Crônicas*] returns to São Paulo," Bo Bardi left the newspaper and her substitute teaching position in Salvador and returned to São Paulo in early November 1958.[38] The motivations for her departure are unclear, but it seems to have resulted mostly from ideological differences within the architecture program. For all the attention she drew among students, her positions did not resonate with the school's ambitions to catch up with the modernist architectural developments from the south of Brazil.[39] Moreover, she antagonized professors in charge of the aesthetics course (her fiercest opponent was Romano Galeffi, an Italian Crocean philosopher). While they did not take her seriously, she criticized them as rhetorical, a confrontation that likely led to the school's decision not to renew her contract.[40] Still, her severance from the architectural program did not separate her from Salvador.

After her application to the Universidade de São Paulo fell through, Bo Bardi returned a few times to Salvador in 1959 and more consistently in 1960 but without connections to professional education or to design practice. Instead, her exposure in Salvador and her relation with Bardi made her a strategic candidate for directing the museum Tavares and Chateaubriand had been planning. During these visits, she benefited primarily from circumstances she perceived as an alternative to the affected and Eurocentric cultural circles of São Paulo, and she eventually played the role of a keen messenger among different worlds, discourses, and scales: south and north, popular and cosmopolitan, modern and traditional, industrial and preindustrial, national and international.

More than becoming a conventional architect, Bo Bardi would find in Salvador new purpose and excitement in acting as a public intellectual. Like others who arrived there with an artistic agenda, she would help modernize and expand local cultural repertoires while simultaneously reinventing herself as a Brazilian artist and thinker. Aside from participating in a radical process of ideological and behavioral transformation, her more extended sojourn in Salvador and her intellectual and physical incursions into the Nordeste would unlock latent interests she had nurtured since the war years in Milan. Above all, it would allow her to live fully by what was important to her.

By the time Lina Bo Bardi flew back to São Paulo in November 1958, she knew Salvador had a lot more to offer her. She would soon return a few times to work with Martim Gonçalves, director of the Escola de Teatro, in whom she had found a new and energizing ally. Aware that her ideas were not finding support among architects in the school of fine arts, she nurtured her interests in the bourgeoning and irreverent performing arts programs at the Universidade da Bahia. Above all, she would later be hired to direct a new museum, which helped mature her worldview as a designer and granted her the autonomy for which she longed.

While still in São Paulo, Bo Bardi helped Gonçalves establish an agreement with Matarazzo in March 1959 to host an exhibition about popular art from Bahia. Gonçalves would represent his Escola de Teatro during the Fifth São Paulo Art Biennial, devoted to informal expressionism and action painting, which was scheduled in six months' time. Soon after, in April, Bo Bardi traveled to Salvador to participate in a seminar directed by Gonçalves and Koellreutter at the drama school. Though she left no notes regarding her teaching, their collaborative course had the intricate title "Conversations about the Historic Continuity of Man's Aesthetic Expression: From Prehistory to Contemporary Art," which attracted, according to the local press, "the same old audience."[1]

In August 1959, she also helped Gonçalves set up a small exhibition about popular cultural practices that opened with an international colloquium of Luso-Brazilian studies at the university.[2] The conference was the flagship in the creation of the Centro de Estudos Africanos e Orientais (CEAO, Center for African and Oriental studies), directed by Portuguese philologist Agostinho da Silva and founded to promote cultural and diplomatic exchanges and studies with Lusophone countries in the Far East and in Africa.[3] In addition, it aimed to reach out to the large local African-Brazilian community generally disregarded as poor and unsophisticated.[4] Not only did that exhibition preface their larger upcoming project at the Biennial, it also inaugurated a prolific dialogue between Bo Bardi and Gonçalves, merging theater and design, as well as educated and popular cultures, which had an enduring effect in the work she produced as a designer later in her life.

During this period, Bo Bardi also began to plan a new monthly magazine based on topics outlined in her recent articles and lectures. She considered naming it *Brasiliana* and noted that "the director," as she described herself, "will write the background article for each issue beyond all the editorial part. No other editors are expected."[5] She studied several graphic design solutions, including a miniature mock-up booklet with several collages highlighting its

Dadaist character with "everything based on comic strips and yellow press, but serious."[6] She hoped to place Brazil in the world and to show its art, architecture, culture, and local themes, highlighting Bahia. The first issue was planned for September 1959 to coincide with the opening of the exhibition at Ibirapuera, but despite her efforts, this experimental editorial project never went to print.

Nonetheless, her return in Salvador to lecture in April 1959 was accompanied by political changes that would eventually benefit her career and her longer stay in the city. On April 7, Juracy Magalhães, one of the commissioners of *Crônicas*, was elected governor of Bahia. He and the mayor of Salvador envisioned a modern capital connected to national development plans, necessitating large infrastructural and institutional projects, which the local press described as an epidemic destruction and construction.[7] Magalhães was also interested in the arts, and on July 22, 1959, his government approved new legislation creating a museum to "promote the state and disseminate the knowledge of arts in general, mainly visual arts and its contemporary developments."[8]

The board of directors brought the governor's old and new political friends together, including Tavares, Chateaubriand, and Edgard Santos, president of Universidade da Bahia. His wife, Lavínia Magalhães, was nominated the museum's president.[9] After some disagreement but with the support of the Magalhães couple, the board members invited Bo Bardi to serve as artistic director in November 1959. They also chose to use the glazed lobby of the modernist Teatro Castro Alves (TCA) as a temporary home. The museum was scheduled to open on January 6, 1960.

Meanwhile, Bo Bardi remained involved in Gonçalves's plan for the *Bahia* exhibition that opened in São Paulo on September 21, 1959. The show was the chief event of several programs fostered by Santos and gave the university national visibility through tour groups to the south of Brazil.[10] Though inaccurately credited to Bo Bardi, according to her statement published in a newspaper article at the time, the exhibition was mainly conceived by Gonçalves and promoted by the political machine involving Magalhães's office, the university, and Chateaubriand's group.[11] Still, Bo Bardi's logistical participation, especially in setting up the show and in drafting the coauthored catalogue text, was instrumental.

According to her, Gonçalves's goal was to "reveal, through a theatrical presentation, the popular roots of the culture of Bahia, in contrast with the cosmopolitan currents that characterize the great São Paulo enterprise [the Art Biennial]." Despite her insightful exhibition display and, until that point, her one brief visit to the hinterland with Mário Cravo Júnior, Bo Bardi had not been very familiar with the various artifacts collected by Gonçalves. "The discovery of those elements of the local culture," she explained, "resulted from my acceptance to direct the Museu de Arte Moderna da Bahia [MAMB, Museum of Modern Art of Bahia]."[12] This discovery also revealed to her the strategic relations between groups from São Paulo and Bahia at the time.

The *Bahia* exhibition was mounted under the concrete canopy at the entrance of the Biennial building designed by Niemeyer at Parque do Ibirapuera. "Not a casual location," Bo Bardi wrote to the Italian readers of *Domus*, since the show contrasted the "polimaterial intuitions" — produced with precarious materials by artists such as Alberto Burri — with what she and Gonçalves called "polimaterial compositions," the survival works made out of leftovers from the northeastern hinterland. The show also contrasted a freedom of expression "full of human reality" with contemporary art "imbided in metaphysics inside the Biennial pavilion."[13] In the exhibition brochure, they noted, "We tried to focus on every fact, even if very small, that expresses poetry in everyday life. We presented a series of ordinary objects treated with great care that offer important examples to modern industrial design."[14]

In her preliminary layout study for *Bahia*, Bo Bardi enclosed the sides of the canopy with dark curtains, creating a long temporary hall with several curved nooks for displaying panels, photographs, and objects (figure 50). The executed version was a variation of the original idea and had a simpler and more orthogonal geometry, but no less carefully choreographed. One entered through a tunnel animated by slide projections of historical and traditional images and the sounds of Afro-Brazilian music.[15] Next, the deep hall opened up to display innumerable images and everyday objects such as hammocks, votives, simple toys, and makeshift and hybrid home utensils loaned from collectors in Salvador and from the drama school.[16]

Complementing the side curtains, Bo Bardi covered the underbelly of the concrete canopy with thin white fabric that diffused the ceiling light like a *velarium*, recalling awnings used in ancient Rome. She also covered the floor with a layer of fresh leaves, a special effect used in popular festivities in Bahia. Large objects, including *carrancas* (carved riverboat figureheads), an armorlike leather garment worn by cattle ranchers in the backcountry, and Afro-Brazilian religious costumes were either placed on cubical stands or stood on their own.[17] Bo Bardi also designed various display panels, including a system of wooden rods sitting atop concrete bases encrusted with seashells and displaying textiles and a photographic documentary, as well as a glass case

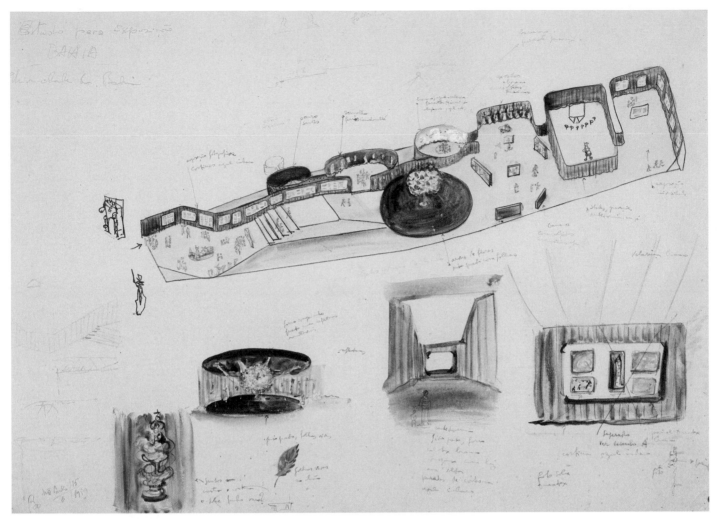

50. Lina Bo Bardi, *Study for Bahia Exhibition (Ibirapuera Park)*, June 15,
1959. Watercolor, ballpoint pen, color pencil, and India and metallic inks
on cardstock, 50.6 × 70.3 cm. ILBPMB Collection.

resembling the *vitrina das formas* (form display case) she designed for MASP and which contained delicate ceramic objects.

The exhibition opened with a performance of Afro-Brazilian dances by actors and students from the drama school and ran for three months. It was an expanded version of the weeklong show of photographs and recordings titled *Dança e teatro popular no Brasil* (Popular dance and theater in Brazil) that Gonçalves presented in Paris in March 1957, during the International Theater Festival organized by UNESCO.[18] As Bo Bardi later wrote, *Bahia* was "a show of cultural anthropology rather than art, [of] popular violence and design novelty: the extreme simplicity of expressive means."[19] Not only did it challenge the establishment and the idea of creative genius presented in the Fifth Art Biennial, it also rejected nostalgic approaches to traditions, which she associated with the new Museu do Folclore (Folklore Museum) in São Paulo. She and Gonçalves reiterated this approach in the exhibition brochure, asserting that those everyday items should not be seen as folkloric documents.

The *Bahia* exhibition materialized an important cultural and ethnographic experiment in tune with works developed at the CEAO in Salvador by anthropologist Vivaldo da Costa Lima — who also collaborated in the show's preparation — and with experiments by anthropologist Darcy Ribeiro, who helped found, in Rio de Janeiro in 1953, the Museu Indígena (Indigenous people museum), focusing on everyday life and culture. The exhibition was especially in line with the Museu de Arte Popular (Museum of popular art) of Recife, created by anthropologist Abelardo Rodrigues and architect Acácio Gil Borsói in 1955. This museum was a precursor of the Movimento de Cultura Popular, which, in the early 1960s, galvanized intellectuals and artists, like Bo Bardi, interested in studying everyday cultural objects of underprivileged populations in the Nordeste and in blending romantic impulses with revolutionary discourse. As Bo Bardi and Gonçalves announced in the exhibition brochure, they conceived *Bahia* "within the framework of living" and invited visitors — especially educated ones, since the invitation was in French — with the words of set designer Adolphe Appia: "Soyons artistes! *Nous le pouvons*" (Let's be artists! *We can do it*).[20]

Bo Bardi's quest started where the exhibition brochure ended. Even before the *Bahia* exhibition closed, she returned to Salvador to quickly remodel the glazed lobby of Teatro Castro Alves for the new Museu de Arte Moderna da Bahia (MAMB). The theater was designed in 1954 by modernist architect José Bina Fonyat's team, and it is still located across praça do Campo Grande from the modernist Hotel da Bahia, where she used to stay and which was designed by Rebouças's team a few years earlier. Both buildings were architectural symbols of the city's modernization, but the theater auditorium mysteriously burned down on July 9, 1958 — five days before its official opening — transforming it into a bizarre half-ruin with glass and white marble walls and a fallen roof.

The theater was an unusual location for a museum, but Bo Bardi was accustomed to improvisation. The transparent, independent lobby was lodged underneath the edge of the monolithic auditorium and lifted slightly from the ground to overlook the leafy plaza. On November 18, 1959, she concluded a series of perspectives, plans, and sections for the renovation. To reduce the problem of direct sun exposure in the lobby and to provide flexible space, Bo Bardi installed floor-to-ceiling curtains around the glazed exhibition hall and sliding curtains to create separable rooms. Also between floor and ceiling, she placed adjustable metal rods to hold flat panels and modular plywood stands in various sizes to hold objects such as statues, ceramic pieces, and even industrial material. With these gestures, she introduced the spatial neutrality she had brought from her exposure to modern Italian exhibition design to local audiences. The white curtains subdivided the lobby into a large area for traveling exhibitions, a small room for works by emerging artists, and a semicircular nook with a raised black platform on the south side reserved for one selected artwork to be displayed on a minimal support, as if an actor on the stage.[21]

Behind the lobby, Bo Bardi carefully converted the ramp leading to the destroyed theater into a small, multipurpose auditorium (figure 51). Two lateral screened walls such as the one she had produced for the expansion of MASP in 1950 both darkened and ventilated the space used for film projections and lectures. Using simple woodwork, she created temporary structures including a podium and rows of interconnected chairs whose back legs were shorter than the front legs so that the chairs would be leveled on the slanted floor. The seats resembled Bauhaus-style furniture, but the wood joints, brass screws, and soft, unfinished leather hanging like hammocks left no doubt about her local references (figure 52). Underneath them, she had the ramp covered with rustic straw mats sewn together to form a carpet, materializing, in different formal vocabularies, the simplification and the vernacular vocabularies she had promoted in previous years.

On January 6, 1960, MAMB opened to the public. It enjoyed political support but lacked sufficient funding. Still, Bo Bardi managed to organize exhibitions and cultural programs strongly relying on MASP's infrastructure and collection and with help from university partners and

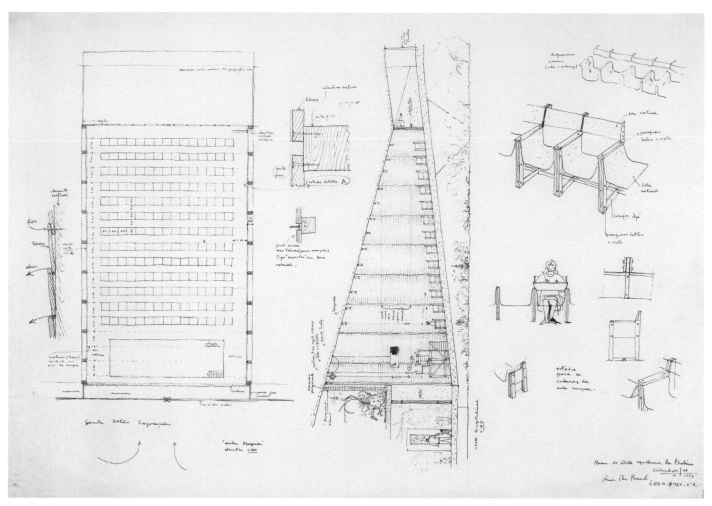

51. Lina Bo Bardi, *Study for Teatro Castro Alves Renovation (MAMB Auditorium, Salvador)*, c. 1959. India ink and tracing paper, 70.2 × 99.2 cm. ILBPMB Collection.

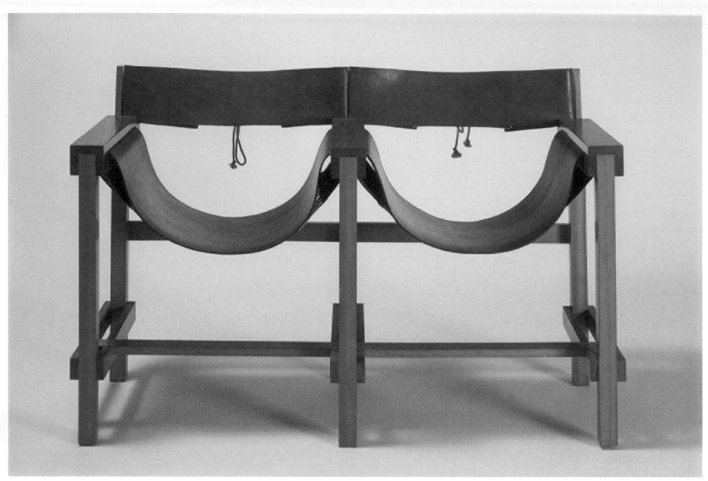

52. MAMB auditorium seats, Salvador, c. 1960. Photograph by Nelson Kon.

local patrons. She also had reliable local assistance during this period. Cravo Júnior executed several of the artwork supports she designed with simple materials such as construction rebar, cast concrete, and plywood. She also hired his son-in-law, anthropologist Renato Ferraz, who acted as her personal assistant and the museum's administrative manager.[22] Working together until 1964, they set up almost a hundred temporary monthly exhibitions (sometimes with more than one running simultaneously).[23]

Bo Bardi wanted to convey a broad understanding of artistic values and production. Visitors were able to view pieces by novice and well-established artists alongside work by iconic national and international figures in solo, pedagogical, and historical exhibitions originally produced by MASP, and even exhibitions commissioned by the state of Bahia.[24] She also displayed works by local artists whom Tavares recommended, though she considered their popular themes to be too folkloristic and contrary to her vision. Meanwhile, she attempted to revive her plan to publish *Brasiliana* magazine, changing the format and title to *Revista B* (B magazine), suitably suggesting Brazil and Bahia and a continuation of her model publication, *A: Cultura della vita*. Her planned board of directors consisted only of regional intellectuals and artists. She hoped to integrate progressive forces throughout the Nordeste. She envisioned a popular magazine that would, "without a doubt, shake up the social and cultural life of Bahia."[25] Without funding, however, the publication was again abandoned in its preliminary stage. Still, her interest in integrating different audiences was met with more success in curatorial and cultural projects.

All were welcomed in the museum. The glass doors remained open to the wide steps that descended toward the square across the street, inviting the public to share in thought-provoking events. Bo Bardi was particularly fond of recalling a time when a street vendor left his basket of delicacies, wrapped in a kitchen cloth, at the front door of the museum and ventured into the exhibition hall. To her, these were signs of interest and curiosity in the arts, and they gave her the gratifying sensation that the museum was achieving its purpose: to bring art to the people.

The museum would soon become a venue for the debate between modern and popular culture in Salvador and for personal quarrels. Whereas Tavares saw MAMB as a vehicle for promoting artists from Bahia, Bo Bardi wanted to develop her own ideas.[26] "This is not a museum," she wrote, echoing her husband's early mission for MASP. "Our museum must be rather called a center, a movement, a school."[27] She considered "Salvador [to be] the only city in Brazil that has cultural tradition. Here, there's an environment and a more refined sensitivity to the problems of art."

However, she overtly criticized a "cultural class established within provincial modes, constituted by celebrity artists united around folkloric groups, the city's tourist aura, and the local press."[28] She saw Tavares as their leader, and it did not take long for hostilities to begin. Bo Bardi's intellectual and political differences with Tavares would evolve into a power struggle that led her to resign from the museum in 1964. It would also allow her to emerge as a contentious opinion-maker.

Bo Bardi aspired to the kind of public intellectual she saw in Gramsci's writings. She expected, as she expressed several times, "to enter the world of true modern culture with the method of technical tools and the force of a new humanism (neither humanitarianism nor *umanesimo* [Renaissance humanism])," recalling the increasingly tense cultural environment in Brazil and especially in Salvador.[29] "A new era has already begun," she declared at the museum's opening.[30] Her aim to create educational programs following her experience at MASP's IAC was clear. Soon after, she noted: "The school-museum will be the point of departure for the attention to things, the respect for everything that mankind represents, its scale, and its authentic humanity."[31]

She questioned the city's cultural establishment, opening the museum's doors to whoever could contribute to her goals. She offered room in the unfinished theater for young filmmakers and a shelter to the Cine Clube da Bahia (Bahia cinema club), a stronghold for experiments such as the national movement Cinema Novo (New cinema).[32] Bo Bardi continued her collaborations with Koellreutter and Gonçalves, bringing the museum and the university closer through the creation of the Escola da Criança (Children's school), which lasted between April 1960 and late 1961, when Gonçalves resigned from the university.[33] Their goal was "not to educate little geniuses" or to promote exhibitions but rather to "introduce them to art and music techniques and to form new audiences."[34] Behind that pedagogical idea was Bo Bardi's desire to create a "popular university," offering technical education to the underprivileged classes. She believed that, if the pioneering works of the educators Anísio Teixeira and Paulo Freire could bring the Nordeste to the forefront of elementary education and literacy programs, she could contribute to the modernization of design education based on the direct contact between local master artisans and design students.

While Bo Bardi tried to create an innovative museum-school in Salvador in 1960, her husband strived in São Paulo to transfer MASP to its new location. With the help of Edmundo Monteiro, administrative director to both the museum and Chateaubriand's press chain, Bardi established an agreement exchanging the support of Diários Associados to Mayor Adhemar de Barros's presidential campaign for the construction of the museum building on avenida Paulista.[35] Bo Bardi was soon called to revise her initial proposal for the disputed Belvedere do Trianon lot, which she would design with the help of engineer Olavo Fonseca and architecture students from the Universidade da Bahia, including Alberto Roiser and Carlos Campos, who drafted the initial construction drawings in Salvador.[36]

The new version was not very different from the previous "home-made model" she had prepared in 1957.[37] It kept the suspended volume covered with rough finishes and plants and even the original idea for a steel-frame structure, which only changed into raw concrete a few years later, during the design-detailing phase and when mainstream São Paulo architects had fully embraced the postwar aesthetics of brutalism. Most of the adjustments Bo Bardi made to the MASP project in 1960 regarded the connections among the museum volume, the civic hall, and the city. She concentrated primarily on the semiburied volume, which would house public offices and was to be built first. She also proposed a sculptural, helicoidal staircase, shaped "like the structure of a leaf," to link the terrace and the museum above.[38] The plinth eventually became more orthogonal and transparent than its first 1957 version, recessed from the street and surrounded by flowerbeds, which suggests a return to her desire to create hanging gardens. These gardens replaced her initial greenhouse idea and the plinth was eventually built with them.

Mayor Barros initially directed public funds to erect the new facility. The site on avenida Paulista was boarded up, and large billboards announcing Heleno & Fonseca Construction Company and a small sign reading "Design: Architect Lina Bo Bardi" were added.[39] Construction broke ground around August and September 1960.[40] The site was excavated all the way down to the level of the lower street, and by February 1961, the retaining walls and the four large footings for the main columns were cast. Soon, however, construction was halted because the new mayor, Prestes Maia, provided little funding for the construction of the Trianon Building. The long-term loan to the museum was irreversible, but Bo Bardi's plans would have to wait until construction resumed fully in 1965 under different leadership.

During the construction of the new MASP in São Paulo and the start of pedagogical activities at MAMB in 1960, Bo Bardi had another groundbreaking design experience through her collaborations with Gonçalves in Salvador. Both had a knack for drama, and she accepted his invitation to collaborate in a production of *The Threepenny Opera* by

Bertholt Brecht and Kurt Weill. She offered the partially destroyed stage of Teatro Castro Alves. The large burned-down and unfinished structure provided a dramatic location for the provocative popular opera, which had been conceived during the convoluted Weimar Republic and restaged during a heated period in the histories of both Salvador and Brazil.

This production was the first of a series of experiences Bo Bardi had in set design — which she preferred to call *arquitetura cênica*, or scenic architecture (figure 53).[41] Her wish for MAMB to become a popular, avant-garde cultural center appeared to be coming true. All the spaces of the building were being used, even if in precarious ways — including Gonçalves's theater production, which ran from November 16 to December 4, 1960; the cinema club, which continued to occupy the improvised ramp auditorium; the basement office rooms, which were used for a few drawing classes; and the glazed lobby still displayed artworks.

Epic and antiheroic, brittle and sardonic, *The Threepenny Opera* was a perfect fit for Bo Bardi's unconventional temperament. She understood that the play challenged both established social values and traditional staging techniques, allowing her to do away with elaborate visual production. She embraced Gonçalves's ideas for the spaces of the performance and the audience to interpenetrate, and to frame the play according to Brecht's first lines: "You are about to see an opera . . . conceived with the splendor only a beggar could imagine." [42] The burned-down theater was rife with sparseness where there was supposed to be ceremony: no comfort, only the rough interior of an exposed armature. Bo Bardi's proposal matched that simplicity. She inserted a temporary wood frame inside the large, empty shell, creating a smaller venue in which the construction process, the actors, and the audience were exposed all at once in a single space.

She carefully studied the five scenes set on a plain stage in three-terraced levels, vaguely suggesting the steep-sited layout for the Chame-Chame House.[43] The simultaneous raw exposure of scenes, objects, musicians, and actors responded to Brecht's anti-illusionist conception and set an important precedent for later theater and exhibition design experiences Bo Bardi had in the following decades. She placed a few props on the stage; others, such as a projection screen, clothes, and banners with popular proverbs, hung from the ceiling. Around the audience bleachers, Bo Bardi designed "wooden scaffoldings like on a construction site" to encompass the audience into the space of the play, erasing the threshold between audience and actors, reality and fiction.[44]

Gonçalves and Bo Bardi's unusual theatrical production of the German opera led, six months later, in June 1961,

53. Lina Bo Bardi, *Study for Teatro Castro Alves Renovation*, c. 1960.
India ink, watercolor, and pencil on cardstock, 38.5 × 50.5 cm. ILBPMB
Collection.

to their presentation of *Caligula*, the controversial play by Albert Camus. This time, she designed both the costumes and the stage set, reusing the adaptive structure she had designed for *The Threepenny Opera*. A large wall, built just a few meters from the bottom of the bleachers, pressed the audience into closer contact with the actors. The rear partition was divided into two levels with openings that held small curtains to conceal the backstage. It was covered with rough plaster, recalling both simple rural constructions and a palace in ruins. On the wooden floor, only a few movable geometric wooden props punctuated a wide, dark carpet.

To give Camus's universal text local appeal, Bo Bardi included objects made by Cravo Júnior and popular pottery from the Salvador bay area.[45] In addition to creating simple pleated togas and small curtains, she used textiles for mood and ambience. She draped a long piece of red fabric over the back wall to suggest blood flowing onto the stage during the murderous second act, an image similar to the thinning red stain that ran from the top edge and down the left side of the folded program she designed for the audience. As well as such graphic gestures, Bo Bardi wrote a short text reflecting Camus's claim that "beyond nihilism, all of us, among ruins, are preparing a renaissance." She was convinced that the work she was doing in Salvador would usher in "a new culture, free of ghosts and myths, in which people will be able to live and build, though never freed from melancholy, aware as they were of nature and history."[46]

Though Bo Bardi's text coincided with emerging movements for the socialization of culture in Brazil, Gonçalves's initiatives were received with reservation.[47] These were extraordinary but difficult times. Cultural disagreements heated up in Salvador between 1960 and 1961, following the rising political and cultural temperature in Brazil. Local elites saw Gonçalves and, to a certain extent, Bo Bardi as troublemakers, while some of the radical groups saw them as distrustful outsiders. The future of Edgard Santos's artistic programs at the Universidade da Bahia was also at stake. Although he propelled the rise of an avant-garde movement in Salvador, his ideological principles were placed under suspicion by left-leaning students who favored the revolutionary impulses beginning to pervade student movements.

During a long student strike that took on national political significance, Santos was coerced to resign his position in June 1961 just as Bo Bardi and Gonçalves completed the production of *Caligula*, causing a devastating domino effect on the university's cultural programs, particularly the drama school. The coalition between cultural and political institutions connecting Santos, Tavares, Chateaubriand, and Governor Magalhães was starting to fall apart in Salvador. Gonçalves was also concerned about his future, since

Tavares had opened fire against him in the press, requesting the university administration restrain his activities. Tavares's crusade soon galvanized students' anger, leading to Gonçalves's resignation in August 1961, less than three months after Santos. Gonçalves returned, in 1962, to Rio de Janeiro, where he founded a new company, Teatro Novo.

In the meantime, Tavares continued to support Bo Bardi, but his attitude would soon change as a new period of increased challenges approached. Among her endeavors was an attempt to negotiate an exchange program among the state government, the university, and the museum. Another was an application to teach in the architecture program at the Universidade da Bahia. Neither proved successful.[48] In the departure of Gonçalves and Santos, Salvador had lost two of its most important cultural leaders, and though Bo Bardi and Gonçalves remained connected, she was now without her closest and most important personal and intellectual ally in the city. She knew that she would need new alliances if she wanted to survive as director of MAMB. Still, despite the changing political situation and the confrontations that threatened to come with it, she chose to embrace more radical alternatives, following the example of growing student and cultural movements in the Nordeste.

As the country geared toward polarization, Bo Bardi's discourse and practice would become more politicized.

The last period of Lina Bo Bardi's time in Salvador, between 1961 and 1964, was marked by her gradual isolation from the cultural establishment that had initially welcomed her, but also by the desire to expand her quest for a new humanism entwined with a national-popular will. Those changes coincided with a radical turn in Brazilian public life after the end of President Kubitschek's term in office. Despite celebrating the inauguration of the new capital, Brasília, Brazilians faced economic crisis, social unrest, and a convoluted political succession that placed the left-leaning nationalist João Goulart in the command seat.[1] Liberals saw him as their hope for necessary reforms, but conservative groups feared his policies and ideology. Emerging progressive leaderships orchestrated an essay of cultural socialization while traditional and hegemonic groups simultaneously prepared a coup d'état under the United States' wary eyes.[2]

In the meantime, Bo Bardi faced new challenges and opportunities. Her support network in Salvador began to shrink after Gonçalves left for Rio de Janeiro and as the unlikelihood of Magalhães's gubernatorial reelection became apparent. She also led an increasingly isolated social life as her hostilities with Tavares grew.[3] Still, she saw the Museu de Arte da Bahia as contributing to a "serious cultural mission and to extreme democracy," and, during its first anniversary, on January 6, 1961, she announced her idea to create a "popular university" to start in the following year.[4]

Bo Bardi imagined artisans and students collaborating in the museum as in pre-Renaissance guilds, with access to a shared curriculum and a visual documentation center. The "production of standard objects" was, at least theoretically, her ultimate goal.[5] Discussions about industrial design were still incipient in Brazil, and she searched widely for international partners to join her efforts in exchange programs, ranging from the Cranbrook Academy in Michigan to the Nigerian College of Art in Enugu but with no success.[6]

Instead, she found hope regionally, when Mário Cravo Júnior introduced her to a group of activist artists from Recife, the largest city in the Nordeste and capital of the state of Pernambuco. The group had started the Movimento de Cultura Popular (MCP, Popular culture movement), which comprised a series of cultural and educational programs for an underprivileged population.[7] Among those activists was Francisco Brennand, whose works Bo Bardi presented in a solo exhibition at MAMB in April 1961 as part of what she described as an initiative to address an "impasse in Brazilian culture."[8] Though she never stated it openly, the events in Recife became the main reference in her work and the springboard for her unrealized plan to connect the whole region.

Unlike Salvador, the political and artistic life of Recife had been modernized in progressive ways as a result of the determination of two consecutive mayors connected to the Partido Social Trabalhista (Social labor party) and the mediation of grassroots cultural programs.[9] The MCP was conceived by artist and community leader Abelardo da Hora in the late 1950s as a popular university, the term Bo Bardi used to describe her plans.[10] The movement became official in 1960, and its headquarters and workshops were housed in the historic Sítio da Trindade (Trindade farm).[11] Influenced by French militant groups such as Peuple et culture (People and culture) and organized by former members of the French Resistance, MCP sought to create a new humanism based on both a cyclical culture connected to everyday life and new pedagogical methods to support it.[12]

These ideas must have sounded irresistible to Bo Bardi. MCP's efforts to promote the practical everyday culture of dispossessed populations contributed to the creation of museums throughout the Nordeste, including the Museu de Arte at the Universidade do Ceará, organized by Lívio Xavier in 1961, and the Museu de Antropologia of Recife, whose work sociologist Gilberto Freyre defined as the quest for a rustic ethnography of the backlands.[13] In addition, young activists in Salvador, especially student leaders who felt left out of Santos's university programs, helped create a national movement called Centros Populares de Cultura (People's cultural centers) that combined politics, culture, and literacy campaigns. Though Bo Bardi left few records about her contacts with these programs, she pursued partnerships in other states of the Nordeste as an alternative to her increasing loss of support in Bahia. "Founding a triangle," she wrote in her diary next to a simple diagram connecting three locations: "Fortaleza (Xavier), Pernambuco (Brennand), Bahia (io [me])," organized around the idea of an "anti-Biennial exhibition" (figure 54).[14]

Her activities in Salvador culminated in 1962–63 with her efforts to create a large documentation, research, and teaching center. In typed notes for the museum, she abandoned the term "popular university" for a new name — Escola de Desenho Industrial e Artesanato (School of industrial design and handicraft) — reflecting MCP's main technical divisions: those of documentation and information and of cultural dissemination and education.[15] Focused on local handicraft and popular festivities, MCP offered workshops ranging from ceramics to printmaking to sculpture, aiming at technical and professional training and the development of domestic industrial production.[16]

Bo Bardi's plan proposed a similar structure for the design school, dividing it into two related institutions: the Centro de Estudos do Trabalhos do Artesananato (CETA, Center for the study of handicraft works), dedicated to documentation, and the Centro de Estudos Técnicos do Nordeste (Center for technical studies of the northeastern region), promoting her vision for an alternative industrial design school.[17] As a preview of these plans, she organized a small exhibition titled *Handicraft and Industrial Design* at MAMB in October 1962. Following the experience of Italian designers such as Gio Ponti, she sought to infuse industrial production with lay knowledge as a way of reenchanting the production process with the aura of handmade objects, as well as with the feeling of deep-seated Brazilianness. Years later, she would reflect on those ideas and replace the word "handicraft" with the term *pré-artesanato* (pre-craftsmanship) to indicate that Brazil lacked an economically organized artisanal production system as defined by Gramsci and found in the traditional Italian context.[18]

For all their potential, Bo Bardi's proposed centers faced a new challenge: they did not fit in MAMB's temporary facilities, and she no longer had contacts at the Universidade da Bahia to negotiate a new venue. Neither could she convince the governor to invest in a new building. An opportunity appeared in 1962 during the construction of avenida do Contorno, an expressway that connected Salvador's historic downtown with Campo Grande district and followed the undulating hills along the bay. The expressway opened access to the Solar do Unhão (Unhão estate), an ensemble of historic buildings that Gonçalves had shown her in 1958. The complex was a hodgepodge of structures that included two plazas and two imposing colonial buildings — a large manor and a chapel — as well as warehouses and shacks covered with mildew and grime and occupied by a few families.[19]

This squalid estate was Bo Bardi's only possibility for relocating the museum. She was not convinced by its potential, according to observations from her assistant, but since she was falling out with Tavares and feared losing government support, she resigned herself to the circumstances. With only about eight months to complete the renovation before the end of Governor Magalhães's term in April 1963, the process was rushed. It was also full of personal and technical hurdles, including disagreements with preservationists. Bo Bardi insisted that the complex could not be restored to its original state, since many of its features had been lost to centuries of invasive alterations without enough documentation to support a reconstruction. Years later, as she talked about the adaptive reuse of her most complex project — SESC Pompeia, in São Paulo — she recalled of her experience with Unhão and of her education in Rome: "In Bahia, I realized, all of a sudden, how deeply I had understood the problems of old factories through the restoration lessons of my professor, Gustavo Giovannoni."[20]

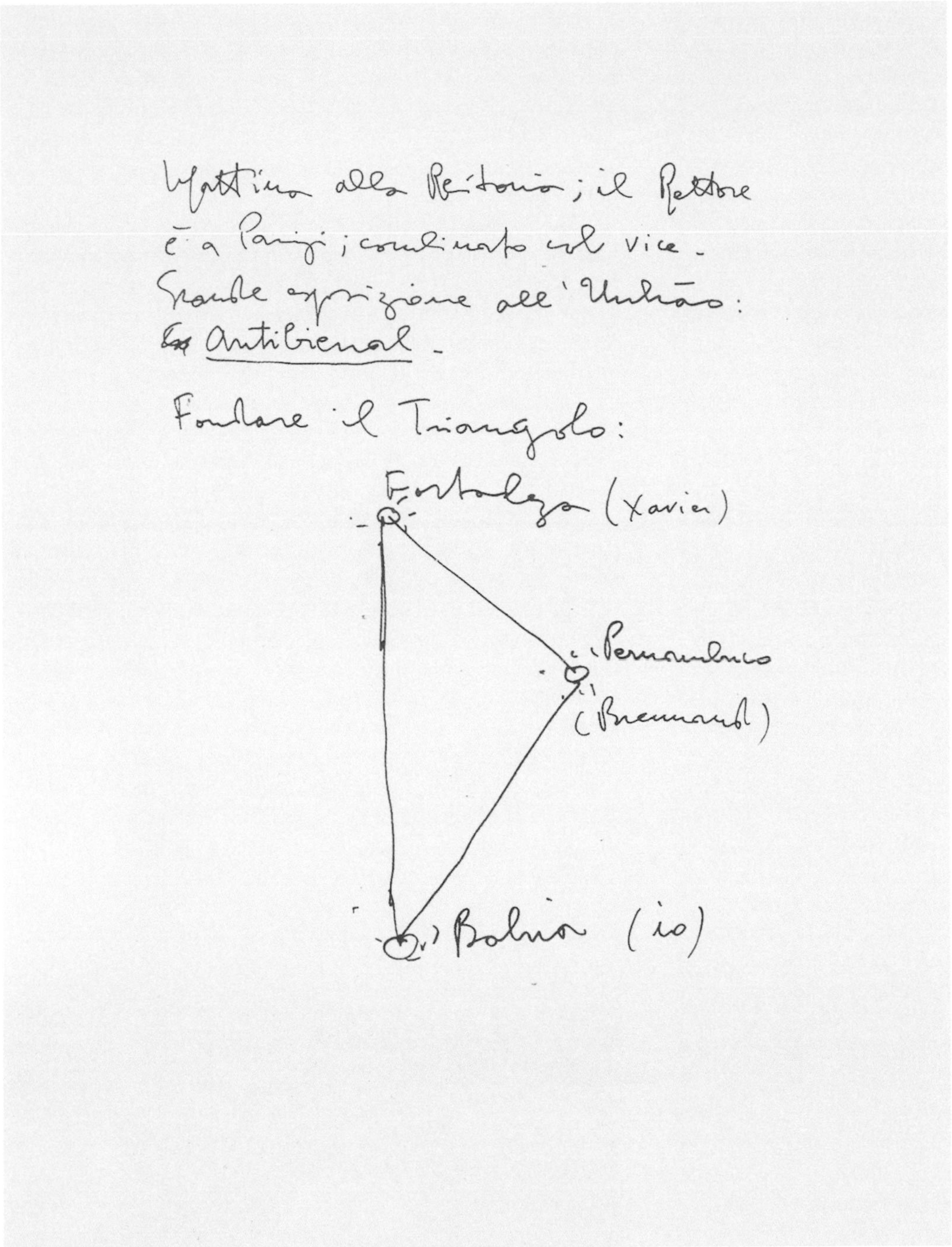

Mattina alla Reitoria; il Rettore
è a Parigi; combinato col vice-
Grande opposizione all'Unità:
Ex <u>Antibienal</u> -

Fondare il Triangolo:

Fortaleza (Xavier)

Pernambuco
(Brennand)

Bahia (io)

54. Lina Bo Bardi, "Founding a Triangle," diary notes, May 31, 1963, p. 6,
15 × 11 cm. ILBPMB Collection.

After settling on the Solar do Unhão, Bo Bardi took great pleasure in its development. She had little practical experience with construction or rehabilitation, especially on the scale the site presented, but she experimented resourcefully with the kind of adaptive reuse of historical buildings that would become recurrent in her work in the 1970s and 1980s. Concerned with more than conservation, she took the liberty of adding new elements. She did not pioneer this procedure, which was conceptually in tune with such Italian contemporaries as Carlo Scarpa and Franco Albini, but Bo Bardi helped disseminate it throughout Brazil, reviving Lucio Costa's heritage works from the 1930s.

In addition to the building revitalization, Projeto Unhão (Unhão project) incorporated conceptual elements from the Recife movement such as its workshops and its permanent exhibition of popular art and handicraft. Though Bo Bardi made no direct analogy with MCP's Sítio Trindade, the adaptation of the old farm and her approach to the Unhão site uncannily resembles choices made by the Recife group. Still, she went a step further, accomplishing architectural results MCP had not dreamed of and which she would later revisit in more depth in the SESC project.

All the superfluous and shabby structures of the Unhão complex were removed, emphasizing the six main buildings (figure 55). Instead of giving them monumental visibility, Bo Bardi neutralized their walls with layers of whitewash in the manner of colonial buildings (figure 56). She dedicated the chapel and the manor to pedagogical and exhibition programs, respectively, and reserved the two large warehouses for the creation of CETA's handicraft workshops, stripping them down to their structural components and daubing larger partitions with plaster as in rural construction. Trellised screens covered transoms, permitting cross-ventilation as well as creating spatial separation between workshops. Educational activities started modestly, with forty-four students from one of Salvador's experimental park-schools distributed among eleven workshops coordinated by local artisans covering different crafts, as in Recife.[21]

Bo Bardi also revived the two existing plazas, enlarging the one next to the water to allow for popular festivities and film screenings. She even produced a preliminary study for a new house resembling the Chame-Chame project for the museum administrator (likely herself) on a secluded slope overlooking the bay. The imposing Unhão manor, which still stands facing the ocean, housed the Museu de Arte Popular (MAP, Museum of popular art), representing the project's greatest investment of material and symbolic resources (figure 57). She replaced the old, interior corner steps with an imposing helicoidal staircase of ype wood connecting both floors in the middle of the existing posts, like a baldachin in the transept of a traditional church (figure 58).[22] A cylindrical mast added to the center of the stairs and held by lateral inclined joists lap-jointed to the wood piers still support the thirty-two triangular steps without risers (figure 59).

The treads twirl up around the pole in two loops that slowly climb 5.5 meters (18 ft.) to the upper floor, resembling the organic shape of other staircases she designed throughout her life (figure 60). The narrow internal ends of the steps rest individually on small woodblocks bolted onto the central mast, while the wider, external edge of each step is notched to create a large horizontal tenon inserted into a mortise cut in the ascending joists (figure 61). To brace the horizontal connection between the joists and the wide

55. Unhão Estate (MAMB and Museum of Popular Art), Salvador, 1963, aerial view of the ensemble from the western side. Computer rendering. Zeuler R. Lima Collection.

56. Unhão Estate (MAMB and Museum of Popular Art), Salvador, 1963, view of the ensemble from the southern side. Photograph by Nelson Kon.

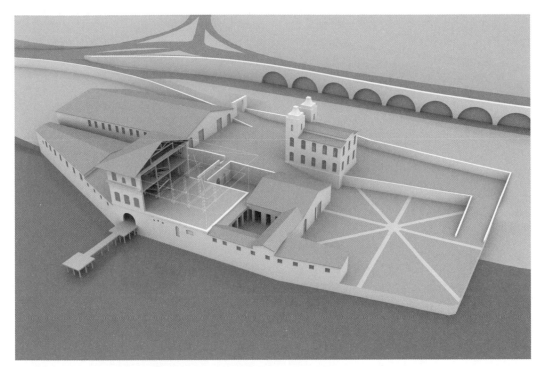

57. Unhão Estate (MAMB and Museum of Popular Art), Salvador, 1963, sectioned view from the western side showing structural logic and new staircase. Computer rendering. Zeuler R. Lima Collection.

58. Unhão Estate (MAMB and Museum of Popular Art), Salvador, 1963, sectioned view of the old manor with added staircase. Computer rendering. Zeuler R. Lima Collection.

protruding tenons, she used small wedges that emulated the construction of oxcarts, an iconic image of creative peasant simplicity. Ingenious from both structural and geometrical viewpoints, the Unhão staircase combines orthogonal and organic forms into simple design and precise use of materials that make it at once open and self-contained.

In addition to renovating the Unhão complex, Bo Bardi produced several drawings for MASP with help from architecture students in Salvador.[23] She continued to travel to São Paulo, where Bardi continued to develop his art dealing business. Progress on the museum on avenida Paulista was slow. She revisited her initial scheme for the suspended hall, but little work was done. Only the concrete structure and ramps of the semiburied civic hall were completed in 1963.[24] Construction would be largely halted until a new mayor took office in 1965.

In 1962 and 1963, she also developed a few unrealized architectural studies in Brazil and even in Italy. Though they never went beyond the preliminary phase, they are examples of her hybrid vocabulary of naturalistic and rationalist references and orthogonal and organic geometries. Among those studies were projects in São Paulo, including a daring cantilevered building for the engineer José Carlos de Figueiredo Ferraz, who had taken over the calculation of MASP's challenging structure.[25] She also produced a preliminary study for a midrise art complex on rua Pamplona, not far from the new museum.[26] This speculative project — perhaps serving Bardi's interest — was a rare incursion into vertical buildings in her career and reiterated her fondness for hanging gardens associated with a raw concrete structure.

In Salvador, meanwhile, the developer Norberto Odebrecht commissioned Bo Bardi to design his family

59. Unhão Estate (MAMB and Museum of Popular Art), Salvador, 1963, general view of added staircase. Photograph by Nelson Kon.

60. Unhão Estate (MAMB and Museum of Popular Art), Salvador, 1963, detailed view of added staircase. Photograph by Zeuler R. Lima.

mausoleum at the historic Campo Santo cemetery.[27] She wished to incorporate Cravo Júnior's sculptures, but Odebrecht did not approve their inclusion, so she designed a solid cubic volume covered with ivy that was completed after she left the city. She also made a study for a project in Tuscany: a marble museum at the quarry of Monte Altissimo, the source for many famous Renaissance sculptures and facades.[28] Of unknown purpose and sparsely documented, this project — to be executed in concrete, glass, and plants — reiterated the laboratory of forms she conducted at this time.

Along with her travels back and forth between São Paulo and Salvador, Bo Bardi took a short trip to the small town of Monte Santo, in the hinterland of Bahia, to see the production of *Deus e o Diabo na Terra do Sol* (Black god, white devil), the award-winning film written and directed by her young friend Glauber Rocha. In her notes, she mixed sketches and comments about the film set with drawings of local plants and expressions of enthusiasm for the way they grew in this arid landscape, comparable to her interest in the human adaptability to the harsh living conditions found in the northeastern backcountry (figure 62).

Above all, she carried on her activities as the artistic director of MAMB, organizing an average of twenty-two exhibitions each year. The Unhão renovation received its official gubernatorial opening on March 31, 1963. Another eight months would pass, however, before its first two exhibitions and the Museu de Arte Popular were opened to the public on November 3.[29] An unassuming exhibition titled *Artistas do Nordeste* (Artists from the northeast) was housed in the adobe buildings near the lower plaza. She reserved the large colonial house for her pet project, the

62. Lina Bo Bardi, "Return to Salvador," diary notes, June 30, 1963, p. 24, 15 × 11 cm. ILBPMB Collection.

61. Unhão Estate (MAMB and Museum of Popular Art), Salvador, 1963, exploded perspective showing the added staircase assemblage logic. Computer rendering. Zeuler R. Lima Collection.

Nordeste exhibition, which expanded the *Bahia* exhibition of four years earlier to comprise the whole region. Handmade everyday objects and utensils of popular origin occupied the two floors of the renovated manor, the beginnings of a documentation center intended for her innovative educational program. As conceived in her plans, "The popular art and handicraft section is located at the access level," she wrote, while "the upper floor presents an exhibition of pieces with African and native influences" from local institutions and collectors.[30]

Among the large objects sharing the space with the wood columns and staircase on the first floor were a full-size woodcarving representing an indigenous Brazilian, a raft built of palm trunks, and rustic, wood-carved mortars with their pestles hanging from the ceiling. Bo Bardi also displayed several carrancas (wood-carved boat figureheads) attached to metal rods cast into reinforced concrete cubes, like those used for the glass easels she designed for the permanent collection at MASP years later. The upper floor, with its lower ceiling, had a more intimate atmosphere and contained more fragile objects such as gourd canteens, improvised kerosene lamps, and coffeepots made out of used cans (figure 63). The centerpiece of the show was a rustic version of her recurrent *vitrine of forms*. Instead of presenting a polished glass menagerie, she stacked several rough pinewood containers transversally across the floor, creating a vivid display of handmade baskets, toys, textiles, ceramic bowls, and religious images.

Bo Bardi's brochure conveyed the radical meanings she attributed to the objects in the exhibition (figure 64). "This show should have been titled 'Nordeste Civilization,'" she wrote, recalling Gramsci and highlighting the difference

63. Makeshift coffee pots initially presented in the *Nordeste* exhibition, Museum of Popular Art, Salvador, 1963, and later in other exhibitions organized by Lina Bo Bardi. MASP Collection.

between "the rhetorical-courtly meaning that goes with the word 'civilization'" and her intention to treat the show as "the practical character of culture" produced in the context of everyday life. "This exhibition," she wrote, "attempts to present a civilization that is thought out in every detail, technically studied." She intended it to document "the life of mankind in its every moment."[31]

In an irreverent line, Bo Bardi wrote: "Waste is the raw material of this exhibition." Below it, she added, "Each object touches the threshold of nothingness, of poverty," insisting on their distinction from folklore. "We critically present this exhibition in the sense of modern reality, as an example of straightforward simplification of forms filled with lively energy and representing both craft and industrial design." Instead of understanding simplification as misery, she saw it as "an indispensable path for finding poetry within the framework of a technical humanism."[32] And poetry, to Bo Bardi, had nothing to do with sentimentalism.

The *Nordeste* exhibition was mounted at a time of escalating political struggle in Brazil. The idea of a coup d'état had been germinating since its promotion in 1961 by conservative groups, and in October 1963, the military announced a national state of emergency.[33] Despite this charged environment, Bo Bardi's brochure concluded with an even more provocative statement, one that resonated with the inflamed pronunciations by the cultural left during Goulart's reformist presidency and even with Zevi's description of *A* magazine, which had coincided with her gradual political awakening in postwar Italy. "This exhibition is an accusation," she declared, celebrating the creative survival skills of the Brazilian people. "It is the flipside of the desperate struggle of everyday culture against degrading living conditions."[34]

For all the indisputable value of Bo Bardi's curatorial work and her desire to constitute the new school-museum on a technical foundation, the makeshift objects on display were organized in a less scientific way than she suggested — that is, they followed more aesthetic than anthropological criteria. According to her museum assistants, the material formed an uneven mosaic of objects hastily assembled through the generous cooperation of old and new interlocutors, such as from Gonçalves's private and theater collections (including the carrancas), Cravo Júnior's votive collection, and Xavier's contributions from cultural institutions in Ceará. Bo Bardi also benefited from help from the artists Francisco Brennand (once her guest at MAMB) and Abelardo da Hora, in Recife, who added other pieces such as small ceramic figurines.[35] She planned to publish a catalogue with texts from several authors, including da Hora and Xavier, but never did. Some of the material would be

NORDESTE

Museu de Arte Popular do Unhão, Bahia, Brasil

Esta exposição que inaugura o Museu de Arte Popular do Unhão deveria chamar-se Civilização do Nordeste. Civilização. Procurando tirar da palavra o sentido áulico-retórico que a acompanha. Civilização é o aspecto prático da cultura, é a vida dos homens em todos os instantes. Esta exposição procura apresentar uma civilização pensada em todos os detalhes, estudada técnicamente, (mesmo se a palavra técnico define aqui um trabalho primitivo), desde a iluminação às colheres de cozinha, às colchas, às roupas, bules, brinquedos, móveis, armas. É a procura desesperada e raivosamente positiva de homens que não querem ser "demitidos", que reclamam seu direito à vida. Uma luta de cada instante para não afundar no desespêro, uma afirmação de beleza conseguida com o rigor que sòmente a presença constante duma realidade pode dar.
Matéria prima: o lixo.

Lâmpadas queimadas, recortes de tecidos, latas de lubrificantes, caixas velhas e jornais. Cada objeto risca o limite do "nada" da miséria. Êsse limite e a contínua e martelada presença do "útil" e "necessário" é que constituem o valor desta produção, sua poética das coisas humanas não-gratuitas, não criadas pela mera fantasia. É neste sentido de moderna realidade que apresentamos criticamente esta exposição. Como exemplo de simplificação direta de formas cheias de eletricidade vital. Formas de desenho artesanal e industrial. Insistimos na identidade objeto artesanal-padrão industrial baseada na produção técnica ligada à realidade dos materiais e não à abstração formal folklórico-coreográfica. Chamamos êste Museu de Arte Popular e não de Folklore por ser o folklore uma herança estática e regressiva, cujo aspecto é amparado paternalisticamente pelos responsáveis da cultura, ao passo que arte popular (usamos a palavra arte não sòmente no sentido artístico mas também no de fazer tècnicamente), define a atitude progressiva da cultura popular ligada a problemas reais.

Esta exposição quer ser um convite para os jovens considerarem o problema da simplificação (não da indigência), no mundo de hoje; caminho necessário para encontrar dentro do humanismo técnico, uma poética.
Esta exposição é uma acusação.

Acusação dum mundo que não quer renunciar à condição humana apesar do esquecimento e da indiferença. É uma acusação não humilde, que contrapõe às degradadoras condições impostas pelos homens, um esfôrço desesperado de cultura.

LINA BARDI

64. *Nordeste* exhibition flier, Museum of Popular Art, Salvador, 1963.
ILBPMB Collection.

published posthumously thirty years later in a book planned by her in the 1980s and whose title recalled her introduction to Brennand's 1961 exhibition at MAMB: "Design no impasse" (Design at an impasse). Yet, although her displays for *Nordeste* did not follow scholarly principles, her discourse dignified those objects as works produced by creative and resourceful hands. Documentation, to her, had gained strong political meaning.

Despite difficulties and contradictions, the exhibition of makeshift everyday objects allowed Bo Bardi to draw attention to the region's cultural and social problems and to reorient her personal and intellectual affiliations. Above all, it supported her idea of creating an innovative technical school aimed at the value of manual work, the integration between design and execution, and shared knowledge. She rejected nostalgia and sentimentalism associated with folklore and the arts and crafts tradition, as well as the utopian abstraction linked to the Bauhaus and Ulm schools, which she considered useless in an underdeveloped country. Imbued with the mythology emerging from the harsh realities of the Nordeste, she believed that the study of the region's artisanal activities "should be the foundation for the aesthetic education of future national industrial design.[36] Ultimately, she wanted Brazilian industrialization to develop out of the skills that were literally at the hand of the common people, who, she believed, retained authentic creativity. She avoided using the term "popular culture," because of the potential for it to be misunderstood as folklore. She equated culture with everyday life and approached the artifacts produced by uneducated people as expressions of authentic human ability and aesthetic discernment. She expected to stress what she and some of her contemporaries saw as authentic values by which Brazilians went about their daily needs and chores: from eating to dressing and working to resting.

The *Nordeste* exhibition was a starting point for Bo Bardi's evolving ideas for MAP, as were other events, including her undeveloped plan for four ethnological exhibitions — titled *Africa-Bahia*, *Brazilian Indians*, *São Paulo by Immigrants*, and *Europe and the Iberian Peninsula* — to be developed with ethnophotographer Pierre Verger, anthropologist Darcy Ribeiro, and sociologist Octavio Ianni, respectively.[37] However, MAMB and MAP were gradually losing their cultural reach in Brazil's increasingly turbulent political landscape, and though she would try several times in the following decades to revive her plans for the Unhão complex, incorporating curatorial and design ideas into other projects, she would not see them materialized until the 1980s, when she mounted a series of similar shows at SESC Pompeia in São Paulo.

Although her activities slowed, Bo Bardi did not give up easily. Between January and April 1964, as MAMB director, she contacted institutions seeking additional venues for the *Nordeste* exhibition around the country and abroad.[38] For example, in February, on a trip to Rome, Zevi invited her to present the Unhão project at the Roman school of architecture. She accepted but felt that the audience misunderstood her intentions. She was particularly offended that his students had laughed at slides of carrancas and mistaken them for the carnival floats of Viareggio, unable to see that, recalling old times with Zevi, the "Unhão exhibition is not the glorification of popular culture . . . but an accusation and a denunciation."[39]

She also tried — both in person and through letters — to obtain support for her curatorial plans from economy minister Celso Furtado, the mastermind of national reforms during and after Kubitschek's presidency. After hearing that "Itamarati [the Brazilian ministry of foreign affairs] was organizing an exhibition of handicraft from the Nordeste to be exhibited in the countries of the European Economic Community," she wrote to the minister asking for help.[40] In a polite but firm response on April 5, 1964, Furtado cautioned her to avoid isolating traditional cultural practices of handicraft at the risk of perpetuating an immobile social structure.[41] Despite being mired in misunderstanding, her message likely found its destination and her request, a supportive response, because her *Nordeste* exhibition was selected to represent Brazil in Europe later that year.

Bo Bardi's struggle for the simplification and socialization of Brazilian design happened during a period of profound political crisis. President Goulart's reform policies faced increased polarization between progressive movements and right-wing sectors of society, which brought the country to the verge of a popular revolution and led to his overthrow by a military junta on March 31, 1964.[42] The coup d'état yielded a sequence of military presidents who replaced two decades of populist democracy with a conservative, authoritarian modernization model, as well as escalating opposition between right and left and persecutions and violence, until the return of democratic rule in 1985.[43]

When the coup d'état occurred, Bo Bardi was lecturing at the Universidade de São Paulo.[44] She was safe at home but uncertain about the continuation of her work in Salvador. The Movimento de Cultura Popular had been dismantled in Recife and several of its leaders arrested.[45] Similar events unfolded throughout Brazil, and Salvador was not spared.[46] Later in life, she suggested that the military forced her to leave MAMB, a story that easily transformed her into a political martyr. The situation was more complex, however, and seems to have been motivated more by personal than by political conflicts.

At the outset of the military coup, two army representatives showed up at MAMB looking for Bo Bardi. Her museum assistant, Renato Ferraz, sent Bo Bardi a ciphered telegram telling her to remain in São Paulo while he worked on appeasing conspirators about her association with subversive causes.[47] In a letter to her friend Zevi, she indicated that she was uncertain about her return and lacked access to the material she had left in Bahia, as her hopes for developing the Unhão complex started to languish.[48] Meanwhile, Ferraz reported being concerned with the security of loaned artworks and the possibility of vandalism against the glazed theater lobby, given its proximity to the university and the governor's palace, both under suspicion by the military junta. Through sinuous contacts in government offices, her assistant managed to get the military to allocate soldiers to protect the collection for a few days. Still, the army also took this opportunity to place retired artillery pieces on the sidewalk in front of the theater symbolically aimed toward the nearby governor's palace, where the new state leader was being held under suspicion of sympathizing with President Goulart. Ferraz took photographs before the cannons returned to the military quarters and gave them to Bo Bardi when she returned to Salvador in July 1964, since she had not seen the pieces personally.[49] She kept them as bitter souvenirs of the denouement of her intimate contact with the city's cultural life.[50]

On arriving back in Salvador, she was worried because Tavares viewed her return with mixed feelings. Like Ferraz, he had offered the military favorable testimony about her political leanings, waiving her from involvement with what they considered to be suspicious activities. However, Tavares did not agree with her plans for the museum. Vulnerable in her position, Bo Bardi felt that he was using her, but instead of trying to placate him, according to her assistant, she continued to dismiss him as "merely a collector."[51] Likely sensing problems, she wrote him a letter stating, "I have no personal interest in holding the directorship of MAMB, in spite of the five years of hard work under difficult conditions."[52]

The situation became untenable when the armed forces requested to use the lobby for an exhibition celebrating "Soldier's Day."[53] After refusing them several times, she gave in to their intimidating persistence. The military set up a show with old artillery from the nearby armory mixed up with objects and documents confiscated from resistance groups and presented as subversive material to intimidate further opposition.[54] Bo Bardi tried to avoid the opening on July 30, 1964, staying just long enough to greet the chief officer before slipping out. In the following days, Tavares's *Diário de Notícias* published a spiteful article showing Bo Bardi shaking hands with a general.[55] Furious, concerned about her safety, and likely humiliated, on August 3, she resigned as director of the museum at the sign of what seems to have been a shrewd and well-articulated checkmate.

On August 7, Tavares published another article, maliciously announcing, "Lina leaves Bahia," even before she had left Salvador.[56] Five days later, she requested access to the material displayed in the Unhão complex for use in another exhibition.[57] Within weeks of her resignation and return to São Paulo, MAP was closed. MAMB remained, but its links with MASP were severed, as was Bo Bardi's friendship with Cravo Júnior, whom she never forgave for having taken over the museum directorship after her.[58]

The period Bo Bardi spent in Salvador, especially the almost five years she served as MAMB director, had an enduring effect on her outlook. She renegotiated her identity as a designer, Brazilian architect, and public intellectual. She opened herself up to new dialogues and partnerships, and in spite of political and personal crises, she continued to see Brazil's popular roots and the ongoing movements that would continue for a few years more as conveyors of "a cultural ferment and violence in the true historical sense of a country."[59] She did not abandon her desire to turn the association between handicraft and industrial design into a regenerative social force, believing that the material and symbolic foundation of the country's everyday reality could be reinvented. Though her project for the Unhão complex remained incomplete, she continued to long for a shared prosperity associated with accessible aesthetics and a new humanism.

Bo Bardi, like many other Brazilian artists and intellectuals of this period, struggled with the rapidly changing scenario after the 1964 presidential overthrow, revising and even radicalizing her position. In the years after leaving Salvador, she repositioned herself both conceptually and politically. With the embrace of Marxist ideology, she expanded her definition of popular art and culture beyond material artifacts and into the productive forces and the social relations that structure them. She left Salvador but not the experience she gained there. As she later declared to Zevi, the "disappointment that followed the coup d'état did not deter me from attempting to build something provoking and unconventional."[60]

Lina Bo Bardi's life changed profoundly when she resigned from MAMB in August 1964. About to turn fifty, she now faced an uncertain professional career. Although she suggested that her resignation was due to military persecution rather than her growing struggles with Odorico Tavares, later in life she reminisced about the coup d'état in a way that clarified her political view. "What happened in 1964 was not, as it may appear, the military takeover of the country," she said. "It was a civil reaction," adding that "the military only established the order." Her real concern was that "the dangerous people, the civil reaction, continued to retain power."[1] Though she had to leave Salvador, she did not let go of either the Nordeste or her desire to continue the work she started there.

For at least two years she would receive small commissions and try to establish new partnerships, especially in Rio de Janeiro, before returning permanently to São Paulo to complete the revision for MASP's project on avenida Paulista, which continued to advance at a slow pace. Although the mayor who replaced Adhemar de Barros prioritized financing urban infrastructure over the new museum, his secretary of public works, engineer José Carlos de Figueiredo Ferraz, ran the firm responsible for the museum's structural project and became an important agent in the process. With his acting in both supporting roles, the museum site reopened, after several interruptions, in February 1964. The construction process was slow but steady, with the casting of the four colossal piers completed by the end of that year.[2] In January 1965, a jungle of lumber with woven branches started to grow on the site to stabilize the casting of the two sets of pre-stressed concrete beams that eventually supported the wide hall suspended above the terrace, giving the museum its unique appearance on completion in 1968.[3]

Meanwhile, in her attempt to replace Salvador with sunnier and more exposed places than her husband's shadow, Bo Bardi strengthened her collaboration with Gonçalves, who was living and working in Rio de Janeiro. In 1963, she had helped her friend and ally set up a small exhibition about Brazilian popular theater in the Museu de Arte Moderna (MAM, Museum of modern art) in that city, and at the end of September 1964, she completed the scenic architecture (as she liked to call it) for his production of John Ford's classic tragedy, *'Tis Pity She's a Whore*.[4] The Portuguese version of this polemical English drama transported the plot line of incest in the bosom of a sixteenth-century Italian family to the tropical Flamengo landfill park with Sugarloaf Mountain and Guanabara Bay in the background.

Set on the unfinished second floor amid MAM's iconic raw concrete structure, Gonçalves's production provisionally

65. La Torraccia Guesthouse (Valéria P. Cirell House), São Paulo, 1964, view from the western side. Photograph by Zeuler R. Lima.

inaugurated the museum's theatrical activities while it was still under construction. According to press coverage, Bo Bardi's costumes, masks, and simple stage were based on Elizabethan amphitheaters with no separation between actors and audience and organized in two L-shaped bleachers with several entries and exits, suggesting the classical architecture of post-Renaissance Italy. Bo Bardi and Gonçalves were staging, once again, the experience they had a few years earlier in the burned-down structure of Teatro Castro Alves in Salvador. The press also praised her decision to retain the "naked walls of the museum," which gave the set "virile and dramatic beauty." [5]

Likely through the influential cultural and political network established around the Flamengo park and museum projects in Rio de Janeiro, Bo Bardi was invited by Governor Carlos Lacerda, one of the masterminds behind the overthrow of President Goulart, to discuss the transformation of the historical Parque Lage (Lage park) — recently declared a heritage site — into a cultural center. [6] Dismissing his political affiliations, she hoped to continue her unfinished plans for the creation of an alternative design school, this time using the site of a large bourgeois manor surrounded by lush gardens at the foot of Corcovado (the rocky hill where the iconic Christ statue stands overlooking the city). Still, it would take her almost a year to visit the site and to start thinking about the project. In the interim, she produced three other architectural studies, combining many of the principles about which she had been writing and lecturing and using the formal vocabulary with which she had

Legacies to Be Remembered

66. La Torraccia Guesthouse and Valéria P. Cirell House on the site, São Paulo. Computer rendering. Zeuler R. Lima Collection.

experimented in previous years. Above all, she revised the *Nordeste* exhibition and sent it to Europe.

In August 1964, likely with the help of Juracy Magalhães, who had moved from Salvador to Rio de Janeiro to occupy two consecutive ministerial positions, Bo Bardi received approval from the Ministry of Foreign Relations to organize "an exhibition of Brazilian Popular Art in Rome and Paris."[7] In addition to seeking support from Minister Furtado, she had contacted several international institutions to host the show and requested a few pieces of handicraft for the exhibition from the Bahia State Museum. After much insistence and a few discreet trips to the Nordeste, she even gained access to the material stored at Unhão.[8] The show's final destination was Rome's Galleria Nazionale d'Arte Moderna, situated next to her former school of architecture. The pieces were shipped to Europe along with several photographic panels. Between December 1964 and early 1965, she followed them, arriving in Italy to set up the show for its scheduled opening on March 10, 1965.

Her curatorial design resembled both the *Bahia* and the *Nordeste* exhibitions with a unifying display feature: a simple pinewood frame with thin slats connecting the different rooms and detaching photographic panels from the walls.[9] The images illustrated the cultural, religious, and economic context in which the works had been produced, as well as a less advertised, photographic review of the new capital, Brasília.[10] Bo Bardi also placed three-dimensional objects such as wood votives, mortars and pestles, and improvised candleholders and kettles on simple pinewood boxes and pedestals, similar to those designed for MAP at Unhão, along with carrancas atop wooden trestles. Hung above the displays, a white electric wire meandered through the rooms with several sockets containing simple one-hundred-watt lightbulbs, emulating makeshift houses in poor areas of Brazil.[11]

Just before the exhibition was scheduled to open, the Brazilian embassy sent Bo Bardi an order to cancel the opening and to pack up the works, which were inconspicuously returned to Brazil a few days later.[12] She suggested that the military regime was behind the decision, but in fact the cancelation was due to the intervention of Brazilian diplomats in Rome, triggered by another contentious event in Italy.[13] A few weeks earlier, between January 21 and 30, the Brazilian cultural attaché and the wife of the Brazilian

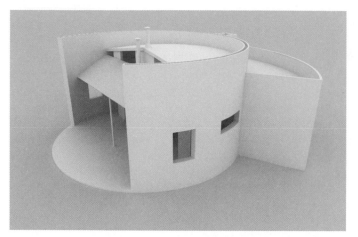

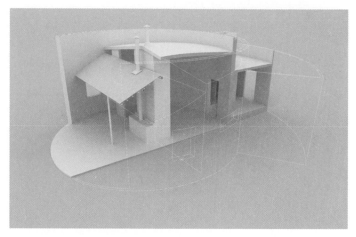

67. La Torraccia Guesthouse (Valéria P. Cirell House), São Paulo, 1964, aerial view from the southern side. Computer rendering. Zeuler R. Lima Collection.

68. La Torraccia Guesthouse (Valéria P. Cirell House), São Paulo, 1964, sectioned view showing interior layout. Computer rendering. Zeuler R. Lima Collection.

ambassador had attended the conference Terzo mondo e comunità mondiale (Third world and the world community) organized in Genoa by the "Columbianum" cultural institute.[14]

Bo Bardi was among the official guests selected by the cultural sector of the Secretaria de Estado de Relações Exteriores (State department) to participate in a roundtable about Brazilian cinema.[15] The presenters included her friend filmmaker Glauber Rocha, who introduced his shattering manifesto *A estética da fome* (The aesthetics of hunger), which was imbued with themes of violence and dispossession in Brazil. Concerned by what they saw and heard in presentations by progressive Brazilian intellectuals and artists, the diplomats returned to Rome. They had walked out on the film *Maioria absoluta* (Absolute majority), a poignant black-and-white documentary about the everyday life of the Nordeste's impoverished, illiterate peasants. The embassy representatives accused the filmmaker of misrepresenting Brazilian society. Amid such tensions, Bo Bardi's exhibition was canceled, very likely after embassy personnel saw the drafts for posters and a critical brochure that she sent to press through their official services.

Italians never saw the *Nordeste* exhibition, but Bo Bardi was quick to let them know about her indignation. In her defense, Zevi signed a long article titled "L'arte dei poveri fa paura ai generali" (Art of the poor, scared generals), which was published on March 14, 1965, in the Roman newspaper *L'Espresso* and reprinted three weeks later in Rio de Janeiro's *Correio da Manhã* under the title "Regime de generais proíbe a exposição" (Generals' regime prohibits exhibition).[16] Zevi's article repeated Bardi's points almost verbatim, including terms in Portuguese with which he was likely not familiar, suggesting that she was anonymously behind the

publication. The article insisted that the objects planned for display had a disturbing meaning and that the negative reaction to the show (that is, the fact that it was confiscated) was because it "referred to the hungry hinterland of the continent, the reality of the country, its misery, and its culture," a sentiment similar to Rocha's presentation in Genoa.[17]

The article briefly mentioned that the objects presented by Bo Bardi had been "recently confused with pop-art in Paris," implying that if the military had indeed been concerned about the show's contents, they would have stopped it earlier in Paris. Still, Zevi publicly represented Bo Bardi's opinion that the works on display were "the opposite of pop-art: not gestures of more or less passive integration by an economically advanced culture, but the desperate efforts of a society condemned to death and which denounces its intolerable existence."[18] Privately, however, Bo Bardi confirmed in a letter to Magalhães's wife, Lavínia, that the exhibition had been canceled by the embassy in Rome, which suggests that the military's involvement was overstated in the press.[19]

As Bo Bardi tried to show the insightful simplicity of Brazilian handmade objects to Europeans, she continued to develop her notion of *arquitetura pobre* (simple architecture) in Brazil. In December 1964, just before traveling to Italy, she designed a guesthouse for the Cirell House (figures 65, 66).[20] Though her initial drawings are slightly different from the built version (likely completed in 1965) and from the later renovation of the current roof, the regular geometrical figures and the separation of a large common area from small service areas hint at her reliance on classical and rationalist layouts (figure 67).[21] Likewise, the imagery of rustic architecture and the use of simple and traditional materials, plants, and rough finishes suggest her interest in local and naturalistic features.

69. La Torraccia Guesthouse (Valéria P. Cirell House), São Paulo, 1964, view from the living room. Photograph by Zeuler R. Lima.

70. Lina Bo Bardi, *Study for Butantan Institute Museum*, May 18, 1964. India ink, gouache, and pencil on cardstock, 28.2 × 46.3 cm. ILBPMB Collection.

The guesthouse's centerpiece consists of a semicircular living room enclosed by a curved masonry wall shaped as three quarters of a circle and covered — like its peer — with pebbles, ceramic shards, vines, and shrubs. A fireplace occupies the geometric center of the building, holding the structure of a semiconical roof, while a eucalyptus frame (originally finished as a thatched roof) covers a small patio facing west (figures 68, 69). On the backside, facing east, Bo Bardi designed an extruded section of a cylinder for a bedroom, a bathroom, and a small kitchen. She nicknamed the guesthouse La Torraccia, invoking the romantic image of a crumbling turret covered with plants while also showing her continued interest in Wright's solar hemicycle house. La Torraccia had an even greater resemblance to that project than did the Chame-Chame House, which had been recently completed in Salvador. Once again, however, her reference was more typological than technical. Had she taken Wright's concern with energy efficiency into consideration, for example, the patio would have faced north and not to the western afternoon sun.

Bo Bardi produced another project in São Paulo in May 1965. Though not residential, it resembled the visual vocabulary for the Cirell House while also building on her adaptive reuse experiences at Unhão. Likely invited by former Mayor Barros, who was now state governor of São Paulo, she developed preliminary studies for a pedagogical museum at Instituto Butantan (Butantan institute), a renowned research center specializing in venomous animals. She produced a few drawings for one of the institute's historical buildings with a courtyard at its center, dividing it into three sections: a U-shaped exhibition room with display cases; a small auditorium; and a new patio with a reflecting pool surrounded by rustic thatched porches and slightly elevated boardwalks supported by a eucalyptus frame. She wanted to create "dioramas with plants, dried trees, leaves, dirt, embalmed animals, and recordings with noises from the Sertão and other natural habitats" (figure 70).[22] In spite of her enthusiasm for the project and its idealized image of the Brazilian wilderness, the governor decided to give the building another purpose and canceled the museum project.[23]

After the Instituto Butantan project halted, Bo Bardi wrote a letter to Zevi lamenting that she did not have enough work other than the conclusion of MASP, which nonetheless

71. Lina Bo Bardi, *Study for Itamambuca Subdivision (House Units and Land Parceling)*, 1965. India ink, oil pastel, and pencil on tracing paper, 27.8 × 27.2 cm. ILBPMB Collection.

Sertão" in Bahia. She described the Unhão complex as "popular architecture like most of the colonial architecture in Brazil." Ultimately, she insisted on an anthropological and historical understanding of the "Brazilian *mezzogiorno*," comparing the impoverished and archaic Nordeste to similar conditions in southern Italy as described by Gramsci.[27]

In São Paulo, between September and October 1965, Bo Bardi prepared studies for workshops and exhibition facilities at Parque Lage. She left few notes about the project other than some colorful drawings illustrating her experimentation with a handful of rustic architectural elements that had already become the basic vocabulary of her arquitetura pobre: rough eucalyptus trunks, wooden trellises, palm thatch, rocks, gravel, and walls covered with plants. She imagined different types of pavilions looking either like tropical huts or Mediterranean cabins on terraced grounds and surrounded by a tall fence of dried treetrunks, stone, and boulders.

On October 11, 1965, shortly after Bo Bardi's initial studies, Governor Lacerda was replaced by his opponent, who showed no interest in her project and who, a few months later, moved the more conventional Instituto de Belas Artes (IBA, Fine arts institute) to Parque Lage. Though Bo Bardi made a formal request to discuss the project, the new governor did not respond. Upset, Bo Bardi sent him a resignation letter on October 14, 1965, and went back to São Paulo. She would not return to work in Rio de Janeiro until 1975, when she would be invited by artist Rubens Gerchman, soon after his inauguration as director of IBA, and set designer Hélio Eichbauer for a short-lived collaboration in their proposal for a new fine arts curriculum.[28]

In addition to her projects for La Torraccia, Instituto Butantan, and Parque Lage, Bo Bardi received a commission to study a seaside resort at Itamambuca Beach on the northern coast of the state of São Paulo. According to her records, she turned in a set of drawings on December 30, 1965, but never heard back from her client until she insisted they return the documentation to her.[29] Though the resort was never built, this study foreshadowed a community resettlement project she would develop ten years later in the Nordeste. The site was located along a small river at the foot of the verdant Serra do Mar range. Bo Bardi emphasized the need to preserve its original configuration, combining a small hotel, a leisure area, and a small subdivision designed as a regular grid of circles with winding diagonal streets and two types of lots and houses (figure 71). She described her plan as the creation of a "natural subdivision."[30]

Both beach house typologies departed from the main block of the Cirell House with a slightly more complex geometrical layout based on a small square rotated diagonally

kept her occupied sporadically for several years.[24] She also mentioned that, having agreed to pursue the art center that Governor Lacerda planned to create at Parque Lage, she had begun to commute between São Paulo and Rio de Janeiro. The project promised to help her find a new place in the discriminating Brazilian cultural establishment, especially in Rio de Janeiro. In June 1965, she finally visited the site at the foot of Corcovado, hoping to continue the interrupted curatorial and pedagogical work she had started in Salvador.[25]

She was preparing for a public presentation about her plans for the park-school project and was unyielding about her recommendations. In a letter to the governor, she even asked for complete control over the project ("professional responsibility" was her term), likely wanting to avoid any problems she had recently faced at MAMB.[26] As part of her endeavors, on August 19, 1965, she lectured about MAP at the Escola Nacional de Belas Artes, the traditional beaux-arts school in Rio de Janeiro, and unveiled her vision for Parque Lage. She spoke extensively about social, economic, and political problems in the Nordeste and about her experience creating "a museum of modern art at the edge of the inside a larger square and with a column marking their matching centers. The larger unit contained an atrium with a central staircase and was surrounded by raised wood verandas with thatched roofs. The smaller unit was internally similar to the Cirell House but externally different from it: the plan rotation allowed for four triangular porches, making the unit look like a tropical and rustic version of a Palladian house. In both cases, the houses were to have trellised doors, epiphytes on the pebble-covered walls, and a crowning roof flowerbed. The Itamambuca complex confirmed, with several variations, the formal palette Bo Bardi had begun to develop in the late 1950s and that recurred in many unrealized studies for different purposes she produced throughout her life.

Except for the completion of the Museu de Arte de São Paulo in 1968, the Itamambuca project would be the last architectural commission she would receive for ten years. Though the new museum granted her increased visibility, the flourishing of her architectural career would have to wait. In the interim, she followed the changing political and cultural life of Brazil and gradually adapted herself to it. She no longer criticized Brasília, as she had done with Niemeyer's buildings in *Crônicas* in 1958. On the contrary, she strongly defended Lucio Costa's plan in a letter to Zevi addressing a conversation she had had with Vilanova Artigas about her Italian friend's criticism of the new capital.[31]

Bo Bardi had shifted her attention from the Italian architectural debate but remained somehow peripheral to the Brazilian professional milieu. Since becoming the target of international criticism in the early 1950s and under the stress of a changing national political panorama, prominent Brazilian architects revised their formal and discursive affiliations. While Niemeyer wrote about simplification and focused on structural aspects of his iconic buildings in Brasília, Vilanova Artigas and some of his followers toned down their revolutionary discourse and critically embraced the rhetoric of development professed by the new regime. Artigas became a major proponent of the use of raw, reinforced concrete as the technological trope of national development plans, as influenced by the late developments of European brutalism, but he disagreed with the movement's appeal to irrationality.[32] Aware of Artigas's work (the two maintained a distant dialogue), Bo Bardi had incorporated raw concrete structures while distancing herself from irrationalist interpretations and developing a different path both professionally and intellectually from her Paulistano colleague.

Though Bo Bardi limited her practice to curatorial and scenic projects until 1975, her ongoing design for MASP and its bold pre-stressed concrete structure marked her

isolated appearance in a scene dominated by Artigas. The architecture for the museum emerged somewhere between Artigas's position and that of European designers, from her growing belief in the coexistence of advanced technology and the poetry and improvisation of everyday life. To her, this intersection produced the intuitive, logical, and symbolic collisions into which her architecture would mature. The construction of MASP progressed haltingly as Bo Bardi tried to find an alternative to solve technical problems that delayed the enclosing of the elevated exhibition hall. The main structure of longspan pre-stressed concrete beams and slabs was cast by the end of 1965. However, the structure remained exposed to the weather until 1967, when glazed curtain walls replaced the solid walls with plants, which she had long but unsuccessfully insisted on keeping.

As the museum entered its final construction stage, Bo Bardi collaborated on a new editorial project launched by her husband in January 1967: the magazine *Mirante das Artes, Etc.* (Art observatory, etc.), a title suggesting Bardi's vision for the new MASP and its privileged location in São Paulo. The publication, which had a psychedelic logo following trends of the time, was part of her husband's commercial endeavors at his private Galeria Mirante, once envisioned by Bo Bardi as a long, all-white space squeezed between an undulating pinewood ceiling and plastic flooring.[33] The magazine was slimmer and simpler than *Habitat* and included a new generation of collaborators with whom she would develop closer relationships, such as that with designer Flávio Império, one of the leaders of emerging cultural and political movements in the city, especially those in theater productions. Throughout 1967, she wrote four articles for the new magazine, the first three of which illustrated her defense of architectural rationalism against unrelenting claims of its demise. The final article was a retrospective evaluation of her experience in Salvador from the increasingly polarized political outlook that grew among artistic, professional, and intellectual groups in Brazil at the time.

Bo Bardi's first article, titled "O que está acontecendo na Améria do Sul depois de Le Corbusier?" (What is happening in South America after Le Corbusier?), criticized a recent issue of *Progressive Architecture*. In it, Bo Bardi refuted the editor's comments about the demise of Le Corbusier's influence and the need, in her critical words, "to look for inspiration in native huts, 'ranchitos,' and slums." Against his paternalistic view, she suggested building housing projects and revisiting progressive values emptied out by the Western postwar economic model "in the hands of monopolistic capitalism." Longing for the early efforts of the Modern Movement at the brink of postmodernism, she defended "the social, political, and revolutionary values that sustained rationalism." She insisted that in order to create a "just and human industrial society it was necessary to base it on humanistic values, exactly those from which Le Corbusier's architecture had emerged." She concluded that "a great legacy cannot be forgotten: the rationalist legacy," specifically focusing on the transformative confluence between aesthetics and politics rather than on the relation between rationality and industrial production.[34]

In the following issue and somewhat in contrast to her opening article, Bo Bardi published "No limite da casa popular" (At the limit of low-income houses), an essay stressing the confluence between rationalization and traditional construction techniques.[35] She turned to a housing experience initiated in 1963 for the resettlement of a large community in Cajueiro Seco outside of Recife, in the Nordeste, but interrupted after by the military coup.[36] Instead of writing about the neighborhood layout designed by architect Gildo Guerra, she described the technical adaptations that architect Acácio Gil Borsói, once related to MCP, had made of local *mucambos* (small, crude wattle-and-daub cabins).

Though not new in Brazil, Borsói's approach came to be regarded as an innovative model for housing projects and, coincidentally, was in line with the suggestions made by the editor of the US *Progressive Architecture* magazine, casting doubt on whether national-popular values implied in Bo Bardi's articles mattered more than technical principles. Her article highlighted Borsói's modular construction system, which used precast panels of adobe built with community participation.[37] She embraced his political discourse, though the houses she had designed in the past ten years had remained mostly an exercise in style. Despite ambiguities, her practice would eventually catch up with her ideological aspirations, especially in her project for the resettlement of the Camurupim community in the Nordeste and for two churches she designed almost a decade later.

Bo Bardi hoped to revive what she considered to be the core values of modern architecture, and her interest in Borsói's references to rural architecture reflected the idea that popular ingenuity was embedded in an authentic rationality and simplicity. In the following two years, she would explore these ideas in a handful of residential studies, including the preliminary project for a private country house based on a U-shaped scheme supporting an unusual, large roof with verandas resembling Brazilian colonial rural architecture.[38] Still, to prove her point while writing the article for *Mirante das Artes, Etc.*, she submitted a provocative entry to an international, low-cost furniture design competition. Her sketches for a roadside chair show seats made of three slender branches tied on top with vine and formed into a

pyramidal frame that holds a thicker branch horizontally tied to two of the legs. The photographs of the prototype she produced for the chair suggest a bus stop in the Brazilian countryside though, in reality, her references came from far away — specifically an article published in a British magazine showing similar seats made for children in an African village. Less concerned about anthropological rigor, she was interested in the rationality of simple, handmade objects. Her prototype is still kept in her archival collection.

She continued to promote rational design in her third article for the magazine, titled "O novo Trianon" (The new Trianon). In it, she presented her most recent aesthetic and political concerns about the museum building nearing its completion on avenida Paulista. Concerned with the reception her peers and critics would have of such a large and daring structure built under an increasingly oppressive regime, she explained: "The Trianon complex will re-propose, in its monumental simplicity, the themes brought forward by rationalism that have become so unpopular." She refuted and perhaps even feared associations of monumentality with grandiosity, especially with projects of authoritarian regimes, like "the buildings of Nazi-fascism, which were arrogant and similar to elephants in their lack of logic, but not monumental." Rather, she stated, "that which I call monumental is not a question of size or ostentation, but just an element of . . . collective consciousness." She wrote in conclusion, "It is necessary to eliminate all elements of perfectionism out of rationalism, which are part of its idealist and metaphysical legacy, and to face the reality of architectural mishaps," likely validating the many inevitable changes that were transforming her original project for MASP both conceptually and physically.[39]

After publishing three articles about rationalization in a time of great political and cultural instability, Bo Bardi wrote a special supplement for the magazine. It is one of her best-known pieces: "Cinco anos entre os brancos," which can be translated as either "Five years among white people" or, considering her isolation as a woman, "Five years among white men."[40] In this article, she offered a selective retelling of her experience as the former director of MAMB. More political than historical, this text erases the ambivalent associations she had with white elites that led her to direct the museum and the different phases of her long and uneven time in Salvador.

Bo Bardi's narrative ensured that her initiatives stood on the same ground as reforms that promoted "a university in expansion" or movements started by the "student body, which, despite acting confusingly against their own interests, was on the right way to political and cultural awareness." Above all, she stressed "the deeply popular character of

Bahia and all the Nordeste," though she did not mention the MCP in Recife as she suggested the originality of her project. She discussed how "MAMB was not a 'museum' in the traditional sense," describing it instead as "a cultural movement that could enter the world of true modern culture by taking on the values of a culture that is historically poor (in a dignifying sense)." She described the museum as a "popular experience (rigorously different from folklore)" based on "the technical instruments, the method, and the strength of a new humanism (neither humanitarianism nor [Renaissance] *umanesimo*)."[41]

She also fine-tuned her criticism of the group organized around Odorico Tavares. "Since the outset," she wrote, "MAMB faced the hostility of a 'cultural class' established according to provincial patterns" and composed of "nationally celebrated artists gathered around folkloric themes and the local press." She declared without modesty: "I started the job by eliminating the city's cultural establishment," dismissing the retaliatory consequences of her actions. Instead, she highlighted her concerns with popular audiences in her ideas for the renovation of Teatro Castro Alves and of the Unhão complex as a documentation center for technically studying "the passage from a primitive pre-handicraft into industrial production" as an alternative "framework to the country's development." She mentioned her desire to carry out a "survey of popular handicraft (pre-handicraft) in the whole country," referring to a large exhibition of everyday handmade objects that she was preparing for MASP's opening. In contrast to her previously stated confidence, she recalled "not [having] an ambitious program, but just a quest."[42] She was likely referring to the unenthusiastic response she received from the influential economist and former minister Celso Furtado, who, just before she completed the article, wrote her a candid letter warning her not to see her plans as a consolation for poverty.[43]

By narrating her past quarrels, "Cinco anos entre os brancos" ultimately introduced Bo Bardi's new public persona to the cultural milieu of São Paulo. It pictured the stage of her martyrdom: "The shadow of cultural reaction, of rancid traditions, of anger, of fear appearing on the horizon." She described the opening scene as "the Sixth Military Region occupied MAMB soon after April of 1964 [and] presented the pedagogical subversion exhibition." And as she edited her memories, she combined that event with another occasion. "In front of the museum: cannons from Amaralina [army headquarters]," she wrote, inaccurately associating the termination of her work directly with the coup d'état rather than her confrontations with Tavares. She also included herself in a selective cast of artists and intellectuals — such as Glauber Rocha, Martim Gonçalves,

and Lívio Xavier — who had operated in the Nordeste during that period and alongside whom she wanted to be remembered. She closed the article in full circle from its title: "Five years of hard work that revealed cowardice, defections, crooked behavior. Five years of collective hopes . . . Five years among 'white people.'"[44]

The personal account of the experiences and aspirations Bo Bardi tried to immortalize in the pages of *Mirante das Artes, Etc.* suggest not only that the legacy of rationalism should be remembered but also that her efforts to humanize it should not be ignored.

The years following Bo Bardi's departure from Salvador concluded her transition from a period of personal examination and growth into a decade of increasing radicalization, and of introspection and melancholy. They also represented the interlude during which the completion of the Museu de Arte de São Paulo on avenida Paulista gave her unprecedented professional visibility after a long and convoluted construction process. Given its symbolic and geographic prominence in São Paulo, MASP became her most visible work, eventually granting her national and worldwide exposure but also eclipsing her unrealized original plans for the building as well as the complex and hybrid features of her other works from the same period (figure 72).

Along with Reidy's Museu de Arte Moderna in Rio de Janeiro and Artigas's school of architecture at the Universidade de São Paulo, Bo Bardi's project was one of the first large public buildings in Brazil to embrace the use of raw reinforced concrete. This technique — as influenced by the works of British and French brutalism — and its structural expressionism would pervade the work of several Brazilian architects during the 1960s and 1970s, though they seldom included Bo Bardi as a peer.

Her initial project for MASP began, as demonstrated before, in 1957, but construction did not start until late 1960. Discontinued the following year, it resumed between 1962 and 1963, when the basic structure and the roof terrace of the Civic Hall that constitutes the plinth for the elevated museum volume were completed. After that, construction halted again, and the site was practically deserted, leaving the unfinished structure exposed to weather. Work resumed in February 1964 after engineer Figueiredo Ferraz, who was responsible for the project's structural project and served as the city's secretary of public works, successfully obtained public funds.[1]

During the erection of the museum's four large piers in 1964, workers mistakenly cut the longer pieces of rebar from the splice lap connections reserved on the terrace slabs as they prepared the casting of the remaining upper section of the structure. To minimize future problems caused by the accident, Figueiredo Ferraz increased the thickness of each pier in order to vertically pre-stress the structure and to create a reinforcement ring around it below the terrace.[2] The piers, completed at the end of September 1964, thus ended up slightly more robust than planned. Soon after the columns were cast, a forest of large wooden scaffoldings emerged from Trianon Terrace, initially sprouting at the outer edges of the lot, offering support for the casting of the four large columns, and later expanding all around the site.

In January 1965, while Bo Bardi was setting up the *Nordeste* exhibition in Europe, the execution of the large

72. MASP, São Paulo, 1957–68, aerial view from the north side with
avenida Nove de Julho in the foreground. Photograph by Nelson Kon.

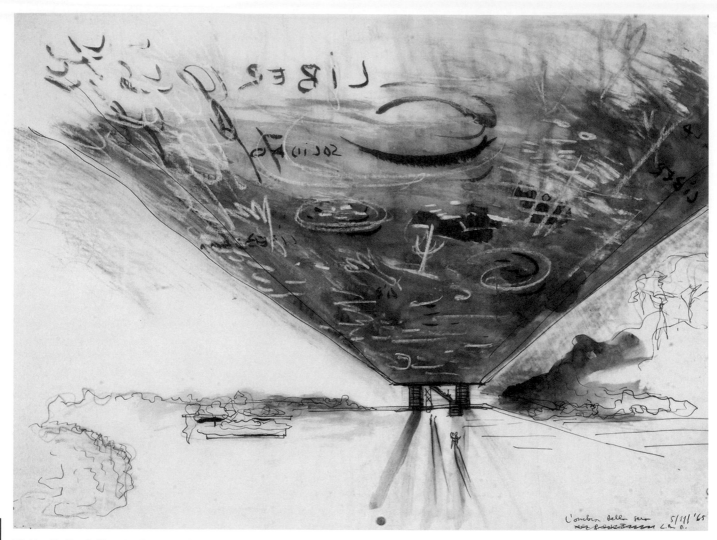

73. Lina Bo Bardi, *"Evening Shadow," Study for MASP Terrace*,
November 5, 1965. India ink and oil pastel on tracing paper, 49.9 × 69.5
cm. ILBPMB Collection.

74. MASP during construction, c. 1967, view from the northwestern side on avenida Paulista. MASP Collection.

pre-stressed concrete beams sped up. As the site was prepared for the casting of the large concrete slab above the plaza, she prepared a large drawing imagining the wide-open space protected under the "shadow of the evening" (figure 73). Construction was spurred further by the election of the new mayor, José Vicente Faria Lima, an air force major-general in civilian attire who became well known for the sheer amount of public works his administration promoted. Mayor Faria Lima dedicated substantial financial support for MASP's completion, setting the stage for a play of epic proportions (figure 74). With the city as audience, MASP as the stage, the designers as protagonists, the public administration in a supporting role, and the construction workers as the stage crew, the show would go on until the museum was officially inaugurated on November 7, 1968, and its first exhibitions finally opened to the public on April 7, 1969.

Until then, the site on avenida Paulista remained an experimental ground for the most modern engineering technology available in the country at the time. Figueiredo Ferraz's patented pre-stressed concrete system allowed MASP to have the longest structure without intermediate supports in Brazil. Behind MASP's structural prowess,

there was a predominantly artisanal construction process. The engineer's pre-stressing system required little mechanization and a relatively small and lightweight jack.[3] As a result, human labor and not conventional industrialized components prevailed on the site.

Bo Bardi herself used the construction office on the site as an unconventional design studio, which allowed her to develop close dialogues with the technical and construction crews and especially the foreman, with whom she had a mutually respectful and helpful collaboration. This unusual way of working resolved many practical issues, given the project's complexity and scale and complex administrative problems. It also nurtured her romantic approach to the construction site as a premodern laboratory, recalling the Italian guilds of masters and artisans, whose division of labor she saw as cooperative rather than alienating. Bo Bardi later suggested that such collaboration "also does away with the ridiculous dichotomy between engineers and architects, allows one to closely check costs, negotiations, and dubious arrangements."[4]

This working scheme also concentrated decision making on the construction site, especially when Bo Bardi was away. By the end of 1965, when she had permanently

75. MASP, São Paulo, 1957–68, sectioned view from the northwestern side showing spatial layout and building logic. Computer rendering. Zeuler R. Lima Collection.

returned from Rio de Janeiro, the building's concrete structure was complete. The wooden scaffolding was removed, revealing three long slabs hanging from straddling legs and spines, waiting for a solution for the enclosure that would bring the elevated exhibition halls into existence. That naked view temporarily exposed the complex and intriguing structural armature that became largely invisible after the building's completion.

Although the building in which MASP continues to operate seems to hover eight meters (26 ft.) above the terrace held only by two large parallel beams spanning seventy-four meters (243 ft.) and with no intermediate vertical piers, it is, in fact, supported by a biarticulated system. In addition to the upper beams, two similar hollow concrete girders transfer the load of both elevated floor slabs to the lateral piers. The internal girders are almost invisible from the outside and hold most of the load in the elevated part of the building. They rest on large consoles cast into the columns, halfway between the terrace and the roof, and

hold twenty-one transversal concrete joists along with the upper-floor slab that cantilevers five meters (16 ft.) on each side (figure 75).

Only the pleated concrete roof slab of the suspended volume is connected to the upper beams. Still, they are both under significant pressure and, in spite of receiving a lower load, exposed to larger temperature variation and dilation, which required that the beams be built to allow for horizontal movements of expansion and contraction. Although one end of each upper beam is directly encased in a column, the other end rests on a hydraulic support created by filling the top of the other columns with oil and pressurizing and sealing them with neoprene.[5] Beneath the pair of central girders, a regular system of steel tie rods with turnbuckles suspends the hollow, fifty-centimeter (20 in.) deep, cast concrete slab, which is six meters (20 ft.) below the collection room and acts as the administrative floor and temporary gallery.[6]

76. MASP, São Paulo, 1957–68, interior view of main lobby in the elevated volume. Photograph by Nelson Kon.

77. MASP, São Paulo, 1957–68, view of interior hallway under pre-stressed concrete beam holding steel rods in the elevated volume. Photograph by Nelson Kon.

The adjustable rods that hold the lower slab are grouped into prismatic bundles of four pieces lined up at each edge of the long beams and coinciding with the transversal joists that support the upper floor. As a result, they create two long, tunnel-like spaces under the girders, which Bo Bardi used as hallways to connect the entry lobby with the administrative offices along the museum's north and south sides (figures 76, 77). Above all, the cables made it possible to build the lower slab in camber, with an upward curvature to compensate for load deflection and to create the plane that seems to hover over Belvedere do Trianon as a canopy, framing the vista of the old terrace toward the city center (figure 78).

This daring armature remained in view from the end of 1965 until 1967 as construction slowed. Figueiredo Ferraz did not support Bo Bardi's intention to enclose the museum's elevated volume with opaque walls, but she did not give up her idea easily. Since the inception of the project, she had imagined it sealed: "a straight volume that I will cover with tropical plants between the interstices of rough cement, just like between the stones of an old cathedral."[7] Between September and November 1965, she produced several studies for the envelope of the raised volume, departing from the solid, white marble or pebble-covered walls she envisioned in her 1959 and 1960 versions. In the newer drawings, she proposed a modular system of eighty vertical pre-stressed concrete panels that contained receptacles for plants and exposed the concrete gutter and both floor slabs framing them.[8] She even imagined having artist Abelardo da Hora (from the former Recife MCP) produce panels for the museum's exterior walls.[9]

Figueiredo Ferraz continued to insist that walls or panels would be too heavy for the cantilevered slabs.[10] He also feared that, though her scheme was theoretically logical, it would be very difficult to execute pre-stressed concrete pieces that could be cast with enough precision and juxtaposed in a stable way.[11] Instead, he recommended a lighter, more flexible solution for enclosing the main gallery and the offices below, but there was no sign of her first alternatives until March 1966, after the beams were concluded and casting of the large slabs was underway.[12] Throughout that year, she produced several drawings considering different materials, proportions, and openings as she envisioned an alternative to the vertical concrete panels while keeping the upper floor enclosed.

But those alternatives were encumbered by technical circumstances, and the final decision was likely a compromise between the architectural ideas Bo Bardi pursued and the varied influences and setbacks she experienced during construction. She gradually went from the idea of "hand-thrown cement as brute as stone" to a window frame measuring almost twelve meters in height all around the long elevated

78. MASP, São Paulo, 1957–68, southwestern view on avenida Paulista.
Photograph by Nelson Kon.

building.[13] By September 1966, one year after she proposed the pre-stressed concrete panel system, she produced her first sketches for telescopic mullions, a system of metal tracks that allowed the glass panes to slide vertically, adjusting to the height variation caused by the movement of contraction and expansion of the concrete structure.[14]

Rather than an aesthetic choice, Bo Bardi's use of a continuous window frame for MASP's elevated volume was the result of a technical compromise between her and the construction team — especially evident when contrasted with the theories and the predominantly solid, opaque, and roughly textured projects she had been developing in the previous decade. MASP's polished and transparent enclosure has placed her work in the international architectural discourse while erasing the ambiguous and hybrid character of her original ideas, which combined rationalist and naturalistic elements. The need to change materials and the time it took to conclude the museum construction has eclipsed,

if not altered, the understanding of her search for simplification and roughness over extravagance and sophistication. Aware of the contradictions brought about by the technical problems in her design, Bo Bardi wrote her article for *Mirante das Artes, Etc.*, clarifying the meanings she attributed to the museum. She also used it to justify her architectural compromises, declaring that she used "transparent walls as compensation for the efforts of the common people."[15]

For all her efforts, however, the final decision seems to have been out of her hands. What remains of the records and letters she penned between 1967 and 1968, while she and her assistants detailed the telescopic mullions, suggests that she was often excluded from the negotiations between the city's department of public works and the construction company, though she wrote letters protesting their decisions. For example, she complained about their choice to have the Liceu de Artes e Ofícios (a traditional school of arts and crafts in São Paulo) produce the window frames for the

79. MASP, São Paulo, 1957–68, interior view of the semiburied Civic Hall with ramped staircases in the background. Photograph by Nelson Kon.

museum.[16] Though Liceu had modernized its pedagogical structure and was a major supplier of mullions and metal-work for the construction of iconic buildings in Brasília, Bo Bardi considered their organization outdated, calling them demoralizing and dilettante.[17] She was also upset that the company contacted landscape architect Roberto Burle Marx to design the plaza without consulting her. She warned that "Belvedere do Trianon will be a square with no garden, a venue for popular meetings, exhibitions, and free outdoor concerts. Nothing else."[18]

Given the construction delay, Bo Bardi was concerned they would not meet the deadline for the museum opening ceremony in July 1968.[19] She continued to press the city administration and contractors for several months, confid-ing in a personal note, "Behind the scenes of every work of architecture, the struggle between the architect (when the architect is worthy of that title) and the owners of the construction company reaches dramatic proportions."[20]

Corroborating her notes, the press printed provocative pieces about the administrative crisis surrounding the site on avenida Paulista and against continuing construction. These obstacles, however, did not affect the work in prog-ress. In addition, Mayor Faria Lima's term was coming to a close, so he intensified the production, setting a new open-ing date of November 7, 1968.

During those months and even beyond, Bo Bardi remained intensely busy with several small projects aimed at the museum opening. Between February and April 1968, she concluded the details for the large-stepped, red ramps connecting the lower hall and the mezzanines of the Civic Hall that had been left unfinished since their casting in 1963 (figure 79). She also designed simple but skillfully articu-lated concrete railings and benches to crown the edges of the exhibition hall.[21] She started to produce studies for the large auditorium and its seats, but they would not be completed until a few months after the museum was in operation.[22]

A Museum Within Everyone's Reach   129

80. MASP, São Paulo, 1957–68, view of the main auditorium with pleated concrete walls. Photograph by Nelson Kon.

She originally planned a central rectangular arena with a movable stage but replaced it with a conventional stage facing a slightly slanted audience (figure 80).

Her initial studies for the theater seats referred to the wood and leather chairs she designed for the improvised ramp auditorium at Teatro Castro Alves in Salvador in 1959. She next experimented with other schemes ranging from individual pieces in wood and fabric to sequential seats in cast concrete with cushions that recalled her early bowl chair. She finally decided on twelve long rows of chairs with beveled backs set in two symmetrical pieces built of waxed peroba, a native hardwood.[23] The city did not approve the budget for her proposal, so in October 1969, after much struggle, she suggested a simple and fast alternative: stringer wooden seats with no upholstery like those used in movie theaters and public schools and produced by Móveis Cimo (Cimo furniture), the largest manufacturer of commercial and institutional furniture in Brazil.[24] Unconvinced, the city administration chose conventional cushioned leather seats instead, but Bo Bardi would not give up and in the early 1980s would propose a variation on her design for the theater seats at SESC Pompeia.

More significant than the chairs, the controversies around the enclosure of the suspended museum volume had finally ended. Once the large window frame enclosing the suspended structure was completed, work began on internal finishes and facilities setup. The exposed air-conditioning ducts were painted, and modular industrial rubber tiles were laid on the slabs of both gallery floors. Bo Bardi and workers rushed to design and execute the tempered glass partitions separating the administrative offices from the hallways beneath the two pre-stressed concrete girders, as detailed in drawings she completed in March 1968.[25] Simultaneously, they finished the floors of the Civic Hall with large square tiles of beige quartzite, a relatively inexpensive and durable Brazilian stone.

81. MASP, São Paulo, 1957–68, southern view of Trianon Terrace from the main staircase. Photograph by Nelson Kon.

The terrace at avenida Paulista was covered with unpolished gray granite tiles with grass growing between them to resemble cobblestones. The stainless steel elevator connecting the Civic Hall below and the museum above was installed next to the concrete staircase, which seemed to fold out of the elevated volume and to delicately touch the plaza as if extending an inviting gesture to passersby (figure 81). In a colorful drawing, Bo Bardi envisioned this public area as a place for large sculptures and a playground: "I tried to create an atmosphere on Trianon Terrace," she wrote. "I'd like for the common people to go there and see outdoor exhibitions and chat, listen to music, watch films." She expected to see "children playing in the morning and afternoon sun. And a band, a kind of popular bad taste, but which could be meaningful" (figure 82).[26]

As planned, on November 7, 1968, though the building was not completely finished, the presidential convertible Rolls-Royce stopped in front of the museum on avenida Paulista. A red carpet stretched from the curb to the bottom of the museum stairs and was lined by the mayor, the governor, and their wives in light dresses, hats, and gloves, there to welcome the guests of honor, Elizabeth II and her consort. Pietro Maria Bardi took the group on a tour of the new museum, culminating with a visit to the upper floor, where the permanent collection was housed. As they emerged from the dimly lit lower floor into the bright and airy space under the pleated roof, the large room and the views of the city opened before their eyes. In it, they saw a colorful and slightly irregular constellation of more than two hundred paintings supported by glass easels designed by Bo Bardi that made it seem as though the paintings hovered in the middle of the large and unobstructed hall (figure 83).

The easels, conceived during the casting of the elevated slabs, were based on experiments from previous curatorial works inspired in the work of Italian designers that eliminated traditional museum walls. More specifically, they went

82. Lina Bo Bardi, *Preliminary Study for Sculptures-cum-Stage-Props on Trianon Terrace, MASP*, May 6, 1965. India ink and watercolor on paper, 56.2 × 76.5 cm. Photograph by Luís Hossaka. MASP Collection.

A Rainha, o dr. Assis e o Museu

P. M. BARDI

O Governador Abreu Sodré, S. M. Elizabeth II, sr. João Monteiro, secretário de Educação e Cultura da Prefeitura Municipal de São Paulo, P. M. Bardi, Brigadeiro Faria Lima, no dia 7 de novembro, em nosso Museu de Arte.

Graças ao prefeito Faria Lima que aplica a recomendação latina de **Acta non verba**, aplicando verbas para a ressurreição de São Paulo, o "Museu de Arte Assis Chateaubriand" e uma esplêndida realidade que todos podem agora ver na Avenida Paulista e muito brevemente visitar. Um Museu para ser identificado, para se incorporar no contexto popular necessita tornar-se antes de mais nada um edifício; como os palácios governamentais, o paço municipal, o forum, a catedral e assim por diante.

Ao longo de vinte e tantos anos vividos nos andares que o dr. Assis em 1946 destinara ao nôvo Museu ali no prédio dos "Associados", advertíamos da falta de comunicação com o público, a integração na vida da cidade. De vez em quando conversávamos de planos com seu Fundador, e êste repetia: — O prédio ganharemos quando a coleção fôr robusta. Por enquanto vamos formando o acervo, sem gastarmos um centavo para o cimento da sede.

Chauteaubriand tinha as antenas voltadas para o que iá acontecer no futuro. Era um homem perspicaz e com tal visão que desconfiar da sua previsão seria ato de pura ingenuidade. Conhecia mais que qualquer financista o zig-zag da inflação; assim soube levantar meios destinados ao maior número possível de obras destinadas ao Museu.

Tendo a honra de receber e de ser o cicerone de S. M. a Rainha Elizabeth II na visita que a soberana fez à Pinacoteca, pude sentir, ao meu lado, o espírito do mágico dr. Assis: eu media as palavras e as ajeitava no papel de um portavoz do homem que criou tudo aquilo que o ilustre hóspede, surprêsa, estava vendo.

A Rainha perguntou-me — Como foi possível reunir todos êstes Impressionistas? — Majestade — respondi sintético —, foi "jeito" do Embaixador Chateaubriand. Traduzi jeito para "ingenuity". Estávamos diante da "Marta Berard" de Renoir; outras cinco obras dêste mestre estavam alinhadas de um lado enquanto outras seis estavam um pouco distanciadas; a escultura da "Vênus Victorieuse" perfilada diante dos vidros que deixavam entrever a crista do Parque Siqueira Campos. A Rainha fêz um imperceptível gesto de cabeça, como a demonstrar recordações e raciocínio. Pode ser que o souvenir era de um senhor dinâmico, quase elétrico de olhos foudre que a preenteava. Não Coroação, com um colar de águas mari-

nhas especialmente confeccionado para Ela no longínquo Brasil. Num instante explodia, ao pronunciar o nome Chateaubriand, um fôgo de artifício, lampejando o trabalho e as extravagâncias de um embaixador que palmilhou os salões da Côrte de Saint James, autêntico e generoso; e mais, o único embaixador no mundo a criar uma Ordem de Cavalaria, a Ordem do Jagunço, imposta a pouquíssimos como o caso de Winston Churchill; um embaixador que ao champanhe de um ágape no Ritz de Londres, quando tinar para a exposição do acervo na Tate Gallery, dizia ser um cristão de primeira porque um saxônico antepassado, um índio, comeu o bispo Sardinha. Londres das elites adorava o Dr. Assis e devorava feijoadas e carnes sêcas de sol, tudo em honra do pitoresco diplomata que no momento oportuno sabia demonstrar seu conhecimento da história inglesa como se fôra um professor de Oxford.

Tínhamos pôsto o "Salão Azul" de Churchill bem defronte o elevador. Recebi a Rainha com êste primeiro encontro balanceado entre a museugrafia e a história, a cortesia e o "esprit". A Rainha ignorava que o dr. Assis havia arrematado a peça em Londres. Mostrei a prancha técnica colocada atrás da placa de cristal com um autógrafo do Defensor da Europa. Chateaubriand, certa noite, me telefonou do Savoy para anunciar que o disputou com o ator Montgomery, isto num leilão da Christie's. Gritou: — Professor, é uma pintura arco-da-velha; trate-a com carinho!

A Rainha gostou do destaque dado ao quadro. Simples, com aquele jeito de mulher que deixa a gente despreocupada em relação à etiqueta, olhou as pinturas com a curiosidade natural com que qualquer europeu se defronta, vis-a-vis, uma obra de arte. Eu um comentário para os inglêses: Gainsborough, Reynolds, Lawrence, Constable e para um grupo de obras de londrinos moços: Kitay, Blacke, Scott, Tilson, Procktor, Paolozzi, além de dois belíssimos Sutherland, um dos quais, o "Admirante Nelson". Cada obra com uma história; o imaginoso dr. Assis tanto fez que convenceu o pintor a lhe produzir um retrato do Almirante, resultando numa perfeita cédula de identidade à la Bertillon.

A Rainha olhou-me interrogativamente. Expliquei-lhe — Chateaubriand... (De fato o dr. Assis dois anos antes pediu-me

para ir à Londres e trazer uma autêntica safra de inglêses para os Museus Regionais. Quando voltei confiei ao chefe que uma parte da colheita fôra armazenada no Museu pilôto. Reservei a apresentação pública destes bons inglêses para quando da visita real. A Rainha ficou contente ao saber que nós matutos afinal estamos ao corrente, como é de nosso dever, do que se passa na Ilha. Aliás um dos seus assessores, deve tê-la informada que um brasileiro afirmou no "Ilustrate London News" que, na Europa, Londres havia tomado o lugar de Paris no campo da jovem pintura, dividindo com Nova York a liderança da Escola Contemporânea.

Nosso Museu, apesar de alguns ignorantes chamá-lo de "moderno", não é múmia: é "moderno" mesmo, se com êste adjetivo pe quiser dizer que somos conservadores também de vivência e não sòmente de coisas dos tempos antigos. Tanto é verdade que, dulcis in fundo, a gentilíssima senhora inglêsa, foi homenageada por seis artistas brasileiros — Maria Helena Chartuni, Nelson Leirner, Tomie Ohtake, Sheila Brannigam, Bernardo Cid e Caciporê Tôrres. Cada um ao lado da sua obra cumprimentou e respondeu as perguntas da Rainha às vêzes veladas de estupor pelas aventuras das formas que em mãos originais podem vir a criar. Nelson mexeu na sua "Construção", uma genial escultura em movimentos sôbre rolamentos. O Principe Philip, mais à vontade na imposição do protocolo pôde fazer observações ou mesmo soltar uma das suas piadas só em parte aceitáveis, comentou "se não seria possível fazer um objeto menor". Não provocou sorrisos.

O quadro que a Rainha mais apreciou foi o "Retrato do artista Desbutin", de Manet: compreendeu-o logo com a exclamação imediata. A soberana não se deteve diante dos Modigliani e fato a lenda do "maudi" está estragando o valor da substância pictórica. Agradaram-lhe os Renoir e, naturalmente, as esculturas de Degas. E a "Ressurreição" de Rafael foi ensejo para que Elizabeth II estabelecesse um paralelo entre a obra prima do mestre ali exposta e a cópia desgraçada da "Madonna della Seggiola", cortada retangularmente e que foi colocada no dormitório que a soberana ocupou no casarão do Morumby pelo arrumador.

Aqui, o Espírito do anfitrião infelizmente ausente mas entre nós presente pela sua prepotente vitalidade que como um êco e como um relâmpago se expande pelo espaço, teria certamente contado a história da compra de Rafael que começou nas redondezas de Picadilly.

Vi muitas gente com lágrimas nos olhos entrando na Pinacoteca, notadamente senhoras. Ah se o dr. Assis ali estivesse, mesmo numa cadeira de rodas, com as pupilas que tudo abrangiam e circunscreviam, cheias de fascinante carinho! Forçoso concordar da injustiça do destino que teve. Mas estava ali naquela sala, dominante, contemplando o vale do Saracura-pequeno, acompanhando a Rainha símbolo do país que ardentemente admirava, feliz da graciosa visita, contente com a inscrição que Menotti del Picchia bolou, com aquele soberbo "Assis Chateaubriand — Criador de Monumentos". Não estavamos diante do imenso seixo quando o Governador do Estado traduziu os dizeres para a Rainha. Mas certamente a soberana compreendeu que monumento significava "Diários Associados", a revista "O Cruzeiro", as Campanhas da Aviação, Puericultura, dos Cafés finos, do Algodão, e dêste Museu que os brasileiros irão apreciar melhor agora que está em casa própria. E estas notas, alinhavadas ainda sob o calor do acontecimento histórico, com as imagens que o meu caro assistente Luiz Sadaki conseguiu tirar na Pinacoteca sem fotografar, querem tão sòmente lembrar mais uma vez o fantástico asceque que foi o dr. Assis, premiado pela presença da "sua" Rainha e pela vontade construtora do prefeito Faria Lima, homem da têmpera dêle.

Eis a primeira composição da Pinacoteca do Museu de Arte de São Paulo, apresentada à Rainha Elizabeth II, dia 7 de novembro, quando do ato inaugural. Como se vê na foto cada obra está apoiada numa placa de cristal temperado; no verso de cada obra foi colocada uma prancha de Duratex, com texto e ilustrações didáticas, que ilustram a pintura e fornece dados biográficos a respeito do autor. É a primeira vez que o sistema é aplicado em um museu, eliminando o "parede". A pintura colta à sua primeira vivência, o cavalete. De fato um artista realiza sua obra num cavalete; depois o adquirente pendura a obra na parede e então passa a ser vista como objeto. A direção do Museu desejou fazer com que a pintura voltasse à sua origem, quando do seu nascimento, deixando-a viver livremente no ar. O sistema já recebeu, naturalmente, mas críticas, mas bastante compreensão.

O Museu de Arte de São Paulo está agora na sua sede definitiva. Não está contudo ainda aberto ao público, o que vai acontecer logo que o conjunto de ar condicionado seja definitivamente instalado. Aqui publicamos algumas fotos do conjunto da Pinacoteca, realizada pelo fotógrafo Jacock.

A direção do Museu de Arte atribui especial atenção à didática. Cada obra tem no seu verso uma prancha explicativa da pintura, com referências à obra e florilégios indicativos do autor e do período que a êle se refere.

12

13

83. "A Rainha, Dr. Assis, e o Museu," *Mirante das Artes, Etc.* 12 (November–December 1968), 12–13. Zeuler R. Lima Collection.

back to the art galleries Bardi once ran in Italy, the exhibition in the MES building in Rio de Janeiro, the couple's projects for the original MASP, and, more recently, Bo Bardi's own museum work in Salvador. Still, it was the first time she had used a transparent material, matching the new building enclosure, to hold paintings. This insightful exhibition layout was groundbreaking in Brazil. It simplified the display of artworks, as Bo Bardi had expected, to its bare essentials. Each easel consisted of a vertical rectangular piece of tempered glass inserted into a roughly cast concrete cube with a triangular notch turned upward, with both glass and cube stabilized by a wooden wedge. By making the supports symbolically imperceptible, she magnified the presence and the visibility of the artworks in the large, transparent hall (figure 84).

All the paintings were turned toward the east side of the long glass prism to face incoming visitors as they dispersed through a dynamic, multicolored constellation. Rather than touching its easel directly, each piece leaned against a white piece of plywood trimmed to the exact proportions of the frame and bolted discreetly onto the glass. No labels, captions, or graphic information were displayed around them. Instead, they offered themselves as human creation, documents for present discoveries, not monuments of the past. Photographs and texts were placed on the backside of the easel, compressed between the plywood and the glass and providing pedagogical information about the artwork for those who considered it necessary. This innovative display — sometimes criticized for its nonconformity with expected standards and even abolished by the administration that followed Bardi — did away with physical and historical hierarchies among artworks, avoiding distinctions between early and modern art, though the collection is predominantly realistic and figurative in its composition. The clear supports contradicted the idea that a museum should reproduce the opaque walls of a bourgeois interior and instead be as transparent socially and politically as they were physically.

Bo Bardi declared herself, in an interview for *O Estado de São Paulo* newspaper, to be "the designer of the museum and of the crystal easel project (paintings are born in the air)." She insisted: "Let me clarify that my intention was to destroy the aura that surrounds museums," confirming her desire to "present the artwork as work and as a prophecy within everyone's reach."[27] Those comments came several months after she had announced in the *Diário de São Paulo* newspaper on the opening day in November 1968 that "many people will be shocked by the brutal appearance of the building." Aware of the controversies she and Bardi were generating, Bo Bardi maintained that the museum's appearance, which "does not hide the construction elements and

leaves raw concrete on display, should be based on a technique reduced to its essentials."[28]

Though the building and the events surrounding its opening were intensely documented, Bo Bardi herself appears in none of the photographs taken during the opening. Another player was missing from the pictures and the event itself. Seven months earlier, on April 4, 1968, Assis Chateaubriand, the polemical press magnate who idealized the creation of MASP and fought to bring it to avenida Paulista, died of a heart attack, after having struggled eight years with debilitating paralysis. Mayor Faria Lima officially named the Trianon Building after Chateaubriand.

Bo Bardi also paid him an unspoken tribute. On the terrace, facing the stairs and the totem that marked the museum's entrance, she had a large, stocky boulder mounted vertically into the ground to symbolize the chubby man who had given her so many opportunities in her new country. She surrounded the boulder with a small garden of plants from Chateaubriand's native Nordeste (and her mythical land). She found a special place for a *mandacaru*, a tall, slender, and very resistant cactus with vertical branches that grows in the area in Nordeste where Chateaubriand was born and which had been an iconic plant among early Brazilian modernists who used to meet in the ballroom that once stood on the museum lot.[29] She could not get all the mineral and floral elements she wanted to cover MASP, but with this homage of a rock and a plant, she was able to condense their meaning into a single and powerful gesture greeting visitors.

For all the pomp and circumstance of the official opening in November 1968, the public had to wait to visit the museum until the Civic Hall was completed, furniture was installed, and the first temporary exhibition was set up in the lower gallery of the elevated volume. On the evening of Friday, April 7, 1969, the last day of Mayor Faria Lima's five-year term, MASP welcomed selected guests.[30] The people, Bo Bardi's targeted audience, finally entered it over the weekend that followed this ceremony.

Whether approached from the valley of avenida Nove de Julho as if it were an acropolis or from the top of avenida Paulista as if a surprising hiatus in the dense line of buildings, MASP created a new reference in the physical space and collective life of São Paulo. It gave the contested site of the historic Belvedere do Trianon new meaning and the city a reinvented public space. The Bardis created a unique, innovative museological program as well as a new cultural magnet open to anyone who wished to venture inside as protagonists of their architectural and artistic creation.[31] Moreover, as the city grew vertically and horizontally, the span of MASP (as the void underneath the glazed museum is called) incorporated the terrace into a dense urban fabric

84. MASP, São Paulo, 1957–68, view of the original layout of the
collection room with glass easels. MASP Collection.

with few open public spaces. Consequently, the plaza became a referential meeting point and landmark in the city in addition to providing an outlook to the surrounding landscape.

From the outset and despite its success, the museum faced maintenance challenges that only grew over time. Though the Bardi couple sometimes blamed the contractors for bad waterproofing, most problems derived from the combination of a difficult construction process with innovative technology, as well as from institutional and financial setbacks. Even before the main galleries opened to the public in 1969, water leaks appeared in the upper floor and supporting piers. Faithful to her desire to leave the concrete structure as raw as possible and to the widespread belief at the time of construction that pre-stressed concrete structures were naturally impermeable, Bo Bardi had authorized treating only the unexposed concrete roof slab and joists against water.[32]

Leaching and structural problems continued to develop with a few in-house attempts to resolve them throughout the 1970s until the museum was temporarily closed in 1988 for repairs. By then, problems included not just water leaks but cracks in the concrete structure, rusting mullions, and even lack of funding, which put the collection at great risk. To Bo Bardi's dismay, consultants from Figueiredo Ferraz's office suggested, at the time of the renovation, removing and redoing the old waterproofing and insulation system and recovering the concrete structure wherever it presented problems.[33] As as result, the beams and piers that supported the elevated block could no longer be left in their raw state. They could be covered with transparent sealing, but their rough appearance would be changed. Instead of trying to disguise the inevitable visual effect of the waterproofing treatment, Bo Bardi compromised on a striking chromatic effect, having the external piers and beams stained with a semigloss acrylic red paint just as she had portrayed the structure of the São Vicente museum on the cover of *Habitat* in 1951.[34] The idea for the colored structural elements was also present in a few of her original drawings for MASP, before being discarded in favor of raw concrete at the height of the brutalist vogue among São Paulo architects. Forty years later, at the end of 1991 and just a few months before Bo Bardi's death, the red painting was finally completed (figure 85).[35]

After her passing, the museum suffered other changes as the result of a complex set of fiscal and administrative conditions, especially after a new board of directors replaced Pietro Maria Bardi following his retirement in 1994 from his almost lifelong position as museum director. With the Bardis gone from MASP, emergency responses to inherited budget

and operational problems and a much narrower museological vision — especially during architect and developer Júlio Neves's long tenure as director — dramatically affected the museum's original spatial layout and its mission as a cultural center. Since then, among the unrealized ideas proposed by succeeding administrators to raise funds for the museum, Neves's administration envisioned an electronic billboard set up on the elevated volume and, between 2004 and 2007, a project to build a tall tower topped by a restaurant on the adjacent site that would have dwarfed the museum. Meanwhile, administrators did carry out renovation work, but they radically transformed its interior. The remodeling projects were primarily concerned with the necessary safety and conservation of the building and with the need to update technical equipment and spaces. In effect, however, they grossly erased the museological features that gave the museum its unique aesthetic and spatial identity. Among the problems that have resulted from the renovations are the drastic changes in the previously open access to the museum and in the layout of the permanent collection hall, which has since generated many — though ineffective — protests.

Instead of promoting technical solutions that combined conservation improvements for the collection and the preservation of the unique display and architecture, the board of directors who came after Bardi opted to replace the transparent easels with a maze of ordinary opaque partitions. Not only did this decision introduce conventional museum walls in a transparent space and block the visibility between the elevated hall and the city, it erased the unique atmosphere of the permanent collection and the nonhierarchical character of the original — and now historical — museological project. Moreover, justified by the concern with budget and property and personal safety, new administrators closed the main staircase that gave access to the elevated volume, restricted the museum entrance, and began to charge admission fees. Such uncompromising actions found shortcuts to minimize practical problems at the cost of the collective and popular purposes the Bardis had imagined for the museum.

Still, despite all the financial problems, layout changes, and restrictions on public use, MASP and Belvedere do Trianon did not lose their symbolic presence in the collective identity of São Paulo and in the physical space of avenida Paulista. On the contrary, the convergence between them and the city continues to enjoy a privileged position without equivalence in the social, cultural, and political life of the metropolis. And though the changes made to the museum have disfigured the Bardis' contribution and legacy to São Paulo's cultural life, the architecture, with its beguiling boldness and welcoming clarity, persists. "The wide span of MASP was not an 'architectural affectation,'" Bo Bardi

85. MASP, São Paulo, 1957–68, southeastern view of the elevated galleries and plinth with red column. Photograph by Zeuler R. Lima.

the early themes of rationalism that have become so unpopular."[37] In reaction, she compared the brutality of the raw concrete and the museum's naked shapes to "eliminating the cultural snobbery that is so dear to contemporary intellectuals and architects."[38]

Despite the obstacles and ambiguities in its design and construction process, the MASP building on avenida Paulista produced innovative and unmatched spaces as well as visual narratives that translate an unusual sense of social inclusion in São Paulo. As such, it became a key reference in the city and in Bo Bardi's small but powerful body of work. "Intellectuals did not like it," she reflected about her project late in life, "but the people did." She would likely have been satisfied to see that the spontaneity of everyday life is powerful and that people continue to play an important role as protagonists of her architecture. "I was not looking for prettiness," Bo Bardi noted. She was looking for something authentic and human: "I looked for freedom."[39]

insisted at the end of her life. "I looked for simple architecture, an architecture that could immediately communicate that which, in the past, was called monumental, meaning the sense of collective, civic dignity." In agreement with Bardi's vision and contradicting the new board of directors' decision to clutter the collection hall and surrender MASP to private interests, Bo Bardi had maintained: "A new museum should open its doors, let in fresh air, new light."[36] And so it did, against the odds.

The museum conceived by the Bardis enjoyed a successful public reception soon after its opening, though it was long neglected by the mainstream media and established architectural scholars. Bo Bardi was aware of the resistance the museum and her project for it caused among modernist São Paulo architects. They had likely not paid attention to her article about it in *Mirante das Artes, Etc.*, in which she said, "The Trianon complex repositioned, in its simplicity,

With the ingenuity of everyday people in mind, Lina Bo Bardi celebrated the public opening of MASP in April 1969 by staging a large temporary exhibition, which her husband titled *A Mão do Povo Brasileiro* (The hand of the Brazilian people).[1] Although the museum collection crowned the new building with its crystalline display of international masterpieces, this hefty but unpretentious show opened the gallery below, where the Bardis promoted all kinds of aesthetic creation in Brazil. The new gathering of popular objects on display expanded the *Bahia* and *Nordeste* exhibitions with additions from different regions gathered by P. M. Bardi and his assistants, whose individual contributions were lost over time.[2] This tribute to everyday creation paved the way for shows Bo Bardi would organize more than a decade later at SESC Pompeia cultural and leisure center.

After this exhibition, however, Bo Bardi became less involved with her husband's work in the museum.[3] At the same time, her professional activities were increasingly affected by the social tensions that rose around the country in response to an increasingly repressive regime. The melancholy that Bo Bardi had expressed in a letter to Zevi a few years earlier would eventually lead to disenchantment and even a short exile from Brazil.[4] Though the new MASP building corresponded to the rising brutalist aesthetics embraced by São Paulo architects, she received no substantial commissions between the late 1960s and the mid-1970s and instead engaged in radical artistic experiences as a curator and worked on theater and film productions. Despite this long-term distance from the drawing board, she did not give up on her belief that architects should engage in actions with collective relevance, which she developed in other media.

The exhibition of popular artifacts inaugurating the museum followed that goal and was, like the permanent collection, a great public success. Lines of curious visitors meandered under the wide concrete canopy and slowly climbed the stairs to enter the temporary exhibition hall.[5] The large room recalled many of Bo Bardi's drawings from previous curatorial projects. The symmetrical perspective of the deep space was framed by three large, anthropomorphic figures at the entrance. Flanking the wide door, two tall plaster and papier-mâché puppets with oversized heads and long, striped floral gowns gazed solemnly at each other above visitors' heads. At the center of the perspective, they announced a large baroque image of Saint George sitting on a wooden trestle covered with fabric to imitate a horse. Above this unusual composition, a small altar canopy hung from the ceiling, adorned with colorful paper-cut flags. This larger-than-life icon seemed to lead a carefully organized regiment of simple, handcrafted objects as though they could march right out of the museum and onto the streets (figure 86).

86. *The Hand of Brazilian People* exhibition, MASP, São Paulo, 1969, view from the entrance. Photographed by Hans Günther Flieg. Instituto Moreira Salles Collection.

In contrast to the industrial materials chosen for mounting the permanent collection, Bo Bardi placed the objects for this show on simple handmade stands. Against the whitewashed concrete wall at the back of the hall, she displayed seven large colorful quilts and covered the side walls with wooden shelves and panels, as at the Unhão complex in Salvador. These held small items such as kitchen utensils, farm tools, toys, and ceramic pieces. On the rubber floor, she placed a grid of low-rising pinewood platforms of different sizes organized in nine transversal rows with four longitudinal corridors between them. She reserved the platforms for large pieces, including a rustic childbirthing chair,

flowerpots made of old rubber tires, and canoes. She even presented Gonçalves's large carrancas on the same three-legged trestles she had designed for their display in Rome.

According to Bo Bardi, *A Mão do Povo Brasileiro* was the "presentation of creativity and possibilities of everyday craft" rather than a collection of "art as consolation to poverty." "I did not want it to be interpreted that way," she insisted. As a result, the exhibition allowed her to work out her concerns about a letter she received in 1967 from former minister Celso Furtado, in which he criticized her plan to document Brazilian handmade objects. He warned her about "the risk of stopping at the identification phase and ending up like the literature produced about the Nordeste, which only tangentially addressed problems and served as a tranquilizer for those who can't sleep during their afternoon nap."[6] She was upset that he had compared her intent to a "sentimental vision of the Nordeste that is well suited to middle-class mentality." But she declared, agreeing with his original suggestion: "I am convinced that everything that makes poverty acceptable must be destroyed."[7]

From this point on, Bo Bardi distanced herself from initiatives to preserve handicraft and insisted on calling them "popular facts" and "pre-craftsmanship" instead of popular art. She had difficulty giving the exhibition a political connotation as she tried to avoid associations with the compliant meaning suggested by Furtado. As the Bardis' collection of handmade objects grew, it gradually lost the value Bo Bardi attributed to it as the result of the everyday struggles of anonymous people in the country's backlands. Though enthusiastic about the accomplishments of the exhibition, she began to see signs of a conceptual and practical impasse that would lead to gloomier conclusions a decade later.

While still preparing the show, Bo Bardi left town between November and December 1968 to pursue another project, in different media but facing similar issues.[8] She traveled back to her beloved Nordeste, this time to the small town of Brejo Seco in the hinterland of Pernambuco state. She finally had the chance to spend a long period in the semiarid Agreste while working on the film production of *A compadecida* (Our Lady of Compassion), for which she produced the set design, or scenic architecture, as she preferred to call it.

The director of this unusual film was George Jonas, a Hungarian-born Jewish cinema enthusiast and creator of the first film laboratory in Brazil.[9] His film was based on the acclaimed 1955 theatrical tragic comedy *O auto da compadecida* (The penance of Our Lady of Compassion) by writer Ariano Suassuna, a staunch defender of Nordeste culture. The satiric story of two poor, cunning friends who try to fool local religious and political leaders and suffer the consequences depicts an allegory of the region's endemic problems. Jonas, Bo Bardi, and Francisco Brennand — with his allegorical regional costumes — turned the story into a colorful pantomime set in the quintessential Brazilian rural community of Brejo Seco. Lying at the bottom of a bowl-shaped valley amid rocky hills was the main stage Bo Bardi depicted in her drawings: the town's arid plaza scorched by the sun and squared off by houses with arched doors and windows, a church, and the courthouse (figure 87). In the middle of the plaza, she displayed makeshift market and amusement stalls built, like the objects in the exhibition at

MASP, produced with simple materials and profuse colors (figure 88).

The interior sets were sparsely furnished with chairs, a hammock hanging from nails on the wall, and simple, locally found objects. Just outside the town square, a small blue circus tent framed the opening scene, showing the female protagonist riding around the ring on horseback.[10] In such simple sets, Bo Bardi created spaces that were visually choreographed but had no clear sign of a conventional designer, only the implied hands of local people.

The film had its first screening in November 1969, when Bo Bardi was again involved with theatrical productions.[11] The press complimented her work, but the production itself received negative responses from both sides of a polarized public.[12] Progressive critics dismissed the film as too lighthearted for the confrontational standards of Cinema Novo, while a reactionary priest spearheaded a public campaign against it, calling it offensive to family and clerical structures.[13]

Those contrasting viewpoints illustrated the increasingly tense atmosphere in Brazil that culminated on December 13, 1968, with the decree of the Fifth Institutional Act (AI-5). The act curtailed civil liberties and rights, consolidating the ambition of hard-line military leaders who refused to relinquish power to democratic rule. While radical militants incited uprisings and armed struggles, the military persecuted dissidents, and the situation remained particularly critical and brutal until March 1974, the end of the third military president's term. This period, known as the Years of Lead, was accompanied by a technocratic development model legitimized in the slogan "Economic Miracle" and through propaganda of Brazil as a great power.[14]

Until the first international oil crisis in 1973, when that optimistic image started to dissolve, the dictatorial regime favored public planning offices and engineering and construction firms, leaving architects in a bind. To make a living out of design, one had to decide whether to comply with the system. In a Faustian dilemma, progressive Brazilian architects, artists, and intellectuals felt tormented by seeing themselves as bearers of progressive values amid economic underdevelopment, social conservatism, and political repression.[15] Like some of them, Bo Bardi viewed conventional architectural practice as a bourgeois activity to be questioned and even refuted.

The waning utopian energies of the late 1950s and early 1960s and the image of a national-popular culture yielded ideological conflicts across all political orientations in Brazil.[16] However, from the springboard of her sympathy for leftist causes, Bo Bardi plunged headlong into

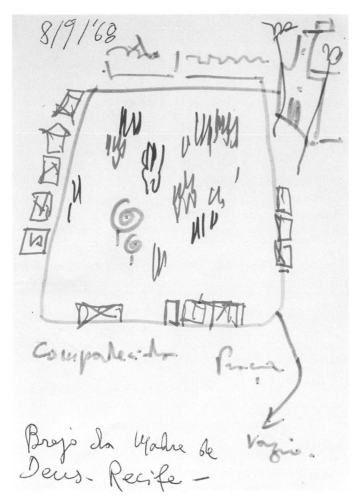

87. Lina Bo Bardi, *Staging the Main Square of Brejo da Madre de Deus*, diary notes on the production of *A compadecida*, September 8, 1968, p. 103, 15 × 11 cm. ILBPMB Collection.

88. Lina Bo Bardi, article about the production of *A compadecida*, highlighting Bo Bardi's scenic architecture and Brennand's costume design, *Mirante das Artes, Etc.* 12 (November–December 1968), 18. Zeuler R. Lima Collection.

the undercurrent of revolutionary debate and found new company among a younger, politicized generation. Now, in her maturity, she did what she had flirted with in her youth: she sharpened her convictions and her image as an activist designer, emulating the politicized Italian architects and intellectuals who were partisans in the resistance and whom she had admired during the war years, retrospectively suggesting her participation in the Italian liberation movement. She shed all vestiges of the elegant woman in high heels for the bohemian outlook she had begun to develop in Salvador. She collected Maoist poetry and Che Guevara photos and changed her reading habits to leftist literature.[17] She claimed to be a Stalinist, dismissing the Bolshevik revolutionary's authoritarianism and remembering him instead as a pragmatic leader and war hero.

As Bo Bardi changed her political discourse, she radicalized her design aesthetics and experiences, moving away from architecture for several years — her final study marking that transition was a preliminary project resembling a colonial rural house — and toward organizing events and, especially, stage productions.[18] In 1969, she was invited to design a stall for América Fabril at Fenit, the national textile fair, leaving a couple of sketches for a floating canopy of colorful fabric over a helicoidal catwalk.[19] Above all, she started working with José Celso Martinez Corrêa, director of Teatro Oficina (Workshop theater company), after being introduced by their common friend, filmmaker Glauber Rocha. The Oficina group (represented by an anvil) was a revolutionary cyclone, pushing political discourse and counterculture off the stage. With them, Bo Bardi moved from intellectually irreverent productions with Martim Gonçalves to ideologically and physically brutal plays. Later in life, when talking about her experience with scenic production, she said, "Theater is my way of participating in politics."[20]

Martinez Corrêa, whose company was a stronghold of resistance against the military regime, invited Bo Bardi to collaborate with him in the production of Bertolt Brecht's tragic drama *In the Jungle of Cities*. Their shared anticonformist outlook brought them together both intellectually and aesthetically. On the one hand, she joined him in July 1969, searching for experiences with design simplification. On the other hand, he offered her the ideas of Polish director Jerzy Grotowski's "poor theater," in which everything superfluous must be eliminated, especially the separation between stage and audience. Later in life, she remembered, "I think my ideas on poor theater, which I identify with the most modern ideas of poor architecture . . . , coincided with the type of production [Corrêa] wanted for the young Brecht's play."[21]

Aggression and anarchism, the basic drives of the play, permeated Teatro Oficina's lengthy performance. Bo Bardi found a bare space with a central revolving platform, an exposed structure, and no curtains in the company's long, narrow building, which had been renovated because of a fire that partially destroyed it in 1967.[22] After reading Brecht's introductory notes about a "wrestling match between two men and . . . the downfall of a family" and having produced a few expressive watercolors, Bo Bardi transformed the theater into a boxing ring for a production set in eleven rounds.[23] She had the rotating stage removed and replaced with a podium and added an extra set of stepped seats on the other side of the platform, unfolding the original proscenium into an arena with two auditoriums facing each other. With this design, she finally succeeded in creating the central stage she had wanted for MASP, setting a precedent for the theater she would design for SESC Pompeia more than a decade later.

To accentuate the play's aggressive atmosphere, Bo Bardi evoked images of the mystical northeastern sertão and included objects found in neighborhood dumpsters and debris from the construction site of the large elevated expressway across the street — nicknamed "Minhocão" ("big earthworm," one of São Paulo's most unpopular urban eyesores).[24] She also had graffiti painted on the sidewalls, using words and phrases she had heard from uneducated construction workers and protesting student leaders.[25] She even included the slogan coined by Mayor Faria Lima (who backed the expressway) for his administration — "To São Paulo, the city that humanizes itself" — mocking its intention by presenting it as graffiti and conveniently forgetting his administration's financial support of MASP. With rocks, improvised furniture, old cans, and cheap perfume, Bo

Bardi brought together onstage the aesthetics of hunger, the aesthetics of rubbish, and the aesthetics of a red-light district.

Around the city, posters advertised the play with such catchphrases as "Watch a violent fight between two men" and "An experience in hell," while middle-class crowds crammed the small theater to watch performances that ran nearly four hours.[26] At the end of each "round for the destruction of everything," actors engaged in hand-to-hand fighting and smashed many of the scenic objects in fury, leaving a growing pile of rubble next to the stage-ring.[27] Bo Bardi's design for the play temporarily reduced her discourse on rationalism from its formal principles to little more than its political impulse. Instead of organizing objects, as for the museum collection, she set them up to be shattered in the theater. While the Oficina troupe took on almost suicidal performances, she engaged in the death of the conventional architect as form-giver.

In the Jungle of Cities closed in São Paulo on October 5, 1969, and moved to Teatro João Caetano in Rio de Janeiro, reaching Belo Horizonte, capital of Minas Gerais state, a few weeks later. However, the production ended prematurely when the leading actress was accidentally thrown several meters into the audience through the violent action of her costars and injured. The line between reality and fiction collapsed both on stage and in the company's emerging internal crisis. Though many of the actors left Martinez Corrêa after that incident, a few of his followers engaged in a new film and another play production in the next two years, again inviting Bo Bardi to contribute with her design skills.

One collaboration was *Prata Palomares*, a controversial film directed by André Faria Júnior. The plot involves two guerrilla leaders who hide in the chapel of a small fishing village and wait for an opportunity to escape. In 1970, Bo Bardi traveled to Florianópolis, the coastal capital of southern Santa Catarina state, to help Faria and his assistant, Carlos Ebert, in the production. She organized a very simple setting. Among the records she left are a few photographs and a note showing the use of existing buildings, new and old, alongside found objects and dramatic lighting. Again, she distanced herself from an abstract conception of design and engaged in direct action. The film was scheduled for release in 1971, at the height of the combat between guerrilla leaders and the military, but the Brazilian government censored it, and although a clandestine copy was screened at the Cannes Film Festival, it received little public exposure in Brazil.

Also in 1970, Bo Bardi designed another unusual scenic project, not for a theater or film company, but for the Fifth International Congress of Psychodrama, held in August at MASP for three thousand participants. When the organizers contacted her, she was hesitant but finally agreed to do it after identifying herself with the libertarian political philosophy of the creator of psychodrama, Jacob Levy Moreno.[28] With cultural initiatives such as Paulo Freire's book *Pedagogia do oprimido* (Pedagogy of the oppressed) and Augusto Boal's militant philosophy "Teatro do Oprimido" (Theater of the oppressed) under censorship by the military, the congress was cathartic for participants though it was carefully monitored for suspicious activities.[29]

Bo Bardi embarked on this adventure with gusto and turned the museum's Civic Hall into a large, horseshoe-shaped amphitheater that could be transformed by moving simple platforms, chairs, and props. On the plywood partitions surrounding the theater, she inscribed thought-provoking sentences from Moreno's books in red paint.[30] She also designed six mobile, wood-framed stands for public workshops and role-playing sessions. Through this experience, she found a new dimension to the relationship among theater, architecture, and lived space that had been suggested in the lectures she gave in Salvador a decade earlier. New protagonists were introduced to the scene, re-creating, to her enjoyment, the museum's physical and existential space. She was delighted that about three thousand people had filled up the spaces of the museum she had designed in search of freedom. A couple of months later, she would return to that concept as she designed an exhibition of Cândido Portinari's works at MASP based on a grid-ded wooden scaffolding to support the works and allow for random movement among paintings. Her aesthetic quest had gained political overtones.

The theater and film productions and the psychodrama event were not the only risky flirtations Bo Bardi made toward the wary eyes of the military regime. Soon after the congress ended, a policeman representing the Serviço Nacional de Informações, the Brazilian intelligence agency, appeared at her door. He had an order for her to testify about a compromising episode that had taken place in 1968, when she opened her house to a secret meeting among leaders of armed guerrilla groups. In her official testimony, she said she was merely responding to a request made by activist Dulce Maia (a frequent presence in MASP's inner circles) to discuss the preparation of a modern art exhibition for the new museum with the presence of her acquaintance architect Sérgio Ferro, who was also involved in radical political activities.[31] On December 9, 1970, Bo Bardi presented herself for a three-hour cross-examination at the Second Army Command in downtown São Paulo.[32]

The interrogation was part of several investigations organized by the military police to intimidate the cultural left.[33] According to Bo Bardi's defense documents, which appeared between 1972 and 1973, she stated that she did not participate in the meeting and did not know the nature of its discussion. She mentioned later having heard Maia had been arrested like Ferro. Bo Bardi also said she only recognized the other individuals who had been in her house when she saw a picture of one of the guerrilla leaders in the newspaper after he was killed. Finally, she stressed that, in the cross-examination, Ferro confirmed her statements. However, she did not feel safe.

After the questioning, Bo Bardi quietly prepared her luggage for a trip to Italy. Just over a week later, on December 19, 1970, she showed up at her sister's apartment in Milan by surprise.[34] She spent several months away from Brazil traveling between her family and a weekend apartment in a building that sat on a cliff overlooking a small plaza and the sea in the village of Bogliasco, just outside Genoa.[35] During this period, she read new literature, including works by Roland Barthes, Claude Lévi-Strauss, and Franz Boas.[36] She continued to think about handicraft in an anthropological light, writing, "Handwork (art) in the Nordeste expresses the passage from nature to culture," and, noting soon after, "the art produced by the people is always beautiful."[37]

Just as Bo Bardi's crisis with Tavares at MAMB had caused her to leave the Nordeste, so her sympathy for revolutionary groups led her out of Brazil.[38] Eventually, Bardi flew to Italy to help prepare his wife's legal case. In late 1971, at the height of military action against guerrilla groups, she returned to São Paulo, where she remained mostly quiet and, with the help of a defense attorney, studied the Brazilian civil code, under an investigation that would endure for two years.[39] Still, her judicial case did not keep her from engaging in new and irreverent theatrical experiences with Martinez Corrêa.

In 1972, Teatro Oficina produced a collective play, *Gracias, señor* (based on fragments of texts by modernist author Oswald de Andrade), inaugurating the group's new configuration and philosophy. Since the company's breakup after *In the Jungle of Cities*, its remaining members had been producing happenings and street performances around the country. *Gracias, señor* took them back indoors. However, Martinez Corrêa wanted the production to be an open play, with action spread throughout the whole space and directly engaging viewers.[40] In response, Bo Bardi's design organized simple, void spaces for improvisation in two different productions in Rio de Janeiro and São Paulo, in February and April 1972, respectively.[41]

In both productions, Bo Bardi emphasized people, not architectural forms, as protagonists. For the Rio de Janeiro production, she left the stage in its raw state, adding only simple props and graffiti protests on the walls. Above the

89. Lina Bo Bardi, *Study for Piolin Circus at MASP*, April 3, 1972.
Watercolor, felt pen, and ballpoint pen on cardstock, 32.1 × 47 cm.
ILBPMB Collection.

stage, she hung a large straitjacket from the ceiling with ropes and pulleys, which allowed actors to transform it into a large sail.[42] In São Paulo, she incorporated a large hole in the stage, left from a previous production, and added two watchtowers, scaffoldings, and bleachers around the square stage.[43] The play's lengthy performances (eight hours on two consecutive days) pushed the boundaries of theater into psychodrama and open aggression, dividing audiences and critics around its hostility.[44] Still, the controversy was short-lived, since the play was censored in June 1972 and never completed its planned tour around the country. Bo Bardi would later work with Martinez Corrêa in renovating his theater, but she would no longer collaborate in his dramatic productions.

While *Gracias, señor* opened in São Paulo, Bo Bardi gravitated toward MASP with another thought-provoking idea to celebrate the fiftieth anniversary of the 1922 Semana de Arte Moderna (Modern art week), a cultural milestone in Brazil conceived in the restaurant of the original Belvedere

do Trianon, now replaced by the museum's Civic Hall. Instead of focusing on the erudite and anti-academic aspects of the event, she sought out its popular roots. In a reverential and, at the same time, irreverent gesture, she had the popular Circo Piolin (Piolin circus) temporarily installed in the middle of the plaza beneath the museum's large concrete slab.[45] Piolin, the circus owner, was an actor, acrobat, and clown whom early modernists imbued with nationalist and folksy characteristics and who was regarded as an authentic Brazilian popular artist. In her colorful project notes, Bo Bardi described the event as "the greatest spectacle in the world" (figure 89).[46]

More than a year later, between August 17 and September 3, 1973, and without much design work despite having considered participating in two international competitions — the urban renovation of the city center of Santiago, Chile, and the new opera house of Belgrade, Yugoslavia — Bo Bardi paid another tribute at MASP. With the help of Carioca set designer Hélio Eichbauer, she organized a retrospective exhibition about Eros Martim Gonçalves's life-long contribution to Brazilian drama. It had been almost six months since her friend and close collaborator in Salvador had died. She was still mourning the loss of one of her main intellectual allies during a difficult period of her life as the military investigation against her was coming to an end.

Subject to pervasive tensions around the country, the military regime was entering a long crisis and losing its tight control of political persecution, but it continued to hold power. Bo Bardi was disillusioned about the Brazilian political situation and her prospects as a designer. For at least three years, she had no work in sight. With the exception of a series of small, unidentified sketches for a large cubic library drawn on a newsprint block in 1972 with a few notes in Italian, no other dated records of her building design exist until 1975. Meanwhile, she maintained a growing number of friends and acquaintances among like-minded artists and intellectuals, including old collaborators like art critic Flávio Motta and young people like designer Flávio Império, who began migrating toward her company in long weekly lunches at the Glass House.[47] During this time, and in line with their discussions, she discovered and devoured the work of thinkers such as Karl Marx and Herbert Marcuse.[48]

Among the few trips she took during this period were some of her last visits to Italy. In encounters with her friends Fabrizio Clerici and Bruno Zevi, she described longing for her youth in Milan, and during a visit to a Milanese doctor she was diagnosed as "suffering from depressive syndrome."[49] Zevi was sensitive to Bo Bardi's struggles and published an article about their conversations in his weekly column for *L'Espresso* newspaper in February 1973. He described her time in Bahia as an "encounter with the authentic Brazil," and mentioned that her project for MASP "reflects its architect's anxious temperament," and, "though rationalist . . . it reveals a message full of contradictions." He also wrote that "Lina is on trial for an unknown subversive action, but she does not even think about returning to Italy. Here everything seems bland and compromising, she cannot stand the resigned attitude of her old friends."[50]

Several months later, in April 1974, Bo Bardi wrote to Zevi criticizing his latest book *Il linguaggio moderno dell'architettura* (The modern language of architecture). She considered his concern with modernism as a language as a "pseudo-problem." She protested, "The problem is of a different kind. It does not matter whether architecture is 'modern' or not; it is important that it is valid." Instead of establishing abstract invariants as he proposed, she insisted, "The question is to CHANGE architecture as it has never been done before." She was aware that cultural resetting would likely not happen and said: "Authentically creative

spirits have never gone back to zero, they have violently revolutionized; and a revolution is the subversion of what exists, plus the future." Her letter ended as it started, stressing that the international crisis of architecture in the face of postmodern developments was not aesthetic but political. To her, architects still had an irreplaceable role in the pursuit of collective goals. "After all," she concluded, "since 1945, I know we cannot do without it."[51]

In August 1974, Zevi published Bo Bardi's letter as a manifesto in his magazine *L'Architettura: Cronache e Storia*, adding a response to her ideas. He explained his theoretical points and warned readers with wit and affection: "You should never want to argue with Lina Bo Bardi. She has such fury, generous impetuosity, and restless quest for a true, stark reality. Especially since living in Brazil, she no longer tolerates European, and especially Italian, intellectual acrobatics." He was especially aware that "when she returns to Milan and Rome, she is always impatient. She wants to scratch the surface of things to see if, behind them, there is still something authentic."[52]

Rehearsing an Anthropological Quest

The uncertainty Lina Bo Bardi experienced after the conclusion of her project for MASP was pervasive among Brazilian architects in the mid-1970s. A decade of authoritarian rule had altered the country. The atmosphere remained one of fear, but as economic hardships triggered by failed national programs and the international oil crisis increased, the regime's propaganda of Brazil as a great power fell apart. It became hard for the military to justify the state of national security, and the government was forced to alter its hard-line policies and begin the long, slow process that eventually led to a return to democratic rule.

The Brazilian cultural milieu was affected, too, destabilizing some of the ideas and hopes so dear to Bo Bardi. With the turn toward mass production and individualism, many artists no longer struggled for political causes and instead worked for the cultural industry. The notion of a national-popular culture pursued by a previous generation was increasingly discarded as mere populism. Romantic-revolutionary energies dissipated, and a generalized disenchantment nurtured an epistemological crisis that ended the radical efforts for the socialization of Brazilian culture. Still, for all those collective hurdles and personal struggles, Bo Bardi did not give up on her longing for socially and culturally sensitive design, and she gradually found new motivation in her work between 1974 and 1975. At age sixty, she was entering the most productive phase of her career.

Bo Bardi kept scratching the surface of the realities around her, looking for the survivors of preindustrial manufacturing and trying to bring the everyday world into her work and, whenever possible, into the museum. Among the younger crowd she charmed in those years was Edmar José de Almeida, an artist from Uberlândia (in the western part of Minas Gerais state) who was living in São Paulo.[1] She became interested in the tapestry workshop he coordinated in Martinésia, a small, rural village twenty kilometers (12 mi.) north of his hometown, with a group of local artisans (most of them uneducated women), and he arranged with Bardi to exhibit their work at MASP. In August 1974, Bo Bardi and de Almeida began planning a show titled *Repassos* (Weaving patterns) that opened just over a year later, on September 9, 1975, and ran for three weeks.[2] Meanwhile, they traveled with a group of friends to Uberlândia to visit the workshop and collect documentation for the show. Artist Flávio Império filmed a documentary about the activities of tapestry weavers. Psychoanalyst Alan Meyer and curator Luís Hossaka handled the photography, while de Almeida commanded the manufacturing team and Bo Bardi organized the exhibition setup.

Bo Bardi saw this as an opportunity to revisit and to expand her incomplete project for the Museu de Arte Popular in Salvador. The exhibition focused less on products than on the process for creating and handing down graphic weaving patterns particular to the central region of Brazil. Aside from large tapestries hanging from the ceiling, photographic panels and a film projection produced by the team depicted the simple and self-sustained work the weavers of Martinésia performed in the face of economic scarcity. The documentation of the artisans' daily work was complemented by a loom with baskets and rolls of yarn on its side placed in the middle of the hall with live demonstrations during the opening ceremony. Anticipating what would later become the practice of art installations, but also denouncing the economic inequities of industrial capitalism, Bo Bardi described this award-winning exhibition as an "environment-space."[3]

In a simple manila brochure, she cautioned visitors: "This is not an exhibition of religious art." "In difficult times in the history of a country," she added, "mysticism is the last resort to drive one away from passivity." Instead, she described it as a "document-exhibition" of human work created under adverse conditions and not artistic skill or spiritual sentiment. She was interested in expressing the "urge to make things, to put one's creativity at someone else's service, and [in expressing] the search for a more dignified human situation." The show extended her call for "a collective form of self-criticism," she wrote, explaining that "Edmar simply registered things, facts, and possibilities in the cerrado [savanna backlands of Minas Gerais]." To her, this was "a small contribution to the great collective awareness [to] denounce the perversity of a[n economic] system that believed in 'industrial design' as a purifying force."[4]

By documenting that work, Bo Bardi honed her evolving theoretical approach to design, describing it as "an anthropologically framed artistic research."[5] With that goal in mind and through her friendships with a younger generation of artists and designers, she regained interest in developing other projects. During the preparation of the Repassos exhibition, she accompanied architect Joaquim Guedes on a trip to Madrid, where he participated in the Twelfth World Congress of the International Architects' Union in May 1975. Though she was skeptical about the congress's debates about technology, describing them as "a Babel Tower," she met prominent Spanish and Portuguese architects who demonstrated knowledge of her work and who shared her political concerns.[6] She extended her trip with stops in Morocco, Barcelona, Paris, Rome, and Milan, all of which reinvigorated her confidence and reawakened her dormant interest in design practice.[7]

In August 1975 artist Rubens Gerchman invited Bo Bardi to return to Rio de Janeiro. He had been named director of the Fine Arts Institute at Parque Lage and had renamed it Escola de Artes Visuais (EAV, Visual arts school), instituting a new curriculum based on the idea that artistic practices should not be limited to traditional in-studio creation. Gerchman offered her the project of designing new workshop spaces and wished to discuss interdisciplinary collaborations with her. It is thought that Bo Bardi produced drawings for the workshops, but, even though she left a few unidentified drawings, it is not clear whether her studies for EAV are among them. The school operated out of an old manor house, but it soon became a hothouse of avant-garde aesthetics in Brazil, and Bo Bardi returned a year later to introduce a retrospective exhibition about the pedagogical work of artist and set designer Hélio Eichbauer, one of the school's leading instructors. She described his experience as developing "design as total behavior," instead of traditional and smothered, in all scales of production, by consumption and power relations. She also advocated ideas from her youth in Italy that still resonated in Brazil. Her introduction stressed the need to "achieve freedom: collective freedom, not individual freedom. To replace 'Me' with 'Us.'"[8]

With those ideas in mind, Bo Bardi joined the design team for a community resettlement project in her beloved Nordeste on September 9, 1975, the same day the Repassos exhibition opened. The Camurupim Community Project, as it was called, aimed to relocate rural populations around Propiá, a poor village about one hundred kilometers (62 mi.) north of Aracaju, the state capital of Sergipe, and on the border of Alagoas. Through personal contacts with MASP's staff and board members, she signed a contract with the Brazilian subsidiary of the Italian engineering firm ELC Electroconsult, which was responsible for dams, irrigation, and agricultural development projects in Brazil.[9] Bo Bardi was in charge of architecture and urban design and of lodging for three hundred farmers and one hundred other workers and their families.

The company's plan for Propriá had been in motion since December 1973, when the military government, during the international oil crisis, started to study a large irrigation project associated with the creation of hydroelectric power plants along the lower valley of the São Francisco river in the semiarid Agreste.[10] Loosely modeled after the US Tennessee Valley Authority project developed during the Great Depression, the Brazilian plan aimed at economic development while guardedly containing the potential for rural uprisings in the region. Oblivious to the broader political ambiguities of such a project, Bo Bardi remained involved with the technical team for two years, until November 1977, when her project was canceled because of disagreements about her concepts and methods. Though her ideas for the community never materialized, they represent both her return to architecture design after having been without concrete commissions for ten years and her renewed effort to ground her practice and discourse in environmental and social advocacy.

This was Bo Bardi's first urbanization project. Soon after signing her contract, she traveled initially to Recife to meet with Electroconsult regional representatives and the engineering team and from there to Propriá. During her visit, she intuitively observed how the community adapted to harsh geographic and economic conditions rather than conducting rigorous scientific assessments.[11] Later, she received photographs and a survey of living habits and standards prepared by the company.[12]

Her initial studies, produced between October and November 1976 and one year after signing the contract, show a rural agglomeration of about 2.5 square kilometers (1 sq. mi.) with about four hundred circular, modular lots measuring 3,000 square meters (32,300 sq. ft.) displayed around the slopes of a bluff.[13] She located the community center with institutional buildings atop the hill. According to Bo Bardi's drawings and notes, her references came from diverse sources and not just from an empirical understanding of local conditions. For example, the "radial lots with a house at the center" should accommodate the steep topography through terraces built according to the "system of short stone walls on the slopes of Liguria," the region of Italy where she had recently spent an extended period at the outset of her military investigation in Brazil (figure 90).[14]

This circular parceling scheme resembled the Itamambuca Beach resort of 1965, while the square and symmetrical houses with rustic materials and plants again emulated the Cirell House. Bo Bardi also considered an alternative house typology with a more spontaneous layout consisting of a rectangular footprint with irregular enclosure walls surrounded by a single porch and simple furniture produced on site. She insisted that the units were critical to the project's success, and — no longer praising mud construction techniques as she had in her 1967 article about Acácio Gil Borsói's resettlement experiment in Recife — she stressed that a brick house was the populace's highest dream. Still, she kept a principle also used by Borsói — that their reproduction would be executed on a sweat-equity system, a method seen at the time as an empowering solution to housing problems.[15]

On the larger scale, Bo Bardi was sensitive to create lots that organically fit the irregular topography, but on the smaller scale, her plans for the community center on top of the hill — as the housing units to be distributed around the site — were based on orthogonal and functionalist diagrams. A long, linear canopy connected the open and the enclosed social facilities bordering the covered walkway. At one end, she proposed a plaza surrounded by collective sports and health facilities and agricultural workshops, at the other end a small open market, a church, and a school. Along the way, she drew placeholders for leisure and commercial facilities as well as the city hall and a jail. The Camurupim project evolved slowly and, like her frustrating experience with the creation of the Museu de Arte Popular in Salvador, never went beyond the conceptual phase.

Despite being incomplete, the project remains relevant to Bo Bardi's career in that it exercised her beliefs about the ethical purpose of architecture and transposed her concepts of a new humanism into pragmatic action attempting to combine anthropological elements with an otherwise primarily technical approach. "Architects must be deeply connected with living, since it is everything," she stated later. "I saw wonderful things in the Camurupim community. From fishing nets to pieces of furniture made by just placing a few wooden slats together . . . , things made by the people . . . , an invitation to survey our own Brazilian needs."[16] She had not given up on the idea of a national-popular culture as many of her contemporaries had.

The Camurupim project also marked her return, after ten years, to building design, and it gradually reintroduced her voice, now with a fresh tone, into the countercurrent of the Brazilian architectural debate. She began to write and publish again and to receive commissions that would allow her to reignite her belief in modern rationality, to reengage her search for the humanization of the built environment, and to attempt to reconcile them into concrete design proposals.

While working on the resettlement project, Bo Bardi wrote about her provocative political and aesthetic thoughts on design, collective freedom, and Brazilian culture. From her handwritten notes titled "Arquitetura e desenho industrial: Depois do Sturm und Drang" (Architecture and industrial design: After the Sturm und Drang), she published an article in the second of the three issues of *Revista Malasartes*, a short-lived experimental art magazine.[17] She titled the piece "Planejamento ambiental: O desenho no impasse" (Environmental planning: Design at an impasse) after her careful reading and notes of the book *La speranza progettuale: Ambiente e società* (Design, nature, and revolution: Toward a critical ecology), published in 1970 by designer and theorist Tomás Maldonado, the Argentinean Italian disciple of Max Bill.[18]

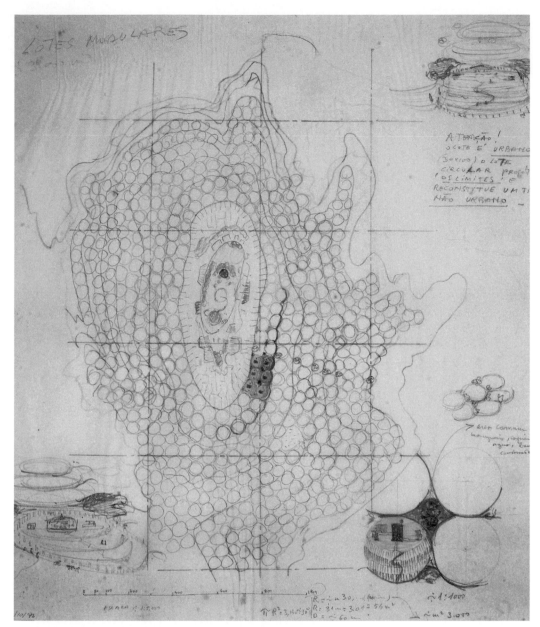

90. Lina Bo Bardi, *Study for Camurupim Rural Community (Propriá, Sergipe)*, October 26, 1976. Color pencil, felt pen, and ballpoint pen, on tracing paper, 57 × 49.5 cm. ILBPMB Collection.

Maldonado's text, which was an important reference among Italian designers, drew attention to a theme that had been pervasive in recent Brazilian architectural debates and even in Bo Bardi's 1957 thesis: the relation between design and society. He introduced two interrelated notions that had become central in Bo Bardi's thinking and remained so until the end of her life. The first was the idea that design had socio-anthropological roots, and the second was the need to reinfuse design with trust in the renewed revolutionary role of rationality.[19] Aware of the crisis in Western architecture, Bo Bardi's article called for the renewal of the "rationalist metaphor, . . . the principles that informed the modern movement, interrupted by World War II, and later abandoned as outdated." [20]

She cautioned against sentimentality and irrationality and criticized the cooption of planning — to her, the "great fundamental idea" of the modern movement — by technocrats, who emptied it out and transformed it into the

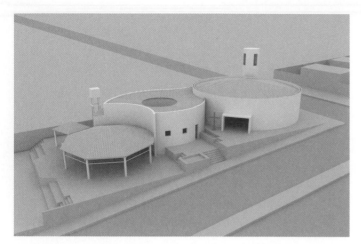

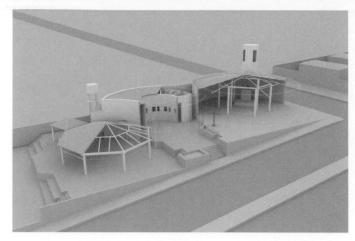

91. Cerrado Church, Uberlândia, Minas Gerais, 1976–82, view from the northern side showing the general ensemble. Computer rendering. Zeuler R. Lima Collection.

92. Cerrado Church, Uberlândia, Minas Gerais, 1976–82, sectioned view from the northern side showing spatial layout and building logic. Computer rendering. Zeuler R. Lima Collection.

"fetishism of abstract [economic] models that considers the world of numbers and the world of mankind to be equal." Despite ongoing cultural, political, economic, and professional crises, Bo Bardi claimed that the role of designers continued to have societal relevance. "This is what Brecht called the ability to say 'no,'" she insisted, reminding her readers that "the artist's freedom has always been 'individual,' but true freedom can only be collective: [the kind of] freedom aware of social reality." And recalling Gramsci, she wrote: "While economists and sociologists can easily produce diagnosis, the artist must act as an intellectual integrated into an active society."[21]

By this point in her life, Bo Bardi resented that the work she had initiated as a director of MAP in Salvador was no longer possible. The political and social conditions she had found there in the early 1960s had changed. Still, to her, the authentic source of Brazilian culture was a "generosity within reach of our hands, a unique anthropological wealth with tragic and fundamental historic events." She saw the task of environmental planning (understood as a relation between design disciplines and everyday culture) as replacing the philosophical "aesthetic quest" — "the concentration camp of Western civilization" — with an "anthropological quest." She proposed to embrace cultural reintegration and simplification along with "the great conquests of scientific practice (not [to be confused with] technology decayed into technocracy)." She realized that the country and the world faced new challenges, but she did not lose her desire to battle. She called for the "restart from a new reality" and more than ever asserted: "Art (as well as architecture and industrial design) is always a political operation."[22]

Despite its predicaments, Bo Bardi's article was a springboard for the kind of design-in-action she would develop as she regained her creative energies and started to entertain new projects. In July 1976, while writing her article about the impasse of design and studying the Camurupim proposal, and almost a year after the set up of the *Repassos* exhibition at MASP, Bo Bardi returned to Uberlândia to visit her friend Edmar de Almeida. She was entering the last and most productive sixteen years of her life, which legitimized and propelled her career as a distinctive architect. During her short stay there, he introduced her to a group of Franciscan priests led by the Sicilian friar Egidio Parisi who wanted to build a small church in the low-income neighborhood of Jaraguá on the outskirts of town.[23] It took some effort to convince Bo Bardi that the priests shared values similar to hers.[24] In a letter after her visit, de Almeida appealed to her: "Make it beautiful and simple; a picture of this good people."[25] He included a plan for the small, slanted lot on avenida Mognos and detailed information for a modest play area for children and three interconnected buildings: a shed for community activities and a residence for two nuns to be built first and a midsized chapel to follow. There was little money, so the spaces needed to be flexible and the building materials and techniques simple to allow for community participation and minimal cost.

The complex was officially named Igreja do Divino Espírito Santo (Church of the Divine Holy Spirit), but it is generally known as Igreja do Cerrado (Cerrado Church), relating it to the region's highland savannas and paying tribute to Bo Bardi's affection for the Brazilian hinterland. She accepted the proposal and started work in September 1976, but like many of her architectural projects, the church took

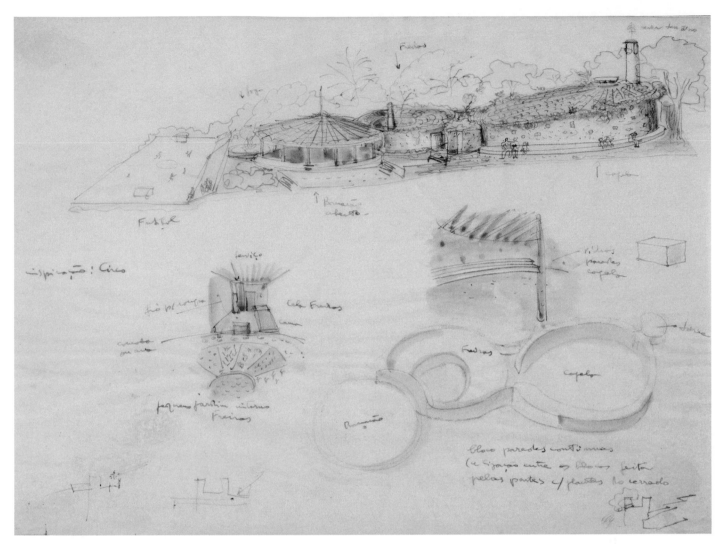

93. Lina Bo Bardi, *Study for Cerrado Church, general perspective and details*, October 26, 1976. Watercolor, pencil, and India ink on paper and Mylar, 23.4 × 32.5 cm. ILBPMB Collection.

a long time to be completed. The basic project was approved in December 1978, but work started only in 1979 with initial funds received from German charity groups.[26] Most of the construction details were developed between 1980 and 1981 with the assistance of the young architects who would accompany Bo Bardi until the end of her life. The basic structure was completed in 1982, but construction extended until 1996, after her death.

Between September and October 1976, Bo Bardi conceived the general terraced layout that would guide the church construction in the following years. Instead of designing a single, monumental, or symmetrical building, the articulation among three smaller structures on the slanted site eased the gradual construction and occupancy

and maximized earthworks, safety, and privacy. She had recently experimented with a similar scheme in the abandoned study for a private house to be built out of semiburied raw concrete walls, creating several terraces.[27] As for the church, she located the two volumes that would serve local residents (the chapel and the community hall) at the upper and lower ends of the site so that they faced the main avenue, and she placed the parochial house at a slight recess between them. The three volumes thus framed a small churchyard accessible through concrete steps set perpendicular to the sidewalk and concentrating all access points on the middle terrace (figures 91, 92).

"Inspiration: circus," Bo Bardi noted on the left-hand side of her first perspectives in watercolor (figure 93).[28] The

Rehearsing an Anthropological Quest

94. Cerrado Church, Uberlândia, Minas Gerais, 1976–82, view from the western, rear side of the ensemble. Photograph by Zeuler R. Lima.

95. Cerrado Church, Uberlândia, Minas Gerais, 1976–82, view of the church and altar with tapestry by Edmar de Almeida. Photograph by Zeuler R. Lima.

chapel was supposed to be a venue for community gatherings and social activities from religious masses to movie projections and celebrations. She investigated the simplicity and the geometry of structures ranging from early Christian churches — reminiscences from her childhood in Rome — to tents, cabins, and vernacular buildings from different geographical origins.[29] Her decision to use roof frames with tree trunks covered with interlocked barrel tiles required special attention and was resolved with references found in *Shelter*, the illustrated book edited by Lloyd Kahn a few years before and brought in by her young assistants, who helped prepare most of the construction drawings.[30]

Aside from a circus, the chapel, still located on the highest point of the site, evokes her project for La Torraccia guesthouse. Its surrounding wall, built with a regular reinforced concrete structure with brick infill, is crowned by a double concrete ring with a flowerbed and a cantilevered gutter invisible from the outside. The ring supports the outer edge of the independent six-pitched roof, which is laid out on a hexagonal frame of slender wooden piers and

joists.[31] She imagined the sanctuary (the largest building she ever designed based on circular geometries) without side windows but lit by a skylight in the conic roof and with unrealized small, irregular holes covered with colored glass and screens displayed randomly around the circular wall.[32]

For the furniture, Bo Bardi studied wooden chairs based on Portuguese tripartite sewing seats, which were later developed and built by her assistants but never used in the church.[33] The altarpiece adorning the interior is simple: a concrete-and-brick platform, a back wall, and a table supported by a robust tree stump. Behind the chapel stands a short, cylindrical bell tower whose base was transformed into a small sacristy when the building was consecrated as a parish church (figures 94, 95). In addition, the outdoor terrace railing was built with a series of welded vertical and horizontal rebar pieces cast into the concrete retaining wall, insightfully translating her interest in simple, improvised solutions.

Her choice of a layout with cylindrical volumes easily led to a courtyard typology for the parochial residence,

96. Cerrado Church, Uberlândia, Minas Gerais, 1976–82, view of the patio in the original dormitory area. Photograph by Zeuler R. Lima.

which she associated with an ancient Roman *compluvium* (a space left unroofed over a small courtyard to collect rain into a water pool, or *impluvium*). The small house is organized around a modest patio with gravel and plants, also recalling the rusticity of whitewashed rural houses (figure 96). The interior is plain but comfortable, with rooms separated by radial partitions with hardwood floors in individual areas and cement flooring in communal areas. While she designed the interior of the residential suites with careful furniture details, her assistants diligently worked on the ceramic tile roof, whose irregular geometries made it difficult to maintain the same incline, match the tiles, and avoid leaks.[34] In spite of the team's design efforts, the nuns lived in the house for only a year after construction was completed, leaving the house to the community.[35]

On a lower terrace, wedged against the central cylindrical volume of the parochial house, Bo Bardi located the octagonal community hall — which she called "quiosque" (kiosk or pavilion) or "salão de festas" (entertainment hall).[36] Though its pitched roof made it harder to match the

concave wall placed between the two buildings, it favored regular sections that were more suited to the ceramic tile technique. It also allowed for a helpful solution taken from a similar example in *Shelter* magazine: a wooden cap piece shaped like a diamond bracing the joists, eliminating the need for a central support for the pavilion.[37] Over time and for maintenance and security reasons, the original dirt flooring was changed into the glossy cement finish common to the vernacular of Brazilian domestic architecture. The railings were also replaced by translucent partitions of eucalyptus trunks set next to one another, maintaining the simplicity and natural ventilation of the original proposal and adding a textured effect of filtered sunlight (figure 97).

As requested by the community, Bo Bardi left the lower, fourth terrace untouched so that children could use it for a small soccer field and playground. As the construction reached its initial completion phase, she added service entries to the back of the parochial house and placed a water tower on raw concrete stilts, the entirety of which she imagined covered with flowering vines in her design.

Rehearsing an Anthropological Quest

97. Cerrado Church, Uberlândia, Minas Gerais, 1976–82, interior view of
the community hall. Photograph by Zeuler R. Lima.

98. Angels' Chapel, Vargem Grande Paulista, São Paulo, 1978, external view. Photograph by Nelson Kon.

Though many of the simple details in her studies were never built, her design for a wooden cross standing on a conic pile of concrete and stones, like the one she made for George Jonas's film *A compadecida* in 1968 or even those for panels in the 1959 *Bahia* exhibition, was accordingly executed next to the chapel entrance.

Faithful to the idea expressed in her recent article that humanistic and not formal principles should guide the renewal of Brazilian design, Bo Bardi noted that "the most important thing during the construction of the Holy Spirit Church was the possibility of a joint effort between architect and the workforce." [38] As she returned to architecture practice in the mid-1970s, she echoed the debate promoted by progressive São Paulo architects who had been concerned with labor conditions on the construction site especially in the late 1960s. Among them were Rodrigo Lefèvre and Sérgio Ferro, who had once kept a studio with her friend Flávio Império but who, in the case of Lefèvre, had moved to a large, state-run construction company and, in Ferro's case, had left architecture practice altogether for exile in France and a career in painting. In the meantime, Império

remained her close friend and developed a career as a prolific artist and set designer. Aware of impasses, Bo Bardi took up where the three young men had left off.

She did not give up on architectural practice, but she did not want her approach to be seen as folkloric either. She insisted that her image as a designer be connected to the community: "In no way was [the church] a project prepared in the architect's office and merely sent along for construction, since there was close, permanent contact between the designer, the construction team, and the people who helped build it." [39] The raw quality of the building pushed the aesthetics of brutality to a new limit and, above all, gave symbolic visibility to the hands of the people who built it. Finally, she could show in architecture what she had rehearsed in her exhibitions, including the *Repassos* show that led to the Uberlândia project. More than MASP, the Cerrado Church provided convincing images of her desire for freedom over beauty. It also opened up the opportunity for her to simultaneously design another building under similar conditions.

99. Angels' Chapel, Vargem Grande Paulista, São Paulo, 1978, external view. Computer rendering. Zeuler R. Lima Collection.

100. Angels' Chapel, Vargem Grande Paulista, São Paulo, 1978, sectioned view showing spatial layout and building logic. Computer rendering. Zeuler R. Lima Collection.

In 1978, Edmar de Almeida once again demonstrated his support to his friend. He introduced Bo Bardi to Bruna Sercelli, a charity worker connected to a Franciscan fraternity that wanted to build a chapel outside of São Paulo.[40] The site for a small sanctuary dedicated to Our Lady of the Angels was located in their retreat camp in Vargem Grande Paulista, a low-income residential district in the town of Ibiúna surrounded by a semirural landscape. Sercelli self-consciously told Bo Bardi that they had little resources for a new building, unaware that she would be excited about such a restriction. Bo Bardi rejected the studies her new client had hired from an engineer, saying they would be too expensive to build, and accepted the challenge asking her just to build a "poor chapel."[41]

The project went quickly, and by comparison, the construction was effortless despite their limited resources. Over a weekend in October 1978, Bo Bardi produced a series of architectural drawings and perspectives. She designed a very simple building associating her experience with the Cerrado Church and the vocabulary of square-based plans and austere volumes from her previous residential projects. Like the Uberlândia sanctuary, she located the chapel on a slight incline, which she cut into a terrace accessible through simple concrete steps from left and right and below. The flattened ground supported a solid and almost cubic volume surrounded by a tiled porch built with tree trunks and originally covered with thatched grass, which resembled an enlarged version of the Cirell House (figure 98).[42]

However, unlike in the house for her friend, Bo Bardi placed the entrance at the corner of the chapel. This gesture led her to orient the interior space diagonally and to chamfer the two corners at each end of the axis, accommodating the main door and the altar, respectively, and maximizing the scale and experience of the space both vertically and horizontally (figures 99, 100). She also placed two vertical windows at the edges of the walls flanking the altar, lighting the interior spaces more warmly and offering a slightly more polished treatment of sealed cement flooring, plastered walls painted in white, and a wooden ceiling (figure 101). Externally, she chose not to paint the solid volume built with a reinforced concrete frame and cinder blocks but to finish it with a mixture of sand, cement, and dirt removed from termite earth houses found in the area and whose dark red color gave the plaster a pink tone. "This is another one of our cheap projects," she later described the chapel with affection. "As usual, there was no money. But the result was surprising. Inside, the sound reverberates, creating mysterious voices during masses."[43]

Both the Cerrado Church and the Angels' Chapel materialize the ideas Bo Bardi had pondered after a decade away from the practice of building design. They condense, with limited resources, her Italian classical education and incursion into rationalism, her desire to associate architecture with nature, and her intent to develop a collectively relevant aesthetics of simplification, which she called "arquitetura pobre." Still, by pushing the material and formal boundaries in her effort to create buildings that represent the notion of social life untainted by consumption and industrialization, she also faced dilemmas.

101. Angels' Chapel, Vargem Grande Paulista, São Paulo, 1978, interior view and altar. Photograph by Nelson Kon.

These two churches (like her naturalistic houses) reveal the flip side of the impasse faced by modernist buildings in early twentieth-century Brazil. While artisanal techniques emulated the unavailable industrial technologies that made European flat roofs possible (by hiding, for example, ceramic tile roofs behind ledges as Gregori Warchavchik did), Bo Bardi moved into the opposite direction. She built structures with a mixture of industrial and artisanal materials, creating ambiguous solutions and simulating traditional techniques with modern materials, such as using rammed earth in the walls of Angels' Chapel or employing barrel tiles for circular roofs in the Cerrado Church.

Though her practice echoed the dilemmas to which she pointed in her theory, Bo Bardi relentlessly pursued her desire for the humanization of architecture. As she quoted Brecht in the article about environmental planning she wrote for *Malasartes* magazine in 1976, she did not say "no" to experimentation, as did many of her contemporaries. Above all, as she insisted that designers, though striving for individual artistic freedom, should aim at promoting collective freedom, she did not say "yes" to compliance, which, according to her, was "the 'no' of imbeciles."[44]

As Lina Bo Bardi began studying the Cerrado Church in 1976, she unexpectedly received a commission that would become her ultimate accomplishment and give her greatest visibility. She was invited to renovate an old factory in São Paulo, an endeavor that would produce the most complex and meaningful project of her career. During the following decade she would work with a large team to combine collective everyday, cultural, and pedagogical activities at what would become SESC Pompeia Leisure Center. At last she would be able to consolidate many of the goals she had pursued since arriving in Brazil thirty years before.

In SESC (Serviço Social do Comércio, Trade social services), a not-for-profit entity maintained by Brazilian trade leaders, she found her best client and patron. Created in September 1946 to promote political appeasement through community education and cultural and health programs when Brazil's growing industrial and commercial sectors were concerned with potential uprisings, SESC achieved great success and popularity over the decades through its facilities around the country, many of which were designed by renowned architects. Bo Bardi's project for the old factory in the traditional immigrant and working-class Pompeia neighborhood of São Paulo is a tour de force that both she and the organization share, though she was not the first designer to present a proposal for the complex.

Her clients initially had different plans when they acquired the old steel barrel factory through public auction in 1971. They were going to tear it down. Built in 1938 with a modular structure based on French engineer François Hennebique's prefabricated reinforced concrete system and with an exposed brick enclosure, the factory closed thirty years later after its last industrial occupant, a refrigerator manufacturer, left. SESC started to use the structure informally in 1973 for sports and children's activities. A year later, it hired architect Júlio Neves (who was then in his forties and would later direct MASP and alter the Bardis' museum's mission and layout) to present a project for a new leisure center. Neves's February 1975 proposal suggested leveling the old structure and replacing it with new buildings, but his ideas were abandoned as being too costly.[1]

In August, SESC and its sibling organization SESI (Serviço Social da Indústria, Industry social services) organized a national conference about leisure and culture, which led SESC's president, José Papa Júnior, and its regional director, sociologist Renato Requixá, to create a research team and innovative seminars aimed at introducing a humanistic approach to sports, leisure, and recreation as a right of all social classes.[2] Seeking economical uses for the building, Requixá visited the converted industrial site of Ghirardelli Square in San Francisco, California, and returned to Brazil with the idea of transforming the old Pompeia factory in a similar way. During a conversation with Pietro Maria Bardi, Papa Júnior mentioned the new idea for SESC, and Bardi immediately suggested that they talk to his wife, highlighting her previous adaptive reuse experience at Unhão in Salvador.[3]

A few months later, Papa Júnior contacted Bo Bardi, and after visiting the site, she agreed to design the Pompeia project for SESC without tearing down the existing building, though she would not start work on it until April 1977.[4] When the complex was completed in 1986, she described her first encounters with the building: "As I entered the abandoned steel barrel factory at the Pompeia neighborhood for the first time in 1976, the rationally displayed sheds drew my attention." She returned a few days later, on the weekend, to discover an even more exciting scene: "During my second visit, on a Saturday, the environment was different: no longer was there just the elegant and solitary structure but also a joyous crowd of children, parents, and elderly people moving from one pavilion to the next."[5]

"I thought all of that would have to continue as it was, with all that joy," she added.[6] She suggested that the existing structure should simply be cleaned and maintained as a historic example of industrial architecture and, above all, that it should embrace the existing uses of the building as they were. Aside from being a site for social and architectural experiments, Bo Bardi embraced SESC Pompeia with all of the skills and interests developed in her practice: architecture, furniture design, education, heritage, popular festivities, exhibitions, and theater, aiming at developing a comprehensive Brazilian design identity grounded on everyday and collective life.

The activity program organized by SESC's technical staff gave Bo Bardi the opportunity to bring many previously curtailed ideas and experiments back to the drawing board, to the construction site, and into the building, revisiting her ideas for MAP in Salvador. Though financed by large capitalist groups that used to be associated with social injustice by left-leaning cultural groups such as those Bo Bardi had worked with in the 1960s, SESC was (and is) a forward-thinking institution, and her ideas benefited greatly from their collaborative relationship and institutional support. Together they negotiated the creation of an unconventional collective facility. They aspired to approach culture as a comprehensive, flexible field and to transcend aesthetic and intellectual production by incorporating everyday life and embracing the educated, popular, and mass cultures within their educational and leisure programs. Ultimately, they wanted to encourage new audiences to be active and creative groups and individuals.[7]

Bo Bardi's SESC Pompeia project offers an essential key to understanding her quest to humanize architecture, to make it welcoming and collective, "to dignify human presence." She stressed that her design for the project "started from the desire to create another reality." Paraphrasing an unidentified Polish architect and urban restorer who later visited SESC and commented that she had done so much with so few elements, she liked to say, "We just added a few things: a water pond and a fireplace. The less junk, the better."[8]

Despite that apparent simplicity, the old factory site offered complex design conditions. The lot, which took up more than half of a large urban block, contained many factory sheds that needed to be preserved at the northwestern corner of rua Barão do Bananal and rua Clélia on the north. The main entrance on rua Clélia gave access to an internal street running north-south and dividing the factory into two blocks on either side. This street slanted slightly toward a narrow, built-up flood valley on the south end with a small creek running east-west between rua Barão do Bananal and avenida Pompeia, the only area originally left open for new buildings. However, an environmental protection ordinance kept a narrow surface along the channeled stream from being built on, substantially reducing the possibilities for locating new structures behind the existing factory.

SESC administrators favored using the sheds as a Centro de Convivência (Gathering center), housing all the educational and leisure activities, including a theater, a restaurant, a library, and exhibition rooms, aware that the buildings' horizontality would make spontaneous social integration easier.[9] Consequently, all the sports facilities, including a large swimming pool, sports courts, and support rooms, would have to fit into the exiguous site behind the sheds and along the flood area, creating a real design challenge, a condition Bo Bardi faced with excitement (figures 102, 103).

With the church in Uberlândia and the possibility of such a large commission in sight, Bo Bardi decided to hire two energetic senior students from the school of architecture at the Universidade de São Paulo, Marcelo Carvalho Ferraz and André Vainer, following the recommendation of their professor and her friend, architect Joaquim Guedes. In their company, Bo Bardi, now sixty-two, embarked on the most fruitful and prolific journey of her mature years. Though Vainer collaborated very little with her after this project, leaving Bo Bardi to hire other young enthusiastic interns like architect Marcelo Suzuki, Ferraz would maintain an enduring cooperative relationship with her until the end of her life. For the SESC project, both Vainer and Ferraz translated her ideas into orthographic drawings, which

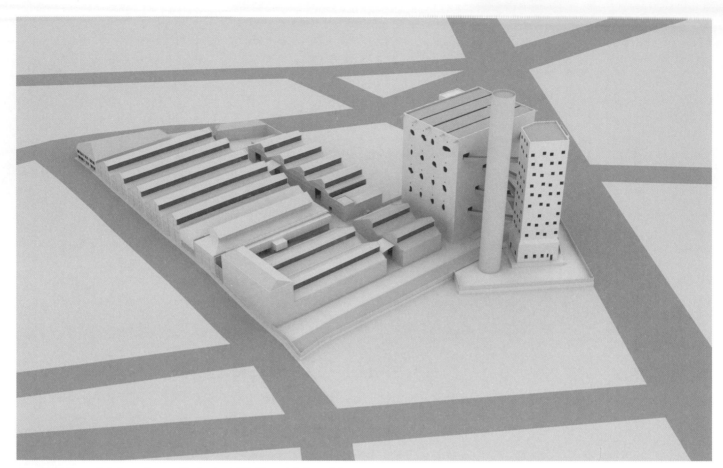

102. SESC Pompeia Leisure Center, São Paulo, 1977–86, aerial view of the ensemble showing the existing factory and the added towers. Computer rendering. Zeuler R. Lima Collection.

freed her to approach her sketches more spontaneously and expressively.

In addition to hiring technical support, Bo Bardi began spending more time in the office set up by the construction company on the SESC site, especially during the long construction process. Most of her meetings with Vainer and Ferraz as well as with engineers and contractors took place there, a practice she had casually initiated during the construction of MASP on avenida Paulista and which she claimed served as a bridge between designers and builders. She liked to call the shed *Catetinho*, referring to a simple wooden building on stilts designed by Oscar Niemeyer as the first presidential residence during the construction of Brasília.

Though Bo Bardi's team completed the basic project in a few months, the building process was divided into two consecutive phases that took much longer, sometimes made more difficult by Bo Bardi's constant changing of construction details, including tearing down complete parts of

it.[10] The factory renovation itself took place between 1978 and 1982, when SESC was partially opened to the public, allowing her to organize a few pedagogical exhibitions. The sports facilities were finally built between 1982 and 1986.

According to archival records, Bo Bardi concluded the preliminary studies and basic project for the whole complex between April and December 1977. Her notes show that she established the rules and shapes for the adaptive reuse of the old factory — which consisted of nineteen industrial sheds clustered into seven juxtaposed blocks of various sizes — and for the construction of the three new towers and flyovers for the sports complex. Among the many drawings and documents produced during the project's nine years of design and construction, Bo Bardi also kept photomontages and sketches with her initial ideas.[11] Her first section of the industrial sheds, titled "Landscape" (in English), shows elevated wooden platforms on two levels connected by ramps permeated by plants and playgrounds, while her first sketch representing the sports courts shows an elevation of five

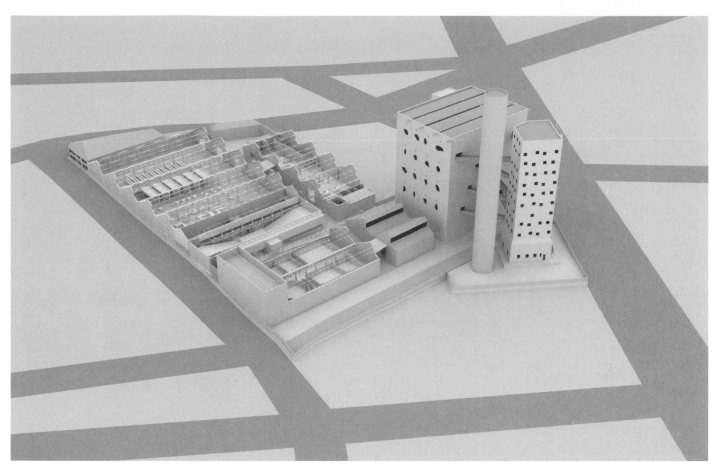

103. SESC Pompeia Leisure Center, São Paulo, 1977–86, sectioned aerial view showing factory renovation and spatial layout. Computer rendering. Zeuler R. Lima Collection.

stacked concrete slabs of different lengths surrounded by a large metal screen.[12] She revised those ideas several times, often trying to keep naturalistic elements in the foreground (figure 104). She gradually morphed her original landscape idea into art workshops and an elevated library in the industrial sheds. Instead of a single block for the sports facilities, she accepted the building constraints over the channeled creek and split them into separate towers articulated by intertwined skywalks.

Between 1978 and 1981, once the renovation work was underway, Bo Bardi and her young team complemented the basic design with building details, furniture design, and visual communication for the largest block (commonly known as the "general activities pavilion"). In 1984, after a short building lull, they concluded the construction drawings for the articulated towers, whose large pre-stressed concrete structure was mostly cast by 1985. That same year, they added final peculiar details, such as sculptural elements and delicate textures, to contrast with the brick and raw concrete structures, reintroducing the human hand and size into SESC's monumental scale and giving SESC Pompeia its unique architectural identity.

These features are visible on the approach to the complex, either by glimpsing its tall concrete towers with red shutters emerging out of the neighborhood's irregular landscape of valley and hills, small townhouses and large buildings, or by walking along the brick walls with windows covered by wooden lattice. Once through the varnished wooden gate on rua Clélia, visitors are welcomed by a tall signage post with printed boards offering directions followed by a sketched hand with a pointing finger, the image Bo Bardi had used since her youth whenever she wanted to draw attention to a detail.[13] Beyond the signpost, the lively internal street presents itself as the backbone of the complex (figure 105). It measures 134 meters (440 ft.) in length and is flanked by the brick sheds and open gutters lined with auburn river pebbles, which Bo Bardi chose to heighten the sound of rainwater collected from the wide industrial

A Bowl of Soup for the People   161

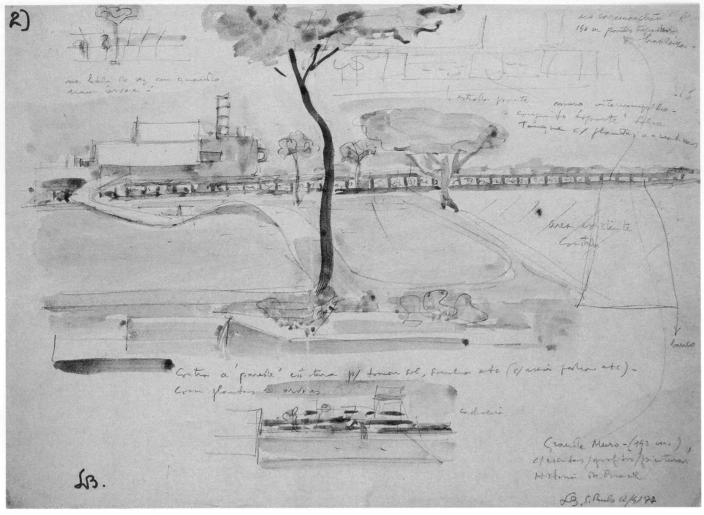

104. Lina Bo Bardi, *Study for SESC Pompeia Leisure Center*, first idea for
the area along the flood area and large wall, April 12, 1977. Watercolor
and pencil on cardstock, 23.4 × 32.5 cm. ILBPMB Collection.

105. SESC Pompeia Leisure Center, São Paulo, 1977–86, view of entrance into the central street between factory sheds with information totem in the foreground. Photograph by Zeuler R. Lima.

roofs and delivered into the Águas Pretas creek. Visitors meandering along the street, in and out of the sheds, with or toward other groups of people, experience the rich, mutating day-and-night activities that animate the center and open themselves to the discovery of new places and experiences.

To the west of the entrance, beyond the administrative offices, the largest block with five sheds — known as the "general activities pavilion" — is the heart of the complex (figure 106). In it, adults, children, and elderly groups from all over the city continue to stage the everyday life of a traditional neighborhood plaza in a city that needs more spaces of collective interaction and in an area increasingly occupied by residential highrises and shopping malls. With subtle physical divisions marked by the rational layout of the original concrete piers, the south side of the pavilion contains an

open exhibition hall, a large lounge with modular couches, a fireplace, and a meandering reflecting pool with rolled stones covering its shallow waters. On the north side, one bay is reserved for exhibitions, and at the center of the pavilion, two bays contain a small library. The remaining sheds are used as a lounge for changing activities.

While an arterial, sinuous reflecting pool draws attention to the lounge floor, the elevated library platforms focus attention to the roof, as if to suggest the variations between a light-colored valley, in Brazilian quartzite, and gray mountains, in raw concrete. In order to turn Bo Bardi's landscape metaphor into habitable space, she and her team devised an insightful orthogonal geometry of twelve elevated "reading slabs."[14] They are organized in six perpendicular bays on two levels and articulated through

A Bowl of Soup for the People

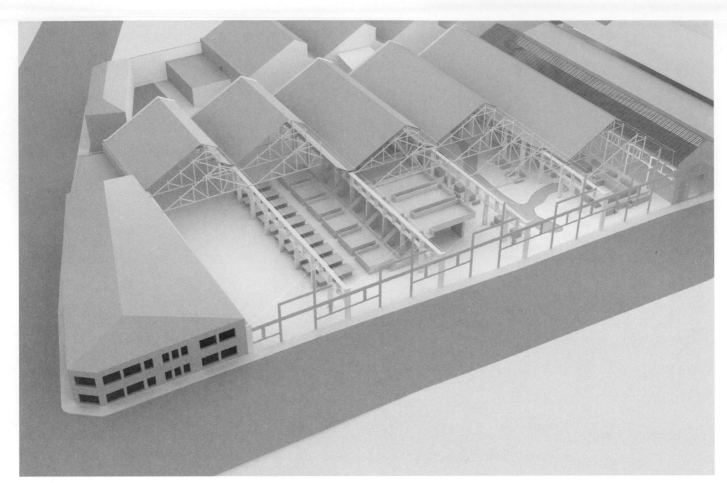

106. SESC Pompeia Leisure Center, São Paulo, 1977–86, sectioned aerial view or renovated factory sheds showing the exhibition, library, and lounge areas. Computer rendering. Zeuler R. Lima Collection.

the existing building structure by bridging stairs along both sides of the concrete posts between the second and third sheds of the main factory pavilion (figure 107). The six raised platforms are supported by large piers to create a room contiguous to the lounge, and the six lower platforms look like concrete volumes rising from the ground, resembling some of Bo Bardi's cubic buildings. Parallel to them, the library stacks are placed directly on the floor, adjacent to the lounge. Bo Bardi saw this open configuration for the library as an inviting alternative for people to study, read, or even play board games.[15]

Along with the library, the reflecting pool is a prominent feature of the large general activities pavilion (figure 108). It is Bo Bardi's most conspicuous tribute to her beloved but already distant Nordeste. Originally designed in zigzag form, the areas around the pool were to suggest the rolling geography of the São Francisco River, which was fresh in her mind after her recent project for the Camurupim

community. In addition to the shallow water container, she considered creating low platforms with modular seats and "artificial trees," based on Mário Cravo's dry trees and on artworks to be designed by other friends, such as Rubens Gerchman, Flávio Império, and Edmar de Almeida.[16] Though not accomplished, her goal was to emulate the islands and banks along the river.

Across the internal street from the large hall, a buffet restaurant serves home-style lunches to over one thousand people daily (figure 109). In the evening, it is transformed into a popular beer garden, with live shows on a stage surrounded by large, abstract tapestries that Edmar de Almeida prepared with weavers from Martinésia. On the opposite side of the restaurant and farther down, in the middle of the complex's west side, Bo Bardi transformed the secondary entry to the old factory into a translucent space covered with a glass-tiled roof that reveals itself to visitors through large trellised floor-to-ceiling partitions at either end (figure 110).

107. SESC Pompeia Leisure Center, São Paulo, 1977–86, library bays in concrete inserted amid the structure of the renovated factory sheds with lounge in the foreground. Photograph by Nelson Kon.

108. SESC Pompeia Leisure Center, São Paulo, 1977–86, lounge area with reflecting pool, a tribute to São Francisco River. Photograph by Nelson Kon.

109. SESC Pompeia Leisure Center, São Paulo, 1977–86, restaurant and beer garden with tapestry by Edmar de Almeida in the background. Photograph by Zeuler R. Lima.

110. SESC Pompeia Leisure Center, São Paulo, 1977–86, theater foyer with access to galleries and dressing rooms in the foreground. Photograph by Zeuler R. Lima.

111. SESC Pompeia Leisure Center, São Paulo, 1977–86, theater with central stage and seats facing each other. Photograph by Nelson Kon.

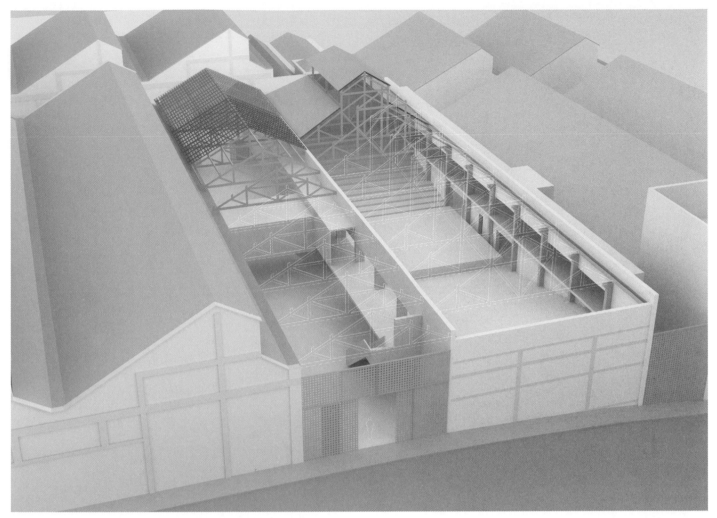

112. SESC Pompeia Leisure Center, São Paulo, 1977–86, sectioned aerial view of renovated factory sheds showing theater and foyer areas. Computer rendering. Zeuler R. Lima Collection.

Aside from giving access to the auditorium, this transitional hall also serves as an exhibition room and informal stage, which Bo Bardi referred to as "terreiros," large dirt yards found in small towns and on rural properties in Brazil.[17]

Because the larger, adjacent shed was not tall enough to contain a regular theater with a proscenium or an arena, Bo Bardi decided, after attempting different alternatives, to create a central stage with two audiences face to face as in the set she designed for Martinez Corrêa's production of *In the Jungle of Cities* in 1969. This configuration maximized audience visibility without resorting to ground excavation or changes in the shed structure (figure 111). She designed two bleachers with twelve steps, a central aisle, and two symmetrical rows of interconnected wooden seats based on her original ideas for chairs in MASP's auditorium in

1968. This mirrored layout also allowed for bathrooms and machinery to be placed under the concrete bleachers and entrances to serve both sides, as well as the stage, either from the atrium shed at the north or from the service alley at the south. In addition, she had the building internally reinforced with the help of engineer Figueiredo Ferraz, her previous collaborator in the MASP project, allowing for the creation of a looping circulation around the second floor with cantilevered galleries shaped like tubular volumes in raw concrete lining both sides of the shed structure (figure 112).[18]

A similar tubular volume that seems to hover perpendicularly in the middle of the auditorium foyer and fitting the concrete gallery contains the dressing rooms. At either end of the translucent atrium, stairs in raw concrete give access to the upper-floor galleries and the general audience.

A Bowl of Soup for the People   167

113. SESC Pompeia Leisure Center, São Paulo, 1977–86, art workshops separated by cinderblock walls. Photograph by Nelson Kon.

At the bottom of each staircase, Bo Bardi added a block of roughly cut granite to create a transition between exterior and interior spaces, as in the traditional Japanese architecture she had seen on recent trips to that country. She also paid special attention to the combination of rough, polished, natural, and artisanal materials subtly covering the main floor, from irregular cobblestones with a runner of polished granite leading into the foyer to colorful ceramic shards in the restrooms.

In addition to these architectural elements, Bo Bardi designed most of the furniture and visual communication for these areas of the complex. For all her talk about inclusive participation in the design process, she strove to control every detail of so large a project as was SESC Pompeia, and between 1980 and 1981, once the cleaning and construction of the old factory structure was in motion, she produced an exhaustive series of colorful drawings ranging from preliminary ideas to fully developed projects, many of them never executed. She imagined each area of the converted factory as having its own details, using different materials to create props, signage, and uniforms, as well as pieces dedicated to children's play and study. She even conceived a promotional newsletter, *Jornal do SESC*, and designed a logo for the center that showed "the smokestack giving out flowers."[19]

Satisfying her idea for a total design, she fashioned all the furniture in use in the pavilions, including several library and restaurant tables and chairs, modular lounge couches with cushioned seats originally covered in green tarp, and auditorium seats. She was especially interested in designing furniture for children, such as an articulated desk-and-chair piece in pinewood, which she nicknamed *caixotinho* (little wooden box).[20] This small cubic piece is separated diagonally into two matching elements placed on wheels to create different use combinations. Conceived with simple shapes and assemblage techniques, her furniture for SESC Pompeia is sturdy and still in use after several decades, thanks to its bulkiness and the materials she used, including plywood, laminate wood, and concrete. With the exception of the children's movable pieces, however, most of her furniture is also heavy and some of it not very comfortable, especially the theater seats, which she impudently described as motivation for the audience not to be passive. Not only did design face an impasse, as she claimed, but her quest for an anthropological approach in these cases prioritized the discourse about collective appropriation over individual ergonomics. Unlike her furniture design, however, her architecture is noticeably welcoming and accommodating.

Farther down from the theater, the two smaller warehouses that border the southern bottom end of the internal street contain technical facilities and a shed with several pedagogical workshops for art techniques ranging from ceramics to printmaking. Each workshop — used for work without losing sight of the enjoyment she saw in architect Aldo van Eyck's playgrounds — is surrounded by cinderblock partitions laid with coarse mortar. They provide basic enclosure at eye level and diffused light from above (figure 113). Not only are there no doors between them, but the programs in them are, like other educational and sports activities in the center, subsidized so that participation and the opportunity to work with renowned artists can be affordable and accessible to all.

Past the workshops, at the end of the promenade that cuts across the leisure center, the internal street abruptly abuts the middle of a long wall and a simple boardwalk covering the channeled Águas Pretas creek. This narrow and potentially floodable valley runs almost 150 meters

115. SESC Pompeia Leisure Center, São Paulo, 1977–86, general aerial view of the ensemble from the southeastern side with the sports towers in the foreground. Photograph by Nelson Kon.

114. SESC Pompeia Leisure Center, São Paulo, 1977–86, general western view of the sports towers and boardwalk over Águas Pretas Creek. Photograph by Nelson Kon.

(492 ft.) between rua Barão do Bananal to the west and avenida Pompeia to the east, surrounded by none of its original natural features beyond the channeled stream. Bo Bardi considered several alternatives for the area, including landscaped terraces along an open canal and small bridges covering the stream and flanked by a large wall to be finished with either large stones or cyclopean concrete with plants growing in its middle.[21] After she saw pictures of the Atlantic City Boardwalk along the New Jersey coast, she came up with a much simpler solution.[22] She left the back wall in its original masonry structure, whitewashed it, and covered the flood channel with a slightly elevated boardwalk while finishing the ground pavement between the towers and the factory sheds with cobblestones and quartzite tiles.[23] With a simple gesture, Bo Bardi created "a long boardwalk that extends throughout the forbidden land with a waterfall to the right, a kind of

collective outdoor shower," a metaphysical but lively beach in the middle of a dense urban landscape of brick and cement.[24]

Looking east onto the boardwalk toward avenida Pompeia, the visitor sees a slender water tower protruding seventy-five meters (245 ft.) into the sky (figure 114). Next to it, the two large, raw concrete towers containing the sports facilities seem to erupt from the ground and to embrace each other with the arms of four double footbridges that crisscross the sky (figures 115, 116). Bo Bardi described the sublime gap between them as "one second of amazement" (figure 117).[25] Before their construction started, she declared in the press: "I hope the sports complex will be ugly, uglier than MASP. It is a silo, a bunker, a container, and more, divided by an area where nothing can be built."[26] In designing the towers, she said: "I thought about the wonderful architecture of old Brazilian military forts lost near the seashore," most

116. SESC Pompeia Leisure Center, São Paulo, 1977–86, the four sets of pre-stressed concrete skywalks between the sports towers seen from the boardwalk. Photograph by Nelson Kon.

117. SESC Pompeia Leisure Center, São Paulo, 1977–86, the "moment of amazement" described by Lina Bo Bardi about the space between the sports towers. Photograph by Zeuler R. Lima.

likely referring to prominent structures she had seen in and around the bay of Salvador.[27]

She realized early in the design process that her first ideas for staggered slabs or boxy volumes would not work, given the site's legal constraints, which she took, as in MASP's case, to be the "architect's best friend."[28] The available area for building along the flood valley was divided into two relatively small sections, which posed a significant challenge to the large program. The only possible solution was to stack up the sports facilities into two interconnected buildings, and her design team resourcefully devised a simple footprint based on legal setbacks, the irregular geometry of the site, the surrounding streets and lots, and the continuity with the existing sheds.

For all those constraints, the result is remarkable. The tower on the north side contains the larger facilities with a rectangular plan measuring thirty by forty meters (98 × 131 ft.). It lines up with the footprint of the lower industrial sheds and extrudes into a rough-looking, robust, but hollow concrete tower with pre-stressed concrete waffle slabs. On the ground level, it contains an indoor swimming pool; above it are four stacked, double-height floors containing basketball, volleyball, and soccer courts, which, as Bo Bardi stressed, should be used only for leisure, not for competition. The swimming pool — which she originally planned to be made of pebble-encrusted concrete, emulating a northeastern weir, and to be surrounded by wall paintings, evoking the sky — is the only part of the north tower with direct access from the boardwalk. Users wishing to access the sports courts must enter through the adjacent service tower and travel along the skywalks (figure 118).

A Bowl of Soup for the People

170

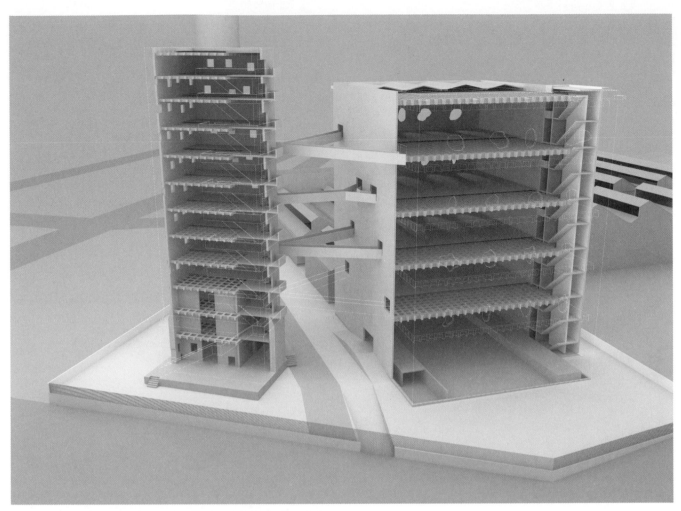

118. SESC Pompeia Leisure Center, São Paulo, 1977–86, sectioned view of the sports tower showing structural, spatial, and circulation logic. Computer rendering. Zeuler R. Lima Collection.

Instead of conventional windows, she designed sixteen large, irregular openings on both the east and west walls of the largest tower. From the outside, they resemble the punched holes she had conceived for an unrealized study for Teatro Oficina during the casting of the SESC sports facilities.[29] From inside each sports court, the opposite rows of four two-meter-tall (6 ft.) irregular openings give the impression of a cavernous space, which she described as a primitive form of inhabitation.[30] "I am horrified by air conditioning as much as I am by carpeting," she declared soon after the complex opened. "So, I suggested the prehistoric holes of caves with no glazing, nothing."[31]

The windows had been designed as rectangular shapes until Bo Bardi returned from a trip to Japan, invigorated and desiring to experiment with new ideas. She showed a sketch to her assistant Marcelo Ferraz pointing out the irregular holes she had in mind for him to develop. After presenting a study drawing to her and commenting that he had never done anything similar, she responded: "Never? Well, neither have I. Let's do it."[32]

Bo Bardi had a knack for creating these irregular shapes, often referring to them in Italian as "fustella" — a die-cutting instrument — to describe her preferences. In addition, the window holes were carefully studied and cast with polystyrene foam forms and beveled corners so that rainwater would drip and run away from the interior floors. Though those openings were initially conceived to be uncovered, Bo Bardi's team added large but simple wooden trellises in square frames sliding between two horizontal tracks against the interior walls (figures 119, 120). Despite their size, they can be easily moved, even by children, allowing for constantly changing patterns of sun and light in the

A Bowl of Soup for the People

171

119. SESC Pompeia Leisure Center, São Paulo, 1977–86, sports court inside the larger tower showing waffle slabs and hole-windows. Photograph by Nelson Kon.

space, contrasts between gray concrete and red trellises, and surprising and dramatic views of the city.

Opposite the blank concrete wall of the bulky sports building, the smaller and almost triangular area south of the Águas Pretas creek received a more compact but taller tower. Bo Bardi rotated it almost forty-five degrees in relation to its companion, making it parallel to avenida Pompeia, and squared off its north corner as she had done with the Franciscan fraternity's Angels' Chapel. The south tower consists of eleven floors stacked onto three slightly different tiers and houses the support services for the courts and swimming pool, exercise and locker rooms, medical facilities, and even, originally, an elliptical snack bar on the ground floor, which was later removed to house a few offices.[33] Although the interior of this tower is mostly plain

and regular, its external walls are arranged with square, irregularly distributed windows that seem to move around the facades, creating unexpected views from each floor.

This taller tower also acts as the main artery of the sports complex, with the public vertical circulation on the chamfered north side consisting of two elevators and a red helicoidal staircase, which she called a "cage-staircase" because of the vertical metal rods running throughout the eleven floors.[34] The halls of the third, fifth, seventh, and ninth floors give access to the four sets of open skywalks leading to the sports courts in the north tower. Though the flyovers are shaped like a solid channel in pre-stressed concrete, keeping users safe and avoiding intermediate supports, each set has a different layout. This arrangement accentuates the complex's sculptural appeal and the sublime experience

120. SESC Pompeia Leisure Center, São Paulo, 1977–86, interior view
of one of the hole-windows in the sports towers covered with a trellised
shutter. Photograph by Zeuler R. Lima.

of moving between the two towers. It also helps users identify each floor, as did the color palettes of the sports courts,
which Bo Bardi had based on the conventional representation of the seasons of the year.[35]

The water tower is the tallest structure on the site and
represents Bo Bardi's desire to emulate not only anonymous
infrastructure but also Mexican architect Luis Barragán's
use of concrete.[36] After seeing his tall sculptural pieces
at the entrance of Ciudad Satélite in a copy of the 1976
MoMA exhibition catalogue of his work sent to Bardi,
Bo Bardi decided to replicate their irregular, striped, and
rough appearance. With the help of engineer Toshio Ueno
and much on-site experimentation, Bo Bardi developed
a system of four sliding pieces with interior and exterior
wooden forms shaped like two half-circles with slightly conic

sections. Each ring was one meter (3 ft.) high, which allowed
one section of reinforced concrete to be cast per day. This
system also allowed workers to place burlap sacks in the gap
between the previously cast section and the bottom of the
circular form just before they poured concrete into it. On
removal of the forms, an irregular bas-relief emerged from
each successive step, creating the image of running concrete
around the tower, which suggests the imprint of human
hands on an otherwise mechanical process.

Once the towers were completed, the whole complex was
open to the public. Bo Bardi imagined a colorful exhibition
about soccer for the opening ceremony, but the show did not
happen.[37] Still, users filled the complex with lively activities similar to those she had seen on her first visits to the site
almost ten years before. Later in life, she considered the old

A Bowl of Soup for the People

factory to be "a document of human work to be respected," while "SESC Pompeia is the new building we designed; it is the water tower that became a landmark."[38] But still, she noted concern with conviviality, "This is a different building. It is not for competition, it is for friendship — sports, joy, children — it is dedicated to Garrincha [a legendary Brazilian soccer player], who made people who lost the competition happy."[39]

Bo Bardi had a difficult time leaving SESC Pompeia after the building was finished and the makeshift office was taken down. Although her partnership with the SESC staff was productive at first, conflicts arose, especially after the old factory opened and she became involved in a series of pedagogical exhibitions. She formally criticized their plans as "against Lina Bo Bardi's will" and complained of the need to instruct visitors about the "correct use of spaces and the conservation of the center's assets."[40] She even threatened to resign from the project before the towers were completed. Though the directors supported her during the building process despite her domineering presence and intolerance, she was discreetly released from the center's programming efforts after the construction ended in 1986.

Still, Bo Bardi's name has remained deeply associated with the leisure center. SESC Pompeia, like MASP, continues to serve as one of the main references in the bustling everyday and cultural life of São Paulo. Despite significant changes after the Bardis' departure, the museum continues to elicit a ceremonial approach. Meanwhile, the leisure center invites all the senses to collective life and individual delight as she imagined for it and as it was created by a committed administrative team. Like her experiences in Italy and the Brazilian Nordeste, SESC Pompeia represents an important realization in her life and in her career. It is the summation of three decades of work and bears witness to her affection for handmade work, to the use of innovative construction technology, and to her understanding that modernization does not preclude the incorporation of history and tradition. She continued to see human beings as the protagonists of buildings and to define architecture as a "collective service."[41]

As a shared space, the complex on rua Clélia promotes lived experiences in several — sometimes overlapping, sometimes juxtaposed — situations of social and cultural contact, circumstances for which Bo Bardi continuously searched with great personal and political effort. She stressed that "'poor architecture' was the leading idea for restoring the ensemble," defining "poor not as penury, but as the maximum of communication and dignity while employing fewer and humbler means."[42] In addition, she admitted that the expressionist character of the towers "comes from my European background, but I never disregard the surrealism of the Brazilian people, their inventions, their pleasure in getting together."[43]

The factory rehabilitation and the new towers gave Bo Bardi long overdue recognition as the architecture debate reopened in Brazil and the country faced a different reality in the aftermath of the military regime. SESC Pompeia, more than MASP, shook the ground of Brazilian architecture, accustomed as it was to worn-out modernist vocabularies. The project reinvigorated Bo Bardi's desire to work and served as her response to the international architectural crises in the late twentieth century. She disagreed with the growing distance between architects and social causes and vehemently opposed the formal solipsism of European and North American architecture that had been propelled by historicism and postmodernism. She considered those developments to be "the complex of impotence faced by the impossibility of escaping from one of the most appalling human feats in the West." Frustrated, she insisted that modern avant-gardes were left to "live off eating the remains of capitalism . . . [and] copying as much as possible the principles of a historical documentation reduced to consumption."[44]

As leisure and culture became commodified worldwide and as Brazil transitioned from a long authoritarian regime into democratic rule in the face of dire social and economic circumstances, SESC Pompeia offered a concrete example of one of Bo Bardi's main pursuits: to show that "culture is a fact of everyday reality," not a special event or even the domain of the educated elite.[45] She described the center as "a light beam, a wind, . . . a bit of joy in a sad city."[46] Above all, SESC Pompeia is her most complete and mature tribute to the Brazilian people, to freedom and democracy, and to social integration.

Bo Bardi imagined it, as many in the center's staff still do, as an antidote to consumer society and a space for human imagination and shared participation. In this context, she liked to refer to anthropologist Darcy Ribeiro, who described the leisure center as a small socialist experiment.[47] "Just take a look at SESC [Pompeia]," she pondered. "When I say that people carry a bowl of soup with a proud outlook as if everybody were looking at them, I feel I was able to do something that serves the collectivity."[48]

A Rugged Field, a Hefty Crop

The experience with SESC Pompeia epitomized Lina Bo Bardi's almost four decades of a circuitous intellectual quest, moving her career into the spotlight of Brazilian architecture. This was a meaningful feat, especially considering that most architects in the country struggled with economic problems and with a professional debate devoid of new energies. It also brought other simultaneous projects and presented new challenges and directions to her activities as a designer. The impetus and political relevance of Brazil's cultural environment had vanished, destabilizing her conceptual goals. The promises of revolution were out, and the tight-knit cultural networks of the past were gone. Progressive artists and intellectuals drifted in a quest for national and popular ideals, still ideologically committed to fighting the bourgeois world despite a belief system in crisis.[1] Conversely, mass culture and consumption were in, reorganizing the conditions for artistic and intellectual production.

Brazil, moreover, was entering another difficult phase as the second international oil crisis took hold between 1979 and 1980. The crisis harshly affected the country's economy and contributed to the demise of the cycle of economic expansion promoted by the military regime. The nation was returning to democratic rule but not to economic and social stability.[2] Despite the pitfalls of Brazil's lost decade, architects returned to the drawing board, seeing that the international push for a postmodern debate provided no consistent alternatives for the realities of underdeveloped countries. Though secluded from the mainstream professional milieu, Bo Bardi's unusual career and collaborative work had given her unique tools to face those challenges. As she approached her late sixties and allied herself with a younger generation, her career as a designer bloomed, albeit with her customary doubt and anxiety but with no less great insight and originality.

As the project and construction of SESC Pompeia evolved, Bo Bardi began organizing a retrospective book about her experiences in Salvador, critically reflecting on the search for an alternative design culture in Brazil. She outlined a storyboard for the publication, dated March 18, 1980, which consisted of two complementary parts.[3] The first part would contain a collection of her essays reconsidering the notions of handicraft and popular art largely based on Gramsci's philosophy. The second part was planned as a selective anthology of texts by iconic artists and intellectuals active in the Nordeste in the early 1960s, such as Abelardo da Hora, Lívio Xavier, and Glauber Rocha.

She quickly became disillusioned with the project, however, and abandoned it within months. Two years after her death, in 1994, her collaborators decided to publish an edited version of the book and titled it *Tempos de grossura: Design no impasse* (Times of roughness: Design at an impasse).[4] In it, she described a stalemate in which the conditions no longer existed for an industrial production adjusted to the country's reality and popular needs. Brazil had chosen refinement, not genuine roughness, in her opinion, turning industrial design into "the most appalling evidence of the perversity of the whole [capitalist] system."[5]

The edited book contains texts from her original list with a few additions. One aspect excluded from the final publication, however, was a small note Bo Bardi intended as the book's epigraph. Originally written in French, it read: "L'Histoire est ce qui transforme des documents en monuments. Michel Foucault. Moi, je crois justement le contraire. L.B.B. [History is that which transforms documents into monuments. Michel Foucault. I believe in exactly the opposite. L.B.B.]."[6] With theoretical wit, she introduced a synthesis of her approach to history and material culture. She also rejected the traditional notion of linear time for a "historical present" — a borrowed linguistic term that frames past events as a present experience — especially associating it with several of the adaptive reuse studies she produced after her experience with SESC Pompeia.

Despite the dilemmas that fed her intellectual frustrations, the privileged situation offered by the leisure and cultural center allowed Bo Bardi to document different aspects of Brazilian culture empirically. She worked with the institution's educational team on the creation of several exhibitions as different sections of the rehabilitated factory gradually opened to the public between January and August 1982. The general activities pavilion opened on April 12, with the first of a series of unusual shows she organized for the center until 1985. She was initially appointed to coordinate the exhibition program, but control was transferred to the SESC staff in 1983 after conflicts grew between the organization and Bo Bardi.[7] During their productive but argumentative collaboration, she planned nine shows, six of which were set up with her assistants in the exhibition hall next to the center's library.

Three of the exhibitions happened in 1982 while she vacillated between preparing and abandoning her book. She dedicated the first exhibition to a critical history of design and manufacturing in Brazil; the second offered a critical commentary on kitsch; and the third showcased Brazilian toys. During this period, she also planned a show about Brazilian dressing habits, but it never happened.[8] After that, she helped set up an irreverent exhibition about Pinocchio in 1983, another show about rural architecture and peasant culture in 1984, and a final one about children and animals in 1985, after abandoning two other ideas, one about cultural habits in the poor outskirts of São Paulo and another about consumer society.[9]

The people who entered the main pavilion of SESC Pompeia for the first time in 1982 encountered the unusual pedagogical exhibition, *Design no Brasil: História e Realidade* (Design in Brazil: History and reality).[10] The show was organized in association with MASP and the Núcleo de Desenho Industrial (Center for industrial design), a research partnership between the Federação das Indústrias do Estado de São Paulo (São Paulo industry federation) and the Ministério da Cultura e da Ciência (Ministry of culture and science).[11] Small and large objects as diverse as indigenous ceramic and textile pieces, artisanal quilts, home appliances, and plane models flooded the space in an expanded version of the 1969 exhibition *A Mão do Povo Brasileiro* (The hand of the Brazilian people), confronting the challenges of industrial production.

The adaptation of the long SESC shed was simple and innovative. A scaffolding system with a long ramp and two floors bordering the library supported the most intimate part of the exhibition while providing panoramic views of the diverse collection of Brazilian objects set on the floor. In the exhibition brochure, Bo Bardi cautioned visitors as usual: "This is not an art exhibition. . . . It is like a torrent, a rigorously planned confusion." With it, she publicly handed down her intellectual project, calling "Brazilian designers . . . to the task of preparing an inventory and a revision." Privately, she noted, "other potentials wait to be discovered and capitalized into an innovative plan that could achieve international relevance."[12]

A few months later, on October 24, Bo Bardi and the SESC Pompeia educational team organized a small, week-long exhibition titled *O 'Belo' e o Direito ao Feio* ("Beauty" and the right to ugliness), with works produced in the handicraft workshops by employees from the Instituto Nacional de Assistência Médica e Previdência Social (INAMPS, National medical and social welfare institute). She transformed the pavilion foyer into a porch covered with aluminum foil that led visitors into a display of handmade furniture, knick-knacks, photographs, and paintings. She also noted: "We do not intend to legitimize kitsch taste, the stigma of the educated bourgeoisie against those who are less fortunate." Instead, translating one of the essays she planned for her book about the impasse of design, she considered the crafters' lack of aesthetic education as "an essential base of many civilizations . . . that never knew the concept of beauty, a concentration camp imposed by the West."

During the display of works by INAMPS employees, Bo Bardi saw to the large exhibition *Mil Brinquedos para a Criança Brasileira* (One thousand toys for

Brazilian children), which stemmed from a research project, "Brinquedos artesanais e expressividade cultural" (Handcrafted toys and cultural expression), promoted by SESC's scientific library.[13] A large team collected an exhaustive inventory of makeshift and industrial objects used in children's play and found on the peripheries of Brazilian cities.[14] Despite improvisation and conflicts, toys of all sizes and shapes filled the exhibition hall, welcoming an enormous crowd at the opening ceremony on the early summer Sunday of December 5, 1982.[15]

"Children's play is a serious thing," Bo Bardi wrote in the exhibition catalogue.[16] With the joyful *Toy Symphony* playing in the background, visitors to the opening filled their eyes with a feast of colorful toys ranging from simple, wood-carved animals and bicycles to a homemade merry-go-round and even a playground piece improvised with large inner tubes.[17] Aside from eliciting fantasies, Bo Bardi hoped that the collection would establish precedents for the design of authentically Brazilian toys, analogous to her plans for the collection of popular artifacts she had started in Salvador two decades before. Her ultimate goal was to create a museum of spontaneous art, following the example anthropologist Ana Maria Beck had set up at Universidade Federal de Santa Catarina (Santa Catarina Federal University).[18]

A few months after the toy exhibition closed, Bo Bardi hosted the traveling exhibition *Pinocchio: História de um Boneco Italiano* (Pinocchio: History of an Italian puppet). The show, held from August 14 to October 15, 1983, celebrated the one-hundredth anniversary of the fictional character. Bo Bardi displayed original material she received from Italy along one side of the exhibition hall and reserved most of the space for a playground of large makeshift animal characters from Collodi's story. She provocatively added a sign at the entrance that read: "Pinocchio: Trombadinha internacional" (Pinocchio: International purse-snatcher), emphasizing the social allegories in the original text. To her, Pinocchio was "not a liar with a long nose who needed to be corrected, but a poor juvenile delinquent," a victim of problems such as those experienced by street children in Brazilian society, not a fairy-tale boy who learns a lesson about honesty.[19]

After her derisive interpretation of Pinocchio's story, Bo Bardi and her assistants collaborated on the preparation for a new, large exhibition planned by the SESC research team. The event was based on a 1980 study of the culture of *caipiras* (traditional peasant groups from the Brazilian central plateau) conducted by anthropologist Carlos Rodrigues Brandão.[20] She turned his inventory of music, religious festivities, and adobe and wattle-and-daub buildings into an exhibition focused on rural architecture and

titled *Caipiras, Capiaus: Pau-a-Pique* (Peasants, bumpkins: Wattle-and-daub).

Opened on June 29, 1984, with musical performances and even live animals, including a cow, the exhibition ran until November 11.[21] The show revisited Bo Bardi's early interest in peasant architecture in Italy and in the hinterlands of the Nordeste, transporting it to closer locations within a three-hundred-kilometer (186 mi.) radius of São Paulo. She set up a full-size diorama of a caipira landscape in two complementary parts. At the entrance of the long hall, a colorful, handpainted "grove of poles" welcomed visitors, emulating the traditional celebration of Saint John's Eve.[22] Beyond those poetic woods, Bo Bardi treated the exhibition hall as a *terreiro*, a farmyard, surrounded by replicas of simple buildings accompanied by slide and film projections on the rear wall.

This rural diorama contained three small houses, a few small barns, rustic domestic utensils and furniture, and a chapel. She paid special attention to the documentation of the onsite construction of the largest of the houses. Coordinated by an elderly caipira couple pictured in the exhibition catalogue, the house recalled the seven-thousand-cruzeiro house she published in *Habitat* in 1951. Instead of folklore, Bo Bardi stressed the exhibition's political aim, disagreeing with UNESCO building recommendations for developing countries. "Well, mud for the Third World, concrete and steel for those above the Equator," she protested in the exhibition catalogue. As she invited visitors to look around the original prefabricated structure of SESC's pavilions, she asserted, hopefully: "Long live Hennebique, pioneer in reinforced concrete!"[23]

Bo Bardi described the caipira exhibition as "a farewell and, at the same time, an invitation to document Brazilian history," as exemplified in the cultural habits and artifacts of a disappearing rural population.[24] Like her abandoned book, this show pointed to the end of her lifelong dedication to the cultural history of design and spoke to the dilemmas in her quest for an architecture of simple means infused with rationalist values and political expectations. She would return to curatorial work only once more, in 1985, at the conclusion of her work with the SESC Pompeia research and curatorial staff.

This final collaboration was titled *Entre-ato para Crianças* (Entr'acte for children) and aimed to expand the two previous large shows and to engage the center's young audience in a fable about animals. Informed by her experiences with theater productions, Bo Bardi described the show as an invitation into children's imaginative universe and out of the world of monsters and scarecrows created by adults. After five preparatory months, the show opened

121. Lina Bo Bardi, *Study for "Entr'acte for Children" Exhibition*, SESC Pompeia Leisure Center, preliminary study, December 27, 1984. Ballpoint pen, felt pen, and India ink on cardstock, 25 × 35 cm. Márcia Benevento Collection.

on March 24, 1985, with musical performances and several parallel activities dedicated to environmental issues.

Visitors entered the hall to find long, lateral shelves holding several glass cases with preserved insects and mounted animals from local zoology collections, while large papier-mâché animal props produced in SESC's workshops shared the main floor with a handcrafted merry-go-round, hand-carved beasts inside a green fence made by one of the SESC construction workers, and a red gazebo with a long ramp (figure 121). Bo Bardi warned, "This exhibition has nothing to do with ecology or animal protection."[25] Instead, she wanted it to be "an invitation into science and fantasy."[26] As she helped set up this last cabinet of curiosities, she prepared to bid farewell to nine years of work with SESC Pompeia. Her long experience with the institution summarized much

of the quest, the impasse, and the insights in her development as a designer, which she applied to the several projects she planned during and after that period, though only a few of them were executed.

Among these projects were the studies Bo Bardi produced between 1977 and 1980 for a cosmetics factory owned by entrepreneur Aparício Basílio da Silva, a member of MASP's board of directors. Her preliminary ideas for undulating roofs covered with gardens responded to his desire to create "a great park of violets with water and flowers." Revisited in November 1980, during a harsh economic crisis in Brazil, the project became much simpler. Bo Bardi alternatively proposed regular and concentric geometries, but her ideas never went beyond these initial studies. Still, she was confident that they were "joyful, beautiful, simple,

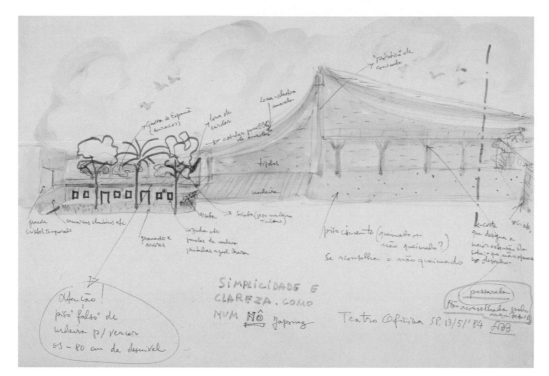

122. Lina Bo Bardi, *Study for Teatro Oficina*, first idea for the theater renovation with yellow tent and hole-windows, May 15, 1984. Watercolor, ballpoint pen, felt pen, and pencil on cardstock, 33.2 × 48 cm. ILBPMB Collection.

and very different from Brazilian architecture, which today is full of hubris."[27]

During that period, after much insistence from her assistants Ferraz and Vainer, Bo Bardi led a team of eight young architects in a public design competition for the historic downtown of São Paulo.[28] The topic was complex: the rehabilitation of Anhangabaú Valley, a park turned into a hub of expressways and mass transportation in the core of the city. Initially hesitant about the site, she eventually saw it as an opportunity to promote collective public spaces. As was usual in her case, after lengthy discussion, the final proposal was drafted in three long days just before the deadline of May 18, 1981.[29]

Unlike the winning proposal, which buried all the transportation systems under a large concrete slab, Bo Bardi and her team's design would have moved most vehicular traffic to an elevated expressway. By proposing two overlapping decks supported by steel columns whose naturalistic form and structural principle were based on large trees with tabular roots, the project's urban impact would be minimized. "Once liberated to pedestrians," she hoped, "the valley will return to life." She imagined that Anhangabaú would become "the Central Park of the people," surrounded by rehabilitated buildings, such as the old post office

transformed into a center for Nordeste immigrants and adding a panoramic restaurant atop the Zarzur Building, the tallest high-rise in the valley. More than a feasible proposal, this project was a consciously designed manifesto for the collective life of the city.[30]

Shortly after the competition and the opening of the rehabilitated Pompeia factory in 1982, Bo Bardi received commissions for cultural facilities from around the country, many of which never happened, such as a proposal to convert the old gas holder in Porto Alegre, capital of the southernmost state of Rio Grande do Sul, into a labor museum.[31] Still, she had more luck with the renovation of the São Paulo Museu de Arte Moderna, previously directed by Matarazzo and then under the leadership of Basílio da Silva, whose factory project had been abandoned. After a long history of institutional instability, MAM had found a permanent location under the canopy near the Biennial Pavilion entrance where Bo Bardi and Gonçalves had set up the *Bahia* exhibition in 1959, a "sacred space," according to her notes.[32]

Aware that the museum had neither a large collection nor resources, she proposed a long, glazed gallery under the cantilevered canopy facing the lawn and backed by support facilities with walls blocking a parking lot. Her one-point

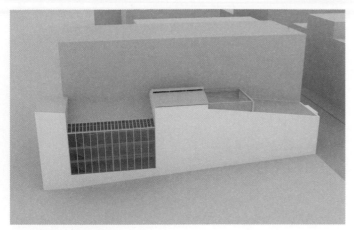

123. Teatro Oficina, São Paulo, 1982–93, exterior western view of the renovated building with side window. Computer rendering. Zeuler R. Lima Collection.

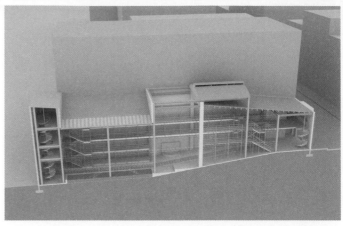

124. Teatro Oficina, São Paulo, 1982–93, longitudinal sectioned view of the renovated building showing structural, spatial, and circulation logic. Computer rendering. Zeuler R. Lima Collection.

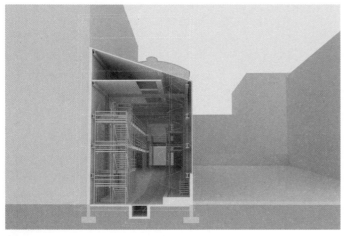

125. Teatro Oficina, São Paulo, 1982–93, cross-section view of the renovated building showing added scaffoldings for audience and street-stage. Computer rendering. Zeuler R. Lima Collection.

perspective in watercolor summarizes her ideas for a single space seen in many of the galleries she designed as a deep void with simple supports for the artworks.[33] The new museum opened in 1983, with its black rubber flooring, its blue-and-gray partitions, similar to MASP, and a large window framing Parque do Ibirapuera — a vitrine of forms and images shared by the exhibition hall and the city.

During the SESC project, Bo Bardi again collaborated with Martinez Corrêa, who had returned from his self-exile in Africa.[34] Between 1980 and 1981, she sketched a renovation project for Teatro Oficina in collaboration with architect Marcelo Suzuki. She proposed catwalks connecting asymmetrical platforms surrounded by individual chairs, but the idea was soon abandoned, and she did not return to the project until May 1984, when Martinez Corrêa planned to purchase a large lot behind his building on rua Jaceguai.[35]

At that point, Suzuki left the project and one of Martinez Corrêa's collaborators suggested that Bo Bardi work with another young architect, Edson Elito.[36]

Together they imagined a wide stadiumlike structure linked to the long and narrow Teatro Oficina, which would be transformed into a covered entryway. Given the lack of resources, however, Bo Bardi limited her efforts to renovating the old building. She imagined a long, yellow plastic tarp stretching up from the entrance to a central roof beam and down to the edge of the stage. This tentlike space was intended to create a physical extension to the street with the stage flooring extending out as a boardwalk toward the back of the site.[37] In addition, she suggested creating irregular openings on the lateral rear wall, referring to them as the holes of cannon balls from the Spanish Civil War, a sign of her sympathies for the struggle against authoritarian regimes

126. Teatro Oficina, São Paulo, 1982–93, interior view of the street-stage with scaffoldings and access door in the background. Photograph by Nelson Kon.

(figure 122).[38] According to Martinez Corrêa, the irregular holes, which became a recurrent theme in her projects in the following years, had originated from a heated conversation between them. He had insisted that the kind of theater he directed transcended walls, to which Bo Bardi responded: "I'm not a witch, I'm an architect. I don't go through walls, I tear them down."[39]

Impatient to see the work concluded and with no previous notice, Martinez Corrêa took her literally, and he and theater members demolished the internal partitions with their own hands, creating an empty shell. This stormy gesture affected the structural integrity of the building, as well as his relationship with Bo Bardi, who designed an alternative of movable lateral galleries but grew frustrated with the process and eventually lost interest in the project. The work progressed slowly and was halted for lack of funding until

1987, when Elito would lead, almost independently from her, the initiative until the project was completed in 1989. By then, though the project was technically Bo Bardi's responsibility, she had distanced herself from Teatro Oficina.[40] Symbolically representing the collective and convoluted authorship of the theater design but aware that it did not follow her recommendations, she accepted the street-stage layout bordered by scaffolding-bleachers, a large side window with interior garden, and a retractable roof in the final project (figures 123–126). She died before it was completed in 1993.

In May 1985, a few months after designing the original yellow tent and while setting up her final exhibition at SESC, Bo Bardi was invited to work on a theatrical production with the Ornitorrinco Theater Company, which rehearsed in Teatro Oficina's basement. Director Carlos

127. Lina Bo Bardi's Studio in Morumbi, São Paulo, 1986, exterior northwestern view of the building. Computer rendering. Zeuler R. Lima Collection.

128. Lina Bo Bardi's Studio in Morumbi, São Paulo, 1986, sectioned northwestern view of the building showing structural logic. Computer rendering. Zeuler R. Lima Collection.

Eduardo "Cacá" Rosset wanted her to develop the scenic and costume design for *Physical and Pataphysical Follies*, a musical parody based on French playwright Alfred Jarry's 1896 works about the antihero King Ubu.[41] With the end of the military regime, the political discourse in the arts had changed, but younger groups remained interested in irreverent experimentation, leading her to revisit earlier ideas for audience participation, flexibility, and improvisation such as in the radical production of *Gracias, señor*.

For the production, because the scenic elements needed to be permeable and adaptable, Bo Bardi chose an empty space suggesting Poland's steppes on the stage of Teatro Sérgio Cardoso in São Paulo.[42] Scenes were filled only by actors, light projections, and simple stage props, and costumes were constantly transformed and moved, all to keep the audience in great anticipation. Among the props was a colorful, calico-covered, stellated dodecahedron, based on a similar small object she had found in the Nordeste representing a mandacaru cactus flower. In addition, she designed a surrealist sculpture on wheels — a pink polochon, a large pillow-pig made in papier-mâché with two buttocks, one at each end, and no face.[43] The provocative *polochon* moved between the stage and the lobby, where a photographic exhibition about Jarry's work was displayed with the projection of René Clair's 1924 Dadaist film *Entr'Acte*, the same title Bo Bardi used for the simultaneous exhibition at SESC.

Later that year, she received a telegram announcing her prize for "best set design." In private, she told her assistants: "Set design? I am not a set designer. I've gotten rid of set design."[44] Later, she prepared a formal acceptance note thanking the jury and writing solemnly, "Theater is life," and adding, "In a certain sense, traditional set design is the opposite of architecture, and the absence of a stage set is, as Walter Gropius said, pure architecture."[45]

The theater prize came as her relationship with SESC Pompeia was ending. Still, the leisure center's success brought requests from public representatives for adaptive-reuse proposals, though only a few would materialize into construction projects, one of which came from the city's health department. In December 1986, she presented a preliminary proposal for converting the sheds of a former slaughterhouse, located just a few blocks west of the new SESC facilities, into what she described as a "poor man's Bauhaus," but the project was soon abandoned.[46] Before that, an invitation had come from André Benassi, mayor of Jundiaí, an industrial town sixty kilometers (37 mi.) north of São Paulo. He wanted to rehabilitate the town's historic Teatro Polytheama, which was originally built in 1897 as a simple multiuse pavilion and closed in 1960 after a long life as Jundiaí's main entertainment center.[47] Once again, she referred to the theatricality of everyday life.

In August 1986, just over a year after first visiting the site, Bo Bardi presented a preliminary study to Mayor Benassi explaining that her goal was "to transform [the theater] into a modern space for multiple uses" while preserving its popular social and historic meaning as a collective space.[48] Although she intended simply to neutralize the dilapidated, ornate exterior walls with white paint, she focused great attention on the interior spaces and the next-door lot, which belonged to the state electric power company.

She proposed removing the partitions between individual boxes throughout the horseshoe galleries and transforming them into a large, single balcony recalling the Italian theaters of her youth. (She liked to call the balcony

129. Lina Bo Bardi's Studio in Morumbi, São Paulo, 1986, exterior southeastern view of the building with bamboo grove in the background. Photograph by Zeuler R. Lima.

"barcaccia," which literally means "big boat.")[49] At the back of the stage, she imagined a wide, glazed plane overlooking the city. In addition, she proposed a side concrete volume along the ground floor to expand the atrium and create an exhibition hall. The adjacent landscaped areas would provide access to the upper galleries through an unusual looping tubular structure with circular windows, reminiscent of studies for unrealized bleachers for the SESC swimming pool. On the backside of the theater, she imagined a bar semiburied into the slope — "like a grotto," she wrote — and under a cantilevered roof garden.

The cleanup and renovation of the old structure started in 1988, but the project was completed only after Bo Bardi died, when her longtime collaborator, Marcelo Ferraz, and his business partner, Francisco Fanucci, carried out the proposal with a reduced site and scope. Limited to the existing building, they followed most of her ideas for the theater. Old elements painted in white offered a background to new elements such as the side atrium in raw concrete, the blue walls surrounding the balconies finished in wood, and an abstract glass chandelier. Ferraz and Fanucci were faithful to Bo Bardi's desire to leave the theater's "spirit intact as a symbol of a time and of a city and as part of today's society," materializing her understanding that historical buildings belong in the present and that architecture should enhance collective life.[50]

Another project Bo Bardi temporarily became involved with at this time was the rehabilitation of the old 1912 Urca cable car station on Sugarloaf Mountain in Rio de Janeiro. The historical steel frame was to be converted into a theater and nightclub next to an existing auditorium in which legendary musical artists performed. Between September

130. Lina Bo Bardi's Studio in Morumbi, São Paulo, 1986, interior view of the building. Photograph by Zeuler R. Lima.

and November 1986, her team worked on a preliminary idea to maximize the visibility of the structure. She imagined the building wrapped with white panels for the sidewalls and black panels for the ceiling. Behind the stage, she suggested a transparent double-height wall. "Amazing!" she wrote, hoping the glass would "frame the view toward the open space and the ocean."[51] She decided, in jest, to nickname the project "Wunder Bar," not knowing that this study, like so many of her projects, would not pass the preliminary, wondering stage.

With more projects on the horizon but no room to accommodate her team, Bo Bardi built a small office shed on the site of the Glass House. She nestled this symmetrical rustic cabin, or *casinha* (little house), as she called it, next to a bamboo grove in the lowest part of the steep slope on the north side, allowing for just enough isolation and a separate entrance on rua Bandeirante Sampaio Soares. She conceived of a very simple, inexpensive building measuring just over fifty square meters (538 sq. ft.) and sitting on an orthogonal grid of elevated masonry foundations.

131. Lina Bo Bardi's Studio in Morumbi, São Paulo, 1986, exterior view northeastern view of the building highlighting sliding panels. Photograph by Zeuler R. Lima.

The modular geometry of the plywood panels determines the building layout, rationalizing both materials and space allocation in three transversal bays originally zoned for different workspaces (figures 127, 128). At the back of the building, a square-based masonry volume covered by a small roof garden contains a small kitchen and a bathroom separated by a diagonal partition resembling her interior layout for the Cirell House (figure 129). Several of the panels that enclose the studio, doubled with screens, slide to allow for natural light and ventilation. Rough eucalyptus piers support a pitched roof and area doubled at the center to allow for shelves running longitudinally throughout the building (figure 130). The building's modular construction and its rustic appearance evoke rationalist layouts, rural simplicity, classical architecture, and even traditional Japanese pavilions, all of which were part of Bo Bardi's broad-ranging aesthetic references (figure 131).

To connect her studio to the Glass House several meters above, Bo Bardi added three narrow, stone-stepped pathways and masonry retaining walls covered with gravel and colorful ceramic bits, as she had in other residential projects. As a result of her growing struggles with arthritis, however, she used the studio for only a short time and worked from the Glass House until the end of her life. In the late 1980s, she and Bardi would convert the shed into the offices of Instituto Quadrante (Quadrante institute), which was created to memorialize and disseminate their work and was later renamed Instituto Lina Bo e Pietro Maria Bardi. This unassuming project (the smallest building in Bo Bardi's career) combines educated elements from different historic and geographic citations together with spontaneous improvisation, which, in her opinion, was the most meaningful feature of Brazilian culture.

Aside from those short-lived studies and delayed projects and despite becoming increasingly less accessible to Bo Bardi, her cabinlike studio housed the activities surrounding a new project that would keep her team busy for three years after the conclusion of her work at SESC Pompeia. In early 1986, anthropologist Roberto Pinho, then chief of staff to the mayor of Salvador, Mário Kertész, conceived a plan that would take her back to Bahia after a long hiatus: the rehabilitation of the historic district of Pelourinho. "We need strong spirits like yours," Kertész told her in a letter. Following Pinho's suggestion, he reiterated her discourse to "avoid folkloric superficiality and to reintegrate Salvador into the contemporary world while reaffirming its historic density." Kertész explained his wish for an updated approach to popular tradition in the contemporary cultural context, emphasizing: "I want it new, not a novelty; I want it modern, not modernist." And at age seventy-one, as she started to harvest the results of a long, irregular, but substantial production, Bo Bardi prepared to reconnect with the city that had witnessed her mature into the autonomous designer and intellectual thinker she had become.[52]

This Is Not a Tourist City

After a long hiatus, but with a sense of pride, Lina Bo Bardi returned to Salvador. On April 23, 1986, the newly elected mayor, Mário Kertész, paid tribute to her at an award ceremony, recognizing her for past contributions to the city and promising her a design commission for the Parque Histórico do Pelourinho (Pelourinho historic park). Bo Bardi was about to engage in a new, large project on several sites, combining old experiences in architecture, heritage, furniture, and exhibition design with new ones in urbanism and prefabrication. "More than a simple invitation," Kertész wooed her: "This gesture is an act of justice. . . . Above all, with it, I reopen the doors of this city to welcome you into the house of a people who owe you so many services and so much love."[1] She enjoyed the courtship and responded in kind as she formally accepted the commission.

Salvador was no longer the stage in which she had come of age as a designer and cultural activist. The military regime had turned public investments toward promoting industrial activity and real estate development in the areas around the capital, leaving the downtown area largely neglected. As the country returned to democratic rule, the city tried to contain the deterioration of the district's historical ensemble by registering it as a national heritage site in 1985 and promoting new plans for the area. Mayor Kertész, with the help of his chief of staff, anthropologist Roberto Pinho, transformed the city planning department into an office of special programs with three autonomous but interrelated organizations focused on rehabilitating the historic district. Two of those organizations were charged with creating urbanization projects and sociocultural programs. The third was a plant for prefabricated community facilities coordinated by architect João Filgueiras Lima.[2]

Salvador's historic colonial center is located on a plateau on the city's west side facing the Bay of All Saints. It covers more than thirty hectares (74 acres), comprising forty-two urban blocks and about a thousand buildings.[3] Named Pelourinho (*pillory* in Portuguese) because of a plaza in which African slaves once received public punishment, the area holds this disturbing memory within a vast collection of historical houses and baroque churches and a vibrant everyday life. The goal of Pinho's plan was to preserve the architectural and urban ensemble while nurturing its traditional function as a place for social gatherings, work, and leisure, and aiming at the permanence of the local population, which is heavily low income and African in its roots. Technical surveys revealed that a third of the buildings were either almost destroyed or severely deteriorated and there were several squalid tenements, a state Bo Bardi described as having been caused by a "voluntary earthquake."[4]

Pinho's team first developed an emergency plan to prop up derelict properties. The prospects were daunting and required phased interventions to achieve results before Kertész's short term in office ended in 1989. This deadline forced Bo Bardi and her team into a tight schedule, in which they had to respond to the Program for the Recovery of Historic Sites (Programa Especial de Recuperação dos Sítios Históricos). Based on local, cultural traditions, and everyday life, the program followed the city's official plan to combine work, retail, and housing in a way that fostered an "underground economy" that would protect the population from eviction.[5] Such intentions resonated, forty years on, with the promises of postwar reconstruction that Bo Bardi's Italian generation nurtured with anti-monumental and humanistic sensibilities.

She was against the idea of rehabilitation as "the restitution to a primitive state of time, place, and style," instead affirming that "the social issue is perhaps more important than the architectural restoration." She envisioned a "recovery system that leaves the exterior appearance as well as the 'spirit,' the 'interior soul' of each building, intact."[6] "This is not a tourist project," Bo Bardi warned on another occasion, wanting to avoid "transforming the Pelourinho district into an 'ice-cream' city."[7] Instead, she recommended "attention to men and not just monuments" and proposed to "think

about food, music, dance, simple things but with a high level of sophistication." She strove to "establish a modern mark, rigorously respecting the principles of traditional historic preservation," and declared: "We are not going to touch anything, but we will touch everything."[8]

Bo Bardi's master plan, presented to the city of Salvador in August 1986, consisted of a complex urban rehabilitation project that included public spaces and strategic but abandoned buildings in the two areas north and south of the once-stylish rua Chile — the larger area of the Pelourinho district and the area around the Igreja Barroquinha, respectively. Several of those projects were cultural centers such as Casa do Olodum (Olodum Music Center). Her proposal also anticipated international cooperation projects focused on African heritage, such as Casa do Benin (Benin House) and a sister house, Casa do Brazil no Benin (Brazil House in Benin), Casa de Cuba na Bahia (Cuba House in Bahia) and its sibling, Casa do Brasil em Cuba (Brazil House in Cuba), though only Casa do Benin was realized among those collaborative proposals.[9]

According to her records, Bo Bardi and her team organized the projects chronologically, starting between June 1986 and March 1987, with Belvedere da Sé (Cathedral terrace) at Pelourinho and the Teatro Gregório de Matos next to the Igreja Barroquinha. Later in 1987, they moved

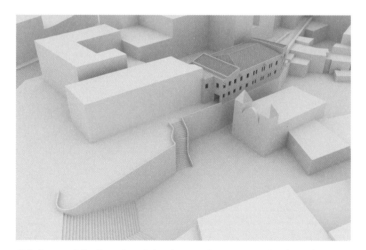

133. Barroquinha Complex, Salvador, southwestern aerial view of the ensemble with movie theater, terrace, staircases, Igreja Barroquinha, and Teatro Gregório de Matos in highlight. Computer rendering. Zeuler R. Lima Collection.

132. Teatro Gregório de Matos, Salvador, 1986–87, the inconspicuous theater entrance with Igreja Barroquinha in the foreground. Photograph by Nelson Kon.

to the recovery of old manors at ladeira da Misericórdia and the Barroquinha community center, though the latter was only partly built. Finally, between late 1987 and early 1988, Bo Bardi and her team worked on Casa do Benin and Casa do Olodum. They continued to produce construction documents, as necessary to support the building process, until mid-1989, even after the election of a new mayor, but their ambitions proved to be much larger than their resources.[10]

In order to give such a dispersed urban ensemble a sense of continuity, Bo Bardi envisioned a single and flexible prefabricated system that would relate isolated buildings while establishing a clear contrast with "the historical part, which will be highlighted by the system's current structure and time."[11] During this period, her team also proposed furniture prototypes and architectural details, but they never developed Bo Bardi's initial plans for the plazas around Terreiro de Jesus, the main square of downtown Salvador, which she envisioned as "a great tapestry in gray granite with inlays of white, blue, and red stone stripes" like in Italian plazas.[12] Other abandoned plans included a preliminary study for the creation of the Pierre Verger Foundation in 1989 after the conclusion of Kertész's term in office.[13]

The first project on Bo Bardi's list was Belvedere da Sé, the cathedral terrace, which had been remodeled by architect Filgueiras Lima a few years earlier and overlooked the placid bay. As with SESC Pompeia, she simply added a few architectural elements to it. Using the simple formal vocabulary of her previous projects, she and her team designed a small snack bar in reinforced concrete with gargoyles covered by a roof garden and a retractable yellow awning. They conceived of sturdy tables in cast concrete resembling the spool-like shape of *caxixis*, chalice-like

popular ceramic miniatures used as children's toys and produced by artisans in the Salvador bay area.[14] Above each table, she placed a large operable yellow tarp umbrella, reflecting the tensile structures she had imagined for SESC Pompeia and Teatro Oficina.

A similar yellow shelter reappeared as a kiosk bar several blocks south of Pelourinho in the reurbanization of the area around the Igreja Barroquinha and just east of the legendary praça Castro Alves. The urban, architectural, and cultural complex idealized by Pinho and Bo Bardi would have occupied (if completed) an urban site on two levels connected by large, sinuous stairs. At the center of the ensemble and in the lower level was the church, originally built in the 1720s and heavily damaged by a fire in 1984.[15] They wanted to transform it into a community center. In addition, on the upper level, a small plaza and two popular bohemian entertainment halls, the Cinema Guarany and the Tabaris Casino Night Club, both closed in the late 1960s, would be recovered as new venues for cinema, theater, and exhibitions.

From the plan regarding this popular cultural center, only the terrace next to praça Castro Alves and the main entertainment halls were rehabilitated and with little interference from Bo Bardi's team. The design team turned the old movie theater into a new cinema complex named in memory of her friend, Glauber Rocha, and added to the plaza a yellow kiosk, an outdoor screening tower, and simple furniture. Most of their attention was dedicated to renovating the old nightclub into Teatro Gregório de Matos, though the building remains almost imperceptible from the street because it is tucked between the church and the old cinema (figures 132, 133). Their plan to transform

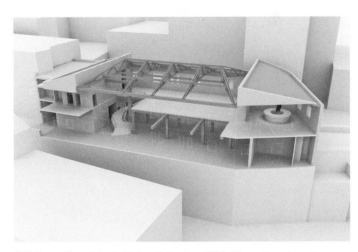

134. Teatro Gregório de Matos, Salvador, 1986–87, southern aerial view of the renovated theater. Computer rendering. Zeuler R. Lima Collection.

135. Teatro Gregório de Matos, Salvador, 1986–87, sectioned southern aerial view of the renovated theater showing structural and spatial logic. Computer rendering. Zeuler R. Lima Collection.

This Is Not a Tourist City

187

a three-story building standing between the two old theaters into a cinema club with a small screening room and archives — similar to what Bo Bardi had improvised on the ramp of Teatro Castro Alves over two decades before — never happened.

Though the church was the architectural centerpiece of the Barroquinha district rehabilitation plan, Bo Bardi's simple but innovative ideas for it remained on paper. Following her habit to neutralize old buildings in white, which had begun with the Unhão complex, she proposed to use the side naves of the ruined structure for community workshops, administration, and bathrooms, while keeping the central nave to be used as a sanctuary. In addition, she expected to rehabilitate old houses and an informal market behind the church, preserving the combination of residential

and commercial uses that animated the area's everyday life.[16] Despite basic building maintenance, cleaning, and structural stabilization in the 1990s, her church rehabilitation project was not completed because of lack of funding and lost its originally planned purpose in later efforts.[17]

Conversely, the inconspicuous Teatro Gregório de Matos, which also housed Fundação Gregório de Matos, the foundation in charge of Kertész's social and cultural programs, became the main focus of the Barroquinha district project. Though unassuming in its approach, the theater reveals itself as a larger venue once visitors pass the discreet entrance at the end of a long walkway overlooking the side of the church. From there, they find a large hall containing a unique staircase like the one in the main building of the Unhão estate. Bo Bardi maintained the exterior walls

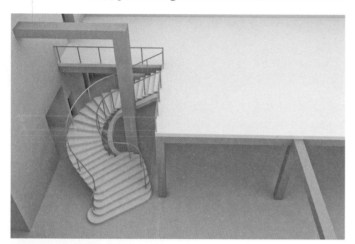

136. Teatro Gregório de Matos, Salvador, 1986–87, sectioned aerial view of the staircase connecting the exhibition hall and the elevated theater floor. Computer rendering. Zeuler R. Lima Collection.

137. Teatro Gregório de Matos, Salvador, 1986–87, structural details of the staircase connecting the exhibition hall and the elevated theater floor. Photograph by Nelson Kon.

138. Teatro Gregório de Matos, Salvador, 1986–87, interior view of elevated theater floor with foldable chairs and hole-window and bar in the background. Photograph by Nelson Kon.

139. Teatro Gregório de Matos, Salvador, 1986–87, interior view of the theater bar area with the hole-window in the background. Photograph by Zeuler R. Lima.

This Is Not a Tourist City

of the building and replaced the collapsed roof with a new wood-truss structure and ceramic tiles, as she proposed for other buildings in the Pelourinho district. She also added a post-and-beam structure in reinforced concrete to stabilize the existing walls and support the performance room on the second floor (figures 134, 135).

The ground floor became an exhibition hall with rooms for the foundation's offices and access to the upper level through a sculptural staircase, the sole feature to which Bo Bardi dedicated special attention inside the bare halls. Given the exiguous space within the gridded structure, she designed an unusually twisted form to serve as a staircase: a "load-bearing arch with ribs (like a fish skeleton). . . pointing everywhere" with "steps folded like a piece of paper," which she associated with "a great structure that I have admired since I was an architecture student: the stair of Berta Stadium in Florence, designed by Nervi."[18] With help from engineer Roberto Röchlitz, a former collaborator who helped calculate the structural frame for MASP, Bo Bardi detailed the stairs in December 1986 with spokelike trapezoidal beams supporting cascading concrete steps (figures 136, 137). Their shape allows for the appropriate connection to the unusual helicoidal beam that receives the entire load and surrounds the main structural column protruding into the space of the theater and standing on a foundation that sinks six meters (20 ft.) into the ground.

The upper level contains the performance room, a stark, open hall with hardwood flooring and no conventional stage or audience seating (figure 138). Only a dark curtain separates the room from a circular bar on the back of the building, where a single, large "hole-window," with sliding solid shutter, reappearing from previous sketches and framing a dramatic view of the surrounding neighborhood (figure 139).[19] In March 1987, before the building rehabilitation was completed and as the Gregório de Matos theater and foundation began operations with Projeto Teatro (Drama project), Bo Bardi suggested organizing an exhibition and a play as a tribute to the work done at the Centro de Estudos Afro-orientais (Center for African and Eastern Studies) in the early 1960s. She titled her proposal *Exposição e Teatro do Extremo Oriente e História da Companhia das Índias* (Exhibition and Theater of the Far East and the history of the India Company).[20] Though not realized, her design for a wooden platform — accessible by a catwalk and surrounded by foldable chairs and banners with oriental motifs hanging from the ceiling — would have combined many elements, including simple props and everyday objects, from her recent scenic and curatorial projects such as those done for Teatro Oficina and MASP.

Still, the flexible performance room offered Bo Bardi the occasion to design pliable chairs based on an idea that she had unsuccessfully pursued before. With the help of her assistants, who encouraged her by testing different mock-ups and prototypes, she arrived at a chair based on the X-shaped structure of the Florentine chairs she and Bardi kept in their personal collection. Instead of the several small, juxtaposed slats seen in the reference pieces, they used eight large boards of araracanga wood in three interconnected parts (figure 140).[21] When folded into an almost flat shape, the chairs can be either stacked or placed against a wall, satisfying the need for flexibility and her aspiration for simple techniques and materials. She decided to name her design Friar Egidio Chair, in tribute to the idealistic priest who had made the Igreja Cerrado possible.

140. Frei Egídio Chair, c. 1987. Photograph by Nelson Kon.

In early 1987, once the theater project was largely complete, Bo Bardi and her team began working at the Pelourinho district, converting the old manors on ladeira da Misericórdia (Misericórdia slope), just a few meters down the cliff from the cathedral terrace, into housing and retail units (figure 141). Until the creation of Lacerda Elevator in the late nineteenth century, the sloped road had been a major connector between the institutional and residential Upper City and the docks and commercial Lower City that still shape the historic downtown. Because the road no longer served as a passageway, it appeared to be abandoned, though it had been known historically to house bohemian and socially marginal activities.[22]

The city wanted to reverse that process and saw great potential in five lots located on the higher, curved end of the hill, where the vacant remains of eighteenth-century houses framed by ruins of old stone walls overlooked the bay (figure 142). The survey team had recommended the area as a pilot plan for commercial use, though the buildings risked physically crumbling down. Bo Bardi did not shy away from the challenge. She embraced the project for ladeira da Misericórdia as an urban and architectural experiment combining structural stabilization, adaptive reuse, and simple construction technology and serving as a model for future developments throughout the Pelourinho district.

Though the project took more than two years to complete, stretching beyond Kertész's term in office, the ensemble on ladeira da Misericórdia is a good example of Bo Bardi's resourceful imagination, search for simplicity, and engagement in collaborative work. The terraced site along the hill was unique in its components, setting, and geometry. Of the massive but plain adobe houses with arched windows originally erected along this descending stretch of the street, only three remained, along with other stone foundation walls

lining the sidewalk (figure 143). Meanwhile, to Bo Bardi's delight, lush vegetation including royal poincianas with dark orange flowers and, especially, a large mango tree sprouted out of the yards and terraces.[23]

In agreement with the city's team to improve the character of the neighborhood, Bo Bardi proposed to maintain the existing site and reuse the buildings to create small retail stores and workshops at street level with low-cost housing above (figure 144).[24] However, time and budget limitations required a strategic building methodology, one that could stabilize, renovate, and transform the many dilapidated structures throughout the historic district in an expedient and economic manner, and with aesthetic continuity. The search for such a unifying and inexpensive method led her team to work with architect Filgueiras Lima, who had been successfully developing experiments with low-cost technology in the community facilities plant he created for the city.[25]

In his workshop, Filgueiras Lima designed and built a system of prefabricated panels and structural elements in ferro-cement adapted to Bo Bardi's ideas for the historic district. Excited about using reinforced mortar cast with a metal mesh on pleated forms, similar to the technology developed by Nervi, which she admired, Bo Bardi was clear about her analogies to naturalistic forms, and interest dating back to her youth, and asked Filgueiras Lima to study alternatives based on the oblong, ribbed leaf of the palm-grass found around her house.[26] His research offered technical support that was invaluable to the success of her architectural and urbanistic vision. Moreover, his focus on labor training and job creation resonated with her ethical concerns, especially since she had little participation in the construction process.

In collaboration with engineer Frederico Schiel, Filgueiras Lima rigorously translated her aspirations into a

141. Lina Bo Bardi, *Study for Ladeira da Misericórdia Housing and Commercial Complex*, February 15, 1987. Watercolor, ballpoint pen, gouache, pencil, and India ink on Mylar, 29.4 × 118 cm. ILBPMB Collection.

142. Ladeira da Misericórdia Housing and Commercial Complex, Salvador, 1987–88, northwestern view of the urban ensemble. Photograph by Nelson Kon.

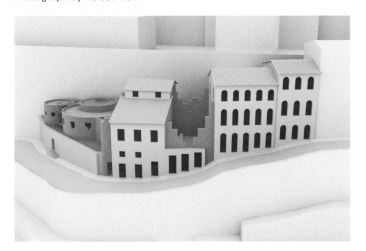

143. Ladeira da Misericórdia Housing and Commercial Complex, Salvador, 1987–88, general western view of the ensemble. Computer rendering. Zeuler R. Lima Collection.

144. Ladeira da Misericórdia Housing and Commercial Complex, Salvador, 1987–88, sectioned view western view of the ensemble highlighting restaurant and one of the housing units. Computer rendering. Zeuler R. Lima Collection.

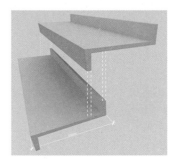

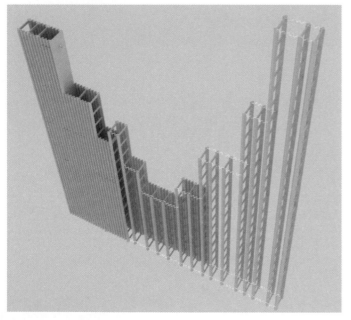

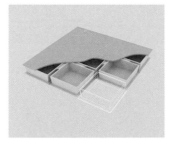

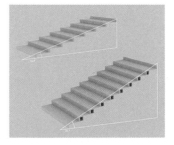

145. Ladeira da Misericórdia Housing and Commercial Complex, Salvador, 1987–88, general scheme of prefabricated ferro-cement components (studs and pleated panels). Computer rendering. Zeuler R. Lima Collection.

146. Ladeira da Misericórdia Housing and Commercial Complex, Salvador, 1987–88, general assemblage of prefabricated ferro-cement components (studs and pleated panels). Computer rendering. Zeuler R. Lima Collection.

147. Ladeira da Misericórdia Housing and Commercial Complex, Salvador, 1987–88, curved geometric patterns formed by prefabricated ferro-cement panels. Computer rendering. Zeuler R. Lima Collection.

148. Ladeira da Misericórdia Housing and Commercial Complex, Salvador, 1987–88, scheme for the use of prefabricated ferro-cement panels as buttresses. Computer rendering. Zeuler R. Lima Collection.

149. Ladeira da Misericórdia Housing and Commercial Complex, Salvador, 1987–88, prefabricated ferro-cement waffle slab components. Computer rendering. Zeuler R. Lima Collection.

150. Ladeira da Misericórdia Housing and Commercial Complex, Salvador, 1987–88, prefabricated ferro-cement staircase components. Computer rendering. Zeuler R. Lima Collection.

151. Ladeira da Misericórdia Housing and Commercial Complex, Salvador, 1987–88, geometric variations with prefabricated ferro-cement staircase components. Computer rendering. Zeuler R. Lima Collection.

modular system, composed of double studs and wall panels to be mounted and filled with either concrete or dirt (figure 145). They reduced the thickness of the pleated concrete pieces to just sixteen millimeters (¾ in.) so that they could easily be cut and staggered or bent, like an accordion, to fit the varying linear and curved geometries of Bo Bardi's projects (figures 146, 147).[27] The triangular ends of the bracing studs in reinforced concrete were designed to tightly connect to the perpendicular plates, resulting in seamless ribbed exterior surfaces and sturdy walls and buttresses stabilizing the existing structures (figure 148).

Filgueiras Lima also developed a complementary system of light partitions, prefabricated slab elements, and adjustable steps, especially adaptable to the different interiors of the houses on ladeira da Misericórdia (figures 149–151). This additional system replaced damaged interior structures and stairs that separated the floors of the colonial houses. Ferro-cement elements proved to be a viable technical solution that balanced Bo Bardi's praise for the efficiency of rational and scientific means with her interest in an organic architectural vocabulary. The elements provided the formal contrast, the structural precision, and the geometric freedom she privileged, and they were strong and easy to handle, to transport, and to assemble. They were conceptually and materially an ideal match.

After using the ferro-cement panels to prop up the three buildings on ladeira da Misericórdia with catenary buttresses topped by flower beds, Bo Bardi's team used the

152. Ladeira da Misericórdia Housing and Commercial Complex, Salvador, 1987–88, *general western view of the ensemble. Computer rendering.* Zeuler R. Lima Collection.

153. Ladeira da Misericórdia Housing and Commercial Complex, Salvador, 1987–88, *sectioned view western view of the ensemble highlighting restaurant and one of the housing units. Computer rendering.* Zeuler R. Lima Collection.

154. Ladeira da Misericórdia Housing and Commercial Complex, Salvador, 1987–88, *northern view of Coati Restaurant surrounding the mango tree with Misericórdia slope in the foreground. Photograph by* Zeuler R. Lima.

This Is Not a Tourist City

193

additional modular elements to remodel the houses inside (figures 152, 153). They designed new floor slabs connected with light stairs and subdivided with thin partitions, creating retail spaces on the street level and, above them, seven small apartments, each measuring between thirty-five and sixty square meters (377 and 646 sq. ft.). The internal layout required spatial compromises, and the upper units facing back toward the old city wall received small terraced backyards to compensate for the lack of a bay view.[28] In addition, they converted the triangular terraced lot into a restaurant and nightclub and used the small lot in the middle of the houses for a bar, hoping to promote more controlled nightlife and to avoid illicit activities (figure 154).

According to archival records, Bo Bardi's team worked diligently on the restaurant project between March and November 1987 and during the detailing for the construction phase in 1989. They searched for a layout that allowed a complex set of existing and new elements, levels, and geometries to occupy a small triangular site. They were able to develop the building layout with concentric rings of ferro-cement walls around the prominent mango tree standing in the middle of the unusual lot, and even to leave part of the roof slab open, allowing the branches to create a leafy canopy to shade the upper terrace. Behind the main hall, a smaller cylindrical volume houses the kitchen at the northern corner of the site with a helicoidal staircase that leads into a semicircular underground storage room with separate street access (figures 155, 156).

The restaurant on ladeira da Misericórdia is the most idiosyncratic building Bo Bardi designed for the rehabilitation of the Pelourinho historic district, taking full advantage of the existing trees and of the innovative construction system created by Filgueiras Lima (figure 157). The place was originally named Restaurante Coati, in tribute to the tropical relative of the raccoon. Seen from the street, the building looks like a wavy, ribbed cement wall with nine irregularly shaped windows, similar to SESC's cutout holes, and a catenary profile buttressing against the house next door. More than an agile climbing mammal, these meandering naturalistic shapes suggest the image of a "lizard lying on rocks in the sun," recalling a reference Bo Bardi made three decades earlier in her lecture about architecture and nature.[29] The restaurant also resembled the curvilinear Chame-Chame house, which had been recently torn down and replaced by an apartment building.

Between December 1987 and April 1988, soon after completing the project on ladeira da Misericórdia, Bo Bardi began work on Casa do Benin, her most accomplished project in the Pelourinho district. This African-Brazilian cultural center was part of a plan envisioned by Pinho's team to create a bilateral agreement between Salvador and the Republic of Benin, the origin of the largest contingent of African slaves brought into Bahia. Their idea was based on French-Brazilian ethnophotographer Pierre Verger's lifelong study of the Western African diaspora during the colonial period.[30] Pinho also planned to create a counterpart in Benin, Casa do Brasil, to pay tribute to Brazilian customs and practices carried by many freed slaves who returned to Africa. Though his team chose a site for a potential building in the small town of Ouidah (forty kilometers, 25 mi., west of the country's capital, Cotonou), Bo Bardi's project for

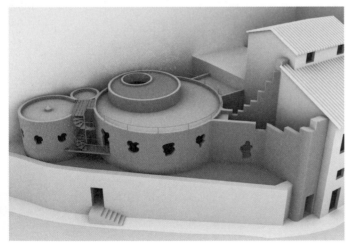

155. Ladeira da Misericórdia Housing and Commercial Complex, Salvador, 1987–88, aerial view of Coati Restaurant surrounding the mango tree. Computer rendering. Zeuler R. Lima Collection.

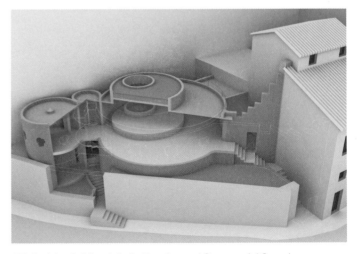

156. Ladeira da Misericórdia Housing and Commercial Complex, Salvador, 1987–88, sectioned view of Coati Restaurant showing the structural and spatial logic of the two main parts of the buildings. Computer rendering. Zeuler R. Lima Collection.

157. Ladeira da Misericórdia Housing and Commercial Complex,
Salvador, 1987–88, interior view of Coati Restaurant surrounding the
mango tree. Photograph by Nelson Kon.

Africa never went beyond a few initial sketches prepared in 1990 after the end of Kertész's term in office.

Her project for Casa do Benin in Salvador consisted of two complementary parts using the remains of three adjacent eighteenth-century buildings at the prominent corner of praça do Pelourinho and rua Flores. The larger and better-preserved corner manor was used for the cultural and study center, while the remaining street facades of the two smaller adjacent buildings gave more freedom to create a courtyard restaurant on the ground floor and a house for a Benin cultural representative on the upper floors (figures 158, 159). She had the exterior walls of the whole ensemble whitewashed, neutralizing their ornamentation under the tropical sun of Salvador in an effort to give the historical buildings a shared identity and contemporary appeal.

Facing praça do Pelourinho, the cultural center of Benin occupies the imposing corner manor, which the city had salvaged after the fire by building an internal, reinforced concrete structure. Bo Bardi dismissed the jungle of piers from the previous remodeling around which she had to work and adapted the ground floor into an exhibition hall, taking advantage of the twelve large double doors that open toward the street. She reserved the two upper levels and the attic, with its balconies and arched window, for the African-Brazilian studies center, which included a library, a conference room, administration offices, and lodging for scholars, with the attic being accessible through a separate steel staircase on top of the vertical atrium (figure 160). Adjusting to what she called a "clumsy structural renovation," Bo Bardi removed all finishes from the back wall and separated it from the concrete structure above with a slit of glass, exposing, as she often did, the construction technique as a historical document.[31]

There were too many concrete columns for such a small space as the ground floor, so she had the existing central staircase moved to the narrow space between the columns and the old stone wall, creating a "linear ascent like during colonial times."[32] In addition to those historical notes, the project abounds in naturalistic references, from a small tree-shaped column supporting the cascading steps to cylindrical handwoven cases of palm leaves, fibers, and bamboo all wrapping the existing concrete piers and even, in one of her sketches, the banisters of the staircase (figure 161).[33]

Just around the corner from the extroverted cultural center, on rua Flores, behind the imposing manor, Bo Bardi's team made the most of the remaining facades of two heavily damaged lower houses and created a new building for commercial activities on the ground level and a house for Benin's diplomatic representative to Salvador on the upper floors (figure 162). She used the same prefabricated system of ribbed wall panels proposed for ladeira da Misericórdia to build a new load-bearing wall rising from the foundations of the destroyed houses, holding the concrete slabs of the new building, and creating a semipublic courtyard.

The ground floor of the renovated building was designated for a retail shop opening toward the street and flanked by a kitchen and bathrooms serving the patio. The two upper floors and a roof garden could be reached through a sinuous staircase resembling a cowrie (a shell used in African-Brazilian divination rituals). In addition to coconut trees shading the courtyard, Bo Bardi proposed a small elliptical shelter with fourteen conic columns and curved partitions made of a mixture of soil and cement and freely evoking rural sub-Saharan architecture. This structure was originally used for the restaurant and covered with an elaborate truss system of slender eucalyptus trunks lifted above the walls to support a finely woven thatched roof that was destroyed in a fire within a few years of operation. She also added a wooden stove, a waterfall, and a small pond to complement the yard's African-Brazilian ambience.

Inside the pavilion, Bo Bardi placed an elliptical communal table made in solid angelim wood with a central opening to accommodate more than thirty people around both its interior and exterior perimeters.[34] To accompany it, she and her team designed a stackable chair based on a three-legged stool, which generated a similar table project. One of the legs of the stool rose above the seat level and was bent slightly to create stability and to hold a short, horizontal board that served as the back (figure 163). They named their creation Giraffe Chair because of its slender zoomorphic silhouette and in tribute to the African continent the furniture celebrated.

The Benin House opened to the public in May 1988, a few months before Kertész's mayoralty ended. To complement the architecture of the main building, Bo Bardi organized a permanent pedagogical display of handicraft from Benin, representing, according to her, "a reduced version of my program for the Unhão complex," as well as an extension of many handcraft exhibitions she had organized since then. Despite the predicaments she had pointed out regarding contemporary design, she continued to describe those handmade objects as not only "poor, but rich in fantasy, in invention, the premise for a free, modern future, which may, with the advancement of scientific practices, safeguard the values of a history of hardship and poetry at the outset of a new civilization."[35]

She originally lined up a series of glass display cases and wooden platforms along the wooden floor of the main hall, showing objects collected from Benin. Undulating above them were long, colorful textile pieces suspended from the

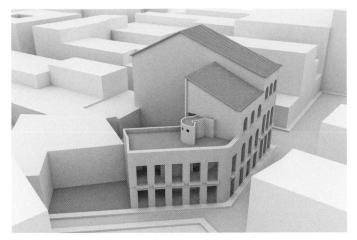

158. Casa do Benin, Salvador, 1987–88, aerial northern view of the ensemble showing the exterior of the three recovered buildings. Computer rendering. Zeuler R. Lima Collection.

159. Casa do Benin, Salvador, 1987–88, aerial western view of the ensemble showing the patio formed by the three recovered buildings. Computer rendering. Zeuler R. Lima Collection.

160. Casa do Benin, Salvador, 1987–88, sectioned view of the cultural hall on Largo do Pelourinho showing its structural and spatial logic and restaurant kiosk on the ground-floor patio. Computer rendering. Zeuler R. Lima Collection.

161. Casa do Benin, Salvador, 1987–88, interior view of the ground-floor exhibition hall opened toward Largo do Pelourinho. Photograph by Nelson Kon.

ceiling. She reserved the second floor for display cases and a panel of Pierre Verger's photographs of Benin and created a vertical opening by removing slabs above the main entry door and letting a series of unrolled bolts of African fabric fill the space, defying gravity and making the atrium look even more dramatic and vertiginous.

For all the changes the center suffered after the end of Kertész's term in office, Casa do Benin revived the interrupted plans and partnerships Bo Bardi had developed in Salvador in the early 1960s and allowed her finally to collaborate with Verger. She described the project as the "living document" of his book *Fluxo e refluxo* (Flow and reflow), which was published in Portuguese translation just as the African-Brazilian studies center opened.[36] She and Pinho's team planned to pay the ethnophotographer another tribute by converting a nearby manor on Pelourinho Square into the Pierre Verger Foundation, a project that consisted mostly of the interior renovation for an archival and research center but that was abandoned by the subsequent city administration.

By then, Bo Bardi had only the chance to complete her last project in Salvador, Casa do Olodum — a not-for-profit

organization created to improve the life of marginalized children and adolescents through workshops and cultural activities and focused mostly on African-Brazilian music, percussion instruments, and theater. The selected building was a derelict two-floor colonial manor at an unusually sharp street corner in a seedy area known as Maciel. Bo Bardi's proposal was both plain and insightful, with her usual neutralized whitewash facades and an unusual triangular internal layout. Given her desire to keep the organization open to the city, she placed a bar on the lower, semipublic level marked by six generous doors on rua Maciel de Baixo (figures 164, 165).

She transformed the second, larger floor into a multipurpose lounge and music practice room and created an intermediate, more intimate level for educational activities (figure 166). To reorganize the building both spatially and structurally, she added a wall to the backside of the upper floor, using the same ribbed ferro-cement elements as in her other Pelourinho district projects. This new wall stabilized the building's external walls, supported the new wooden roof frame, and created the space for a V-shaped staircase connecting the two floors and the mezzanine, which was

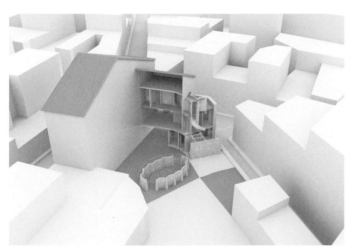

162. Casa do Benin, Salvador, 1987–88, sectioned view of the residential building showing its structural and spatial logic and restaurant facilities on the ground-floor patio. Computer rendering. Zeuler R. Lima Collection.

163. Giraffe Chair, c. 1988. Photograph by Nelson Kon.

This Is Not a Tourist City

covered by a skylight shaped like a pyramid, remotely resembling her forsaken initial sketches for MASP. Completed in 1991, Casa do Olodum promoted programs related to and useful for the local population, materializing Bo Bardi's quest for an architectural design that was simultaneously simple, produced with reduced space and material resources, and relevant to collective social life.

Still, for all of Bo Bardi's appreciation for Salvador's everyday culture and her optimistic intentions, at age seventy-one and in weakening health, she lacked the immersion into the city's reality with which she had approached her experience there two decades before. Neither did she have the direct contact with the construction site she so often praised. Her visits to Salvador were limited and brief because of her increasing complications from arthritis, which made traveling difficult. The design work was, for the most part, carried out in her studio with the help of architects Ferraz and Suzuki (who had replaced Vainer) and engineer Röchlitz coordinating the work in São Paulo and of architect Filgueiras Lima in Salvador.

Bo Bardi started the rehabilitation projects in Salvador with enthusiasm. She had hoped to preserve the city's popular character, but in the end she was disappointed. The lack of effective logistical and financial support from the municipal and state administrations hindered the transposition of those concepts into reality.[37] Her ability to influence political decisions had waned despite her recognition as a designer, and after Kertész's mayoralty ended with a large public debt followed by accusations of corruption, subsequent administrations quickly abandoned the project to rehabilitate the historic district in line with Pinho's ideas and Bo Bardi's master plan. While Teatro Gregório de

Matos, Casa do Benin, and Casa do Olodum kept some of the features and uses from her proposals, the buildings along ladeira da Misericórdia remained abandoned until, during the first decade of the twenty-first century, a new restaurant, a police station, and an environmental organization filled the spaces. None of them, however, shared the plan as initially proposed.

To Bo Bardi, the converted buildings in the Pelourinho district should have served merely as the entryway into and the armature of the livelihood of the area, its inhabitants, its traditions, and its social reality. The lack of continued and efficient public administration prevented the project from achieving its intended purpose. The popular soul of the city she had expected to revive was gradually replaced by the transformation of the historic district into a tourist destination. Nevertheless, the fragile remains of her team's contributions still offer valuable examples of the use of a low-cost and flexible prefabricated system and of her nonconformist approach to the adaptive reuse of historic buildings — examples that became endangered by the same voluntary earthquake that transformed the city from what she had admired in the late 1950s into what it had become in the 1980s.

When Bo Bardi accepted the invitation to reverse that process and develop the Pelourinho rehabilitation project, she declared she wanted to dedicate it "to the people of Bahia, whom I love."[38] She did not know then that her tribute to them would also be an unannounced farewell.

164. Casa do Olodum, Salvador, 1988–89, western street view of the recovered building. Computer rendering. Zeuler R. Lima Collection.

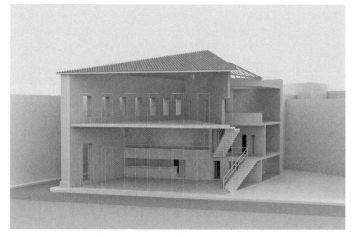

165. Casa do Olodum, Salvador, 1988–89, sectioned view of the recovered building, showing its structural, spatial, and circulation logic. Computer rendering. Zeuler R. Lima Collection.

166. Casa do Olodum, Salvador, 1988–89, interior view of the community
hall on the upper floor. Photograph by Nelson Kon.

During her last years, Lina Bo Bardi's declining physical health took its toll. She became more withdrawn and frail, but she did not lose her intellectual vitality. At last she had collected the material that was absent at age twenty-five, when she dreamed of writing her memoirs. But she never wrote them. She left only sparse notes, many with hints of her imaginative embellishments. She agreed to few interviews, but most were never published, and only a few transcripts of those conversations remain among her records.

Brazilian architects and the press finally granted Bo Bardi national recognition in the late 1980s, and she stayed active until the end of her life. Collaborators kept her engaged in design competitions, and the reputation of the works she developed for SESC Pompeia and the historic district of Salvador brought in a wave of new public commissions. Unfortunately, most projects were never realized. Many of her later ideas comprise no more than preliminary notes, sketches, and models. In one of her last interviews, she said: "Architecture needs life to fulfill its purpose."[1] The life that these ideas needed was just not always there.

Among her completed projects was an exhibition. Her work on Casa do Benin had brought her closer to ethno-photographer Pierre Verger. It also brought Verger, Bahia, and Africa to São Paulo. On May 11, 1988, in the presence of representatives from Brazil and Benin, Bo Bardi opened the show *África Negra* (Black Africa) at MASP.[2] She organized a simple yet meaningful layout around a central open space that suggested a Candomblé yard surrounded by glass display cases showing African cult objects alternating with totemlike woven coconut tree leaves and unrolled bolts of African textile hanging from the concrete ceiling of the museum's Civic Hall. "We are going to invade São Paulo and Bahia with this exhibition," she told the press.[3]

Bo Bardi also wanted to invade MASP with another of her creations, though it would only be built posthumously as a temporary exhibition about her work.[4] With the help of Suzuki's meticulous construction drawings, she made a study of a zoomorphic pushcart named *Grande Vaca Mecânica* (Great mechanical cow). Combining metal office cabinets, flat files, and a few customized storage pieces and assembling them onto a four-wheeled chassis, the movable bovine vitrine recalled a patchwork of her visual repertoire, ranging from her 1943 lithograph *Architect's Room* to the animals featured in SESC Pompeia's recent exhibitions.

Along with those imaginative exercises, Bo Bardi accepted architect Joaquim Guedes's invitation to join his competition team for a project to rehabilitate the industrial Milanese neighborhood of Bicocca into a "technological pole," or development area for large corporations. This was one of four competitions in which she participated, albeit halfheartedly, at the end of her life. Her ambivalence was especially strong in the competition for Milan, whose focus neighborhood evoked disturbing wartime memories for her of the shooting of partisans in empty factories on the city's periphery.[5] She contributed a few sketches in ballpoint pen and watercolor in 1987 for three large buildings, one of which she designed to resemble a swastika pulled into pieces. Guedes did not include them in his final proposal.

In early 1988, she and Guedes again engaged in an international design competition, this one for the Belém Cultural Center in Lisbon. The site, located near the historical Manoeline Jerónimo monastery at the delta of the Tagus River, had a peculiar history: in 1940, during António de Oliveira Salazar's dictatorial regime, it had housed a large exposition celebrating Portuguese navigations, displaying the nationalist and folkloric view of popular culture Bo Bardi refuted. Though disagreements led the pair's collaboration to be severed in only a few weeks, her initial sketches and notes for the project offer a thought-provoking collage of her later brutalist and naturalistic design experiences.

She conceived the main pavilion as a solid, tubular exhibition hall in pre-stressed concrete intended to measure "three hundred meters [984 ft.] in length and thirty-five meters [115 ft.] in width without columns," to be supported only by short buildings at each end and covered with plants. At the building's center, she imagined a tall tower in concrete and clay surrounded by a self-supporting ramp wrapping the building like a serpent. Calling it the "lighthouse of discoveries," she imagined laser beams projecting from the rooftop and crisscrossing the Lisbon sky with images that served as a "beacon to sailors."[6]

Her notes questioned the site's integralist history by defining culture as "free choice, freedom of gathering and meetings and not as a double to captive work." She recommended that the center be issued for "culture as leisure, a serious issue," and that the first exhibition should be about "A Thousand Toys for the Portuguese Children," translating her experience from across the Atlantic Ocean at SESC. She also suggested that any structure for temporary activities should be spontaneous and follow "the rigorous (poetic) principles of 'non-white' rationalism," echoing her ongoing design for Casa do Benin. Still, she had modern rationalism in mind when she invoked the "Lisbon of Voltaire's '*Poème [sur le désastre] de Lisbonne*,'" suggesting how the French philosopher was deeply moved by the humanitarian crisis that erupted among European Enlightenment intellectuals after the 1755 Lisbon earthquake. She praised objectivity and human action in "the courageous anti-Leibniz Lisbon, [and] the strong and strange [marquis de] Pombal." "I would have loved it," she wrote, as she withdrew from the

167. LBA Leisure Center, Cananéia, 1988–90, interior view of the original community hall. Photograph by Nelson Kon.

competition and turned her attention to other projects and abandoned sites.[7]

In December 1988, she began work on a concrete, though much smaller, project in the small coastal town of Cananéia, an old fishing town in the southernmost area of the state of São Paulo. She received a commission to design a low-budget leisure center for the Legião Brasileira de Assistência (LBA, Brazilian aid legion), a federal organization originally created in 1942 to provide assistance and services to the families of Brazilian veterans and later to dispossessed families. The site is located on rua Tristão Lobo, one of the main roads of the town's historic center, and consists of the stone ruins of two houses with arched, street-facing doors and windows, which were whitewashed in the renovation.

With the assistance of architects Suzuki and Ferraz, Bo Bardi stripped the original stucco down and converted the remaining house shell into a lounge, giving it a new roof, a fireplace, and couches like those in SESC Pompeia (figure

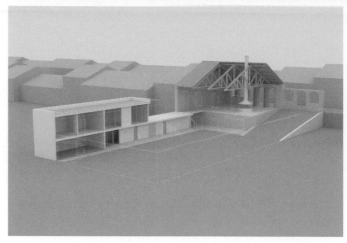

168. LBA Leisure Center, Cananéia, 1988–90, general view of the ensemble from the back highlighting existing and added structures. Computer rendering. Zeuler R. Lima Collection.

169. LBA Leisure Center, Cananéia, 1988–90, sectioned view of the ensemble highlighting existing and added structures. Computer rendering. Zeuler R. Lima Collection.

167). She recommended keeping the site next door for a garden and a passage, "so that one can see the house's old structure — very beautiful stone walls."[8] Along the south, rear party wall, she had a narrow two-story addition built to incorporate the old house's remaining foundations that sat on the backyard (figure 168). This addition connected the lounge facing the street with a new volume for services, administration, and multipurpose rooms facing the verdant backyard, where she added a small waterfall and a rustic merry-go-round — elements previously featured in other projects (figure 169).

The center opened on February 2, 1990, with a ceremony designed but not attended by Bo Bardi. Once again, pitanga leaves covered the floor as a visual trope, no longer associated with Candomblé yards. Colorful fabric hung from the ceiling truss and was agitated by a fan to enhance its theatrical effect.[9] "We tried to create a functional and poetic space for people's spare time; something anti-bourgeois," she wrote, defining "culture as living together, free choice."[10] And so it served the community for about half a decade. Despite her generous efforts, Bo Bardi's project was short-lived because LBA had been the object of an administrative and political crisis that led to the organization's extinction in 1995. As a result, the building remained closed for several years and was eventually renovated as the town's museum with many of the features and goals, as she envisioned them, either removed or neglected.

While she was making studies for the LBA Center and gradually distancing herself from Teatro Oficina, Bo Bardi received, in early 1989, an unusual commission to design an open-air theater over the scattered remains of a historic coffee plantation manor. Located in Barão Geraldo, one

hundred kilometers (62 mi.) north of São Paulo, the property belonged to Renato Magalhães Gouveia, an influential art dealer connected to Pietro Maria Bardi. Bo Bardi conceived preliminary ideas for a "Teatro das Ruínas" (Theater on ruins) with no conventional structures, only "poor bleachers" facing a tentlike stage covered by colorful pyramidal tips and surrounded by duffel curtains, all of which sat atop the orthogonal geometry of the house's wrecked foundations.[11] The Teatro das Ruínas did not go beyond preliminary ideas, but hundreds of kilometers away, the Teatro Gregório de Matos opened in August 1989. Unable to attend her project's opening ceremony because of her frail health, she prepared a letter summarizing her view about design simplification and the need for direct contact between actors and audience: "Where are the armchairs, aisles, stage, props, and spotlights? What we see here is an open and bare space like a square."[12] Her voice would have resounded in the void, poignantly summoning her long-held idea that people should be the protagonists of architecture.

Shortly before the theater was inaugurated in Salvador and after decades of organizing exhibitions, Bo Bardi was honored, for the first time, with an exhibition of her work at the Salão Caramelo (Caramelo hall) in the school of architecture at the Universidade de São Paulo. Her assistants organized the show, displaying several panels with photographs and drawings representing her career as a designer in Brazil. They included examples of her chairs (from the modernist Bardi Bowl to the crude 1967 roadside seat) and the theatrical, pink "polochon," displayed on simple wooden platforms. The exhibition opened on April 14, 1989, with her last public lecture, which filled the school's auditorium with a curious audience.[13]

A Wonderful Tangle

In her talk, Bo Bardi shared ideas she had pursued since writing her thesis, *Contribuição propedêutica* — presented to the university thirty-two years before — as well as her latest opinions about architecture and design. Aside from condemning contemporary architectural criticism and education, which she complained focused more on formal patterns than on ideas, she stressed her concern with architecture as a historical manifestation. She rejected the recommendation by early rationalists like Walter Gropius to "throw away the past and all of its history." Instead, she said, "It is necessary to consider the past as a historical present, still alive, a present that helps us avoid traps [and] forge another 'true' present."[14]

Borrowing the notion of historical present from literature, she defined her architectural voice by working with buildings in ruin and developing strategies for adaptive reuse that largely contributed to her prominence as a designer. "In practice," she warned the audience, "the past does not exist." But she clarified her point, saying, "That which still exists today and has not perished represents the historical present; that which we have to save — or, instead, preserve — is a set of features that are typical to a time period but still belong to humankind."[15] Her progressive historical approach recalls a short note from a few years earlier in which she explains "time": "Linear time is a Western invention. It is a wonderful tangle in which, at every moment, one can choose points and invent solutions with no beginning and no end."[16] Even when most uncertain of her future, she believed in the coexistence of different temporal dimensions.

With such convictions in mind and a few months after this final lecture, Bo Bardi responded to another public commission to create a leisure center out of a historic building. This time it would be the old Guanabara train station in Campinas, a large city eighty kilometers (50 mi.) north of São Paulo. The small terminal was originally created in 1893 and gained covered steel structure platforms in 1915, but following the national dismantling of train transportation during the military regime, it was deactivated in 1974. Finally, in 1990, the state of São Paulo granted UNICAMP (State University of Campinas) rights to use the deserted building for thirty years.[17]

When the university administration contacted Bo Bardi to propose cultural uses for the old station, she selected the industrial platform over the ornate passenger terminal, suggesting they replace it with a new structure. "Liberated from the old masonry building, the 1915 roof — the original English steel structure transformed into a glass volume," she wrote, "will house great exhibitions, meetings, and performances." Her characteristically deep one-point perspective drawing illustrated her vision for the new hall. In it, she

suggested covering the lower part of the roof with a "transparent velarium," as in the pavilion housing for the 1959 *Bahia* exhibition, and surrounding objects and banners with diaphanous light.[18]

Bo Bardi initially wanted to replace the terminal with three cylindrical structures — like "short silos," according to her notes — lined up with the axis of the transparent pavilion and connected by an elevated bridge, but she soon changed that scheme for a solid horizontal volume slightly staggered from the glazed exhibition hall. In it, she imagined a beer garden, an auditorium, offices, and two symmetrical courtyards, invisible from the outside and containing trees growing above a flat-roof garden. She associated the building's stern white wall facing the neighborhood plaza with references to the vernacular Mediterranean architecture appearing in Federico García Lorca's mournful verses. Not only did such references echo her European generation's neorealist sensibility, but the rough finishes of the solid volume also suggested her criticism of the polished minimalism that was fashionable at the time of her project. Finally, she noted that the old rail tracks could be reactivated as part of the center's cultural programs, idealistically proposing that "the 'Unicamp Train' will leave [the station] loaded with permanent [sic] exhibitions to visit all the state of São Paulo and Brazil."[19] With no sponsors to support Bo Bardi's ideas, her proposal, like most of her late projects, did not leave the station.

Soon after producing her preliminary studies for the university's Centro Cultural Guanabara (between April and July 1990), Bo Bardi was approached by Hospital Umberto I, which served the Italian-Brazilian community, to propose a renovation project that included a large underground garage, and by the city administration of the coastal town of Peruíbe to design a tourist park with several cultural facilities along the beach. Neither proposal went beyond preliminary conversations, but she was more successful when she received a commission from another prominent woman, a progressive outsider like herself: Luiza Erundina de Sousa. Erundina de Sousa was the mayor of São Paulo and a social worker with deep roots both in the Nordeste and in political activism, and she wanted Bo Bardi to design a new city hall — she had decided to transfer her administration from the leafy and affluent Parque do Ibirapuera back to the imposing historic Palácio das Indústrias (Industry exposition pavilion) downtown. The Italianate brick-and-steel pavilion had been built in 1924 to house agricultural and industrial expositions. It represented a symbolic catalyst in the rehabilitation plans for Parque Dom Pedro II, an important but neglected downtown public space. This would be the last of Bo Bardi's projects to leave the drawing board, though

170. São Paulo City Hall, São Paulo, Industry Pavilion Recovery, 1990–92, interior view of staff offices. Photograph by Nelson Kon.

it would never be fully completed. Had it been, it would have stood as one of her most idiosyncratic projects next to MASP and SESC Pompeia.

By the time Bo Bardi approached the project in June 1990, little was left of the park's early twentieth-century manicured gardens, replaced over time by a complex traffic interchange of expressways and overpasses. Still, the pavilion, designed by Italian-Brazilian Beaux-Arts architect Domiziano Rossi, was intact. With such a large program for a relatively small building, she proposed the adaptive reuse of the historic pavilion for the mayor's offices, support staff, and public ceremonies, which was completed after her death, and a new building for municipal departments configuring a new public square, which was never built.

Bo Bardi referred to the pavilion as the Coppedè Building, in reference to the ornamented Quartiere Coppedè, a Roman housing ensemble built during her adolescence. Once again, she approached the conservation from the perspective of a historical present. Whereas she respected the building's ornate exterior — exceptionally choosing not to whitewash its terra-cotta facades — she gave herself more freedom in the treatment of its interior

spaces. She had the inner walls and ceilings cleaned, as she had done at SESC Pompeia, to expose the carefully crafted wooden trusses and brick finishes (figure 170).

Although Mayor Erundina de Sousa approved Bo Bardi's preliminary proposal in a meeting on October 19, 1990, renovation did not begin until July 22, 1991, when the city administration finally signed an agreement with the state government to transfer the city hall to the Palácio das Indústrias. The project was not completed until November 28, 1992, after Bo Bardi's death. Still, it fulfilled her specifications. The large basement was rehabilitated for various services and reinforced with new retaining walls that doubled as a flood-drainage system. In contrast to the terra-cotta tones of the everyday working spaces, Bo Bardi reserved a surprise for the core of the pavilion. She had the central ceremonial hall on the second floor painted in fresco-like blue, giving it a startlingly celestial appearance. This single hue toned down wall reliefs and highlighted the hall's grand scale, its colorful, stained-glass doors, and the large restored chandelier at the center of the room, to which only blue chairs and large mural paintings were added (figure 171).

171. São Paulo City Hall, São Paulo, Industry Pavilion Recovery, 1990–92, interior view of ceremonial hall. Photograph by Nelson Kon.

The pavilion's structural intactness allowed for relatively easy renovation. However, the long J-shaped addition planned by Bo Bardi for several of the city's departments was not built because the overpass it was supposed to replace was never demolished. Had the site been vacated, a long, bent volume measuring over two hundred meters (656 ft.) and elevated five meters (16 ft.) from the ground would have reconfigured the northwestern corner between rua da Figueira and rua São Vito (figure 172). The new structure — which she related to the Lisbon cultural center competition studies — would have been supported by three solid vertical volumes containing elevator shafts, stairs, and services.[20] It would have also held the building's pre-stressed concrete frame, as well as two staggered, zigzagging, and open interior floors for small-scale offices above a free-plan public floor.

Bo Bardi imagined an opaque wall facing the park with no openings but supporting a large vertical garden, as in her preliminary ideas for the MASP building four decades earlier. She produced a long, colorful elevation covered with flowering vines, agaves, and bromeliads to complement a roof garden with tropical plants, representing her vision for the

background to be a vast paved plaza between the new building and the pavilion. She associated this open space with a classical Greek exedra, a semicircular niche for philosophical debates that enjoyed great popularity in ancient Roman public buildings and in the successive neoclassical and baroque references to them. She described the space between the two buildings as "a plaza for children" and a place for "the participation of popular life," with the domesticity of hanging gardens in mind. She idealized it as an "anti-Kafkian City Hall," promoting the confluence between formal political spaces and everyday uses, between the archetypal intimacy of an exedra and the grandiosity of a forum.[21]

In one of her last and almost abstract drawings, Bo Bardi traced the main facade of the pavilion in pencil and covered it with fast brushstrokes of watercolor. The study illustrated her general ideas for the site and especially showed how large red, yellow, and blue spotlights should be placed at the bottom of the building to give the impression that flames were engulfing it (figure 173). Her theatrical montage, which she was not able to see finished, suggested that "fire had represented the birth of industry since antiquity."[22] More than in industrial aesthetics, she was interested

172. Lina Bo Bardi, *São Paulo City Hall, Industry Pavilion, Plaza, and New Office Building*, 1991, model photographed by Marcelo C. Ferraz. ILBPMB Collection.

in the idea that industry — like craft — was the expression of human work, an idea she had diligently emphasized throughout her life. Despite her efforts, however, and with the addition absent, the renovated pavilion did not work properly — its layout had been altered at the last minute to accommodate the redistribution of administrative functions. Consequently, the pavilion housed the city hall only until 2004. It then moved to the Matarazzo Building, located in the Anhangabaú Valley and, coincidentally, designed in the 1930s by her former professor Marcello Piacentini. In 2009, a state science center moved into the pavilion, adding exhibition props that made the walls of the blue hall invisible, erasing another meaningful testimony to Bo Bardi's work.

While developing the city hall renovation, Bo Bardi's assistants persuaded her to lead their design team in a large national competition for the pavilion that would represent Brazil at the 1992 Universal Exposition of Seville in Spain. Aside from not feeling well, she had reservations about competitions, especially because she did not believe in spectacular presentations driven by image rather than by content.[23] Still, starting in January 1991, the team embraced the project's challenging task: to address the celebration of the five-hundredth anniversary of European exploration of the Americas since Christopher Columbus's first travels. She talked, and they drew.

Like her original project for MASP and other recent studies, the exposition pavilion was based on a single

volume. The model prepared by her assistants showed an opaque orthogonal volume lifted from the ground by two smaller solid blocks, and she placed a bundle of colorful pipes and a couple of waterspouts protruding from the side of the elevated building (figure 174). She described the pavilion as a "Great Box lined with white Brazilian marble [and] completely enclosed," with no windows, not even holes.[24] As she predicted, however, the jury did not pay attention to her simple though visionary proposal, which can be perceived through the careful reading of the project description but not through its unassuming images.

Bo Bardi conceived the boxy building with another kind of discovery in mind: the traces of prehistoric life found in the state of Piauí, in her beloved Nordeste. She had been interested in the groundbreaking archaeological excavations at Serra da Capivara national park in Raimundo Nonato that gave origin to the Museu do Homem Americano (Museum of the American man) in 1986 and a UNESCO World Heritage Site. Behind its unassuming external shape, her pavilion proposal was supposed to conceal a surprise. Visitors would have to enter it through a large, encased helicoidal staircase to appreciate the provocative fact that the building took them back not to the European mercantile renaissance but to a time before Western history. Instead of celebrating the conquest of the Americas, the pavilion should "display what Brazil and all the Americas were like before the Discoveries."[25]

173. Lina Bo Bardi, *Study for São Paulo City Hall, Industry Pavilion, and Office Building Garden Wall*, July 30, 1990. Watercolor, ballpoint pen, pencil on tracing paper. ILBPMB Collection.

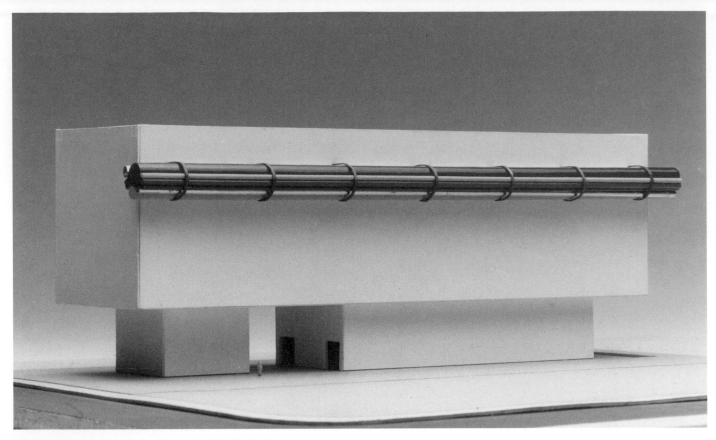

174. Lina Bo Bardi, *Brazilian Pavilion at the 1992 Seville Universal Exposition*, 1991. Model in photographic reproduction. ILBPMB Collection.

Her description of the pavilion suggested a restaurant on the ground floor, with collective tables, serving Brazilian food in use since pre-Columbian times, like "cassava, corn, fruit . . . , and vegetables," though this time she did not represent her ideas with colorful sketches — as she so often did for other projects — discouraged as she was by her weakening health. Above the restaurant and independently accessible from the street, she proposed an auditorium for conferences, multimedia shows, and performances like those of the "Pankararu Indians from the state of Pernambuco, whose ritual dance reproduces the same gestures seen in twelve-thousand-year-old cave paintings." [26]

The opaque hall crowning the pavilion was to contain "a rather unusual exhibition: that of a fantastical, spectral, chimerical human being." [27] She hoped to exhibit documents illustrating cave paintings and everyday objects up to fifty thousand years old. As a centerpiece, she imagined the oldest human remains on the American continent — a ten-thousand-year-old female skeleton, which had been found a few months earlier by the excavation team in Piauí. [28] Her plan was to establish a direct link between prehistory and the present, between artifacts and everyday life, aimed at "the origin of culture, of history, of things; practically the origins of mankind" that were still alive in Brazil. [29]

Instead of representing the feat of the European conquistadors, Bo Bardi intended her project to be a "memorial to the man of the Always-New World." [30] She was becoming physically frailer, but she was still strongly convinced by her search for a new humanism. Her proposal revealed four of her inseparable postulates: that she did not trust the ascendancy of Western values; that the identity of a country comes from its history of everyday manifestations; that simple things and practices are meaningful; and that architecture should celebrate collective existence.

The competition jury members who overlooked Bo Bardi's vision mistakenly awarded an honorable mention to an armadillo-shaped project expecting to pay tribute to her. The equivocation may have proven her apprehension against superficial judgments right. Yet it did not take away from the force of her idea, at the edge of death, to celebrate human existence.

Bo Bardi received her final design commission on December 20, 1991. Mayor Maurício Soares of São Bernardo do Campo, an industrial town in the metropolitan region of São Paulo, envisioned buying the vacant structures of the former Empresa Cinematográfica Vera Cruz (Vera Cruz movie studios), an important feature of the history of Brazilian cinema and originally owned by Matarazzo. Mayor Soares wanted to convert it into a municipal leisure center, like SESC Pompeia, which enjoyed broad success, exposure, and, at the time, a sense of novelty. [31]

Given the low budget of the project, he wanted to maximize the use of the two hectares (5 acres) located in a central urban area near a large expressway. Bo Bardi's study considered keeping only the three large existing structures with ample interior spaces but without the same urban or architectural qualities found in the old Pompeia factory. [32] The two original studio warehouses at the center of the lot were reserved for the leisure center, and a small vaulted ceiling pavilion flanking the avenue on the southern side would be transformed into Vera Cruz Cinema and would include the old studio's archives.

In weakening health, Bo Bardi coordinated the conceptual work but limited her participation in the project's production, leaving the drawing and drafting work in her assistants' hands. As with the LBA leisure center, their preliminary ideas for the Vera Cruz cultural and leisure center (Centro de Convivência Cultural Vera Cruz) were informed largely by the SESC factory rehabilitation, though without its same scale and impact. They proposed to subdivide the square plan of the studios into complementary quadrants devoted to a leisure lounge, a spacious theater-auditorium, exhibition galleries, and a restaurant and beer garden large enough to serve three hundred people.

The most original feature in the project was a sizable helicoidal, cantilevered staircase measuring fourteen meters (46 ft.) in circumference and connecting the lounge to the theater's upper galleries. The carefully detailed stairs were to be built around a single central column with encased steps swirling around it. This knurled shape would have given the staircase the appearance of a tropical inflorescence, such as an anthurium or a heliconia, which Bo Bardi had intended for an unrealized staircase at MASP three decades before. [33] Her team completed the preliminary study drawings in February 1992, but the project was soon halted.

When the team presented the Vera Cruz proposal to Mayor Soares, Bo Bardi was confined to her glazed house and to the use of a wheelchair. After living with great intensity and remaining faithful to her own rules, she had entered the 1990s feeling cheerless and restrained by her declining health. [34] During that period, mobility problems from arthritis had increased, and in late 1990, her difficulty in walking had caused her to fall and break her lower tibia near the joint at her heel (an uncanny coincidence for someone whose first name was Achillina). In recovering from the accident, she suffered from an arterial clot caused by a fragment of the broken bone, which led her to be hospitalized in intensive care for several weeks. After that, she could hardly leave her house. [35]

On the morning of March 19, 1992, after much persistence from her friends, she decided to leave the wheelchair, which she apparently no longer needed, despite walking with difficulty. She gained some enthusiasm and talked about wanting soon to complete her projects for São Paulo's city hall and the Vera Cruz leisure center.[36] In the middle of the night of March 20, 1992, however, she woke up experiencing respiratory failure, a symptom of the pulmonary embolism and the chronic obstructive pulmonary illness that took her life that night. She was seventy-seven years old.[37]

For all the frequent changes in her career, Lina Bo Bardi had strived to develop a creative path in a permanent quest for a shared well-being. Educated in classical and modern values but also among antifascist sensibilities, she believed that the advancement of architecture and design as cultural fields could be limited neither to single contributions of isolated individuals nor to self-standing buildings or objects. Though herself an exceptionally capable individual, she preferred to think of the practice of design as an endeavor with a shared purpose serving the collectivity. She aspired to a humanism that was neither sentimental nor elitist.

Her design and thinking combined practices and culled principles from multiple and sometimes contrasting sources, but she was not interested in solidifying them into immutable canons. She believed that design emerged out of existing conditions and needs, and that is how she designed: out of imaginative curiosity, ethical concerns, and conscientious discipline. She was suspicious of self-indulging aesthetic and intellectual rhetoric.

To Bo Bardi, there was no gentle agreement or acceptance. On the contrary, she often provoked dissent. She was an irreverent and strong-minded woman, despite her personal generosity to others. Her work, her actions, and her thoughts were motivated by reevaluation, though her approach did not preclude contradiction and ambiguity. She developed a process for entering and leaving modernity by actively observing what was considered marginal to the modern world and placing that at the center of her concerns and of mainstream cultural and architectural debates.

Her invitation to take aesthetic and even personal risks for ethical purposes is part of the dialogue she left open to contemporary designers, helping to reverse the process by which architecture is generally perceived. Her basic methods were the simplification of means and vocabulary, along with the hybridization of modern and nonmodern, rational and spontaneous elements and practices, constantly weaving them in and out of each other. She developed a particular approach to architecture based on the need to investigate and to transform the program as the origin of any building design. She went to the meaning and the uses of the spaces first and to material and physical features later.

Bo Bardi's beliefs and forms of practice were not short on paradoxes. Her humanistic, anthropological, and empirical goals were sometimes at odds with her formal and idealistic aspirations. For example, her concept of simplification of means sometimes required technical complexity and customization such as the contrast between the appearance of simplicity and the large financial and material resources it occasionally took to make that possible. The choice she and her educated generation made for popular, lay culture did not always embrace the people as the key agent in their decision-making process, given the complex power relations that permeate professional and cultural institutions, and though altruistic, their liberal discourse about life's hardships was often accompanied by social and political privilege.

No matter how conflicting those beliefs and practices were, they revealed aspects that modernity and modernization tend to conceal. Her work exposed the asymmetrical power relations that are present in the modern world and, more generally, how those relations appropriate and transform the physical environment and enable or hinder human use, material forms, and symbolic meanings. Lina Bo Bardi defended modern architecture to the end of her life. She pursued the modern aspiration for universality, singularity, and wholeness, but she also showed in her many works and in many forms that modernity has no simple and fixed origin, place, or shape. Her works and thinking were, like her definition of time, a wonderful tangle. And she was indeed, as she described herself to a journalist at the end of her life, "somehow special."[38]

Epilogue

A few months before her death, in October 1991, Bo Bardi had shown evidence that, despite her declining health, she kept her intellectual strength. Overcoming her mobility constraints, she had decided to accept an invitation to be one of the honored participants of a round table at the Thirteenth Congress of Brazilian Architects organized in São Paulo. The meeting was titled "Architecture, City, Nature," a theme she had long embraced. She left her house for the local branch of the Instituto de Arquitetos do Brasil downtown and for her last public appearance.

She had prepared notes for a short presentation, what was essentially a testament to her life experiences, her beliefs, and, despite her frail condition, her will to live. She cited leaving Italy as an important step: "When I arrived here [in Brazil] in 1946, shortly after the end of World War II, I brought with me years of bitterness as did everybody in my generation. My generation lived through tragedy. Nothing was built, only destroyed." In contrast, she said: "I had never before seen the kind of spirit of freedom that exists in this country [Brazil]. It seemed natural to all of the Brazilian people." She still felt fascinated by a kind of "purity of expression that can also be very poor, usually produced with simple means" with which she associated the "wonderful things that can be found from the north to the south of the country and that are sometimes full of invention, full of courage."[1]

Bo Bardi also spoke in defense of the origins of modernism, stating that the term "'modern' in architecture does not mean that which is contemporary, because 'modern' has the sense of plenitude." She especially encouraged younger generations to "reconsider some of the aspects—including hope—disowned by the generations that followed the modern movement," and she insisted, "The contemporary panorama presents hopes and possibilities to arrive at an architecture that is truly a step forward in the production of human things." She did not mean to ignore the visual appeal of architecture or even its complex aesthetic references. Instead, she only saw reason in looking for beauty if were "truly serving the collectivity."[2]

"This is what I wanted to say," she declared as she concluded her last appearance in public. "I'm not a lecturer. I am an architect," she told her audience. "Let's have a dialogue."[3]

May the conversation continue.

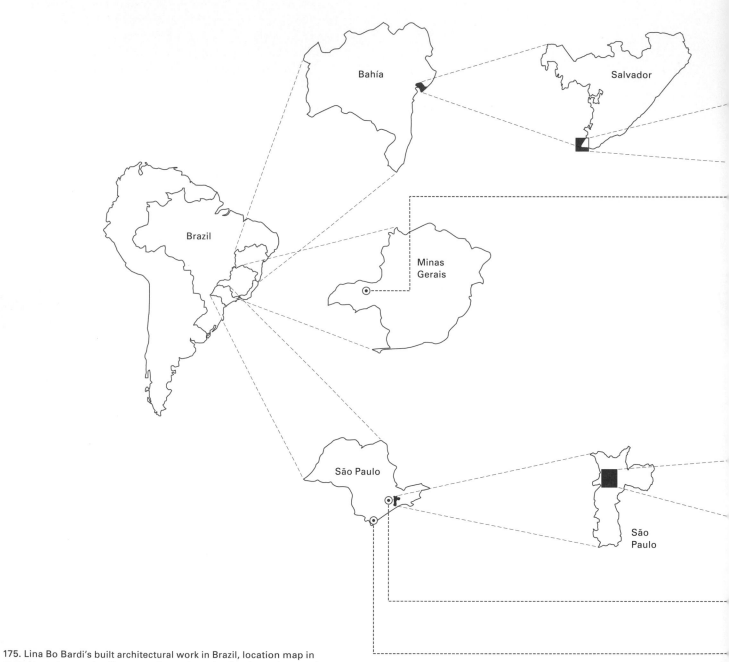

175. Lina Bo Bardi's built architectural work in Brazil, location map in complementary scales (by state, city, and area), with chronology and external views. Computer rendering. Zeuler R. Lima Collection.

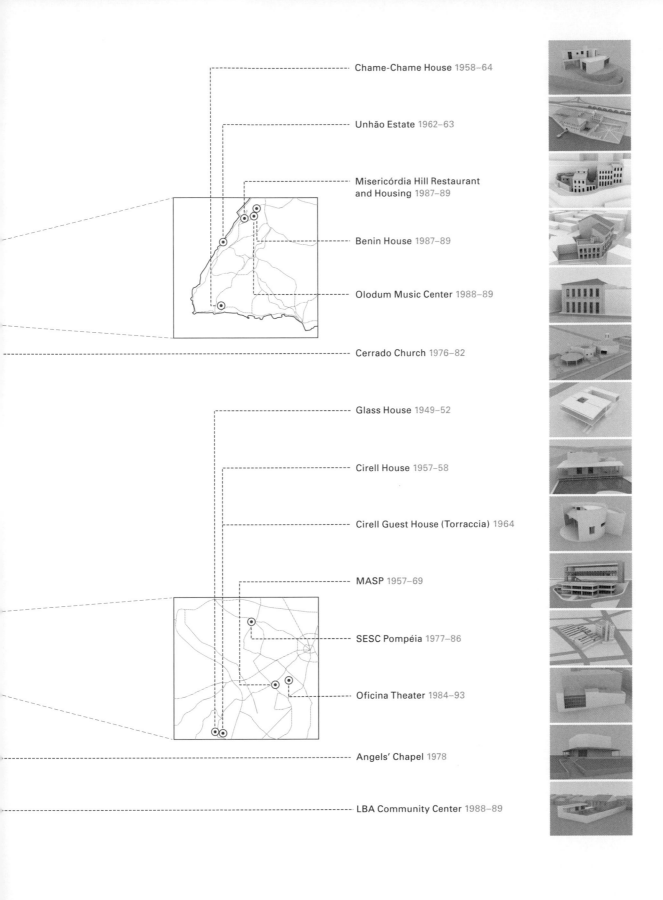

Chame-Chame House 1958–64

Unhão Estate 1962–63

Misericórdia Hill Restaurant
and Housing 1987–89

Benin House 1987–89

Olodum Music Center 1988–89

Cerrado Church 1976–82

Glass House 1949–52

Cirell House 1957–58

Cirell Guest House (Torraccia) 1964

MASP 1957–69

SESC Pompéia 1977–86

Oficina Theater 1984–93

Angels' Chapel 1978

LBA Community Center 1988–89

Abbreviations

AFC	Archivio Fabrizio Clerici
FAUUSP	Faculdade de Arquitetura e Urbanismo, Universidade de São Paulo
FBZ	Fondazione Bruno Zevi
IAC	Instituto de arte contemporânea
ILBPMB	Instituto Lina Bo e Pietro Maria Bardi
LBA	Legião da Boa Vontade
MAM	Museu de Arte Moderna
MAMB	Museu de Arte Moderna da Bahia
MAP	Museu de Arte Popular
MASP	Museu de Arte de São Paulo
MIAR	Movimento italiano architettura razionalista
MSA	Movimento studi architettura
RAC	Rockefeller Family Archives, Rockefeller Archive Center
SESC	Serviço Social do Comércio

Notes

Foreword

1. Lina Bo Bardi, "Sulla linguistica architettonica," *L'Architettura* 226 (August 1974), translated into English as "On Architectural Linguistics" in Olivia de Oliveira, *Lina Bo Bardi: Obra Construída / Built Work* (Barcelona: 2G, 2002), 218.
2. Lina Bo Bardi, "Design ambiental," *Malasartes* 2 (December 1976–February 1977), translated into English as "Ambient Planning: Design Impulse" in Oliveira, *Lina Bo Bardi*, 223.
3. Olivia de Oliveira, "Interview with Lina Bo Bardi" (1991), in Oliveira, *Lina Bo Bardi*, 241.
4. Bo Bardi, "On Architectural Linguistics," 220.

Preface

1. The ILBPMB planned to make a digitized collection of Bo Bardi's archival drawings available for consultation online during the production of this book. Their website at the time of this printing is www.institutobardi.com.br.

Prologue

1. Lina Bo Bardi, lecture at FAUUSP, April 14, 1989, transcript, 5, ILBPMB.
2. Ibid., 5–7.
3. Ibid., 7–8.
4. Ibid., 8.
5. Marcelo C. Ferraz, interview, São Paulo, August 4, 2006.
6. Lina Bo Bardi, interview with Silvio Giannini, "Mostra reúne pela primeira vez obra de Lina Bo Bardi," *Folha de São Paulo*, April 10, 1989, ILBPMB.
7. Lina Bo Bardi, "Arquitetura como movimento," lecture notes, Dance School, Salvador, August 1958, ILBPMB.
8. Lina Bo Bardi, lecture at FAUUSP, 7.
9. Bo Bardi interview.

A Girl in Pants

1. Bo Bardi affirmed that many of her original documents were lost in one of the 1943 bombings of Milan. Her name is listed as Achillina di Enrico Bo in her college certification in 1939. One version of her birth certificate, reissued by the city of Rome on August 24, 1946, reads Achillina Giuseppina Bo, whereas a 1951 version reads only Achillina Bo.
2. Victoria de Grazia, *Le donne nel regime fascista* (Venice: Marsilio, 1993), 56–58.
3. Lina Bo Bardi, interview with Fábio Malavoglia, Centro Cultural São Paulo, March 14, 1991, transcription of tape 1, side B, 4, ILBPMB.
4. Bo Bardi to Fabrizio Clerici, February 18, 1973, AFC.
5. Ibid.; obituary, "Lina Bo Bardi, 1914–1992," *O Estado de São Paulo*, March 21, 1992.
6. Francesco Tentori, *Quattro architetti brasiliani e un uomo eccezionale* (Venice: IUAV, 1995), 21.
7. Edmar de Almeida, interview, Uberlândia, August 6, 7, 2006.
8. Graziella Bo Valentinetti, "Una sorella molto 'speciale,'" in *Lina Bo Bardi, architetto*, ed. Antonella Gallo (Venice: Marsilio, 2004), 11.
9. "MASP," *Revista DC*, May 1992, 30; Claudio Bo Valentinetti, interview, Brasília, September 6, 2009.
10. Lina Bo Bardi, "Currículo literário," in *Lina Bo Bardi*, ed. Marcelo Ferraz (São Paulo: ILBPMB, and Milan: Charta, 1994), 3; Bo Valentinetti interview.
11. De Almeida interview.
12. Lina Bo Bardi, "Como aguentar P. M. Bardi," handwritten notes, c. 1989, 1, ILBPMB.
13. Tentori, *Quattro architetti brasiliani e un uomo eccezionale*, 22.
14. Bo Valentinetti, "Una sorella molto 'speciale,'" 11.
15. Bo Valentinetti interview.
16. Lina Bo Bardi, "Enrico Bo," *Habitat* 7 (July–September 1952), 36.
17. Lina Bo, "Pittura, a Milano, la prima mostra di Enrico Bo da Barbaroux," *A: Cultura della vita* 1 (January 1945), 16.
18. Bo Valentinetti, "Una sorella molto 'speciale,'" 11.
19. Ibid.
20. Olivia de Oliveira, "Interview with Lina Bo Bardi" (1991), in Olivia de Oliveira, *Lina Bo Bardi: Obra construída / Built Work* (Barcelona: 2G, 2006), 233.
21. Graziella Bo Valentinetti, interview, São Paulo, June 20, 21, 2004; Claudio Bo Valentinetti interview.
22. Attilio Wanderlingh and Ursula Salwa, *Storia fotografica d'Italia*, vol. 2 (Naples: Intra Moenia, 2007), 48.
23. Giuseppe Belluzzo, "Sul vestire delle signore insegnanti e delle alunne nelle scuole, Circolare n.35, Ministero della Publica Istruzione, Roma, 12 Febbraio 1929," in *La scuola fascista: Istituzioni, parole d'ordine e luoghi dell'immaginario*, ed. D. Montino and G. Gabrielli (Bologna: Ombre Corte, 2009), 25.
24. Francesco Tentori, interview, Venice, February 18, 2006.
25. Ibid.
26. Lina Bo Bardi, handwritten notes to journalist Luiz Carta, no date, ILBPMB.
27. Vicenzo Fasolo, *La Facoltà di Architettura di Roma (nel suo trentacinquesimo anno di vita)* (Rome: Facoltà di Architettura, 1955), 9.
28. Lina Bo Bardi, "Curriculum vitae," typescript, 1957, 2, ILBPMB.
29. Guido Zucconi, "Gli architetti e la storia della città: Il contributo italiano," in *VII Seminário de História da Cidade e do Urbanismo, Proceedings*, vol. 1 (Salvador: PPGAU/FAUUFBA, 2002), 89.
30. Michelangelo Sabatino, "Back to the Drawing Board? Revisiting the Vernacular Tradition in Italian Modern Architecture," in *Annali di Architettura*, no. 16 (Vicenza: Centro di Studio Andrea Palladio, 2004), 176; Isabella Cruciol and Juliana H. Suzuki, "Considerações sobre patrimônio histórico e cultural," in *Revista Terra e Cultura*, no. 42 (Londrina: Centro de Estudos Superiores, 2004), 30.
31. Francesco Tentori, *P. M. Bardi* (São Paulo: ILBPMB, 1990), 40; Claudio M. Valentinetti, *Il viaggio di Pietro Maria Bardi* (Brasília: ENPULLCJ/EEJ, Instituto de Letras, UnB, 2000), 4.
32. Tentori, *P. M. Bardi*, 40.
33. Tentori, *Quattro architetti brasiliani e un uomo eccezionale*, 21; Lina Bo Bardi notes to Carta.
34. Fasolo, *La Facoltà di Architettura di Roma*, 9.

1. Gianfranco Cimboli Spagnesi, "Storia, storiografia ed insegnamento dell'architettura," in *L'architettura nelle città italiane del XX secolo: Dagli anni venti agli anni ottanta*, ed. Vittorio Franchetti Pardo (Milan: Jaca Book, 2003), 362–66.

2. Leonardo Benevolo, *Storia dell'architettura moderna: Il movimento moderno* (Bari: Laterza, 1997), 568–70; Richard Etlin, *Modernism in Italian Architecture, 1890–1940* (Cambridge, MA: MIT Press, 1991), 64.

3. Paolo Nicoloso, *Gli architetti di Mussolini: Scuole e sindacato, archietti e massoni, professori e politici negli anni del regime* (Milan: Franco Angeli, 1999), 20.

4. Maristella Casciato, "The Italian Mosaic: The Architect as Historian," *Journal of the Society of Architectural Historians* 62:1 (2003), 94–96.

5. Lina Bo Bardi, *Contribuição propedêutica ao ensino da teoria da arquitetura* (São Paulo: ILBPMB, 2002), 19, 52.

6. Benevolo, *Storia dell'architettura moderna*, 571.

7. Nicoloso, *Gli architetti di Mussolini*, 18; Luciano Patetta, "Libri e riviste d'architettura in Italia tra le due guerre," in *Il razionalismo e l'architettura in Italia durante il fascismo*, ed. Silvia Danesi and Luciano Patetta (Venice: La Biennale Edizioni, 1976), 12.

8. Casciato, "Italian Mosaic," 92; Nicoloso, *Gli architetti di Mussolini*, 17, 18, 105.

9. Giorgio Ciucci and Francesco dal Co, *Architettura italiana del '900: Atlante*, Documenti di Architettura (Milan: Electa, 1995), 100.

10. Francesco Tentori, *P. M. Bardi* (São Paulo: ILBPMB, 1990), 40, 29.

11. Riccardo Marianni, *Razionalismo e architettura moderna: Storia di una polemica* (Milan: Comunità, 1989), 43.

12. Vittorio Gregotti, "Milano e la cultura architettonica tra le due guerre," in Danesi and Patetta, *Il razionalismo e l'architettura in Italia durante il fascismo*, 16–21.

13. Francesco Tentori, *Quattro architetti brasiliani e un uomo eccezionale* (Venice: IUAV, 1995), 8, 29.

14. Ibid., 21.

15. Paolo Portoghese, "Un'architettura per tutti," in Gloria Arditi and Cesare Serratto, *Gio Ponti: Venti cristalli di architettura* (Venice: Il Cardo, 1994), ix–xi.

16. Carlo Pagani to Lina Bo, January 9, 1945, ILBPMB.

17. Tentori, *Quattro architetti brasiliani e un uomo eccezionale*, 22.

18. Fasolo, *La Facoltà di Architettura di Roma*, 10.

19. Bo Bardi, "Curriculum vitae."

20. Ibid.

21. Bo Bardi, *Contribuição propedêutica ao ensino da teoria da arquitetura*, 19.

22. Bo Bardi, "Curriculum vitae."

23. Fasolo, *La Facoltà di Architettura di Roma*, 10.

24. Tentori, *Quattro architetti brasiliani e un uomo eccezionale*, 25.

25. Francesco Giovanetti and Francesca Romana Stabile, *Vicenzo Fasolo: Primato del disegno e dell'ambientismo* (Rome: Gangemi, 2005), 129–55.

26. Lina Bo Bardi, interview with Fábio Malavoglia, Centro Cultural São Paulo, March 14, 1991, transcription of tape 1, side B, ILBPMB.

27. Tentori, *Quattro architetti brasiliani e un uomo eccezionale*, 21.

28. Bo Bardi interview.

29. Tentori, *Quattro architetti brasiliani e un uomo eccezionale*, 21.

30. Ibid.

31. Francesco Sturlini, *Lina Bo Bardi* (Florence: Facoltà di Architettura, Università degli Studi di Firenze, 1994), 4.

32. Federico Chabod, *L'Italia contemporanea (1918–1948)* (Turin: Einaudi, 2002), 86, 93.

33. Borden W. Painter Jr., *Mussolini's Rome: Rebuilding the Eternal City* (New York: Palgrave Macmillan, 2007), 73.

34. John McKean, *Giancarlo de Carlo: Layered Places* (Stuttgart: Axel Menges, 2004), 10.

35. Edoardo Persico, "Gli architetti italiani," in Maurizio Grandi and Attilio Pracchi, *Milano: Guida all'architettura moderna* (Milan: Zanichelli, 1980), 161, 166.

36. Edoardo Persico, *Scritti d'architettura (1927–1935)* (Florence: Vallecchi, 1968), 117.

37. Antonnino Saggio, *Nuove sostanze: L'informatica e il rinovamento dell'architettura* (Rome: Carocci, 2007), 1.

38. D. Medina Lasansky, *The Renaissance Perfected: Architecture, Spectacle, and Tourism in Fascist Italy* (University Park: Pennsylvania State University Press, 2004), 200.

39. Giorgio Muratore, "Dalla 'bonifica' alla ricostruzione: Nuovi insediamenti in Italia, 1935–1955," in *Arquitectura, ciudad e ideología urbana* (Pamplona: T6 Ediciones, Escuela Técnica Superior de Arquitectura, Universidad de Navarra, 2002), 39–40.

40. Benevolo, *Storia dell'architettura moderna*, 577.

41. Bo Bardi interview.

42. Sturlini, *Lina Bo Bardi*, 2.

43. Bo Bardi interview.

44. Facoltà di Architettura di Roma, *La Facoltà di Architettura di Roma nel suo trentacinquesimo anno di vita* (Rome: Facoltà di Architettura, 1955), 215; Bo Bardi, "Currículo literário," 9.

45. Bo Bardi, "Currículo literário," 9.

46. Tentori, *Quattro architetti brasiliani e un uomo eccezionale*, 20.

47. Cesare de Sessa, *Luigi Piccinato, architetto* (Bari: Dedalo, 1985), 123.

48. Hanne Storm Ofteland, "Sabaudia, 1934: Materializing the Fascist, Corporate Town" (PhD diss., University of Oslo, 2002), 88.

49. *La Facoltà di Architettura di Roma*, 210–15.

50. Tentori, *Quattro architetti brasiliani e un uomo eccezionale*, 20; Bo Bardi interview.

51. *La Facoltà di Architettura di Roma*, 215.

52. Tentori, *Quattro architetti brasiliani e un uomo eccezionale*, 20.

53. Carlo Pagani, "Allegati alle considerazioni sul 'Curriculum letterario'" (1994), in Renato L. S. Anelli, *Interlocuções com a arquitetura italiana na constituição da arquitetura moderna em São Paulo* (São Carlos: EESC-USP, 2001), 5.

54. Nicoloso, *Gli architetti di Mussolini*, 130.

55. Tentori, *Quattro architetti brasiliani e un uomo eccezionale*, 21.

56. Ibid., 24.

1. Lina Bo Bardi, professional registration, 1940, ILBPMB.
2. Carlo Pagani to Lina Bo Bardi, January 9, 1945, ILBPMB.
3. Lina Bo Bardi, "Currículo literário," in *Lina Bo Bardi*, ed. Marcelo Ferraz (Milan: Charta, and São Paulo: ILBPMB, 1994), 9.
4. Olivia de Oliviera, "Interview with Lina Bo Bardi" (1991), in Olivia de Oliviera, *Lina Bo Bardi: Obra construida / Built Work* (Barcelona: 2G, 2002), 235; Carlo Pagani, *Architettura italiana oggi / Italy's Architecture Today* (Milan: Ulrico Hoepli, 1955), 17.
5. Bo Bardi, "Currículo literário," 9; Carlo Pagani, "Allegati alle considerazioni sul 'Curriculum letterario'" (1994), in Renato L. S. Anelli, *Interlocuções com a arquitetura italiana na constituição da arquitetura moderna em São Paulo* (São Carlos: EESC-USP, 2001), 2.
6. *Lina Bo Bardi*, directed by Aurélio Michiles and Isa Grinspum Ferraz (São Paulo: ILBPMB, 1993), video.
7. Emily Braun, "The Visual Arts: Modernism and Fascism," in *Liberal and Fascist Italy, 1900–1945*, ed. Adrian Lyttelton (Oxford: Oxford University Press, 2002), 207.
8. Lina Bo and Carlo Pagani, "Stanza per due ragazzi," *Domus* 155 (November 1940), 68–69.
9. Lina Bo and Carlo Pagani, "Un giardino disegnato da Bo e Pagani," *Domus* 156 (December 1940), 42–43.
10. Massimo Martignoni, *Gio Ponti: Gli anni di stile, 1941–1947* (Milan: Abitare Segesta, 2002), 15.
11. "Semplicità," *Lo Stile* 3 (March 1941), 1.
12. Lisa Ponti, "Stile è un'isola," in Martignoni, *Gio Ponti*, 7.
13. Lina Bo and Carlo Pagani, "Arredamenti," *Lo Stile* 1 (January 1941), 88.
14. Francesco Sturlini, *Lina Bo Bardi* (Florence: Facoltà di Architettura, Università degli Studi di Firenze, 1994), 4.
15. Lina Bo, "Recensioni: Un importante libro sull'architettura," *Lo Stile* 10 (October 1941): 34.
16. Francesco Tentori, *Quattro architetti brasiliani e un uomo eccezionale* (Venice: IUAV, 1995), 18–19.
17. Lina Bo and Carlo Pagani, "Ambienti per bambini," *Cordelia* 1 (February–March 1942), 13–14.
18. Lina Bo and Carlo Pagani, "In campagna," *Grazia* 161 (August 1941), 17.
19. Enrico Pea, "Magoometto," *L'Illustrazione Italiana*, August 16, 1943, xx.
20. Lina Bo to Carlo Pagani, December 1, 1942, ILBPMB.
21. Pagani to Bo, December 1, 1942, ILBPMB.
22. Marcello Piacentini to Bo, October 18, 1942, written on Reale Accademia Italia stationery, ILBPMB.

23. Piacentini to Bo, Rome, April 2, 1943, written on his personal stationery, 1–2, ILBPMB.
24. Riccardo Mariani, interview, Florence, February 20, 2008.
25. Graziella Bo Valentinetti, "Una sorella molto 'speciale,'" in *Lina Bo Bardi, architetto*, ed. Antonella Gallo (Venice: Marsilio, 2004), 12; Pagani, "Considerazioni sul 'Curriculum letterario,'" 2.
26. Lina Bo, "Casa e nuclei abitativi in Roma," *Lo Stile* 20 (July 1943), 15.
27. Bo Valentinetti, "Una sorella molto 'speciale,'" 20.
28. Bo to Pagani, May 10, 1943, in Carlo Pagani, "Allegati alle considerazioni sul 'Curriculum letterario,'" 8.
29. According to Bo Bardi, the building was completely destroyed. Envelopes sent to her after that period, however, show that the address remained active, and a later survey classified the address on via Gesù 12 as "severely damaged." Mauro Colombo, "I bombardamenti aerei su Milano durante la II guerra mondiale," *Storia di Milano*, http://www.storiadimilano.it/Repertori/bombardamenti.htm.
30. Oliveira, "Interview with Lina Bo Bardi," 236.
31. L.B., "Architettura e natura: La casa nel paesaggio," *Domus* 194 (February 1944), 464–71.
32. Dr. Grace L. McCann Morley, "Western Living: 5 Modern Houses," *California Arts and Architecture* 59 (1942), 23–25.
33. Albert Frey, *In Search of a Living Architecture* (New York: Architectural Book Publishing), 1939.
34. "Case sui trampoli," *Domus* 194 (February 1944), 272–74.
35. Lina Bo, "Sistemazione degli interni," *Domus* 198 (June 1944), 200–201.
36. Pierrefeu e Le Corbusier, "La casa degli uomini: Interpretazioni e commenti di Diotallevi e Marescotti," *Domus* 197, 198 (May, June 1944), supplements.

1. Lina Bo Bardi, "Currículo literário," in *Lina Bo Bardi*, ed. Marcelo Ferraz (Milan: Charta, and São Paulo: ILBPMB, 1994), 11.
2. Lina Bo to Bruno Zevi, July 6, 1945, FBZ.
3. Graziella Bo Valentinetti, interview, São Paulo, June 20, 21, 2004.
4. Francesco Tentori, *Quattro architetti brasiliani e un uomo eccezionale* (Venice: IUAV, 1995), 24.
5. Ibid.
6. Tilina Rota to Bo, June 23, July 7, 1943, sent from Mondadori Editori at Arona to via Gesù 12, ILBPMB.
7. Carlo Pagani, "Allegati alle considerazioni sul 'Curriculum letterario'" (1994), in Renato L. S. Anelli, *Interlocuções com a arquitetura italiana na constituição da arquitetura moderna em São Carlos: EESC-USP, 2001), 5.
8. Tentori, *Quattro architetti brasiliani e un uomo eccezionale*, 23.
9. Bo Bardi, "Currículo literário," 9.
10. Marcelo C. Ferraz, interview with the author, São Paulo, August 4, 2006.
11. Pagani, "Considerazioni sul 'Curriculum letterario,'" 10.
12. Bo Bardi, "Currículo literário," 11.
13. Pagani, "Considerazioni sul 'Curriculum letterario,'" 35.
14. Matilde Baffa, Corinna Morandi, and Sara Protasoni, *Il movimento di studi per l'architettura: 1945–1946* (Bari: 1995), 83–105.
15. Olivia de Oliveira, "Interview with Lina Bo Bardi" (1991), in Olivia de Oliveira, *Lina Bo Bardi: Obra construida / Built Work* (Barcelona: 2G, 2002), 237.
16. Maristella Casciatto, "Neorealism in Italian Architecture," in *Anxious Modernisms*, ed. Sarah W. Goldhagen and Réjean Legault (Montreal: CCA; and Cambridge, MA: MIT Press, 2000), 49.
17. Maristella Casciatto, "Wright and Italy," in *Frank Lloyd Wright: Europe and Beyond*, ed. Anthony Alofsin (Berkeley: University of California Press, 1999), 76–99.
18. Bruno Zevi, "A Recollection," in Goldhagen and Legault, *Anxious Modernisms*, 66.
19. "Rassegna del primo convegno nazionale per la ricostruzione edilizia," in Fabrizio Brunetti, *L'architettura in Italia negli anni della ricostruzione* (Florence: Alinea, 1998), 194.
20. Penny Sparke, "'A Home for Everybody?': Design, Ideology and the Culture of the Home in Italy, 1945–1972," in *Modernism in Design*, ed. Paul Greenhalgh (London: Reaktion Books, 1990), 186.
21. Pagani, "Considerazioni sul 'Curriculum letterario,'" 12.
22. Bo to Bruno Zevi, July 6, 1945, FBZ.
23. Bruno Zevi to Pietro Maria Bardi, Ortensio Gatti, Bo, and Pagani, October 29, 1945, 1, FBZ.

24. Bruno Zevi, "Idee per A" and "Per Bardi e Pagani," typed notes, c. October 1945, FBZ.
25. Bruno Zevi in http://www.fondazionebrunozevi.it/19892000/frame/pagine/simposiowright.htm.
26. Zevi, "Idee per A."
27. Pagani to Zevi, May 10, 1946, 1, FBZ.
28. A, February 15, 1946, cover page.
29. "In cerca di mobili," A: Cultura della vita 8 (June 1, 1946), 8–9.
30. Ibid.
31. Bruno Zevi, "Lina Bo Bardi: Un architetto in tragitto ansioso," Caramelo 4 (São Paulo: FAUUSP, 1992), 36.
32. Sparke, "'A Home for Everybody?'" 187.
33. Oliveira, "Interview with Lina Bo Bardi," 237.
34. "Al Palazzo dell'Arte: Stoffe," Domus 213 (September 1946), 26–27.
35. Tentori, Quattro architetti brasiliani e un uomo eccezionale, 18–19. According to Lina Bo Bardi, she returned to Rome to create a weekly magazine early in 1946; Oliveira, "Interview with Lina Bo Bardi," 236. According to Carlo Pagani, Bo Bardi was already in Rome when A magazine came out in January 1946; Pagani, "Considerazioni sul 'Curriculum letterario,'" 5. Letters between Zevi and Pagani demonstrate that Lina Bo was also working with Pagani in the editorial office in Milan; correspondence regarding A magazine, 1945–46, FBZ.
36. Riccardo Marianni, Razionalismo e architettura moderna: Storia di una polemica (Milan: Comunità, 1989), 9.
37. Bo Valentinetti, "Una sorella molto 'speciale,'" 13; Marianni, Razionalismo e architettura moderna, 9.
38. Fernando Morais, Chatô: O rei do Brasil (São Paulo: Companhia das Letras, 1994), 476.
39. Mariani, interview.
40. Bo Bardi, interview with Fábio Malavoglia, Centro Cultural São Paulo, March 14, 1991, transcription of tape 1, side B, ILBPMB.

1. Federico Mengozzi, "Lina Bo Bardi," Folha de São Paulo, July 18, 1991.
2. Fernando Morais, Chatô: O rei do Brasil (São Paulo: Companhia das Letras, 1994), 476; Pietro Maria Bardi, 40 anos de MASP (São Paulo: Crefisul, 1986), 9.
3. Lina Bo Bardi, Largo Getúlio Vargas, watercolor, October 20, 1946, MASP.
4. Lina Bo Bardi, handwritten note, c. 1990, ILBPMB.
5. Francesco Tentori, P. M. Bardi (São Paulo: ILBPMB, 1990), 172.
6. Lina Bo Bardi, "Pequena carta ao Artigas," handwritten note, c. 1984, ILBPMB.
7. Carlos F. Martins, "Construir uma arquitetura, construir um país," in Jorge Schwartz et al., Brasil, 1920–1950: Da antropofagia a Brasília (São Paulo: Cosac Naify, 2002), 373–82.
8. Lina Bo Bardi, "Athos Bulcão," handwritten note, c. 1989, ILBPMB.
9. Bo Bardi, handwritten note, c. 1990.
10. Teresa A. Meade, A Brief History of Brazil (New York: Facts on File, 2003), 145.
11. Daryle Williams, Culture Wars in Brazil: The First Vargas Regime, 1930–1945 (Durham, NC: Duke University Press, 2001), 15.
12. Zilah Quezado Deckker, Brazil Built: The Architecture of the Modern Movement in Brazil (London: Spon, 2001), 15.
13. Ibid., 60, 81.
14. Otávio Leonildo, Carradas de Razões: Lucio Costa e a arquitetura moderna brasileira, 1924–1951 (Rio de Janeiro: PUC-Loyola, 2007), 190–214.
15. Lélia Coelho Frota, Alcides Rocha Miranda: Caminho de um arquiteto (Rio de Janeiro: UFRJ, 1993); Adriana Irigoyen, Wright e Artigas: Duas viagens (São Paulo: Ateliê/FAPESP, 2002), 62–65.
16. Sergio Miceli, Intelectuais e classe dirigente no Brasil, 1920–1945 (São Paulo: Difel, 1979), 34–35.
17. Deckker, Brazil Built, 29.
18. Nelson A. Rockefeller, letters and documents regarding Latin America and Brazil, 1930s to 1950s, folders 1461, 1467, box 148; folders 1469–1471, box 149, RG 4, NAR Personal Documents, Museums; folder 100, box 17, RG 4, NAR Personal Documents, Countries, RAC; Deckker, Brazil Built, 111–26.
19. Williams, Culture Wars in Brazil, 89.
20. Yves Bruand, Arquitetura contemporânea no Brasil (São Paulo: Perspectiva, 1997), 115, 151.
21. Lina Bo Bardi, interview with Fábio Malavoglia, Centro Cultural São Paulo, March 14, 1991, transcription of tape 1, side B, 3, ILBPMB.
22. Lina Bo Bardi, "Sobre a 'forma na arquitetura' de Oscar Niemeyer," July 9, 1978, typescript, ILBPMB.

23. Geraldo G. Ferraz, "Lina, a poética da instransigência," Revista DC (May 1992), 30–31.
24. Lina Bo Bardi, directed by Aurélio Michiles and Isa Grinspum Ferraz (São Paulo: ILBPMB, 1993), video.
25. Mário Pedrosa, "Dos primitivos à primeira Renascença italiana," in Mário Pedrosa: Modernidade lá e cá, ed. Otília Fiore Arantes (São Paulo: EDUSP, 2000), 37.
26. Pietro Maria Bardi, Sodalício com Assis Chateaubriand (São Paulo: MASP, 1982), 14.
27. Bardi, 40 anos de MASP, 12.
28. Fernando Morais, Chatô: O rei do Brasil (São Paulo: Companhia das Letras, 1994), 456; Bernardo Kucinski, A Síndrome da Antena Parabólica (São Paulo: Perseu Abramo, 1998), 45–47.
29. Maria Cecília F. Lourenço, Museus acolhem moderno (São Paulo: EDUSP, 1999), 97.
30. Assis Chateaubriand to Rockefeller, March 20, 1946, folder 100, box 17, RG 4, NAR Personal Documents, Countries, RAC.
31. Morais, Chatô, 477.
32. Mengozzi, "Lina Bo Bardi," 11.
33. Lina Bo Bardi video.
34. Bardi, Sodalício com Assis Chateaubriand, 12.
35. Morais, Chatô, 479.
36. P. M. Bardi, "Building a Museum on Virgin Soil," Art News 33 (March 1957), folder 1465, box 148, RG 4, NAR Personal Documents, Museums, RAC.
37. Lina Bo Bardi, "Na Europa, a casa do homem ruiu," Rio 92 (February 1947), 53–55, 95. Quotations in the following three paragraphs are from this article.
38. Bardi, 40 anos de MASP, 12.
39. Bo Bardi, "Na Europa, a casa do homem ruiu," 95.
40. Morais, Chatô, 478.
41. Bardi, Sodalício com Assis Chateaubriand, 12.
42. Ibid.
43. Ferraz, "Lina, a poética da instransigência," 30–31.
44. "Lina Bo Bardi, 1914–1992," O Estado de São Paulo, March 21, 1992.

1. Fernando Morais, *Chatô: O rei do Brasil* (São Paulo: Companhia das Letras, 1994), 479.
2. Pietro Maria Bardi, *40 anos de MASP* (São Paulo: Crefisul, 1986), 16.
3. C. S. Smith to Nelson A. Rockefeller, April 17, 1947, folder 1464, box 148, RG 4, NAR Personal Documents, Museums, RAC.
4. Pietro Maria Bardi, "An Educational Experiment at the Museu de Arte, São Paulo," *Museum* 1 (December 1948), 3, 4, 142, 212.
5. Maria Cecília F. Lourenço, *Museus acolhem moderno* (São Paulo: EDUSP, 1999), 97.
6. Morais, *Chatô*, 479–485.
7. Bardi, *40 anos de MASP*, 14.
8. Tentori, *P. M. Bardi* (São Paulo: ILBPMB, 1990), 184.
9. Bardi, *40 anos de MASP*, 14.
10. Lina Bo Bardi, "O Museu de Arte de São Paulo—Função Social dos Museus," *Habitat* 1 (October–December 1950), 43.
11. *Dalbergia nigra*, a valuable Brazilian hardwood.
12. Bardi, *40 anos de MASP*, 14.
13. Lina Bo Bardi, notes and photographs for *Habitat* editorial work, early 1950s, MASP.
14. Brazilian cherry or grumichama, *Eugenia brasiliensis*, a valuable hardwood endemic to Brazil.
15. Lina Bo Bardi, "Uma cadeira de grumixaba e taboa é mais normal do que um divã de babados," *Diário de São Paulo*, November 13, 1949.
16. Bardi, *40 anos de MASP*, 14.
17. E. Kneese de Melo to Smith, April 27, 1947, folder 1467, box 148, RG 4, NAR Personal Documents, Museums, RAC.
18. Lourenço, *Museus acolhem moderno*, 114.
19. Nelson A. Rockefeller to F. Matarazzo So., March 5, 1948, folder 1471, box 149, RG 4, NAR Personal Documents, Museums, RAC.
20. P. M. Bardi, "Building a Museum on Virgin Soil," *Art News* 33 (March 1957), folder 1465, box 148, RG 4, NAR Personal Documents, Museums, RAC.
21. Bo Bardi, "O Museu de Arte de São Paulo," 17, 42.
22. Arthur Vandenberg Jr. to Louise Boyer (NAR's executive assistant and trusted adviser), c. 1950, folder 1471, box 149, RG 4, NAR Personal Documents, Museums, RAC.
23. Bo Bardi, "O Museu de Arte de São Paulo," 42.
24. Renato Magalhães Gouveia, *Masp, 60 anos: A história em três tempo* (São Paulo: MASP, 2008), 39.
25. IAC–MASP, promotional flier, 1950, ILBPMB.
26. Ethel Leon, "IAC, Instituto de Arte Contemporânea: Escola de Desenho Industrial do MASP (1951–53), Primeiros Estudos" (PhD diss., University of São Paulo, 2006), 24.
27. Pietro Maria Bardi to Siegfried Giedion, December 7, 1948, ILBPMB.
28. Lina Bo Bardi, "Sobre a 'forma na arquitetura' de Oscar Niemeyer," manuscript, July 9, 1978, ILBPMB.
29. Ibid.
30. *Habitat* publication records, ILBPMB and MASP.
31. Flávio Motta, Bo Bardi's assistant at the time, attributed six unsigned articles about rural and anonymous architecture published in *Habitat* between 1950 and 1953 to her in Maria de Fátima M. B. Campello, *Lina Bo Bardi: As moradas da alma* (São Carlos: EESC-Universidade de São Paulo, 1997), 27.
32. Lina Bo Bardi, "Casas de Vilanova Artigas," *Habitat* 1 (October–December 1950), 3.
33. "Amazonas: O povo arquiteto," *Habitat* 1 (October–December 1950).
34. Assis Chateaubriand, "O índio e o homem do Planalto," *Habitat* 14 (January–February, 1954), n.p.
35. Pietro Maria Bardi, "Frei Lodoli e a cadeira," *Habitat* 1 (October–December 1950), 52–58.
36. "Ex-votos do Nordeste," *Habitat* 1 (October–December 1950), 50–51.
37. Pietro Maria Bardi, "Para uma nova cultura do homem," *Habitat* 2 (January–March 1951), 1.
38. The essay is translated as "New-born child" in the English summary of the magazine. Lina Bo Bardi, "Bela criança," *Habitat* 2 (January–March 1951), 3.
39. Abelardo de Souza, "A nossa arquitetura," *Habitat* 2 (January–March 1951), 5.
40. Bo Bardi, "Bela criança."
41. Ibid.
42. Campello, *Lina Bo Bardi*, 158–59.
43. "Por que o povo é arquiteto?" *Habitat* 3 (April–June 1951), 3.
44. "Casa de sete mil cruzeiros," *Habitat* 3 (April–June 1951), 18.
45. Edoardo Persico, *Scritti d'architettura (1927–1935)* (Florence: Vallecchi, 1968), 117.
46. Maristella Casciato, "Wright and Italy: The Promise of Organic Architecture," in *Frank Lloyd Wright: Europe and Beyond*, ed. Anthony Alofson (Berkeley: University of California Press, 1999), 92.
47. "O povo é arquiteto," *Habitat* 10 (January–February 1954).
48. "Taba Guaianases," *Habitat* 14 (January–February 1954), 52; Lina Bo Bardi and Pier Luigi Nervi, "Il complesso Guajanazes a San Paolo," *Domus* 282 (May 1953), 4–7.
49. "A segunda Bienal, uma exposição para o grande público," *Habitat* 14 (January–March 1954), 29.
50. "Casas, eles também precisam," *Habitat* 14 (January–February 1954), 28.
51. Lina Bo Bardi, "A catedral," *Habitat* 14 (January–February 1954), Polêmica, C.
52. Lina Bo Bardi, P. M. Bardi, and Rodolfo Klein, "Declaração," *Habitat* 15 (March–April 1954), 1.
53. Ibid.

1. P. M. Bardi, "Building a Museum on Virgin Soil," *Art News* 33 (March 1957), 33–34.
2. Sylvia Ficher, *Os arquitetos da Poli: Ensino e profissão em São Paulo* (São Paulo: EDUSP, 2005), 248.
3. Maria Lúcia Bressan Pinheiro, "Rumo ao Moderno: Uma historiografia da arquitetura moderna em São Paulo até 1945," *III Seminário Docomomo/SP* (São Paulo, 2005), 4.
4. Anat Falbel, "Immigrant Architects in Brazil: A Historiographical Issue," *Docomomo Journal* 34 (2006), 58–65.
5. Hugo Segawa, *Arquiteturas no Brasil, 1900–1990* (São Paulo: Edusp, 1998), 139.
6. Temporary resident visa issued to Achillina Bo Bardi, January 29, 1948 (Brazilian consulate general in Rome).
7. Paubrá business card, ILBPMB.
8. Eros Renzetti, interview held in Rome, February 10, 2007.
9. Paubrá firm registration, February 3, 1949, ILBPMB. Bo Bardi appears as the only official representative of the firm, along with assistant Euclides Faria; the firm closed in December 1950. Quotation from Lina Bo Bardi, notes on Estúdio Palma, c. 1949, ILBPMB. Lina Bo Bardi, "Móveis novos," *Habitat* 1 (October–December 1950), 50–58.
10. Lina Bo Bardi, "Desenho industrial," *Habitat* 1 (October–December 1950), 62.
11. Bo Bardi, notes on Estúdio Palma.
12. Lina Bo Bardi (attributed), "Um restaurante," *Habitat* 2 (January–March 1951), 28–29.
13. Enrico Bo, *Notte a Parma*, 1943, Claudio Bo Valentinetti private collection.
14. Leila K. Moreno, "Nossa cidade em três décadas," *Jornal da Tarde*, August 25, 1987, 12.
15. Pietro Maria Bardi, "Em meio ao verde a casa do Morumbi," *Casa Vogue* 3 (May–June 1984), 160–63.
16. Lina Bo Bardi. "Jardim Morumbi—Terreno reservado para Instituto de Arte de São Paulo," map with handwritten notes, c. 1949, ILBPMB.
17. The purchase of two lots is confirmed by notes written by the Bardis on Jardim Morumbi sales map, Companhia Imobiliária Morumbi, ILBPMB. "Contrato de compromisso de venda e compra de terreno," Companhia Imobiliária Morumby, São Paulo, signed by Lina Bo Bardi and Pietro Maria Bardi, December 19, 1949, ILBPMB.
18. Moreno, "Nossa cidade em três décadas," 12.
19. City permit quoted on the plan for the construction of the housekeeper's house. "Processo n. 285, alvará n. 25.353, tudo de 5 de 7 de 1951," ILBPMB.

20. The building contract signed on May 22, 1951, between Bo Bardi and Sociedade Comercial e Construtora S/A, directed by engineer Heitor Portugal, indicates that the reinforced concrete structure should have been built within a hundred days at a cost of 40,000 cruzeiros. An invoice sent on April 29, 1952, requests payment of more than 166,000 cruzeiros for "building administration expenses taken place during the months of February and March of 1952 regarding the construction to which the heading referred [Residence at Jardim Morumbi]," respectively in "Contrato de construção por administração," May 22, 1951, and in "N/Obra Residência no Jardim Morumbi—OA/216-14," April 29, 1952, invoice, both from Sociedade Comercial e Construtora S/A, ILBPMB.
21. Companhia Nacional de Investimentos, *Jardim Morumbi*, advertisement brochure, ILBPMB.
22. Ibid.
23. "Morumbi," *Habitat* 5 (October–December 1951), 66.
24. Lina Bo Bardi, "Residência no Morumbi," *Habitat* 10 (January–March 1953), 40.
25. Study drawing for the Glass House, c. 1950, ILBPMB.
26. "Case sui trampoli," *Domus* 194 (February 1944), 272–73. Max Bill's house had originally been published in *Werk* in 1942 and had appeared in *Casabella* in 1943 before appearing in *Domus* in 1944.
27. Maristella Casciato, "Neorealism in Italian Architecture," in *Anxious Modernisms: Experimentation in Postwar Architectural Culture*, ed. Sarah Williams Goldhagen and Réjean Legaut (Cambridge, MA: MIT Press, 2002), 29.
28. Lina Bo Bardi, *Casa de vidro* (Lisbon: Blau, 1999), 4.
29. Moreno, "Nossa cidade em três décadas," 12.
30. Lina Bo Bardi, "Exposição da Agricultura Paulista," *Habitat* 2 (January–March 1951), 42.
31. IBEC, *Daily News Digest*, Brazilian Bulletin, March 15–29, 1951, folder 1464, box 148, RG 4, NAR Personal Documents, Museums, RAC.
32. Pier Luigi Nervi, "Resistência pela forma," *Habitat* 3 (April–June 1951), 1.
33. "Edifício Taba Guaianases," *Habitat* 14 (January–March 1951), 4–10.
34. Lina Bo Bardi and Pier Luigi Nervi, "Il complesso Guajanazes a San Paolo," *Domus* 282 (May 1953), 4–7.
35. "Edifício Taba Guaianases," 8.
36. Charles Forbes's mayoral mandate started in January 1952.
37. Lina Bo Bardi, "Museu à beira do oceano," *Habitat* 8 (July–September 1951), 6–11.
38. Ibid., 10.
39. Ibid., 12.

1. Several letters between MAM representatives and Nelson A. Rockefeller, 1951–58, folders 1469, 1470, box 149, RG 4, NAR Personal Documents, Museums, RAC.
2. Maria Cecília F. Lourenço, *Museus acolhem moderno* (São Paulo: EDUSP, 1999), 115–16.
3. Serafim (attributed to Pietro Maria Bardi and sometimes Lina Bo and Assis Chateaubriand), "Bienal," *Habitat* 5 (October–December 1951), 1.
4. "Correspondência," *Habitat* 6 (January–March 1952), 87.
5. Competition document, Francisco Beck, Director, Department of Architecture, São Paulo City, May, 30, 1952, 1, folder 1478, box 149, RG 4, NAR Personal Documents, Museums, RAC.
6. Affonso Reidy, "Museu de Artes Plásticas, São Paulo." Descriptive memorandum, FLS.21: 757/52, Folder 1478, Box 149, RG 4, NAR Personal Documents, Museums, RAC.
7. Matarazzo to Nelson A. Rockefeller, August 19, 1952; Rockefeller to Matarazzo, September 24, 1952, folder 1478, box 149, RG 4, NAR Personal Documents, Museums, RAC.
8. "O centenário," *Habitat* 6 (January–March 1952), 1. Editorial attributable to Pietro Maria Bardi.
9. Lina Bo and Pietro Maria Bardi (attributed), "Ibirapuera," *Habitat* 11 (April–June 1953), 3.
10. Ibid.
11. Lourenço, *Museus acolhem moderno*, 97.
12. According to Bo Bardi, "Lina was denounced (by Ciccilo [Matarazzo]) as a troublemaker, for not being native and being the director of *Habitat* magazine and Pietro was denounced as an ex-Fascist, while for us youngsters, he was the European hope." Lina Bo Bardi, handwritten notes titled "Artigo sobre Pietro p/ Luiz Carta," 2, c. 1989, ILBPMB.
13. Departamento do Interior e da Justiça, Ministério da Justiça e Negócios Interiores, naturalization certificate by the Brazilian federal government, registered on March 18, 1953, and approved on April 28, 1953, ILBPMB.
14. Renato Magalhães Gouvêa, *Masp, 60 anos: A história em três tempos* (São Paulo: MASP, 2008), 50–51.
15. Max Bill, "O arquiteto, a arquitetura, a sociedade," *Habitat* 14 (January–February 1954), A–B.
16. Walter Gropius, "O arquiteto na sociedade industrial," in "Dois mestres da arquitetura contemporânea falam aos arquitetos brasileiros," *Habitat* 16 (May–June 1954), 25.
17. Abelardo de Souza, "IV Congresso Brasileiro de Arquitetos," *Habitat* 14 (January–February 1954), 23.

18. "Report on Brazil," *Architectural Review* 694 (October 1954), 234–50.
19. Alberto Xavier, ed., *Depoimento de uma geração* (São Paulo: Cosac Naify, 2003), 167.
20. De Souza, "IV Congresso Brasileiro de Arquitetos," 23.
21. Lina Bo Bardi to Bruno Zevi, c. 1955, FBZ.
22. Despite the name, the school offered only an architectural program at the time; the program in urbanism was approved in 1960.
23. Joaquim Guedes, "Casa e cidade: Um mestre da moderna arquitetura brasileira," Summary, *Portal Vitruvius* 014, Year 2 (February 2003).
24. Lina Bo Bardi, handwritten note, c. 1980, ILBPMB.
25. Certificate concerning Bo Bardi's contractual transcript, Faculdade de Arquitetura e Urbanismo, Universidade de São Paulo, September 20, 1957, ILBPMB.
26. Lina Bo Bardi, application letter, September 20, 1957, ILBPMB.
27. According to immigration service stamps on Bo Bardi's passport, ILBPMB.
28. Gouvêa, *Masp, 60 anos*, 54.
29. According to her passport stamps, Bo Bardi obtained entry visas for France and Spain at the French and Spanish consulates in Milan, ILBPMB.
30. Gouvêa, *Masp, 60 anos*, 54.
31. Bo Bardi, passport stamps, ILBPMB. The exhibition opened on March 21, 1957, and ended on June 2, 1957, after a monthlong extension and great success. Exhibition catalogue and correspondence, Metropolitan Museum of Art archives.
32. Bo Bardi, passport stamps.
33. Fernando Morais, *Chatô, O rei do Brasil* (São Paulo: Companhia das Letras, 1994), 586.
34. Money transfer receipt, in ibid., 589.
35. Lina Bo Bardi, handwritten note, c. 1980, ILBPMB.
36. Lina Bo Bardi, "Concurso em Cantù," *Habitat* 46 (January–March 1958), 20–21.
37. Lina Bo Bardi, lecture at FAUUSP, April 14, 1989, transcription, n.p., ILBPMB.
38. Lina Bo Bardi, MASP, sketches and notes, c. 1957, ILBPMB.
39. Lina Bo Bardi, MASP, sketches for structural and material alternatives, c. 1957, ILBPMB.
40. Lina Bo Bardi, lecture at FAUUSP, published as "Uma aula de arquitetura," *Projeto* 149 (1992).
41. Pietro Maria Bardi, *História do MASP* (São Paulo: Instituto Quadrante, 1992), 30–31.
42. Gouvêa, *Masp, 60 anos*, 54.
43. P. M. Bardi, "Building a Museum on Virgin Soil," *Art News* 33 (March 1957), 33.
44. Lina Bo Bardi, MASP, handwritten note, c. 1984, ILBPMB.

1. Lina Bo Bardi, *Contribuição propedêutica ao ensino da teoria da arquitetura* (São Paulo: Habitat, 1957); reprinted in 2002 by ILBPMB on the tenth anniversary of Bo Bardi's death.
2. Ibid., 4.
3. Geoffrey Scott, *The Architecture of Humanism: A Study in the History of Taste* (New York: W. W. Norton, 1999).
4. Bo Bardi, *Contribuição propedêutica*, 6.
5. Ibid., 63.
6. Ibid., 40, 78.
7. Ibid., 39–40.
8. Ibid., 49.
9. Ibid., 67.
10. Ibid., 68.
11. Ibid., 70–71.
12. The position was "Professor Catedrático," a term formerly used to describe a professor who holds a chair. Lina Bo Bardi, FAUUSP, application letter, September 20, 1957, ILBPMB.
13. Cover letter filed by FAUUSP on September 21, 1957, along with letters of recommendation by Ponti, Zevi, and Zanuso and professional certificate (Lombardy), all signed between September 1 and 11, 1957, ILBPMB.
14. Júlio Katinsky, interview, São Paulo, August 16, 2005.
15. Note on Bo Bardi's returned application cover letter, September 23, 1957, ILBPMB.
16. Júlio M. Stanato to Pedro Bento Gravina (University Council), September 22, 1958, ILBPMB.
17. Paulo Ormindo de Azevedo, interview, in Juliano Pereira Trindade, *A ação de Lina Bo Bardi na Bahia e no Nordeste (1958–1964)* (São Carlos: EESC–Universidade de São Paulo, 2001), 271.
18. Olívia de Oliveira, *Lina Bo Bardi: Sutis substâncias da arquitetura* (São Paulo: Romano Guerra; and Barcelona: Gustavo Gili, 2006), 81.
19. According to the third owner of the house, Maria Luísa D'Orey Macedo Soares, who lived in it from the late 1970s to 2008. Macedo Soares, interview, São Paulo, June 24, 2006.
20. The registration drawings, signed by Achillina Bo Bardi with a seal by Companhia Imobiliária Morumby, were dated June 6, 1958, Cirell House, plans, ILBPMB.
21. Lina Bo Bardi, "Bela criança," *Habitat* 2 (January–March 1951), 3; "Casa de 7 mil cruzeiros," *Habitat* 3 (April–June 1951), 4–6.
22. Rubem and Gilka Nogueira to Lina Bo Bardi, in Oliveria, *Lina Bo Bardi*, 83, 86.
23. Lina Bo Bardi to Rubem and Gilka Nogueira, in ibid., 85.
24. Lina Bo Bardi, "Casa na Bahia," *Habitat* 8 (July–September 1951), 16–17.

25. Lina Bo Bardi, "Arquitetura e natureza ou natureza e arquitetura?" handwritten lecture notes, Salvador, September 27, 1958, 4, ILBPMB.
26. Maristella Casciato, "Neorealism in Italian Architecture," in *Anxious Modernisms: Experimentation in Postwar Architectural Culture*, ed. Sarah Williams Goldhagen and Réjean Legaut (Cambridge, MA: MIT Press, 2002), 47.
27. Azevedo interview, 271. Lina Bo Bardi, Salvador lectures, handwritten notes, Escola de Belas Artes, Universidade da Bahia, April 17–21, 1958, ILBPMB.
28. Azevedo interview, 273.
29. Bo Bardi, Salvador lectures notes.
30. Lina Bo Bardi, first Salvador lecture, handwritten notes, Escola de Belas Artes, Universidade da Bahia, April 17, 1958, ILBPMB.
31. Ibid.
32. Lina Bo Bardi, second Salvador lecture, handwritten notes, Escola de Belas Artes, Universidade da Bahia, April 19, 1958, 5, ILBPMB.
33. Ibid., 7.
34. Marcelo Ridenti, *Em busca do povo brasileiro: Artistas da revolução, do CPC à era da TV* (São Paulo: Record, 2000), 12–13.
36. Azevedo interview, 273.
36. Júlio Katinsky, "Lina Bo Bardi," *Jornal do Brasil*, March 29, 1992, 6.

1. Marc W. Herold, "Between Sugar and Petroleum: Bahia and Salvador, 1920–1960," *Revista Espaço Acadêmico* 42 (November 2004), 23–24.

2. Eduardo José Santos Borges, "Modernidade negociada: Cinema, autonomia política e vanguarda cultural no contexto do desenvolvimentismo baiano (1956–1964)" (PhD diss., Universidade Federal da Bahia, 2003), 26–27.

3. Renato Ortiz, *A moderna tradição brasileira: Cultura brasileira e indústria cultural* (São Paulo: Brasiliense, 1988), 110.

4. Ridenti, *Em busca do povo brasileiro*, 12–13, 52.

5. Lina Bo Bardi, "Cinco anos entre os brancos," *Mirante das Artes, Etc.* 6 (November–December 1967), 19–20.

6. Paulo Ormindo de Azevedo, interview, in Juliano Pereira Trindade, *A ação de Lina Bo Bardi na Bahia e no Nordeste (1958–1964)* (São Carlos: EESC–Universidade de São Paulo, 2001), 270.

7. Lina Bo Bardi, "Arquitetura e movimento," lecture notes, Salvador, August 11, 1958, 7, ILBPMB.

8. Ibid.

9. Ibid., 6.

10. Carlos Nelson Coutinho, personal communication, July 17, 2010.

11. Bo Bardi, "Arquitetura e movimento," 7.

12. Lina Bo Bardi, "Architettura e natura: La casa nel paesaggio," *Domus* 194 (February 1944), 464–71.

13. Ibid., 464.

14. Bo Bardi, "Arquitetura e movimento," 6, 7.

15. Lina Bo Bardi, "Museu de Arte da Bahia," flier, Salvador, n.d., MAMB.

16. André L. Mattedi Dias, "A Universidade e a modernização conservadora na Bahia: Edgard Santos e os institutos científicos," *Revista da SBHC* 2:3 (January 2007), 128.

17. Aldo Trípodi, "Considerações sobre a arte moderna na Bahia," *Revista da Bahia* 40 (March 2006), 38.

18. Maria do Socorro S. Carvalho, *A nova onda baiana: Cinema na Bahia (1958–1962)* (Salvador: EDUFBA, 2003), 77.

19. Carlos Nelson Coutinho, "Conversa com um 'marxista convicto e confesso,'" in *Intervenções: O marxismo na batalha das ideias*, ed. Carlos Nelso Coutinho (São Paulo: Cortez, 2006), 149; Antonio Risério, *Avant-Garde na Bahia* (São Paulo: ILBPMB, 1995), 34–38.

20. Marcos Uzel, "A UFBA e a descoberta cultural da Bahia," in *A ousadia da criação: Universidade e cultura*, ed. Antonio Albino Canelas Rubim (Salvador: UFBA/Facom, 1999), 99.

21. Aninha Franco, *O teatro na Bahia através da imprensa: Século XX* (Salvador: FCIA/COFIC/FCEBA, 1994), 115.

22. Jussilene Santana, *Impressões modernas: Teatro e jornalismo na Bahia* (Salvador: UFBA/Fundo de Cultura, 2009), 187.

23. Mário Cravo Júnior and Renato Ferraz, interviews, in Trindade, *A ação de Lina Bo Bardi na Bahia e no Nordeste*, 233.

24. Lina Bo Bardi, "Cultura e não cultura," *Crônicas* 1, *Diários Associados*, September 7, 1958, 1.

25. Lina Bo Bardi, "arquitetura ou Arquitetura," *Crônicas* 2, *Diários Associados*, September 14, 1958, 1.

26. Lina Bo Bardi, "Inatualidade da cultura," *Crônicas* 3, *Diários Associados*, September 21, 1958, 1.

27. Azevedo interview, 268.

28. Lina Bo Bardi, lecture notes, August 11, 1958, 6.

29. "Exposição pedagógica na Escola de Teatro," *Crônicas* 3, *Diários Associados*, September 21, 1958, 1.

30. Lina Bo Bardi, "Olho sobre a Bahia," *Crônicas* 4, *Diários Associados*, September 28, 1958, 1.

31. Lina Bo Bardi, "Casas ou museus?" *Crônicas* 5, *Diários Associados*, October 5, 1958, , 1.

32. Lina Bo Bardi, "Casas populares," *Crônicas* 6, *Diários Associados*, October 12, 1958, 1.

33. Lina Bo Bardi, "A escola e a vida?" *Crônicas* 5, *Diários Associados*, October 5, 1958, 1.

34. Mário Cravo Jr., interview, in Trindade, *A ação de Lina Bo Bardi na Bahia e no Nordeste*, 229–30.

35. Lina Bo Bardi, "Arte industrial," 1.

36. Ibid.

37. Ibid.

38. Lina Bo Bardi, handwritten note about *Crônicas*, November 1958, ILBPMB.

39. Maurício de Almeida Chagas, "A arquitetura do Teatro Castro Alves," in *II DOCOMOMO N-NE Conference Proceedings* (Salvador, Bahia, June 2008), 5.

40. Azevedo interview, 271.

1. Jussilene Santana, *Impressões modernas: Teatro e jornalismo na Bahia* (Salvador: UFBA/Fundo de Cultura, 2009), 157.

2. Jussilene Santana, "Cumplicidade e parcerias: Lina Bo Bardi e Martim Gonçalves," in *50 anos de Lina Bo Bardi: Na encruzilhada da Bahia e do Nordeste*, Docomomo Conference Proceedings (Salvador, December 2009), 5.

3. Maria de Fátima Ribeiro Maia, *IV Colóquio Internacional de Estudos Luso-Brasileiros: Relações culturais, identidade e interlocução* (Salvador: Universidade Federal da Bahia, 1999), 112–17.

4. Tattiana Teixeira, "Modernismo e modernidade na Universidade da Bahia," in *A ousadia da criação: Universidade e cultura*, ed. Antonio Albino Canelas Rubim (Salvador: UFBA/Facom, 1999), 76.

5. Lina Bo Bardi, "Brasiliana, arte e natura (o arte e vita?)," typed notes, 1959, ILBPMB.

6. Lina Bo Bardi, "Organizzazione redazionale," notes on *Brasiliana* magazine, 1959, ILBPMB.

7. Santana, *Impressões modernas*, 152.

8. State Law 1,152 in *Diário Oficial*, July 25, 1959, MAMB.

9. Maria Cecília F. Lourenço, *Museus acolhem moderno* (São Paulo: EDUSP, 1999), 178.

10. Paulo Ormindo de Azevedo, interview, in Juliano Pereira Trindade, *A ação de Lina Bo Bardi na Bahia e no Nordeste (1958–1964)* (São Carlos: EESC–Universidade de São Paulo, 2001), 271.

11. Lina Bo Bardi, MAMB notes, São Paulo, 1982, ILBPMB; Lina Bo Bardi, letter to the editor, in "Unidade," *A Tarde*, September 11, 1961.

12. Lina Bo Bardi, letter to the editor.

13. Lina Bo Bardi and Eros Martim Gonçalves, "'Bahia,' Esposizione a San Paolo," *Domus* 289 (March 1960), 32–33.

14. Lina Bo Bardi and Eros Martim Gonçalves, *Expo Bahia*, exhibition brochure (São Paulo: Biennial, 1959), 2.

15. Bo Bardi and Martim Gonçalves, "'Bahia,' Esposizione a San Paolo," 33.

16. Hélio Eichbauer, *Arte na Bahia: Teatro na Universidade* (Salvador: Corrupio, 1990), 56–58.

17. Bo Bardi and Martim Gonçalves, "'Bahia,' Esposizione a San Paolo," 33.

18. Eichbauer, *Arte na Bahia*, 4.

19. Lina Bo Bardi, "Cinco anos entre os brancos," *Mirante das Artes, Etc.* 6 (November–December 1967), 19.

20. Bo Bardi and Martim Gonçalves, *Expo Bahia*, 2–3.

21. Sante Scaldaferri, interview, in Trindade, *A ação de Lina Bo Bardi na Bahia e no Nordeste*, 256; Bo Bardi, "Museu de Arte Moderna da Bahia," renovation drawings and notes, November 18, 1959, ILBPMB.

22. Renato Ferraz, interview, in Trindade, *A ação de Lina Bo Bardi na Bahia e no Nordeste*, 222.
23. Lina Bo Bardi, "Exposições no MAMB," typed lists and handwritten notes, 1960–63, ILBPMB.
24. Scaldaferri interview, 265.
25. Lina Bo Bardi, "Revista B," typed notes, 1959, ILBPMB.
26. Azevedo interview, 271.
27. Lina Bo Bardi, "Museu de Arte Moderna da Bahia," inauguration flier, January 6, 1960, ILBPMB.
28. Lina Bo Bardi, *Jornal da Bahia*, January 31, 1960, 6–7.
29. Bo Bardi, "Cinco anos entre os brancos," 19–20.
30. Bo Bardi, "Museu de Arte Moderna da Bahia."
31. Lina Bo Bardi, typed notes on pedagogical programs, c. 1960, MAMB.
32. Maria do Socorro S. Carvalho, *A nova onda baiana: Cinema na Bahia (1958–1962)* (Salvador: EDUFBA, 2003), 70–71.
33. Santana, *Impressões modernas*, 94.
34. Martim Gonçalves, *Diário de Notícias*, May 26, 1960; Santana, "Cumplicidade e parcerias," 4.
35. Lina Bo Bardi, MASP, handwritten notes, c. 1984, ILBPMB.
36. Ferraz interview, 225.
37. Lina Bo Bardi, MASP, model photo with notes, 1957, ILBPMB.
38. "Come il tessuto di una foglia," Lina Bo Bardi, MASP, staircase drawing note, May 6, 1960, ILBPMB.
39. Hans Günther Flieg, MASP, construction photograph, 1960, ILBPMB.
40. Pietro Maria Bardi to Lina Bo Bardi, telegrams, August 1960–February 1961, MASP.
41. "A Ópera de Três Tostões," program, November 1960, 3, ILBPMB.
42. Martim Gonçalves, "Para compor," notes, 1960, 1, ILBPMB.
43. Lina Bo Bardi, "Ópera de Três Tostões," several drawings, 1960, ILBPMB.
44. Lina Bo Bardi, note and drawing for *The Threepenny Opera* design, 1960, ILBPMB.
45. Eichbauer, *Arte na Bahia*, 90–95.
46. Lina Bo Bardi, typescript about Camus, 1961, 1, ILBPMB.
47. Santana, *Impressões modernas*, 186–91.
48. Lina Bo Bardi, Universidade da Bahia application letter, October 13, 1961, MAMB.

1. Boris Fausto, *História do Brasil* (São Paulo: EDUSP, 2008), 451–55.
2. Robert M. Levine, *The History of Brazil* (Westport, CT: Greenwood, 1999), 192.
3. Florisvaldo Mattos, interview, in Jussilene Santana, *Impressões modernas: Teatro e jornalismo na Bahia* (Salvador: UFBA/Fundo de Cultura, 2009), 100.
4. Lina Bo Bardi, handwritten notes as MAMB director, c. 1961, MAMB.
5. Lina Bo Bardi, "Università popolare ed arte minori," handwritten notes, c. 1962, ILBPMB.
6. Lina Bo Bardi, letters signed as director of the Museum of Modern Art of Bahia, c. 1962, MAMB.
7. Abelardo da Hora quoted in *Memorial do MCP* (Recife: Fundação de Cultura da Cidade, 1986), 3–4.
8. Francisco Brennand, exhibition photographs and notes, and Lina Bo Bardi, Brennand exhibition brochure, April 1961, MAMB.
9. Miguel Arraes, "O que foi o MCP?" *Arte em Revista* 2:3 (March 1964), 1.
10. Weydson Barros Leal, *Ensaio com Abelardo da Hora* (Recife: Instituto Abelardo da Hora, 2005), 101.
11. Movimento de Cultura Popular, *Dossier*, Recife Collection, vol. 49 (Recife: Fundação de Cultura Cidade do Recife, 1986), 34–40; Leal, *Ensaio com Abelardo da Hora*, 101.
12. Jean-François Chosson, *Peuple et culture, 1945–1995: 50 ans d'innovations au service de l'éducation populaire* (Paris: Peuple et Culture, 1995), 21.
13. Leal, *Ensaio com Abelardo da Hora*.
14. Lina Bo Bardi, notes on "grande esposizione al Unhão," c. 1962, in *Lina Bo Bardi*, ed. Marcelo C. Ferraz (São Paulo: ILBPMB, 1994, and Milan: Charta), 152.
15. Movimento de Cultura, *Dossier*, 36.
16. Hora quoted in *Memorial do MCP*, 6.
17. Lina Bo Bardi, "CETA," typescript, 1961, MAMB.
18. Lina Bo Bardi, "Discurso sobre a significação da palavra artesanato," in Lina Bo Bardi, *Tempos de Grossura: O design no impasse* (São Paulo: ILBPMB, 1994), 17.
19. Antonio Risério, "Um olhar sobre o Solar," in *Museu de Arte Moderna da Bahia* (Salvador: Petrobrás/MAMB, 2002), 25.
20. Tentori, *Quattro architetti brasiliani e un uomo eccezionale*, 21–22.
21. Ibid., 2.
22. *Tabebuia* sp. or *pau d'arco*, a valuable Brazilian hardwood.
23. Engineer Castanho, MASP, note on structural project, May 22, 1963, ILBPMB.
24. Lina Bo Bardi, MASP, typescript for *L'Architettura: Cronache, storia*, February 16, 1973, 2, ILBPMB.
25. Lina Bo Bardi, house study drawings, c. 1962, ILBPMB.

26. Lina Bo Bardi, art complex on rua Pamplona, São Paulo, drafted plans, elevations, and sections, c. 1962, ILBPMB.
27. Ana Carolina de Souza Bierrenbach, "Lina Bo Bardi e o mausoléu da família Odebrecht: Entre o etéreo e o terreno," *Arquitextos* 58, Year 05 (May 2005).
28. "Parete scultura 'arrampicata.'" Lina Bo Bardi, Marble Museum, wall sketch, 1963, ILBPMB.
29. Jussilene Santana, *Impressões modernas: Teatro e jornalismo na Bahia* (Salvador: UFBA/Fundo de Cultura, 2009), 146.
30. Lina Bo Bardi, "Projeto da Escola de Artesanato," typescript, c. 1962, 2, MAMB.
31. Lina Bo Bardi, *Nordeste*, exhibition brochure, 1963, 3, MAMB.
32. Ibid.
33. Fausto, *História do Brasil*, 456–57.
34. Bo Bardi, *Nordeste*, 3.
35. Mário Cravo Júnior and Renato Ferraz, interviews, in Juliano Pereira Trindade, *A ação de Lina Bo Bardi na Bahia e no Nordeste (1958–1964)* (São Carlos: EESC–Universidade de São Paulo, 2001), 232–33.
36. Lina Bo Bardi, "A escola industrial para projetistas e mestres de ofício," handwritten notes, c. 1962, ILBPMB.
37. Ibid.
38. Brazilian consul, Philadelphia, to Bo Bardi, March 3, 1964, ILBPMB.
39. Lina Bo Bardi to Bruno Zevi, June 15, 1964, 1, FBZ.
40. Lina Bo Bardi to Celso Furtado, March 5, 1964, 1, ILBPMB.
41. Celso Furtado to Lina Bo Bardi, April 5, 1964, ILBPMB.
42. Élio de Gaspari, *A ditadura envergonhada* (São Paulo: Companhia das Letras, 2002), 56.
43. Fausto, *História do Brasil*, 465–67.
44. Bo Bardi to Zevi, 1.
45. Fundação de Cultura Cidade do Recife, *Movimento de Cultura popular: Memorial* (Recife: FCCR, 1986), 49.
46. Marcelo Ridenti, *Em busca do povo brasileiro: Artistas da revolução, do CPC à era da TV* (São Paulo: Record, 2000), 55, 131.
47. Renato Ferraz, interview, 235, 238.
48. Bo Bardi to Zevi, 4.
49. Ferraz interview, 235–39.
50. Lina Bo Bardi, note on the back of Castro Alves Theater photograph, ILBPMB.
51. Ferraz interview, 237.
52. Lina Bo Bardi, notes for letter to Odorico Tavares, August 1964, ILBPMB.
53. Ferraz interview, 238.
54. Maria Cecília F. Lourenço, *Museus acolhem moderno* (São Paulo: EDUSP, 1999), 187.
55. Ferraz interview, 238–39.
56. "Lina deixa a Bahia," *Diário de Notícias*, August 7, 1964, courtesy of Jussilene Santana.

57. Lina Bo Bardi to MAMB board of directors, August 12, 1964, MAMB.
58. Ferraz interview, 238.
59. Lina Bo Bardi, taped conversation with Hélio Eichbauer, c. 1990, courtesy of Hélio Eichbauer.
60. Bruno Zevi, "Incontro con Lina Bo Bardi: Un supervisore con mitra e speroni," *L'Espresso*, May 27, 1973, 28.

1. Lina Bo Bardi quoted in Hélio Eichbauer, *Arte na Bahia: Teatro na Universidade* (Salvador: Corrupio, 1990), 12.
2. Roberto Röchlitz, MASP, construction report, September 30, 1964, archive 6, shelf 4, box 3, folder 7, MASP.
3. Roberto Röchlitz, MASP, construction report, January 1965, archive 6, shelf 4, box 3, folder 7, MASP.
4. Fausto Wolff, "John Ford, ousadias e teatro," *Tribuna da Imprensa*, July 14, 1964, in Martim Gonçalves, *Dossier*, Funarte, courtesy of Jussilene Santana; *Correio da Manhã*, September 27, 1964, courtesy of Jussilene Santana.
5. Wolff, "John Ford, ousadias e teatro."
6. Carlos Lacerda to Lina Bo Bardi, October 5, 1964, ILBPMB.
7. Vasco Mariz to Bo Bardi, Divisão de Difusão Cultural do Ministério de Relações Exteriores, December 1, 1964, ILBPMB.
8. Lina Bo Bardi, handwritten notes about travels during the 1960s, n.d., ILBPMB.
9. *Nordeste* exhibition, Galleria Nazionale d'Arte Moderna, photographs by Oscar Savio, c. February 1965, ILBPMB.
10. Bruno Zevi, "L'arte dei poveri fa paura ai generali," *L'Espresso*, March 14, 1965, 18, ILBPMB.
11. Elteco, Elettrica Telefonica Costruzioni, invoice for electrical installation payment, Rome, February 26, 1965, ILBPMB.
12. Bruno Zevi, "Regime de generais proíbe a exposição," *Correio da Manhã*, April 4, 1965, ILBPMB.
13. Zevi, "L'arte dei poveri fa paura ai generali," 18.
14. Miguel Pereira, "O Columbianum e o cinema brasileiro," *Alceu* 15:8 (July–December 2007), 127.
15. Secretaria de Estado das Relações Exteriores, invitation to Lina Bo Bardi for the *V Resenha do Cinema Latino-Americano do "Columbianum,"* November 26, 1964, ILBPMB.
16. Zevi, "L'arte dei poveri fa paura ai generali."
17. Ibid.
18. Ibid.
19. Bo Bardi to Lavínia Magalhães, July 7, 1966, ILBPMB.
20. Lina Bo Bardi, "Casa Valéria Morumby," 1:50 drawings, December 1964, ILBPMB.
21. The guesthouse was renovated by Marcelo C. Ferraz and Francisco Fanucci in 1998.
22. Lina Bo Bardi, notes on Butantan Institute museum sketch, May 18, 1965, ILBPMB.
23. Lina Bo Bardi, notes on Butantan Institute museum, n.d., ILBPMB.
24. Bo Bardi to Bruno Zevi, June 1, 1965, São Paulo, 2, ILBPMB.
25. Bo Bardi to Lacerda, June 16, 1965, Rio de Janeiro, 1, ILBPMB; Bo Bardi to Zevi.
26. Bo Bardi to Lacerda.

27. Lina Bo Bardi, lecture notes, Escola Nacional de Belas Artes, Rio de Janeiro, August 19, 1965, 4 pp., ILBPMB.
28. Bo Bardi to the governor of Guanabara [Negrão de Lima], October 14, 1965, Rio de Janeiro, ILBPMB.
29. Bo Bardi to Dona Gabriela, March 1, June 6, 1966, Itamambuca project, ILBPMB.
30. Lina Bo Bardi, Itamambuca project drawings and notes, 1965, ILBPMB.
31. Bo Bardi to Zevi, August 17, 1965, FBZ.
32. Hugo Segawa, *Arquiteturas no Brasil, 1900–1990* (São Paulo: Edusp, 1998), 148–50.
33. Lina Bo Bardi, "Galeria Mirante, São Paulo," study perspective, August 9, 1966, ILBPMB.
34. Lina Bo Bardi, "O que está acontecendo na Améria do Sul depois de Le Corbusier?" *Mirante das Artes, Etc.* 1 (January–February 1967), 12.
35. Lina Bo Bardi, "No limite da casa popular," *Mirante das Artes, Etc.* 2 (March–April 1967), 8.
36. Diego B. Inglez de Souza, *Reconstruindo Cajueiro Seco: Arquitetura, política social e cultura popular em Pernambuco (1960–1964)* (São Paulo: Annablume, 2010).
37. Adobe: *taipa* or *barro-armado* in Portuguese.
38. Lina Bo Bardi, "Casa sr. Antônio Raposo Branco," June 24, 1967; "Casa de Campo, sr. Ricardo," registration architectural drawings, March 1969, ILBPMB.
39. Lina Bo Bardi, "O novo Trianon," *Mirante das Artes, Etc.* 4 (July–August 1967), 10.
40. Lina Bo Bardi, "Cinco anos entre os brancos," *Mirante das Artes, Etc.* 6 (November–December 1967), supplement.
41. Ibid.
42. Ibid.
43. Celso Furtado to Bo Bardi, 1967, in Lina Bo Bardi, *Tempos de Grossura: O design no impasse* (São Paulo: ILBPMB, 1994), 63.
44. Bo Bardi, "Cinco anos entre os brancos."

1. Roberto Röchlitz, construction reports, 1963, 1964, folder 6, shelf 4, box 3, file 7, MASP.
2. Ana Clara Giannecchini, *Técnica e estética no concreto armado: Um estudo sobre os edifícios do MASP e da FAUUSP* (São Paulo: FAUUSP, 2009), 163.
3. Ibid., 174.
4. Lina Bo Bardi, lecture at FAUUSP, April 14, 1989, transcript, 4, ILBPMB.
5. Roberto Röchlitz, "A estrutura do Trianon-Museu," typescript, c. 1966, 1–2, ILBPMB.
6. Ibid.
7. Lina Bo Bardi, MASP, sketches and hand-written notes, n.d., ILBPMB.
8. Lina Bo Bardi, MASP, study for main facades, September 13, 1965, ILBPMB.
9. Roberto Röchlitz, interview, in Giannecchini, *Técnica e estética no concreto armado*, 126.
10. José L. Braga Castanho, interview, in ibid., 127.
11. Röchlitz interview, 126–27.
12. Röchlitz, construction report, March 1966, folder 6, shelf 4, box 2, file 5, MASP.
13. Lina Bo Bardi, MASP, handwritten notes on facade studies, n.d., ILBPMB; Lina Bo Bardi, MASP, enclosure study sketches, c. 1966–67, ILBPMB.
14. Lina Bo Bardi, MASP, telescopic mullion, various sketches initiated on September 27, 1966, ILBPMB.
15. Lina Bo Bardi, MASP, handwritten notes, 1966, ILBPMB.
16. Bo Bardi to Maury de Freitas Julião, August 9, 1967, ILBPMB.
17. Marina Cintra Gordinho and Marília Fontana Garcia, *Liceu de Artes e Ofícios de São Paulo: Missão excelência* (São Paulo: Marca d'Água, 2000), 16–17; Bo Bardi to De Freitas Julião.
18. Bo Bardi to Roberto Burle Marx, July 13, 1967, ILBPMB.
19. Ibid.
20. Lina Bo Bardi, "Negocismo contra idealismo," typed note about MASP construction, August 25, 1968, ILBPMB.
21. Lina Bo Bardi, MASP, Civic Hall drawings, 1968, ILBPMB.
22. Lina Bo Bardi, MASP, theater seat sketches, March 27, 1969, ILBPMB.
23. *Aspidosperma polyneuron*, a valuable Brazilian hardwood.
24. Bo Bardi to Sérgio Ugolini (São Paulo secretary of public works), October 14, 1969, ILBPMB.
25. Lina Bo Bardi, MASP, temperate glass partitions, drawings, March 8, 1968 (ILBPMB).
26. Lina Bo Bardi, MASP, notes, c. 1968, ILBPMB.
27. Lina Bo Bardi, "Explicações sobre o Museu de Arte," *O Estado de São Paulo*, April 5, 1970, ILBPMB.
28. Lina Bo Bardi, "Museu de Arte de São Paulo," *Diário de São Paulo*, November 7, 1968, MASP.
29. *Cereus jamacaru*, a Brazilian cactus.
30. MASP, opening invitation, April 7, 1969, ILBPMB.
31. Zeuler R. M. de A. Lima and Vera Pallamin, "Reinventing the Void," in *Ordinary Places/Extraordinary Events: Citizenship, Democracy and Public Space in Latin America*, ed. Clara Irazabal (New York: Routledge, 2008), 59–67.
32. Giannecchini, *Técnica e estética no concreto armado*, 172.
33. Alex Miyoshi, "Entre a origem e a degradação: A primeira reforma do edifício do Museu de Arte de São Paulo," *Revista de História da Arte e Arqueologia* 6 (December 2006), 137–47.
34. Lina Bo Bardi, "Museu à beira do oceano," *Habitat* 8 (July–September 1951), 6–11.
35. Formacor-Glasurit contract, folder 6, shelf 4, box 6, file 8, MASP.
36. Lina Bo Bardi, *Museu de Arte de São Paulo* (Lisbon: Blau, 1997), 7.
37. Lina Bo Bardi, "Cinco anos entre os brancos," *Mirante das Artes, Etc.* 6 (November–December 1967), supplement.
38. Bo Bardi, *Museu de Arte de São Paulo*, 7.
39. Lina Bo Bardi, quoted in *Lina Bo Bardi*, directed by Aurélio Michiles and Isa Grinspum Ferraz (São Paulo: ILBPMB, 1993), video.

1. Pietro Maria Bardi, "Escultores e artesãos," in *Um certo ponto de vista: Pietro Maria Bardi, cem anos*, ed. Emanoel Araújo (São Paulo: Pinacoteca do Estado, 2000), 95; Lina Bo Bardi, "A mão do povo brasileiro," handwritten notes, 1969, ILBPMB.
2. Bo Bardi, "Escultores e artesãos," 93–97.
3. Edmar de Almeida, interview, Uberlândia, August 6, 7, 2006.
4. Lina Bo Bardi to Bruno Zevi, June 1, 1965, 2, FBZ.
5. MASP photograph, 1969, ILBPMB.
6. Celso Furtado to Lina Bo Bardi, 1967, in Lina Bo Bardi, *Tempos de Grossura: O design no impasse* (São Paulo: ILBPMB, 1994).
7. Bo Bardi, "A mão do povo brasileiro."
8. Lina Bo Bardi, inquest defense, typescript, c. 1971, 2, ILBPMB.
9. George Jonas, *A cor da vida* (São Paulo: Editor de Cultura, 2009), 12.
10. Lina Bo Bardi, *A compadecida* set photographs and drawings, 1968, ILBPMB; *A compadecida*, directed by Jorge Jonas, 1969, DVD reproduction, 2009.
11. *A compadecida* film poster, 1969, ILBPMB.
12. Mauricio Rittner, "A alegre festa do circo," *O Estado de São Paulo*, November 18, 1969, ILBPMB.
13. Jonas, *A cor da vida*, 45.
14. Fausto, *História do Brasil*, 470–80, 487–88.
15. Marshall Berman, *All That Is Solid Melts into Air: The Experience of Modernity* (New York: Verso, 1983), 43.
16. Marcelo Ridenti, *Em busca do povo brasileiro: Artistas da revolução, do CPC à era da TV* (São Paulo: Record, 2000), 270–72.
17. Several references in Bo Bardi's personal library, ILBPMB.
18. Lina Bo Bardi, "Casa de Campo, sr. Ricardo," registration architectural drawings, March 1969, ILBPMB.
19. Lina Bo Bardi, "Fenit–América Fabril," stall sketches, August 1969, ILBPMB.
20. Lina Bo Bardi, taped conversation with Hélio Eichbauer, c. 1990, courtesy of Hélio Eichbauer.
21. Lina Bo Bardi, "Na selva das cidades," handwritten notes, n.d., ILBPMB.
22. José Celso Martinez Corrêa, "Teatro Oficina, osso duro de roer," in Lina Bo Bardi, Edson Elito, and José Celso Martinez Correa, *Teatro: São Paulo, Brasil, 1980–1984* (São Paulo: ILBPMB; and Lisbon: Blau, 1999), 26.
23. Bertolt Brecht, *In the Jungle of Cities* (1927), trans. Gerhard Nellhaus, in *Bertolt Brecht: Plays, Poetry and Prose*, ed. Ralph Manheim and John Willett (London: Methuen, 1970), 118; Lina Bo Bardi, "Na selva das cidades," perspective and notes, 1969, ILBPMB.

24. Sabato Magaldi, "Uma luta gratuita na selva de Brecht," *Visão*, October 10, 1969.
25. Ítala Nandi, *Teatro Oficina: Onde a arte não dormia* (Rio de Janeiro: Nova Fronteira, 1989), 134.
26. *Teatro Oficina*, play posters, 1969, ILBPMB.
27. José Celso Martinez Corrêa, "Na selva das cidades," play brochure, São Paulo, August 1969, ILBPMB; Sabato Magaldi, "Na selva das cidades," *Jornal da Tarde*, September 17, 1969; Nandi, *Teatro Oficina*, 136.
28. Vera Márcio de Lima, video interview, ABPS, 1994, in Norival A. Cepeda and Maria Aparecida F. Martins, *MASP 1970: O psicodrama* (São Paulo: Agora, 2010), 67.
29. Livia B. H. Dorna, Aline A. G. da Cunha, and Heliana B. C. Rodrigues, "Do V Congresso Internacional de Psicodrama e Sociodrama ao evento 'Ética e cidadania': Vicissitudes históricas do psicodrama no Brasil," *Mnemosine* 1:2 (2006), 20–28.
30. Cepeda and Martins, *MASP 1970*, 68–69.
31. Lina Bo Bardi, testimony in police investigation, c. 1972, 4, ILBPMB.
32. "Segundo Exército." Bo Bardi, ibid., 3.
33. Ridenti, *Em busca do povo brasileiro*, 111.
34. Lina Bo Bardi, Italy passport entry stamp, December 19, 1970, ILBPMB; Claudio Bo Valentinetti, interview, Brasília, September 6, 2009.
35. Edmar de Almeida, interview, confirmed by Lina Bo Bardi, drawings of Bogliasco, c. 1970.
36. Lina Bo Bardi, index cards with reading notes in Italian, June–July 1971, ILBPMB.
37. Lina Bo Bardi, handwritten notes, June 9, July 2, 1971, ILBPMB.
38. Paulo Ormindo de Azevedo, interview, in Juliano Pereira Trindade, *A ação de Lina Bo Bardi na Bahia e no Nordeste (1958–1964)* (São Carlos: EESC–Universidade de São Paulo, 2001), 277.
39. De Almeida interview.
40. José Celso Martinez Corrêa quoted in Mateus Bertone da Silva, *Lina Bo Bardi: Arquitetura cênica* (São Carlos: EESC-USP, 2004), 312–13.
41. Lina Bo Bardi, *Gracias, señor*, sketches and notes, 1972, ILBPMB.
42. José Celso Martinez Corrêa quoted in *Lina Bo Bardi* video.
43. Lina Bo Bardi, *Gracias, señor*, sketch and notes, April 22, 1972, ILBPMB.
44. Yan Michalsky, *O teatro sob pressão: Uma frente de resistência* (Rio de Janeiro: Jorge Zahar, 1985), 54.
45. Lina Bo Bardi, Piolin circus at MASP, sketches, April 3, 1972, ILBPMB.
46. Piolin Circus, photograph, 1972, ILBPMB.
47. De Almeida interview.
48. Bo Valentinetti interview.
49. Lina Bo Bardi to Fabrizio Clerici, February 18, 1973, AFC; Dr. Gino Farina, health certificate, Milan, December 22, 1972, ILBPMB.
50. Bruno Zevi: "Incontro con Lina Bo Bardi, un supervisore con mitra e speroni," *L'Espresso*, May 27, 1973.
51. Bo Bardi to Zevi, April 10, 1974, 4, FBZ.
52. Lina Bo Bardi, "Sulla linguistica architettonica," *L'Architettura: Cronache e storia* 226 (August 1974), 260.

Rehearsing an Anthropological Quest

1. Edmar de Almeida, interview, Uberlândia, August 6, 7, 2006.
2. Edmar de Almeida to Lina Bo Bardi about tapestry preparation, August 5, 1974, ILBPMB.
3. Lina Bo Bardi, "Edmar—Repassos e as tecedeiras do Triângulo Mineiro," exhibition brochure, September 9–28, 1975, courtesy of Edmar de Almeida.
4. Ibid.
5. "Uma procura artística em nível antropológico." Ibid.
6. Lina Bo Bardi, "Congresso da União Internacional de Arquitetos," personal notes, c. 1975, ILBPMB.
7. Joaquim Guedes, "Lembranças de Lina Bo Bardi," *Caramelo* 4 (São Paulo: FAUUSP, 1992), 34.
8. Lina Bo Bardi, "Design como comportamento total," in Wilson Coutinho, *O jardim da oposição, 1975–1979*, exhibition catalogue (Rio de Janeiro: EVA, 2009), 36.
9. ELC Electroconsult do Brasil Ltda., "Contratação de serviços," São Paulo, September 9, 1975, ILBPMB.
10. CODEVASF, "Projeto de irrigação Propriá, Avaliação ex-post," Brasília, 1990, in Ana Carolina de Souza Bierrenbach, "Os rastros da ausência: O projeto de Lina Bo Bardi para a cooperativa de Camurupim," *Arquitextos* 101.02, Year 9 (October 2008).
11. Lina Bo Bardi, "Camurupim," questionnaire, c. 1975, ILBPMB.
12. Waldemir Mello, "Camurupim," photographic survey, October 19, 1975, ILBPMB; Nelson Serra e Neves et al., "Considerações sobre o planejamento de comunidades rurais nos projetos regionais de desenvolvimento hidro-agrícola" (Fortaleza: DNOCS, October 22, 1976), ILBPMB.
13. ELC Electroconsult, Engineers Múcio, Raffaeli, and Innocenti to Bo Bardi, November 21, 1976, ILBPMB; Lina Bo Bardi, "Modular Lot," Camurupim community, site plan, October 26, 1976, ILBPMB.
14. Lina Bo Bardi, Camurupim community, studies, sketches, and notes, c. 1976, ILBPMB.
15. Lina Bo Bardi, Camurupim community, "house study for family with five children and a newborn," c. 1976, ILBPMB.
16. Lina Bo Bardi, interview with Aureliano Menezes, 1976, ILBPMB.
17. Lina Bo Bardi, "Arquitetura e desenho industrial: Depois do Sturm und Drang," typed notes, 1976, ILBPMB.
18. Lina Bo Bardi, "Planejamento ambiental: O design no impasse," *Revista Malasartes* 2 (December 1976–February 1977), 4–7; Tomás Maldonado, *La speranza progettuale: Ambiente e società* (Turin: Einaudi, 1970).

19. Maldonado, *La speranza progettuale*, 54–57.
20. Bo Bardi, "Planejamento ambiental," 5.
21. Ibid., 5–6.
22. Ibid., 7.
23. At least four priests were involved in the project, named as Friar Egidio, Friar Guido, Friar Fulvio, and Friar Tarcísio; Cerrado Church, documents and correspondence, 1976–80, ILBPMB.
24. De Almeida interview.
25. Edmar de Almeida to Bo Bardi, July 3, 1976, ILBPMB.
26. Frei Egídio to Bo Bardi, March 15, 1979, ILBPMB.
27. Lina Bo Bardi, "Casa Roberto e Eliana," August 20, 1976, ILBPMB.
28. Lina Bo Bardi, Cerrado Church, chapel sketch, and roof and wall study, c. 1976, ILBPMB.
29. Marcelo C. Ferraz, interview, Saint Louis, April 19, 2005.
30. Lina Bo Bardi, traced images from "Shelter," c. 1980, ILBPMB; Ferraz interview.
31. Lina Bo Bardi, Marcelo C. Ferraz, and André Vainer, Cerrado Church, roof detail drawings, July 7–August 16, 1980, ILBPMB.
32. Lina Bo Bardi, Cerrado Church, perspectives, September 15, 1976, building elevation, August 16, 1980, ILBPMB.
33. Lina Bo Bardi, wooden chair, sketches and notes, October 6, 1980, ILBPMB; Lina Bo Bardi, Cerrado Church, pen sketch, "Dona Maria I" sewing chair, traced from Revista do Patrimônio Histórico e Artístico Nacional, MES 1937, as noted on the drawing, ILBPMB.
34. Lina Bo Bardi, Marcelo C. Ferraz, and André Vainer, Cerrado Church, parochial house roof detail drawing, August 16, 1980, ILBPMB.
35. De Almeida interview.
36. Lina Bo Bardi, Cerrado Church, general plan, July 1978, ILBPMB.
37. Lina Bo Bardi, traced drawings from *Shelter* magazine, c. 1980, ILBPMB.
38. Lina Bo Bardi, Cerrado Church, personal notes, n.d., ILBPMB.
39. Ibid.
40. De Almeida interview.
41. Bruna Sercelli, phone interview, August 9, 2004.
42. The thatched grass used was cogongrass, *Imperata cyllindrica*.
43. Lina Bo Bardi, side notes on FAUUSP lecture, 1989, ILBPMB.
44. Lina Bo Bardi, "O não," manuscript written during the SESC Pompeia project, n.d., ILBPMB.

1. Júlio Neves, SESC Pompeia, drawing for construction permit, February 5, 1975, SESC; Marcelo C. Ferraz, interview, Saint Louis, April 24, 2005.
2. Renato Requixá, "Proposta de preservação do prédio do centro cultural e desportivo Pompéia," typescript, January 21, 1977, ILBPMB; João dos Santos Filho and Rodrigo Meira Martoni, "Ufanismo, sandice e galhofa são atributos das políticas públicas de turismo no Brasil," in *Hospitalidade e turismo: A historiografia da hospitalidade e do turismo brasiliero*, June 21, 2009, http://hospitalidadeeturismo .blogspot.com/2009/06/ufanismo-sandice-e-galhofa-sao.html.
3. Ferraz interview.
4. Lina Bo Bardi, SESC initial sketches, April 12, 1977, ILBPMB.
5. Lina Bo Bardi, notes on SESC Pompeia, c. 1986, ILBPMB.
6. Ibid.
7. Eriveldo Busto Garcia, "Quo vadis, Pompéia?" 1982, in *Cidadela da liberdade*, ed. Giancarlo Latorraca (São Paulo: ILMBPMB, 1999), 8–10.
8. Ferraz interview; Lina Bo Bardi, notes on SESC Pompeia, c. 1986, ILBPMB.
9. Requixá, "Proposta de preservação do prédio do centro cultural e desportivo Pompéia."
10. Marcelo C. Ferraz, interview, São Paulo, August 10, 2008.
11. Lina Bo Bardi, SESC, initial sketches, 1977, ILBPMB.
12. Lina Bo Bardi, SESC, preliminary drawings 2 and 5, June 10, 1977, ILBPMB; Lina Bo Bardi, SESC sports complex, first sketch, 1977, ILBPMB.
13. Lina Bo Bardi, signage totem sketch, 1981, ILBPMB.
14. Lina Bo Bardi, André Vainer, and Marcelo C. Ferraz, "Lajes de leitura," construction drawings, February 2, 3, 1978, ILBPMB.
15. Celene Canoas, interview, in Liana Paula de Oliveira, *A capacidade de dizer não: Lina Bo Bardi e a fábria da Pompéia* (São Paulo: Universidade Mackenzie, 2008), 41.
16. Lina Bo Bardi, reflecting pool, artworks, c. 1980, ILBPMB; Lina Bo Bardi, reflecting pool, pencil sketch, n.d., ILBPMB.
17. "Hall-Terreiro," Lina Bo Bardi, "Teatro," SESC, April 22, 1980, ILBPMB.
18. Figueiredo Ferraz, SESC theater, structural studies, February 24, 1981, ILBPMB.
19. Promotional newsletter, *folheto promocional* in Portuguese.
20. Lina Bo Bardi, "Caixotinho," several drawings and prototype, May 1980 and 1981, ILBPMB.
21. Lina Bo Bardi, Águas Pretas Creek treatment, several studies, September and October 1978, and several perspectives and section sketches, 1980–83, ILBPMB.

22. Marcelo C. Ferraz, interview, São Paulo, August 4, 2006.
23. Lina Bo Bardi, solarium, pavement detail, January 23, 1986, ILBPMB.
24. Ibid.
25. Lina Bo Bardi, "Terapia intensiva," *AU Arquitetura Urbanismo* 18 (June–July 1988), 37.
26. Lina Bo Bardi quoted in Frederico Morais, "Lina Bo Bardi," *O Estado de São Paulo*, April 28, 1984, ILBPMB.
27. Lina Bo Bardi, notes for interview with *Casa Vogue* 6, São Paulo, 1986, ILBPMB.
28. Ibid.
29. José Celso Martinez Corrêa, quoted in Fernando Peixoto, *Teatro Oficina (1958–1982): Trajetória de uma rebeldia cultural* (São Paulo: Brasiliense, 1982), 99.
30. André Vainer quoted in *Lina Bo Bardi*, directed by Aurélio Michiles and Isa Grinspum Ferraz (São Paulo: ILBPMB, 1993), video.
31. Bo Bardi, notes on interview with *Casa Vogue*.
32. Marcelo C. Ferraz, interview, August 4, 2006.
33. Lina Bo Bardi, sports tower snack bar, sketches and plans, October 15, 1984, ILBPMB.
34. Lina Bo Bardi, sports tower cage-staircase, sketch, June 3, 1985, ILBPMB.
35. Lina Bo Bardi, sports courts color studies, sketches, September 1985, ILBPMB.
36. Lina Bo Bardi, SESC water tower, personal notes, n.d., ILBPMB.
37. Lina Bo Bardi, notes on sketch "Inauguração Bloco Esportivo," c. 1985, ILBPMB.
38. Lina Bo Bardi, interview with Carolina Lefèvre, transcript with notes, July 1991, ILBPMB.
39. Lina Bo Bardi, handwritten note, c. 1986, ILBPMB.
40. Lina Bo Bardi to Renato Requixá, memo, 1983, ILBPMB; Bo Bardi to Requixá, July 11, 1983, ILBPMB.
41. Lina Bo Bardi, notes for interview with *Casa Vogue*.
42. Lina Bo Bardi, handwritten notes on SESC Pompeia, c. 1986, ILBPMB.
43. Lina Bo Bardi, notes for interview with *Casa Vogue*.
44. Ibid.
45. Fausto, *História do Brasil*, 509; Lina Bo Bardi, interview with Fábio Malavoglia.
46. Lina Bo Bardi, notes on SESC Pompeia, c. 1986, ILBPMB.
47. Darcy Ribeiro testimony in *Lina Bo Bardi* video.
48. Lina Bo Bardi, taped conversation with Hélio Eichbauer, c. 1990, courtesy of Hélio Eichbauer.

1. Marcelo Ridenti, *Em busca do povo brasileiro: Artistas da revolução, do CPC à era da TV* (São Paulo: Record, 2000), 293–97.

2. Fausto, *História do Brasil* (São Paulo: EDUSP/FDE, 2000), 490–95.

3. Lina Bo Bardi, "Tempos de Grossura, Roteiro," script and storyboard, 1980, ILBPMB.

4. Marcelo Suzuki, "Nota prévia," in Lina Bo Bardi, *Tempos de grossura: O design no impasse* (São Paulo: ILBPMB, 1994), 9.

5. Lina Bo Bardi, "Um balanço dezesseis anos depois," in Bo Bardi, *Tempos de grossura*, 12.

6. Lina Bo Bardi, handwritten note for book epigraph, c. 1980, ILBPMB.

7. Lina Bo Bardi to Roberto Pinho, February 1, 1988, ILBPMB.

8. Bo Bardi to Estanislau da Silva Sales, September 9, 1982, ILBPMB.

9. Lina Bo Bardi, "O cinturão da Grande São Paulo," and "A perder e consumo," notes on exhibition projects, c. June 1984, ILBPMB.

10. *O Design no Brasil: História e realidade*, exhibition catalogue (São Paulo: SESC/MASP, 1982).

11. Liana Paula de Oliveira, *A capacidade de dizer não: Lina Bo Bardi e a fábria da Pompéia* (São Paulo: Universidade Mackenzie, 2008), 92.

12. Lina Bo Bardi, handwritten notes about the SESC design exhibition, c. 1981, ILBPMB.

13. "Brinquedos artesanais e expressividade cultural," José Papa Júnior, "Apresentação," in *Mil bringuedos para a criança brasileira*, exhibition catalogue (São Paulo: SESC Pompéia, 1982), 6; Pietro Maria Bardi, "Introduction," in *Mil bringuedos para a criança brasileira*, 6.

14. Papa Júnior, "Apresentação," 5.

15. Lina Bo Bardi to Renato Requixá, handwritten memo for letter, c. November 1982, ILBPMB.

16. Lina Bo Bardi, in *Mil bringuedos para a criança brasileira*, 10.

17. Bardi, "Introduction," 6.

18. Lina Bo Bardi, in *Mil bringuedos para a criança brasileira*, 10.

19. Lina Bo Bardi, *Pinocchio* exhibition notes, 1983, ILBPMB.

20. Carlos Rodrigues Brandão, *O caipira dos sertões de São Paulo* (Campinas: UNICAMP/Secretaria de Cultura de São Paulo, July 1980), ILBPMB.

21. *Caipiras, capiaus: Pau-a-pique*, exhibition catalogue (São Paulo: SESC, 1984), 24–25; Lina Bo Bardi, "Caipiras, capiaus: Pau-a-pique," exhibition opening notes, June 29, 1984, ILBPMB.

22. Lina Bo Bardi, "Caipiras, capiaus: Pau-a-pique," exhibition sketches, May and June 1984, ILBPMB.

23. *Caipiras, capiaus: Pau-a-pique*, 11–23.

24. Ibid.

25. Ibid.

26. Lina Bo Bardi, in *Entre-ato para crianças*, exhibition catalogue (São Paulo: SESC, 1985), 6, ILBPMB.

27. Lina Bo Bardi to Aparício Basílio da Silva, November 5, 1980, ILBPMB.

28. The design team included Lina Bo Bardi, Francisco Fanucci, André Vainer, Marcelo C. Ferraz, Paulo Fecarrota, Guilherme Paoliello, Bel Paoliello, Marcelo Suzuki, and Ucho Carvalho. Lina Bo Bardi, Anhangabaú Valley competition entry, 1981, ILBPMB.

29. Marcelo C. Ferraz, interview, São Paulo, August 4, 2006.

30. Marcelo C. Ferraz, interview, São Paulo, August 4, 2006.

30. Lina Bo Bard, Anhangabaú Valley competition, 1981, ILBPMB.

31. Lina Bo Bardi, handwritten notes, September 15, 1982, ILBPMB.

32. Lina Bo Bardi, MAM renovation, handwritten note, c. 1982, ILBPMB.

33. Lina Bo Bardi, MAM renovation, interior perspective, July 1982, ILBPMB.

34. José Celso Martinez Corrêa, "Teatro Oficina, osso duro de roer," in Lina Bo Bardi, Edson Elito, and Martinez Correa, *Teatro: São Paulo, Brasil, 1980–1984* (São Paulo: ILBPMB; and Lisbon: Blau, 1999), 5.

35. Lina Bo Bardi, Teatro Oficina renovation, notes, sketches, and plan, December 7, 1980, ILBPMB; Edson Elito quoted in Mateus Bertone da Silva, *Lina Bo Bardi: Arquitetura cênica* (São Carlos: EESC-USP, 2004), 295.

36. Edson Elito, "Uma rua chamada teatro," in Bo Bardi, Elito, and Correa, *Teatro Oficina*, 11.

37. Lina Bo Bardi, Teatro Oficina, sketch and notes, May 13, 1984, ILBPMB.

38. Bo Bardi, Elito, and Correa, *Teatro Oficina*.

39. José Celso Martinez Corrêa quoted in Fernando Peixoto, *Teatro Oficina (1958–1982): Trajetória de uma rebeldia cultural* (São Paulo: Brasiliense, 1982), 99.

40. Elito, "Uma rua chamada teatro," 14.

41. The play was titled *UBU, Folias físicas e patafísicas* in Portuguese.

42. Lina Bo Bardi, UBU set and costume design, notes and sketches, May 18, 19, 1985, ILBPMB.

43. Lina Bo Bardi, "Polochon," sketches, May 25, 1985, ILBPMB.

44. Marcelo C. Ferraz quoted in Bertone da Silva, *Lina Bo Bardi*, 346.

45. Lina Bo Bardi, personal notes on UBU scenic design, c. 1985, ILBPMB.

46. Lina Bo Bardi, Galpão Tendal da Lapa, drawings and notes, December 1986, ILBPMB.

47. André Benassi, "Teatro Polytheama: A luta por sua revitalização," in *Teatro Polytheama de Jundiaí* (Jundiaí: Prefeitura Municipal, 1996), 3; Denise de Alcântara, "É vivo o Polytheama," in *Teatro Polytheama de Jundiaí*, 20.

48. Lina Bo Bardi, Teatro Polytheama renovation, personal notes, São Paulo, July 15, 1986, ILBPMB.

49. Ferraz interview.

50. Lina Bo Bardi, Teatro Polytheama renovation, personal notes, São Paulo, July 17, 1987, ILBPMB.

51. Lina Bo Bardi, Urca Station, notes and sketches, November 23, 1986, ILBPMB.

52. Mário Kertész to Lina Bo Bardi, April 22, 1986, ILBPMB.

1. Mário Kertész to Lina Bo Bardi, April 22, 1986, ILBPMB.
2. Juliana B. Knöpp and Mariana L. Albinati, *Políticas culturais de Salvador na Gestão Mário Kertész (1986 a 1989)* (Salvador: Universidade da Bahia, Centro de Estudos Multidisciplinares em Cultura, 2006), 4.
3. Juarez D. Bonfim, *Políticas públicas para o centro histórico de Salvador: O caso do parque histórico do Pelourinho* (Salvador: Universidade Federal da Bahia, Escola de Administração, 1994), 83.
4. Roberto Pinho, interview, in Juliano Pereira Trindade, *A ação de Lina Bo Bardi na Bahia e no Nordeste (1958–1964)* (São Carlos: EESC–Universidade de São Paulo, 2001), 242.
5. Antônio Risério and Gilberto Gil, *O poético e o político entre outros escritos* (Rio de Janeiro: Paz e Terra, 1988), 72.
6. Lina Bo Bardi, manuscript about Pelourinho renovation, March 1987, ILBPBM.
7. Lina Bo Bardi, personal notes on Pelourinho, c. 1986, ILBPMB.
8. Lina Bo Bardi to Celso Furtado; Lina Bo Bardi, notes on Salvador rehabilitation, April 1986, ILBPMB.
9. Bo Bardi, manuscript about Pelourinho rehabilitation.
10. Lina Bo Bardi, Pelourinho and Barroquinha, project chronology, c. 1986, and several drawings and notes between June 1986 and May 1989, ILBPMB.
11. Bo Bardi, manuscript about Pelourinho rehabilitation.
12. Lina Bo Bardi, Pelourinho, master plan board, notes, 1986, ILBPMB.
13. Lina Bo Bardi, House of Brazil in Benin, sketches, March 1990, ILBPMB.
14. Lina Bo Bardi, notes on Belvedere da Sé, c. 1986, ILBPMB.
15. Fundação Gregório de Mattos (FGM), "'Projeto Barroquinha,' memorial para captação de recursos para projeto de espaço cultural," June 1999, Salvador, FGM.
16. "Casario antigo," Lina Bo Bardi, Barroquinha complex rehabilitation, drawing and notes, 1987, ILBPMB.
17. FGM, "Projeto Barroquinha."
18. Lina Bo Bardi, Teatro Gregório de Matos, stairwell sketch, October 16, 1986, ILBPMB; Lina Bo Bardi, "Projeto Barroquinha," *AU Arquitetura e Urbanismo* 11 (November 1987), 23.
19. Lina Bo Bardi, Teatro Gregório de Matos, window drawing, July 1986, ILBPMB.
20. Lina Bo Bardi, "Estudo para uma Exposição e Teatro do Extremo Oriente e História da Companhia das Índias," sketch and notes, March 21, 1987, ILBPMB.
21. Araracanga, *Aspidosperma desmanthum*, a native Brazilian hardwood.
22. Eneida de Almeida, Luis Octávio da Silva, Marta Bogéa, and Yopanan C. Rebello, "Território de contato: Ladeira da misericórdia, Salvador, Bahia," *AU Arquitetura e Urbanismo* 171 (June 2008), 76.
23. Royal poinciana, *Delonix regia*, "flamboyant" in Portuguese.
24. Bo Bardi, lecture at FAUUSP, transcript, 3.
25. Knöpp and Albinati, *Políticas culturais de Salvador na Gestão Mário Kertész*, 4.
26. João Filgueiras Lima to Lina Bo Bardi, March 20, 1987, ILBPMB; palm-grass, *Curculigo capitulata, curcúligo* in Portuguese.
27. Filgueiras Lima to Bo Bardi.
28. Lina Bo Bardi, ladeira da Misericórdia, general plan, c. 1987, ILBPMB.
29. Lina Bo Bardi, "Arquitetura e natureza ou natureza e arquitetura?" lecture notes, Salvador, September 27, 1958, 4, ILBPMB.
30. Knöpp and Albinati, *Políticas culturais de Salvador na Gestão Mário Kertész*, 21.
31. Lina Bo Bardi, "A Casa do Benin na Bahia," *AU Arquitetura e Urbanismo* 18 (August 1988), 14.
32. Ibid.
33. Lina Bo Bardi, Casa do Benin, concrete pier and staircase studies, December 1987, ILBPMB.
34. Angelim, *Hymenolobium petraeum*, a native Brazilian hardwood.
35. Bo Bardi, "A Casa do Benin na Bahia."
36. Ibid.
37. Lina Bo Bardi to Roberto Pinho, March 4, April 19, November 4, 1987, January 19, 1988, February 1, 1988, ILBPMB.
38. "Ao povo da Bahia, que eu amo." Bo Bardi, manuscript about Pelourinho rehabilitation.

1. Lina Bo Bardi, interview, "Na simplicidade, a beleza do projeto," *Dirigente Construtor* 23 (February 1987), 35.
2. *África Negra*, exhibition opening photograph, May 11, 1988, ILBPMB; *África Negra*, exhibition poster, MASP, May 12–June 26, 1988, ILBPMB.
3. Lina Bo Bardi, interview, *Visão* 239 (May 1988), ILBPMB.
4. Antonella Gallo, ed., *Lina Bo Bardi, architetto* (Venice: Marsilio, 2004), 166.
5. Joaquim Guedes, "Lembranças de Lina Bo Bardi," *Caramelo* 4 (São Paulo: FAUUSP, 1992), 20.
6. Lina Bo Bardi, Competition notes for Belém Cultural Center, January–March 1988, ILBPMB.
7. Ibid.
8. Lina Bo Bardi, LBA Center, preliminary study plan, notes, December 9, 1988, ILBPMB.
9. Lina Bo Bardi, LBA opening ceremony, notes, February 15, 1990, ILBPMB.
10. Lina Bo Bardi, LBA Center, personal notes, c. 1990, ILBPMB.
11. Lina Bo Bardi, Teatro das Ruínas, notes on preliminary drawings, January 30, 1989, ILBPMB; Lina Bo Bardi, Teatro das Ruínas, preliminary design, January 30, 1989, ILBPMB.
12. Lina Bo Bardi, Speech-letter, Teatro Gregório de Matos opening, August 15, 1989, ILBPMB.
13. Lina Bo Bardi, lecture at FAUUSP, April 14, 1989, typed transcription, ILBPMB.
14. Ibid.
15. Ibid.
16. Lina Bo Bardi, personal notes, c. 1984, ILBPMB.
17. Centro de Inclusão Social Guanabara, http://www.cisguanabara.unicamp.br.
18. Lina Bo Bardi, Guanabara Station design notes, April 15, 1990, ILBPMB.
19. Ibid.
20. Lina Bo Bardi, "Programa para Prefeitura de São Paulo," June 1990, A, ILBPMB.
21. Lina Bo Bardi, "Prefeitura de São Paulo," design notes, c. July 1990, ILBPMB; John Fleming, Hugh Honour, and Nicolaus Pevsner, *Dizionario di architettura* (Turin: Einaudi, 1992), 78.
22. Lina Bo Bardi, City Hall, drawing and notes, 1992, ILBPMB.
23. Lina Bo Bardi, interview, *Caramelo* 4 (São Paulo: FAUUSP, 1992), 34.
24. "Grande Caixa revestida de mármore branco brasileiro, completamente fechada." Lina Bo Bardi, Brazilian Pavilion competition entry, description, 1991, ILBPMB.
25. Ibid.
26. Ibid.
27. Ibid.

Epilogue

28. Gabriela Martin, "A mulher mais antiga do Nordeste: 10.000 anos, São Raimundo Nonato, PI," in Gabriela Martin, *Pré-história do Nordeste do Brasil* (Recife: Editora Universitária UFPE, 2008), 69–70.
29. Bo Bardi, Brazilian Pavilion competition entry, description.
30. Ibid.
31. Elizabeth Lorenzotti, "O sonho da Vera Cruz," *Entretextos* (São Paulo: ECA-USP, 2009), 17.
32. Lina Bo Bardi, Centro de Convivência Vera Cruz, site strategy, February 1992, ILBPMB.
33. Lina Bo Bardi, MASP, helicoidal staircase sketch, May 6, 1960, ILBPMB.
34. Marcelo C. Ferraz, personal communication, January 7, 2011.
35. "Nem por isso," in "Anote," *Projeto* 139 (March 1991), 27.
36. "Lina Bo Bardi, 1914–1992," *O Estado de São Paulo*, March 21, 1992.
37. Lina Bo Bardi, nurse notes on medical condition, 1991–92, ILBPMB.
38. Lina Bo Bardi, interview with Silvio Giannini, in "Mostra reúne pela primeira vez obra de Lina Bo Bardi," *Folha de São Paulo*, April 10, 1989, ILBPMB.

1. Lina Bo Bardi, notes for keynote lecture at the Thirteenth Congress of Brazilian Architects, October 1991, 1, ILBPMB.
2. Ibid., 2.
3. Ibid.

Index

Rustic architecture, 81, 115. *See also* Simple architecture

S

Salazar, António de Oliveira, 203
Salvador (Brazil): description of, 83; LBB as teacher in, 82–84; LBB's regional role and museum work in (1961–1964), 101–11; LBB's return to (April 1986), 184; LBB visits to (1958–1960), 75, 79–90; LBB writing about experiences in, 175; rehabilitation of historic district, 184–200; urban redevelopment of, 2. *See also* Casa do Benin; Chame-Chame House; Museu de Arte Moderna (MAMB)
Samonà, Giuseppe, 50
Santos, Edgard Rêgo dos, 85, 92, 100, 102
São Bernardo do Campo, 211
São Francisco River, 147, 164, *165*
São Paulo: architects in, 52–54, 155; Art Biennial, 44, 46, 50, 52, 66–68, 72, 84, 91, 94; Bardis' arrival and first years in, 44–51; Bardi's first visit to, 14; Chateaubriand choosing as final site of art museum, 42; Chateaubriand preferring to build art museum in Rio de Janeiro, 40; City Hall, 205–8, *206–9*; cultural climate of, 42, 44, 49, 52, 54; design competition for downtown (1981), 179; dominance in architectural discourse in Brazil, 68; modern architecture in, 38; move to (1946), 4; theater productions in, 143–44. *See also* Morumbi; Museu de Arte de São Paulo (MASP)
São Vicente seashore museum, *63–64*, 65, 136
Saper vedere l'architettura (Architecture as space: How to look at architecture, Zevi), 82
Scarpa, Carlo, 104
Scheier, Peter, 79
Schiel, Frederico, 190
Scott, Geoffrey, 73, 82
Scuola di Architettura (School of architecture, Rome), 10, 11, 12
Seashore museum (São Vicente), *63–64*, 65
Semana de Arte Moderna (Modern art week, 1922), 38, 66, 144
Sercelli, Bruna, 155–56
Sert, Josep Lluís, 31
Serviço do Patrimônio Histórico e Artístico Nacional (National historic and artistic heritage department), 38
SESC (Serviço Social do Comércio, Trade social services), 158, 159
SESC Pompeia cultural and leisure center, 102, 110, 158–74, *160–73*; as "citadel of freedom," 47; exhibitions, 176–78, *178*; reputation of, 202; seats in, 130
SESI (Serviço Social da Indústria, Industry social services), 158
Shelter (Kahn), 152
Silla, Lucio, 15
Silva, Agostinho da, 91
Silva Brito, Mário da, 34
Simeoni, Natale Alberto (Uncle Natalino), 6, 10
Simple architecture, 78, 81, 86, 115
Sindacato nazionale fascista architetti (National fascist union of architects), 10, 16–17
Sindacato nazionale fascista belli arti (National

fascist union of fine arts), 10
Sitio da Trindade (Trindade farm), 102, 104
Sitte, Camillo, 13
Soares, Maurício, 211
Solar do Unhão (Unhão estate), 102, 104
Spontaneous art, 177
Staircases, 78, 80, 98, 104, 106, *106*, 172, *188*, 189, 196, 211
Stalinist views of LBB, 3, 141
Stucchi, Tullio, 62
Studio d'Arte Palma, 34
Suassuna, Ariano, 140
SUDENE (Superintendência do Desenvolvimento do Nordeste [Northeast development authority]), 83
Surrealism, 174
Suzuki, Marcelo, 159, 180, 200, 202, 203

T

Tavares, Odorico, 75, 84, 85, 90, 92, 97, 100, 101, 102, 111, 112, 121
Tavolo degli orrori (Table of horrors, Bardi photomontage), 11, 13
Teatro Castro Alves (TCA), 92, 94, *95*, 98, *99*, 113, 121, 130, 188
Teatro das Ruínas (Theater on ruins, Barão Geraldo), 204
"Teatro do Oprimido" (Theater of the oppressed), 143
Teatro Gregório de Matos (Salvador), *186–88*, 186–89, 200, 204
Teatro João Caetano (Rio de Janeiro), 142
Teatro Novo, 100
Teatro Oficina (Workshop theater company), 141–43, 171, *179–81*, 180–82, 187, 189, 204
Teatro Polytheama (Jundiai), 182
Teatro Sérgio Cardoso (São Paulo), 182
Teixeira, Anisio, 97
Tempo (magazine), 22
Terzo mondo e comunità mondiale (Third world and the world community) conference, 115
Theatrical productions, 4, 98–100, 112–13, 141–44, 181–82
Thirteenth Congress of Brazilian Architects (São Paulo), 213
The Threepenny Opera (Brecht & Weill), 98, 100
'Tis Pity She's a Whore (Ford play), 112
Trencadís (Catalan mosaic technique), 69
Trianon Terrace. *See* Belvedere do Trianon
Twelfth World Congress of the International Architects' Union (1975), 147

U

Uberlândia (Minas Gerais state), 146, 150, 155. *See also* Igreja do Cerrado
Ueno, Toshio, 173
UNESCO, 44, 94, 177; World Heritage Site, 208
Unhão project (Projeto Unhão), 102, 104, *104–7*, 106, 107, 110, 111, 114, 117, 121, 159, 188, 196
UNICAMP (State University of Campinas), 205
United States, tour of MASP collection to, 68, 69
Universal Exposition of Seville (1992), 208, *210*
Universidade de Bahia (University of Bahia), 81, 91, 100
Universidade de São Paulo: architecture school,

53, 68, 122; LBB exhibition (1989), 2–3, 204; LBB's application for position at, 72–74, 82; LBB thesis at, 73–74, 78, 82, 84, 205
Universidade do Ceará's Museu de Arte, 102
Universidade Federal de Santa Catarina (Santa Catarina Federal University), 177
Urbanization, 148
Urca cable car station (Sugarloaf Mountain), 183
USIS (US Information Service), 29

V

Vainer, André, 159–60, 179
van der Rohe, Mies, 11, 13, 65
van Eyck, Aldo, 168
Vargas, Getúlio, 34, 38, 39
Vera Cruz cultural and leisure center, 211–12
Verger, Pierre, 110, 194, 199, 202
Vernacular architecture, 10, 16, 50
Verso un'architettura organica (Toward an organic architecture, Zevi), 29
Vetrina e Negozio (magazine), 22
Vicario, Angelo, 18
Vignola, Giacomo Barozzi da, 14
Vitrine of forms, 108
Vitruvius, 9, 10, 14
Vittorini, Elio, 29
Völcker, Otto, 21
Voltaire, 7, 203

W

Warchavchik, Gregori, 38, 53, 55, 157
Weill, Kurt, 98
Wildenstein, Georges, 69
Workshop theater company. *See* Teatro Oficina
World War II: Italy after, 28, 41; LBB's life during, 5, 20, 24, 27; Nazi occupation of Italy, 24, 26, 27. *See also* Mussolini, Benito; Resistance
Wright, Frank Lloyd, 28, 53, 69, 70, 74, 77, 80, 81, 82, 84, 117
Writings by LBB (or under maiden name Bo): "Contribuição propedêutica ao ensino da teoria da arquitetura" (Introductory contribution to the teaching of architectural theory) (thesis and book), 73–74, 78, 82, 84, 205; *Crônicas* pieces, 86–89, *87–88*; *Domus* solo piece, 25; early pieces with Pagani, 20, 21, 22, 25; *Habitat* pieces, 49, 50–51, *63–64*, 67, 86; *Lo Stile* pieces, 24; *Mirante das Artes, Etc.* pieces, 119, 120–21, 128, 137; *Revista Malasartes* pieces, 148, 157; *Rio* piece, 41; *Tempos de grossura: Design no impasse* (Times of roughness: Design at an impasse, posthumously edited book), 175–76

X

Xavier, Livio, 102, 108, 121, 175

Y

Years of Lead, 140

Z

Zevi, Bruno, 28, 29–32, 34, 49, 68–69, 74, 81–82, 84, 108, 110, 111, 115, 117, 119, 145

Illustration Credits

The photographers and the sources of visual material other than the owners indicated in the captions are as follows. Every effort has been made to supply complete and correct credits; if there are errors or omissions, please contact Yale University Press so that corrections can be made in any subsequent edition.

Computer Renderings
© Zeuler R. Lima: figures 28, 29, 38, 40, 43, 46, 55, 57, 58, 61, 66, 67, 75, 91, 92, 99, 100, 102, 106, 112, 118, 123–25, 127, 128, 133–36, 143–53, 155, 156, 158–60, 162, 164, 165, 168, 169, 175

Photographs
© Juan Esteves: frontspiece

Marcelo C. Ferraz: figure 172

Peter Hans Günther Flieg: figure 86

© Zeuler R. Lima: figures 30, 31, 36, 60, 65, 69, 85, 94–97, 105, 109, 110, 117, 120, 129–31, 139, and 154

Nelson Kon: figures 18, 23, 25, 26, 27, 39, 41, 52, 56, 59, 72, 76–81, 98, 101, 107, 108, 111, 113–16, 119, 126, 132, 137, 138, 140, 142, 157, 161, 163, 166, 167, 170, 171

Hugo Segawa: figures 35, 44, 45

The photographic reproduction of Lina Bo Bardi's drawings in the collection of the Instituto Lina Bo e Pietro Maria Bardi was made by Henrique Luz.